GEORG BÜCHNER w⟨◁⟩ **S0-ALM-014**
17th, 1813 near Darmstadt in Germany, the
son of a physician. He showed brilliant
promise as a young medical student, and
later expanded his interests to embrace literature, philosophy, and history. His historical studies and personal attitudes involved
him in revolutionary politics and a period in
exile began. Integrating his non-scientific interests, he embarked upon an extraordinary
period of literary activity as a political pamphleteer, translator, and playwright. Between the years 1834 and 1837—a period in
which he attracted attention as a researcher
in the field of comparative anatomy—he
wrote three plays, *DANTON'S DEATH,*
LEONCE AND LENA, and *WOYZECK,* the
importance of which has only recently come
to be fully appreciated. These theater works
have exerted a vast influence over the most
important theater movements of the twentieth century. Attempting to combine his
medical research career with his expanding
interests in literature, he became over-
worked and contracted typhus, dying on
February 19th, 1837—just four months past
his twenty-third birthday.

HENRY J. SCHMIDT is Associate Professor
of German at Ohio State University. His
translations of the works of Georg Büchner
are widely read and performed, and his
initial reconstruction of *WOYZECK* was described, by Eric Bentley, as "a model of what
such things should be."

Georg Büchner: The Complete Collected Works

Translations and Commentary by
HENRY J. SCHMIDT

 A BARD BOOK/PUBLISHED BY AVON BOOKS

GEORG BÜCHNER: THE COMPLETE COLLECTED
WORKS is an original publication of Avon Books. This work
has never before appeared in book form.

AVON BOOKS
A division of
The Hearst Corporation
959 Eighth Avenue
New York, New York 10019

First Bard Printing, December, 1977

BARD TRADEMARK REG. U.S. PAT. OFF. AND IN
OTHER COUNTRIES, MARCA REGISTRADA, HECHO EN
U.S.A.

Printed in the U.S.A.

TABLE OF CONTENTS

PART ONE

GEORG BÜCHNER'S WORKS

PART TWO

NOTES AND DOCUMENTARY MATERIAL

Georg Büchner:
The Complete
Collected Works

GEORG BÜCHNER'S WORKS

THE HESSIAN MESSENGER

by Georg Büchner and Friedrich Ludwig Weidig

FIRST MESSAGE

Darmstadt, July 1834

Preface

This paper intends to reveal the truth to the State of Hesse, but he who speaks the truth will be hanged; yes, even he who reads the truth might be punished by corrupt judges. Therefore anyone receiving this paper must take note of the following:

1) He must hide this paper carefully outside his house from the police;
2) he may only pass it on to trusted friends;
3) he may only pass it on anonymously to those who cannot be trusted as one trusts one's own self;
4) if this paper is found in the possession of anyone who has read it, he must confess he was just about to bring it to the District Council;
5) if this paper is found on anyone who has not read it, then he is of course guiltless.

*   *   *

Peace to the huts! War on the palaces!

In the year 1834 it looks as if the Bible had been lying. It looks as if God had created peasants and laborers on the fifth day and princes and aristocrats on the sixth, saying to the latter: have dominion over every creeping thing that

3

creepeth upon the earth—and had included peasants and citizens among the creeping things. The life of aristocrats is a long Sunday; they live in beautiful houses, they wear elegant clothing, they have well-fed faces, and they speak their own language, while the people lie before them like manure on the field. The peasant walks behind his plow, but behind him walks the aristocrat, driving him on with the oxen, taking the grain and leaving the stubble to the peasant. The life of the peasant is a long workday; strangers consume 'his fields before his eyes, his body is a callus, his sweat is the salt on the aristocrat's table.

The Grand Duchy of Hesse has 718,373 inhabitants who pay the state 6,363,364 florins [*sic*] every year as follows:

1)	Direct taxes	2,128,131 fl.
2)	Indirect taxes	2,478,264 fl.
3)	Rent (for use of royal lands)	1,547,394 fl.
4)	Royal prerogatives	46,938 fl.
5)	Fines	98,511 fl.
6)	Various sources	64,198 fl.

6,363,363 fl. [*sic*]
[6,363,436 fl.]

This money is the blood-tithe taken from the body of the people. Some 700,000 human beings sweat, moan, and starve because of it. It is extorted in the name of the state, the extortionists claim to be authorized by the government, and the government says this is necessary to preserve order in the state. Now what kind of powerful thing is this: the state? If a number of people live in a country and regulations or laws exist to which everyone must conform, this is called a state. The state is therefore *everyone;* the regulators within the state are the laws which secure the well-being of *all*, and which should arise from the well-being of *all*.—Now see what has become of the state in the Grand Duchy; see what it means to preserve order in the state! Seven hundred thousand people pay six million for it, that means they are transformed into plowhorses and oxen so that they live in order. Living in order means starving and being oppressed.

4

Who are they who have created this order and who watch over its preservation? The Grand Ducal government. The government consists of the Grand Duke and his highest officials. The other officials are men appointed by the government to maintain order. Their number is legion: state and government officials, county and district officials, church and school officials, treasury and forestry officials, etc., all with their armies of secretaries, etc. The people are their flock, they are its shepherds, milkers, and fleecers; they wear the peasants' skins, the spoils of the poor are in their houses; the tears of widows and orphans are the grease on their faces; they rule freely and exhort the people to servitude. To them you pay your 6,000,000 florins in fees; for that they have the task of governing you; that is, to be fed by you and to rob you of your human and civil rights. Now see the harvest of your sweat.

The Ministries of the Interior and Justice are paid 1,110,607 florins. For that you have a chaos of laws accumulated from arbitrary ordinances of all centuries, written mostly in a foreign language. You have thereby inherited the nonsense of all previous generations; the oppression that victimized them is rolling over you. The law is the property of an insignificant class of aristocrats and scholars who grant themselves authority through their own machinations. This justice is merely a means to keep you under control, so that you can be more easily oppressed; it acts according to laws that you do not understand, principles about which you know nothing, judgments that you cannot comprehend. It is incorruptible, for it lets itself be paid dearly enough not to need any bribes. But most of its servants have sold body and soul to the government. Their easy-chairs stand on a pile of 461,373 florins (total expenses for the courts and penal institutions). The dress coats, sticks, and sabers of their inviolable servants are coated with the silver of 197,502 florins (total cost of the police force, constabulary, etc.). In Germany justice has been for centuries the whore of the German princes. You must pave each step toward her with silver and pay for her verdicts with poverty and humiliation. Think of the red tape, think of cringing in offices and standing in line in front of them. Think of the fees for scribes and bailiffs. You may sue your neighbor for stealing a potato, but just try to sue for the larceny committed on your property every day on behalf of the state in the form of fees and taxes, so that a legion of useless officials may fatten themselves on your sweat; try to sue because you are subject to the whims of a few potbellies and because these whims are called law; sue because you are the plowhorses of the state; sue for your lost human rights: where are the courts that will hear your suit, where are the judges who will administer justice?—The chains of your fellow citizens of Vogelsberg who were dragged off to Rokkenburg[1] will give you an answer.

And if at last one of those few judges or other officials who holds justice and the common good dearer than his stomach and Mammon wants to aid instead of persecute the people, then he will himself be persecuted by the highest officials of the prince.

For the Finance Ministry 1,551,502 florins.

This pays the salaries of the treasury officials, chief revenue officials, tax collectors, and their subordinates. For this they calculate the yield of your fields and count your heads. The ground beneath your feet, the bite of food between your teeth, is taxed. For this the lords sit together in frock coats and the people stand naked and cringing before them, the lords place their hands on the people's loins and shoulders and calculate how much they still can carry, and if the lords are charitable, it is like sparing an animal that should not be completely worn out.

For the military 914,820 florins.

For that your sons get a colorful coat for their bodies, a gun or a drum on their shoulders, and every autumn they may shoot blanks, and they tell you how the men of the court and the misbegotten sons of nobility take precedence over all children of honest people, and they march around with them on broad city streets with drums and trumpets. For those 900,000 florins your sons must swear allegiance to the tyrants and stand guard at their palaces. With their drums they drown out your groans, with their clubs they smash your skulls when you dare to think you are free men. They are legal murderers protecting legal thieves,

---

[1] They were arrested for their presumed complicity in the peasants' revolt, which ended in the "bloodbath at Södel." See Notes, pp. 243 and 258–61.

think of Södel! There your brothers, your children were killers of brothers and fathers.

For pensions 480,000 florins.

For that the officials are put in easy-chairs after they have served the state loyally for a certain time, that means after they have been zealous hacks serving in that organized oppression called law and order.

For the Ministry of State and the State Council 174,600 florins.

Just about everywhere in Germany the biggest rascals stand closest to the princes, at least in the Grand Duchy. If an honest man appears in a State Council, he will be thrown out. But if an honest man could indeed become and remain a minister, as matters now stand in Germany he would merely be a puppet on strings pulled by a princely puppet, and the princely scarecrow is being manipulated by a valet or a coachman or his wife and her favorite, or his half-brother—or all together. The situation in Germany is now as the Prophet Micah writes, Chapter 7, Verses 3 and 4: "The great man, he uttereth his mischievous desire: so they wrap it up. The best of them is as a brier: the most upright is sharper than a thorn hedge." You must pay dearly for the briers and thorn hedges, for in addition you must pay 827,772 florins for the Grand Ducal house and royal court.

The institutions, the people of which I have spoken up to now are merely tools, merely servants. They do nothing in their own name; under their appointment to office stands an "L.," that means *Ludwig* by the Grace of God, and they say with reverence: "in the name of the Grand Duke." This is their battle cry when they auction off your equipment, drive off your cattle, throw you in jail. In the name of the Grand Duke, they say, and this man is called: inviolable, holy, sovereign, Royal Highness. Yet approach this child of man and look through his princely cloak. He eats when he is hungry and sleeps when his eyes grow heavy. Behold, like you he crept naked and soft into the world and like you he will be carried from it hard and stiff, and yet his foot is on your neck, 700,000 human beings are hitched to his plow, his ministers are responsible for his actions, he controls your property through the taxes he decrees, he controls your lives through the laws he

7

makes, around him are noble men and women known as the court, and his divine power is passed on to his children through women of equally superhuman stock.

Woe unto you idolaters!—You are like the heathens who pray to the crocodile that tears them apart. You place a crown on his head, but it is a crown of thorns that you are pressing onto your own heads; you place a scepter in his hand, but it is a rod that flogs you; you place him on your throne, but it is a rack of torture for you and your children. The prince is the head of the bloodsucker that crawls over you, the ministers are its teeth and the officials its tail. The hungry bellies of all elegant gentlemen to whom he gives high positions are the cupping glasses which he applies to the body of the land. That "L." on his decrees is the mark of the animal worshiped by the idolaters of our time. The princely cloak is the carpet on which lords and ladies of nobility and the court roll over each other in their lust—they cover their abscesses with medals and ribbons, and they cover their leprous bodies with costly garments. The daughters of the people are their maids and whores, the sons of the people their lackeys and soldiers. Go to Darmstadt once and see how the lords are amusing themselves there with your money, and then tell your starving wives and children that strangers' stomachs are thriving marvelously on their bread, tell them about the beautiful clothes dyed in their sweat and the dainty ribbons cut from the calluses on their hands, tell about the stately houses built from the bones of the people; and then crawl into your smoky huts and bend over your stony fields, so that your children can go there once as well when a royal heir and a royal heiress want to devise means to produce another royal heir, and your children can look through the open glass doors and see the tablecloth on which the lords dine and smell the lamps that shine from the fat of the peasants. You endure all that because rascals tell you: "This government derives from God." This government derives not from God but from the Father of Lies. These German princes represent no legitimate authority; to the contrary, for centuries they have scorned and finally betrayed legitimate authority, namely the German Emperor, who was formerly freely chosen by the people. The power of the German princes is based on treason and perjury, not on the people's choice, and therefore their existence and actions are cursed by God; their wisdom is illusion, their justice is oppression. They trample down the land and beat up the poor. You blaspheme against God if you call one of these princes a man anointed by the Lord; this means God has anointed devils and made them princes over German soil. These princes have torn Germany apart, our dear Fatherland, they have betrayed the Emperor elected by our free forefathers, and now these traitors and torturers demand your loyalty!—But the realm of darkness is coming to an end. Now oppressed by the princes, Germany will soon arise again as a free state with a government elected by the people. The Scriptures say: "Render unto Caesar the things which are Caesar's." But what things belong to the princes, to the traitors?—*Judas's share!*

For the legislatures 16,000 florins.

In 1789 the people of France were tired of being their king's whipping boy. They rose up and nominated trustworthy men who came together and said: a king is a man like any other, he is merely the first servant of the state, he must be accountable to the people, and if he does his job poorly, he should be punished. Then they defined the rights of man: "No one shall inherit by birth any rights or titles over another, no one shall gain rights over another through property. Supreme power lies in the will of all or of the majority. This will is law, it manifests itself through legislatures or through the people's representatives, elected by all, and anyone may be elected; the elected express the will of their constituents, and the will of the elected majority thus corresponds to the will of the majority of the people; the king is merely responsible for the execution of the laws they enact." The king swore to uphold this constitution, but he perjured himself before the people, and the people sentenced him to die as is proper for a traitor. The French then abolished hereditary monarchy and freely elected a new government, to which every nation is entitled according to reason and the Holy Writ. The men who were to supervise the execution of the laws were elected by the assembly of people's representatives, they formed the new government. Executive and legislative government was thus elected by the people and France was a free state.

9

But the remaining monarchs were terrified of the power of the French people; they thought they might all break their necks on that first royal corpse, and their mistreated subjects might awaken at the French call to freedom. With giant war machines and cavalry they descended upon France from all sides, and a large number of nobles and aristocrats rebelled and joined the enemy. Then the people grew angry and arose in their strength. They crushed the traitors and annihilated the monarchs' mercenaries. This newborn freedom grew in the blood of tyrants, and thrones trembled and nations rejoiced at its voice. But the French sold even their newborn freedom for the glory offered them by Napoleon, and they crowned him Emperor.—Thereupon the Almighty allowed the Emperor's army to freeze to death in Russia and lashed France with cossacks' whips and gave potbellied Bourbons back to the French as kings, so that France would convert from idolizing hereditary monarchy to serving God who had created men free and equal. But when France had paid its penalty and brave men chased the corrupt Charles the Tenth out of the country in July 1830, liberated France nevertheless turned once again to *semi-hereditary* monarchy and set a new scourge on its back in the person of the hypocrite Louis Philippe. There was great joy in Germany and all of Europe, however, when Charles the Tenth was deposed, and the suppressed German states prepared to fight for freedom. Then the princes deliberated how to avoid the wrath of the people, and the cunning ones among them said: let us give up part of our power to save the rest. And they appeared before the people and spoke: we shall grant you the freedom you meant to fight for.—And trembling with fear they threw down a few scraps and spoke of their charity. Unfortunately the people trusted them and quieted down.—And so was Germany deceived like France.

What in fact are these constitutions in Germany? Nothing but empty straw from which the princes have threshed the grain for themselves. What are our legislatures? Nothing but slow-moving vehicles which can perhaps be shoved in the way of the rapacity of the princes and their ministers once or twice, but which can never be used to build a mighty fortress for German freedom. What are our election laws? Nothing but violations of most Germans' civil and human rights. Think of the election laws in the Grand Duchy, where no one may be elected who is not well-to-do, no matter how upright and well-intentioned he may be, yet Grolmann, who wanted to steal two million from you,[2] is elected. Think of the constitution of the Grand Duchy.—According to its articles, the Grand Duke is inviolable, holy, and accountable to no one. His high position is a family inheritance, he has the right to wage war and has exclusive control over the military. He convenes, adjourns, or dissolves the legislatures. The legislatures may not originate laws but must request them, and it is left completely up to the prince's discretion to grant or deny them. He retains possession of nearly unlimited power, except that he may not enact new laws and impose new taxes without the approval of the legislatures. Yet often he does not adhere to this approval, often he is satisfied with the old laws deriving from princely power, and he therefore needs no new laws. Such a constitution is a miserable, deplorable thing. What can be expected from legislatures restricted by such a constitution? Even if there were no betrayers of the people nor craven cowards among the elected, even if they consisted only of determined friends of the people?! What can be expected from legislatures hardly able to defend the miserable tatters of a wretched constitution!—The only opposition they were able to muster was the denial of the two million florins the Grand Duke wanted as a gift from the heavily indebted nation for the payment of his debts. But even if the Grand Duchy's legislatures had sufficient rights, and the Grand Duchy—but the Grand Duchy alone—had a true constitution, this marvel would soon come to an end. The vultures in Vienna and Berlin would stretch their hangmen's claws and destroy this little freedom root and branch. The entire German nation must win this freedom. And this time, dear fellow citizens, is not far off.—The Lord has delivered the beautiful land of Germany—for many centuries the most glorious empire on earth—into the hands of foreign and native oppressors, because in their hearts the German people had

---

[2] Representative Friedrich von Grolmann and others proposed that the State Treasury assume the personal debts of Ludwig II. The motion was defeated (see below).

forsaken the freedom and equality of their ancestors and forsaken the fear of the Lord, because you devoted yourselves to idolizing those many petty lords, little dukes, and kinglets.

The Lord who smashed the rod of the foreign oppressor Napoleon shall also smash the idols of our native tyrants with the hands of the people. These idols may glitter with gold and jewels, medals and decorations, but inside them *the worm does not die, and their feet are of clay.*—God shall give you strength to smash their feet as soon as you repent the error of your ways and recognize the truth: "that there is only one God and no other gods before him who let themselves be called Highness and Majesty, divine and accountable to no one; that God created all men free and equal in their rights; that no government has God's blessing unless it is based on the people's trust and is expressly or tacitly elected by them; but that a government with power but no rights over a nation derives from God only as the Devil derives from God; that obedience to such a devil's government is only valid until its devil's might can be broken; that God, who united a nation into one body through a common language, shall punish in this life and eternally hereafter those murderers of the people and tyrants who draw and quarter the nation or even tear it into thirty pieces, for the Scriptures say: what God hath joined together, let no man put asunder; and that the Almighty, who can create a paradise from a desert, can also transform a land of distress and misery into a paradise, like our treasured Germany before its princes tore it apart and flayed it."

Since the German Empire was decayed and rotten, and the Germans had forsaken God and freedom, God let the Empire go to ruin in order to regenerate it as a free state. For a time He gave "Satan's angels" the power to beat Germany with their fists, He gave "principalities and powers, the rulers of the darkness of this world, spiritual wickedness in high places" (Ephesians 6:12), power to torment citizens and peasants and suck their blood and do mischief to all who love justice and freedom more than injustice and servitude.——But their cup is full!

Look at that monster branded by God, King Ludwig of

12

Bavaria,[3] the blasphemer who forces honest men to kneel before his image and allows corrupt judges to imprison those who speak the truth; that pig who rolled in every puddle of vice in Italy, the wolf who makes corrupt legislatures allot five million every year to his Baal-court, and then ask: "Is this a government with God's blessing?"

> Ha! you'd be a governor of God?
> God bestows on us his grace;
> You rob, oppress, imprison us,
> You're not of God, tyrant![4]

I say to you: the cup of the prince and his like is full, God, who has used these princes to punish Germany for its sins, shall heal it again. "He shall go through the briers and thorns and burn them together." (Isaiah 27:4).

Just as the hunchback with which God has branded this King Ludwig can grow no larger, so can the atrocities of these princes no longer increase. Their cup is full. God will smash their fortresses, and life and strength, the blessing of freedom, shall then bloom again in Germany. The princes have transformed German soil into a great field of corpses, as Ezekiel writes in Chapter 37: "The Lord set me down in the midst of the valley which was full of bones, and lo, they were very dry." But what is God's Word about these dry bones: "Behold, I will lay sinews upon you, and will bring up flesh upon you, and cover you with skin, and put breath in you, and ye shall live; and ye shall know that I am the Lord." And God's Word shall truly come to pass in Germany as well, as the Prophet says: "There was a noise, and behold a shaking, and the bones came together, bone to his bone.—And the breath came into them, and they lived, and stood up upon their feet, an exceeding great army."

As the Prophet writes, so it was until now in Germany: your bones are dry, for the order in which you live is sheer oppression. In the Grand Duchy you pay six million to a

3 Ludwig (1786–1868) was an energetic patron of the arts. His enlightened political views became increasingly reactionary after the Revolution of 1830. He abdicated in 1848.
4 Altered final stanza of "The Peasant: to His Serene Highness, the Tyrant," by the Storm and Stress poet Gottfried August Bürger (1747–1794).

handful of people whose whims govern your life and property, and it is the same for others in fragmented Germany. You are nothing, you have nothing! You are without rights. You must give whatever your insatiable oppressors demand and carry whatever they load upon you. As far as a tyrant can see—and Germany has about thirty of them—land and people wither. But as the Prophet writes, so will it soon be in Germany: the Day of Resurrection is at hand. On the field of corpses there shall be a noise and a shaking, and there will be a great army of the resurrected.

Lift up your eyes and count the little band of your oppressors, who are strong only through the blood they suck from you and through your arms which you lend them against your will. There are about 10,000 of them and 700,000 of you in the Grand Duchy, and that is the ratio of people to their oppressors in the rest of Germany as well. They may threaten with royal armaments and cavalry, but I say to you: all they that take up the sword against the people shall perish by the sword of the people. Germany is now a field of corpses, soon it will be a paradise. The German nation is one body, you are a limb of that body. It makes no difference where the seemingly dead body begins to twitch. When the Lord gives you his signs through the men through whom he shall lead nations from bondage to freedom, then arise, and the whole body will rise up with you.

You cringed for long years in the thorny fields of servitude, then you will sweat for a summer in the vineyard of freedom and shall be free unto the thousandth generation.

Throughout a long life you dug up the earth, then you shall dig your tyrants' grave. You built the fortresses, then you shall destroy them and build the house of freedom. Then you shall be able to baptize your children freely with the water of life. And until the Lord calls you through his messengers and signs, be watchful, prepare yourselves in spirit, pray, and teach your children to pray: "Lord, break the rod of our oppressors and let Thy kingdom come, the kingdom of justice. Amen."

DANTON'S DEATH

CHARACTERS

Georges Danton
Legendre
Camille Desmoulins
Hérault-Séchelles
Lacroix   } deputies of the National Convention
Philippeau
Fabre d'Églantine
Mercier
Thomas Payne
Robespierre
St. Just
Barère   } members of the Committee of
Collot d'Herbois   Public Safety
Billaud-Varennes
Chaumette, procurator of the Commune
Dillon, a general
Fouquier-Tinville, public prosecutor
Amar
Vouland   } members of the Committee of General Security
Herman
Dumas   } presidents of the Revolutionary Tribunal
Paris, a friend of Danton
Simon, a prompter
Simon's wife
Laflotte
Julie, Danton's wife
Lucile, wife of Camille Desmoulins
Rosalie
Adelaide   } grisettes
Marion

Ladies at card tables, Gentlemen and Ladies as well as a
Young Gentleman and Eugénie on a promenade, Citizens,
Citizen-soldiers, Deputies from Lyons and other Deputies,
Jacobins, Presidents of the Jacobin Club and the National
Convention, Jailers, Executioners, and Drivers, Men and
Women of the people, Grisettes, Balladeer, Beggar, etc.

ACT ONE

1

HÉRAULT-SÉCHELLES, *a few women at a card table.*
DANTON, JULIE *somewhat farther off,* DANTON *on a
footstool at* JULIE's *feet.*

Danton.
Look at Madame over there—how sweetly she fingers
her cards. She knows how, all right—they say her husband always gets a heart, the others a royal flush. You
women could even make us fall in love with a lie.

Julie.
Do you believe in me?

Danton.
How do I know? We know little about each other. We're
all thick-skinned. We stretch out our hands toward each
other, but it's all in vain, we just rub the rough leather
off . . . we are very lonely.

Julie.
You know me, Danton.

Danton.
Yes, whatever "knowing" means. You have dark eyes and
curly hair and a nice complexion and you always say to
me: dear Georges. But (*He points to her forehead and
eyes.*) there—there: what's behind that? No, our senses
are coarse. Know each other? We'd have to break open
our skulls and pull each other's thoughts out of the brain
fibers.

A Woman.
(*To* HÉRAULT.) What are you doing with your fingers?

Hérault.
Nothing!

Woman.
Don't twist your thumb under like that! I can't stand it.

17

Hérault.

Just look, it has a very peculiar physiognomy.

Danton.

No, Julie, I love you like the grave.

Julie.

(*Turning away.*) Oh!

Danton.

No, listen! They say in the grave there is peace, and grave and peace are one. If that's so, then in your lap I'm already lying under the earth. You sweet grave— your lips are funeral bells, your voice my death knell, your breasts my burial mound, and your heart my coffin.

Woman.

You lose!

Hérault.

That was a little adventure of love. It costs money as they all do.

Woman.

Then you made your declarations with your fingers, like a deaf-mute.

Hérault.

And why not? Some say that fingers are the easiest to understand. I plotted an affair with a queen. My fingers were princes changed into spiders, you, Madame, were the good fairy, but it didn't work: the queen was always with child, bearing jacks by the minute. I wouldn't let my daughter play games like that. The kings and queens fall on top of each other so indecently and the jacks pop up right after.

(CAMILLE DESMOULINS *and* PHILIPPEAU *enter.*)

Hérault.

Philippeau, what sad eyes! Did you rip a hole in your red cap? Did Saint Jacob look angry? Did it rain during the guillotining or did you get a bad seat and not see anything?

Camille.

You're parodying Socrates. Do you know what that divine man asked Alcibiades when he found him gloomy and depressed one day? "Did you lose your shield in battle? Did you lose a race or a sword fight? Did some-

18

one else sing better or play the zither better than you?"
What classic republicans! Just compare that to our guil-
lotine-romanticism!

Philippeau.

Another twenty victims today. We were wrong: the
Hébertists were sent to the scaffold because they weren't
systematic enough. Maybe also because the decemvirs
thought they'd be lost if just for a week there were men
who were more feared than they.

Hérault.

They want to change us into cavemen. St. Just would be
happy to see us crawling around on all fours so that the
lawyer from Arras[1] could invent beanies, school benches,
and a God according to the formulas of the watchmaker
from Geneva.[2]

Philippeau.

They wouldn't be afraid to add a few more zeros to
Marat's calculations. How much longer should we be
dirty and bloody like newborn children, having coffins as
cradles and playing with human heads? We must act.
The Committee of Clemency must be established and the
expelled deputies reinstated.

Hérault.

The Revolution has reached the stage of reorganization.
The Revolution must stop and the Republic must begin.
In our constitution, right must prevail over duty, well-
being over virtue, and self-defense over punishment.
Each man must be able to assert himself and live according to his nature. Be he reasonable or unreasonable,
educated or uneducated, good or evil—that's not the
state's business. We are all fools: no one has the right to
impose his own folly on anyone else. Everyone must be
allowed to enjoy himself as he likes, but in such a way
that he doesn't seek pleasure at somebody else's expense
or disturb him in his own enjoyment.

Camille.

The government must be a transparent gown that clings
closely to the body of the people. Every pulsing vein,
flexing muscle, twitching sinew must leave its imprint.

---

[1] Robespierre.
[2] J.-J. Rousseau.

Its appearance may be beautiful or ugly—it has the right to be as it is. We don't have the right to cut a dress for it as we see fit. We will rap the knuckles of those who wish to throw a nun's veil over the naked shoulders of that dearest sinner, France. We want naked gods and bacchantes, Olympic games, and from melodic lips the words: "Ah, uninhibited, wicked love!" We won't prevent the Romans from sitting in a corner and cooking their turnips, but they are not to give us any more gladiatorial games. The divine Epicurus and Venus with the beautiful backside must replace Saints Marat and Chalier as door-keepers of the Republic. Danton, you will lead the attack in the Convention.

Danton.

I will, you will, he will. If you live that long, as the old women say. In an hour sixty minutes will have gone by. Right, my boy?

Camille.

What's all that for? That's obvious.

Danton.

Oh, everything is obvious. Who's going to accomplish all these beautiful things?

Philippeau.

We and the honest people.

Danton.

That "and" there is a long word, it holds us pretty far apart. The road is long and honesty runs out of breath before we come together. And what if we do!—to those honest people you can lend money, be their godfather, give them your daughters in marriage, but that's all!

Camille.

If you know all that, why did you begin the fight?

Danton.

Because I loathed certain people. I could never look at such pompous Catonians without giving them a kick. That's the way I am. (*He rises.*)

Julie.

You're going?

Danton.

(*To* JULIE.) I have to. Their politics are getting on my nerves. (*While leaving.*) A parting prophecy: the statue

20

of freedom is not yet cast, the furnace is glowing . . . and we can all still burn our fingers. (*Exits.*)

Camille.

Let him go. Do you really think he could stay away once the action starts?

Hérault.

Yes, but he'd do it just to pass the time, like playing chess.

2

A street.

SIMON. *His* WIFE.

Simon.

(*Beats his* WIFE.) Thou panderer, thou wrinkled contraceptive, thou worm-eaten apple of sin!

Wife.

Hey, help! Help!

People.

(*Running in.*) Get them apart! Get them apart!

Simon.

No—let me be, Romans! I will smite this skeleton to the earth! Thou . . . vestal virgin!

Wife.

Me a vestal virgin? We'll see about that!

Simon.

Thus I tear thy raiment from thy shoulders,
Thy naked carcass I cast into the sun.

Thou bed of prostitution, in every wrinkle of thy body lurketh lechery.

(*They are separated.*)

First Citizen.

What's going on?

Simon.

Where is the maiden? Speak! No, I cannot call her that. The lass! No, not that either. The girl, the woman! Not that, not that either. Only one name is left. Oh, it chokes me! I have no breath for it.

Second Citizen.

That's good. Otherwise the name would stink from brandy.

Simon.

Old Virginius, cover thy bare pate. The raven of shame perches upon it and stabs at thine eyes. Give me a knife, Romans! (*He collapses.*)

Wife.

Oh, usually he's a good man, but when he drinks too much, brandy sticks out a leg and trips him up.

Second Citizen.

Then he walks on three legs.

Wife.

No, he falls.

Second Citizen.

Right. First he walks on three and then he falls on the third until the third falls too.

Simon.

Thou art the vampire's tongue which drinketh the warmest blood of my heart.

Wife.

Leave him be—about this time he always gets sentimental. He'll get over it.

First Citizen.

What happened?

Wife.

You see, I was sitting in the sun on a rock, keeping warm, you see, 'cause we don't have any wood, you see . . .

Second Citizen.

So use your husband's nose.

Wife.

. . . and my daughter had gone around the corner— she's a good girl and supports her parents.

Simon.

Ha! She confesses!

Wife.

You Judas, would you have a pair of pants to pull *up* if the young gentlemen didn't pull theirs *down* with her? You barrel of brandy, do you want to die of thirst when the little spring stops running, hey? We have to work with all our limbs—why not with *that* too? Her mother

22

worked with it when she was born, and it hurt. Can't she work for her mother with it, too, hey? And does it hurt her, hey? You idiot!

Simon.

Ha, Lucretia! A knife, give me a knife, Romans! Ha, Appius Claudius!

First Citizen.

Yes, a knife, but not for the poor whore. What did she do wrong? Nothing! Her hunger goes whoring and begging. A knife for those who buy the flesh of our wives and daughters! Down with those who prostitute the daughters of the people! You have hunger pains and they have stomach cramps, you have holes in your jackets and they have warm coats, you have calluses and they have velvet hands. Ergo: you work and they do nothing. Ergo: you earn it and they steal it. Ergo: if you want to get a few cents back from your stolen property, you have to go whoring and begging. Ergo: they are thieves and must be killed.

Third Citizen.

All the blood they have in their veins they sucked out of ours. They told us: kill the aristocrats, they are wolves! We strung up the aristocrats on the lampposts. They said the Veto eats up your bread. We killed the Veto. They said the Girondists are starving you out. We guillotined the Girondists. But they undressed the dead and we go barefoot and freeze, the same as before. We want to pull the skin off their thighs and make pants out of it, we want to melt off their fat and blend it into our soups. Let's go! Kill anyone without a hole in his coat!

First Citizen.

Kill anyone who can read and write!

Second Citizen.

Kill anyone who turns up his toes!

All.

(*Screaming.*) Kill them, kill them!

(*A* YOUNG MAN *is dragged in.*)

A Few Voices.

He's got a handkerchief! An aristocrat! String him up! String him up!

23

Second Citizen.
What? He doesn't blow his nose with his fingers? String him up on the lamppost!

Young Man.
Oh, gentlemen!

Second Citizen.
There aren't any gentlemen here. String him up!

A Few.
(*Sing.*)

> If you lie within the earth,
> The worms will soon invade your berth.
> Hanging is a better lot,
> Than lying in a grave to rot.

Young Man.
Mercy!

Third Citizen.
It's only a little game with a bit of hemp around your neck. It'll only take a second—we're more merciful than the likes of you. Our life is murdered by work. We hang on the rope for sixty years and twitch, but we'll cut ourselves loose. String him up on the lamppost!

Young Man.
All right, but that won't make things any brighter.

The Others.
Bravo, bravo!

A Few Voices.
Let him go! (*He escapes.*)

(ROBESPIERRE *enters, accompanied by women and sans-culottes.*)

Robespierre.
What's the matter, citizen?

Third Citizen.
What's the next step? Those few drops of blood from August and September haven't reddened the cheeks of the people. The guillotine is too slow. We need a cloud-burst.

First Citizen.
Our wives and children cry out for bread. We want to feed them with the flesh of the aristocrats. Hey! Kill anyone without a hole in his coat!

24

All.

Kill them! Kill them!

Robespierre.

In the name of the law!

First Citizen.

What's the law?

Robespierre.

The will of the people.

First Citizen.

We are the people, and we don't want any law. Ergo: this will is law; ergo: in the name of the law there is no more law; ergo: kill them!

Several Voices.

Listen to Aristides! Listen to the Incorruptible!

A Woman.

Listen to the Messiah, who has been sent to choose and to judge. He will destroy the wicked with his sharp sword. His eyes are the eyes of selection, his hands are the hands of judgment.

Robespierre.

Poor, virtuous people! You do your duty, you sacrifice your enemies. People, you are mighty. You reveal yourselves in lightning and thunder. But you must not be wounded by your own blows; you kill yourselves in your own wrath. You can fall only through your own strength. Your enemies know that. Your lawmakers are watchful, they will guide your hands. Their eyes are infallible, your hands are inescapable. Come with me to the Jacobins. Your comrades will open their arms to you. We will hold a bloody judgment over our enemies.

Many Voices.

To the Jacobins! Long live Robespierre! (*They all exit.*)

Simon.

Woe is me, abandoned! (*He tries to get up.*)

His Wife.

There! (*She helps him.*)

Simon.

Oh, my Baucis, thou gatherest coals upon my head.

Wife.

There—stand up.

Simon.

Thou turnest away? Ha, canst thou forgive me, Portia?

25

Did I smite thee? 'Twas not my hand, 'twas not my arm,
'twas my madness.

His madness is poor Hamlet's enemy.

Then Hamlet does it not, Hamlet denies it.

Where is our daughter, where is my Susie?

Wife.

There—around the corner.

Simon.

Let's go to her. Come, my virtuous spouse. (*Both exit.*)

3

The Jacobin Club.

A Man from Lyons.

Our brothers in Lyons have sent us to pour their bitter
displeasure in your ears. We do not know whether the
cart on which Ronsin rode to the guillotine was the
hearse of freedom or not, but we do know that since that
day Chalier's murderers again walk the earth as if there
were no grave for them. Have you forgotten that Lyons
is a blot on French soil, which we must cover with the
bones of traitors? Have you forgotten that this whore of
kings[3] can only wash away her leprosy in the waters of
the Rhone? Have you forgotten that this revolutionary
torrent must make Pitt's Mediterranean fleets run aground
upon the corpses of the aristocrats? Your clemency is
murdering the Revolution. The breath of an aristocrat is
the death rattle of freedom. Only a coward dies for the
Republic; a Jacobin kills for it. We tell you this: if we
no longer find in you the vigorous leadership of the 10th
of August, of September, and of the 31st of May, then,
like the patriot Gaillard, we can only turn to Cato's
dagger. (*Applause and confused cries.*)

A Jacobin.

We will drink the cup of Socrates with you!

Legendre.

(*Jumps onto the tribune.*) We do not need to turn our
eyes to Lyons. For several days now those who wear silk

---

[3] Lyons.

26

clothes, ride in carriages, sit in boxes in the theater, and speak according to the dictionary of the Academy have felt their heads to be secure on their shoulders. They make jokes, saying that Marat and Chalier should be helped to a double martyrdom by guillotining them in effigy. (*Violent commotion in the assembly.*)

Several Voices.

They are dead men. Their tongues guillotine them.

Legendre.

May the blood of these saints come over them! I ask you members of the Committee of Public Safety: since when have your ears become so deaf . . .

Collot d'Herbois.

(*Interrupts him.*) And I ask you, Legendre: whose voice has given breath to such thoughts that they come to life and dare to speak? It is time to tear off masks. Listen! The cause accuses its effect, the shout its echo, and the premise its conclusion. The Committee of Public Safety is more logical than that, Legendre! Be quiet. The busts of the saints will remain untouched, like Medusa-heads they will turn the traitors into stone.

Robespierre.

I wish to speak.

The Jacobins.

Listen! Listen to the Incorruptible!

Robespierre.

We were waiting only for the cry of discontent to ring out from all sides before we speak. Our eyes were open, we watched the enemy arming himself and rising up, but we did not sound the alarm. We let the people be their own guard. They did not sleep, they took up arms. We let the enemy break from his cover, we let him advance. Now he stands exposed in broad daylight: every blow will strike him. He is dead as soon as you have seen him. I have told you once before that the internal enemies of the Republic consist of two factions, like two armies. Under banners of various colors and in quite different ways they all strive toward the same goal. One of these factions no longer exists.[4] In its presumptuous insanity it tried to throw aside the most proven patriots as worn-out

---

[4] The Hébertists.

weaklings in order to rob the Republic of its strongest arms. It declared war on God and property in order to create a diversion on behalf of the kings. It parodied the illustrious drama of the Revolution in order to compromise it through premeditated excesses. Hébert's triumph would have turned the Republic into chaos, and despotism would have been satisfied. The sword of judgment has struck the traitor down. But what does it matter to our foreign enemies when criminals of another sort remain to accomplish the same purpose? We have done nothing so long as another faction remains to be destroyed. This one is the opposite of the first. It leads us to weakness; its battle cry is: mercy! It intends to rob the people of their weapons and of the strength to fight in order to deliver them up to the kings, naked and unnerved. The weapon of the Republic is terror, the strength of the Republic is virtue. Virtue: for without it, terror is corruptible; terror: for without it, virtue is powerless. Terror is an outgrowth of virtue; it is nothing more than swift, rigorous, and inflexible justice. Some say terror is the weapon of a despotic government, therefore ours resembles despotism. Certainly, but in the way a sword in the hand of a hero of freedom resembles a saber in the hand of a tyrant's minion. If a tyrant rules his animallike subjects through terror, that is his right as a despot. If you destroy through terror the enemies of freedom, you, the founders of the Republic, are no less right. The Revolutionary government is the despotism of freedom against tyranny. Spare the royalists! certain people cry. Spare the wicked? No! Spare the innocent, spare the weak, spare the unfortunate, spare humanity! Only the peaceful citizen deserves the protection of society. In a republic only republicans are citizens, royalists and foreigners are enemies. To punish the oppressors of mankind is kindness—to pardon them is barbarity. It seems to me that every trace of false sentimentality is a sigh that flies to England or Austria. Yet not satisfied with disarming the people, some try to poison the most sacred sources of its strength through vice. This is the most sophisticated, most dangerous, and most deplorable attack against freedom. Vice is the mark of Cain on the aristocracy. Within a republic it is not only a moral but a political crime. The vice-ridden are the political enemies of freedom; the more they seem to accomplish in its service, the more dangerous they are. The most dangerous citizen is the one who wears out a dozen red caps more easily than doing one good deed. You will understand me readily when you think about those who used to live in a garret and now ride in a carriage and fornicate with former marchionesses and baronesses. We may well ask: have the people been robbed or have we grasped the golden hands of the kings when we, the people's lawmakers, display all the vices and luxuries of former courtiers? When we see these marquises and barons of the Revolution marrying rich wives, giving sumptuous banquets, gambling, keeping servants and wearing expensive clothes? We may well be surprised when we hear them being witty, playing the snob, and adopting elegant manners. Quite recently someone shamelessly parodied Tacitus—I could answer like Sallust, and travesty Catiline; but no more brushstrokes are necessary, the portraits are complete. Let there be no compromise, no armistice with those who were only set on robbing the people, who hoped to rob them unpunished, for whom the Republic was speculation and the Revolution a trade. Frightened by the rushing torrent of the examples we have set, they now very quietly seek to cool down our justice. We are to believe that we ought to say to ourselves: "We are not virtuous enough to be so terrible. Philosophic lawmakers, have mercy on our weakness! I don't dare to tell you that I am so wicked—so I'd rather tell you, don't you be inhuman!" Calm yourselves, virtuous people, calm yourselves, patriots: tell your brothers in Lyons that the sword of justice will not rust in the hands of those to whom you have entrusted it. We will set a great example for the Republic. (*General applause.*)

Many Voices.

Long live the Republic, long live Robespierre!

President.

The meeting is adjourned.

4

A street.

LACROIX. LEGENDRE.

Lacroix.

What have you done, Legendre? Do you realize whose head you're knocking off with those busts of yours?

Legendre.

The heads of a few playboys and elegant women, that's all.

Lacroix.

You are a suicide, a shadow that murders itself with its origin.

Legendre.

I don't understand.

Lacroix.

I thought Collot had made himself clear.

Legendre.

What difference does it make? He was drunk, as usual.

Lacroix.

Fools, children, and—well?—drunks speak the truth. Who do you think Robespierre was talking about with his Catiline?

Legendre.

Well?

Lacroix.

It's very simple: the atheists and the ultrarevolutionaries have been sent to the scaffold, but the people haven't been helped. They still go barefoot in the streets and they want to make shoes out of aristocratic leather. The guillotine thermometer must not drop. A few more degrees and the Committee of Public Safety can seek its bed on the Square of the Revolution.[5]

Legendre.

What do my busts have to do with that?

Lacroix.

Don't you see it yet? You have officially announced the

---

[5] The location of the guillotine.

counterrevolution; you have forced the decemvirs to act; you have led their hand. The people are a Minotaur that must have a weekly supply of corpses if it is not to devour them.

Legendre.

Where is Danton?

Lacroix.

How should I know? He's searching for the Venus of Medici piece by piece among all the grisettes of the Palais Royal. He's making a mosaic, as he says. Heaven knows what limb he's at right now. It's a shame that nature has cut up beauty into pieces—like Medea her brother—and has put the fragments into our bodies. Let's go to the Palais Royal. (*Both exit.*)

5

A room.

DANTON. MARION.

Marion.

No, leave me like this. Here at your feet. I want to tell you a story.

Danton.

You could use your lips in better ways.

Marion.

No, let me stay like this. My mother was a smart woman. She always said chastity was a nice virtue—when people came to the house and started talking about certain things, she told me to leave the room. When I asked what they wanted, she said I ought to be ashamed of myself. When she gave me a book to read, I almost always had to skip over a couple of pages. But I read the Bible whenever I liked—there everything was holy; but there was something in there that I didn't understand, and I didn't want to ask anybody about it—I brooded about myself. Then spring came, and around me all sorts of things were going on which I didn't take part in. I was in an atmosphere of my own, it almost choked me. I looked at my body, and sometimes I thought there were two of me which then

31

melted again into one. At that time a young man came to the house—he was good-looking and he often said crazy things. I didn't really know what he wanted, but I had to laugh. My mother invited him often—both he and I liked that. Finally we couldn't see why we might not just as well lie together between two sheets as sit next to each other in two chairs. I enjoyed that more than our conversations, and I didn't understand why one would allow the smaller pleasure and deny the greater one. We did it secretly. It went on like that. But I became like an ocean, swallowing everything and swirling deeper and deeper. For me there was only one opposite: all men melted into one body. That was my nature—who can escape it? Finally he realized it. He came one morning and kissed me as if he wanted to choke me, his arms wrapped tight around my neck. I was terribly afraid. Then he let me go and laughed and said he had almost done a foolish thing, I ought to keep my dress and use it, it would wear out by itself, he didn't want to spoil my fun just yet, it was all I had. Then he left, and again I didn't know what he wanted. That evening I was sitting at the window. I'm very sensitive, and I relate to everything around me only through a feeling. I sank into the waves of the sunset. Then a group of people came down the street, children out in front, women looking out of their windows. I looked down—they were carrying him by in a basket, the moon shone on his pale forehead, his hair was damp. He had drowned himself. I had to cry. That was the only break in my being. Other people have Sundays and working days, they work for six days and pray on the seventh; once a year, on their birthdays, they get sentimental, and every year on New Year's Day they reflect. I don't understand all that. For me there is no stopping, no changing. I'm always the same, an endless longing and seizing, a fire, a torrent. My mother died of grief, people point at me. That's silly. It's all the same, whatever we enjoy: bodies, icons, flowers, or toys, it's all the same feeling. Whoever enjoys the most prays the most.

Danton.

Why can't I contain your beauty in me completely, surround it entirely?

Marion.
Danton, your lips have eyes.

Danton.
I wish I were a part of the atmosphere so that I could bathe you in my flood and break on every wave of your beautiful body.

(LACROIX, ADELAIDE, ROSALIE *enter.*)

Lacroix.
(*Remains at the door.*) Oh, that was funny!

Danton.
(*Indignantly.*) Well?

Lacroix.
The street!

Danton.
And?

Lacroix.
There were dogs on the street, a Great Dane and an Italian lapdog—they were trying to have a go at it.

Danton.
So what?

Lacroix.
I just thought of that and I had to laugh. That was a fine thing! Girls were looking out of the windows—one ought to be careful and not let them sit in the sun or the flies will do it on their hands—that's food for thought. Legendre and I went through almost every cell—the little Nuns of the Revelation Through the Flesh were hanging on our coattails and demanded a blessing. Legendre is making one do penance, but he'll have to fast for a month for that. Here are two priestesses of the body.

Marion.
Hello, Miss Adelaide, hello, Miss Rosalie.

Rosalie.
We haven't seen you for a long time.

Marion.
Yes, I'm sorry.

Adelaide.
Oh God, we're busy night and day.

Danton.
(*To* ROSALIE.) Say, little one, your hips are getting softer.

33

Rosalie.

Oh yes, every day we get more perfect.

Lacroix.

What's the difference between an antique and a modern Adonis?

Danton.

And Adelaide has gotten virtuous—how interesting! A fascinating change. Her face looks like a fig leaf which she holds in front of her whole body. A fig tree like that on such a frequented street throws a refreshing shadow.

Adelaide.

I'd be a cowpath, if Monsieur hadn't . . .

Danton.

I know, just don't get angry, my dear.

Lacroix.

Listen! A modern Adonis isn't torn to pieces by a boar but by sows. He isn't wounded in the thigh but in the groin, and it's not roses that sprout from his blood but buds of mercury.

Danton.

Miss Rosalie is a restored torso. Only her hips and feet are antique. She's a magnetized needle: what the head-pole repels, the footpole attracts—her middle is an equator where everyone who crosses the line gets a sublimate baptism.

Lacroix.

Two sisters of mercy—each serves in her own hospital, that is, in her own body.

Rosalie.

You ought to be ashamed! You're making our ears red.

Adelaide.

You should have better manners.

(ADELAIDE *and* ROSALIE *exit.*)

Danton.

Good night, you beautiful children!

Lacroix.

Good night, you pits of mercury!

Danton.

I'm sorry for them. They'll miss dinner.

Lacroix.

Listen, Danton, I just came from the Jacobins.

Danton.
Is that all?

Lacroix.
The Lyonists read a proclamation, saying that all they could do was to wrap themselves in a toga. Everybody made a face as if he wanted to say to his neighbor: Paetus, it doesn't hurt! Legendre cried that some want to shatter the busts of Chalier and Marat. I think he wants to redden his face again. He's completely turned away from the Terror—on the street children tug at his coat.

Danton.
And Robespierre?

Lacroix.
Drummed on the tribune and said, "Virtue must rule through terror." That cliché made my neck hurt.

Danton.
It's planing boards for the guillotine.

Lacroix.
And Collot yelled like a madman that it's time to tear off masks.

Danton.
The faces will come off with them.

(PARIS *enters.*)

Lacroix.
What's new, Fabricius?

Paris.
From the Jacobins I went to Robespierre. I demanded an explanation. He tried to make a face like Brutus sacrificing his sons. He spoke in generalities about duty, said that concerning freedom he makes no compromises, he would sacrifice anyone—himself, his brother, his friends.

Danton.
That was clear. If you reverse the order, he'll stand below and hold the ladder for his friends. We owe Legendre thanks. He made them talk.

Lacroix.
The Hébertists aren't dead yet and the people are impoverished—that's a terrible lever. The scale of blood must not rise if it is not to become a lamppost for the

35

Committee of Public Safety. It needs ballast—it needs a weighty head.

Danton.
I know that. The Revolution is like Saturn, it devours its own children. (*After some thought.*) But they won't dare.

Lacroix.
Danton, you are a dead saint, but the Revolution is not interested in relics. It has thrown the bones of kings out into the street and all the statues out of the churches. Do you think they'd let you stand as a monument?

Danton.
My name! The people!

Lacroix.
Your name! You are a moderate, I am one, Camille, Philippeau, Hérault. For the masses weakness and moderation are the same. They kill the stragglers. The tailors of the red-cap faction will feel all of Roman history in their needles if the Man of September[6] was a moderate to them.

Danton.
Very true, and besides—the people are like children. They have to break everything open to see what's inside.

Lacroix.
And besides, Danton, we are vice-ridden, as Robespierre says, that is, we enjoy ourselves; and the people are virtuous, that is, they don't enjoy themselves, because work deadens their organs of pleasure. They don't get drunk because they don't have any money, and they don't go to whorehouses because their breath smells of cheese and herring and that disgusts the girls.

Danton.
They hate the pleasure seekers as a eunuch hates men.

Lacroix.
They call us scoundrels, and (*Leaning toward* DANTON's *ear.*) between us, there's a grain of truth to that. Robespierre and the people will be virtuous, St. Just will write a novel, and Barère will tailor a carmagnole and hang a mantle of blood over the Convention and . . . I see it all.

Danton.
You're dreaming. They never had courage without me.

6 Danton.

They won't have any against me. The Revolution isn't over yet. They might still need me—they'll keep me in the arsenal.

Lacroix.
We must act.

Danton.
We'll see.

Lacroix.
You'll see when we're lost.

Marion.
(*To* DANTON.) Your lips are cold, your words have stifled your kisses.

Danton.
(*To* MARION.) To have lost so much time! As if it were worth it! (*To* LACROIX.) Tomorrow I'll go to Robespierre —I'll provoke him. Then he can't remain silent. Until tomorrow! Good night, my friends, good night, I thank you.

Lacroix.
Out, my good friends, out! Good night, Danton, the thighs of that woman will guillotine you, the mound of Venus will be your Tarpeian Rock. (*Exit.*)

6

A room.

ROBESPIERRE. DANTON. PARIS.

Robespierre.
I tell you, whoever tries to stop me when I pull my sword is my enemy. His intention is of no concern. Whoever prevents me from defending myself kills me as surely as if he attacked me.

Danton.
Murder begins where self-defense stops. I see no reason to continue the executions.

Robespierre.
The social revolution is not yet achieved. Whoever carries out a revolution only halfway, digs his own grave. Aristocracy is not yet dead; the healthy strength of the peo-

ple must replace this class, decadent in all respects. Vice must be punished, virtue must rule through terror.

Danton.

I don't understand the word "punishment." You and your "virtue," Robespierre! You've never taken money, you've never been in debt, you've never slept with a woman, you've always worn a decent coat, and you've never gotten drunk. Robespierre, you are appallingly upright. I'd be ashamed to walk around between heaven and earth for thirty years with that righteous face just for the miserable pleasure of finding others worse than I. Isn't there something in you that sometimes whispers secretly: you lie, you lie!

Robespierre.

My conscience is clean.

Danton.

Conscience is a mirror before which an ape tortures itself. We preen ourselves as best we can, and we go looking for pleasure each in our own way. As if it were worth the trouble to get in each other's hair: everyone can defend himself when someone else spoils his fun. Do you have the right to make the guillotine a basket for other people's dirty laundry and to make their decapitated heads into scrubbing balls for their dirty clothes just because you always wear a cleanly brushed coat? Yes, you can defend yourself when they spit on it or tear holes in it, but what difference does it make to you as long as they leave you alone? If they don't mind walking around as they do, do you have the right to lock them up in a grave? Are you the military policeman of heaven? And if you can't stand the sight of it, as God can, then put a handkerchief over your eyes.

Robespierre.

You deny virtue?

Danton.

And vice. There are only Epicureans, either crude or refined. Christ was the most refined of all. That's the only difference I can discern among men. Each one acts according to his nature, that means he does what is good for him. Isn't it cruel, Mr. Incorruptible, to pull the rug out from under you like this?

Robespierre.

Danton, at certain times vice can be high treason.

Danton.

You can't outlaw it, for heaven's sake—that would be ungrateful. You owe vice too much for providing a contrast to you. By the way, in keeping with your terminology, our blows must serve the Republic: the innocent must not be struck down with the guilty.

Robespierre.

Whoever said that an innocent person was struck down?

Danton.

Do you hear that, Fabricius? No innocent person was killed! (*Leaving, to* PARIS.) We don't have a moment to lose, we must show ourselves! (DANTON *and* PARIS *exit.*)

Robespierre.

(*Alone.*) Go ahead! He wants to stop the horses of the Revolution at the whorehouse, like a coachman his trained nags. They'll have enough strength to drag him to the Square of the Revolution. "To pull the rug out from under me!" "In keeping with your terminology!" Wait! Wait! Is it really that? They will say his gigantic figure threw too much of a shadow on me, and for that I made him leave the sunlight. And if they're right? Is it really that necessary? Yes, yes! The Republic! He must go. It's ridiculous how my thoughts watch over each other. He must go. Whoever stands still in a mass moving forward opposes it as much as if he would move against it. He'll be trampled. We will not let the ship of the Revolution be stranded on the shallow calculations and the mudbanks of these people; we must cut off the hand that tries to stop it, and even if he seized it with his teeth! Down with a society which took the clothes away from the dead aristocracy and inherited its leprosy! "No virtue!" "Virtue: a rug under me!" "In keeping with my terminology!" How that keeps coming back. Why can't I escape that thought? It's always pointing there, there! with a bloody finger. I can wrap as many rags around it as I like, the blood keeps seeping through. (*After a pause.*) I can't tell what part of me is deceiving the other. (*He steps to the window.*) Night snores over the earth and wallows in wild dreams. Thoughts, hardly perceived wishes, confused and formless, having crept shyly from daylight, now take

39

shape and steal into the silent house of dreams. They open doors, they look out of windows, they become almost flesh, their limbs stretch out in sleep, their lips murmur . . . And isn't our waking a more lucid dream? Aren't we sleepwalkers? Aren't our actions dreamlike, only clearer, more certain, more complete? Who can reproach us for that? The mind accomplishes in one hour more acts of thought than the sluggish organism of our body can carry out in years. The sin is in our thoughts. Whether thought becomes action, whether the body carries it out—that is pure chance.

(ST. JUST *enters*.)

Robespierre.

Hey—who's there, in the dark? Hey—lights, lights!

St. Just.

Do you know my voice?

Robespierre.

Oh, it's you, St. Just! (*A maid brings a light*.)

St. Just.

Were you alone?

Robespierre.

Danton just left.

St. Just.

I met him on the way in the Palais Royal. He made his revolutionary face and spoke in epigrams. He spoke familiarly with the sansculottes, the grisettes were on his heels, and people were standing around whispering what he had just said in each other's ears. We will lose the advantage of the attack. How much longer are you going to hesitate? We will act without you. We are resolved.

Robespierre.

What do you want to do?

St. Just.

We will call a formal session of the Committees of Legislature, of General Security, and of Public Safety.

Robespierre.

Quite a bother.

St. Just.

We must bury the great corpse with proper decorum, like priests, not murderers. We dare not chop it up; all its limbs must fall with it.

40

Robespierre.

Speak more clearly.

St. Just.

We must bury him in full armor and slaughter his horses and slaves on his burial mound: Lacroix . . .

Robespierre.

A confirmed scoundrel, formerly a law clerk, presently lieutenant general of France. Go on.

St. Just.

Hérault-Séchelles.

Robespierre.

A handsome head.

St. Just.

He was the nicely painted capital letter of the Constitutional Acts. We have no further need of such ornaments. He will be erased. Philippeau, Camille . . .

Robespierre.

He too?

St. Just.

(*Hands him a piece of paper.*) I thought so. Read that!

Robespierre.

Aha, *The Old Franciscan*, is that all? He's a child, he was laughing at you.

St. Just.

Read it, here, here!

Robespierre.

(*Reads.*) "Robespierre: a Messiah of Blood on his Calvary between the two thieves Couthon and Collot, upon which he sacrifices and is not sacrificed. The devotees of the guillotine stand below like Mary and Magdalene. St. Just lies at his heart like St. John and reveals to the Convention the apocalyptic revelations of the Master. He carries his head like a monstrance."

St. Just.

I will make him carry his like St. Denis.

Robespierre.

(*Reads on.*) "Are we to believe that the clean shirt of the Messiah is the shroud of France and that his thin fingers, twitching on the tribune, are guillotine blades? And you, Barère, who said our coinage is being minted on the Square of the Revolution. Yet—I don't want to dig up that old sack again.[7] He is a widow who had half a dozen husbands and helped bury them all. Who can help that? That is his talent: he sees a death's head on people half a year before they die. Who would want to sit with corpses and smell the stench?" You too, then, Camille? Away with them! Quickly! Only the dead do not return. Have you prepared the accusation?

St. Just.

It will be easy. You made allusions to it at the Jacobins.

Robespierre.

I wanted to scare them.

St. Just.

I merely have to carry out your threats. The Forgers are the soup and the Foreigners the nuts. They will die from the meal, I promise you.

Robespierre.

Then quickly, tomorrow. No long death agony! I've become sensitive lately. Quickly!

(ST. JUST *exits*.)

Robespierre.

(*Alone*.) That's true, Messiah of Blood who sacrifices and is not sacrificed. He redeemed them with His blood and I redeem them with their own. He allowed them to sin and I take the sin upon myself. He had the ecstasy of pain, and I the agony of the executioner. Who denied himself more, I or He? And yet there is something foolish in that thought . . . Why do we always look only toward Him? Truly the Son of Man is crucified in each of us, we all struggle in bloody sweat in the Garden of Gethsemane, but not one of us redeems the other with his wounds . . . My Camille!—They're all leaving me—all is desolate and empty—I am alone.

---

[7] A pun on Barère de Vieuzac.

ACT TWO

1

A room.

DANTON. LACROIX. PHILIPPEAU. PARIS. CAMILLE
DESMOULINS.

Camille.
Hurry, Danton, we have no time to lose.

Danton.
(*Getting dressed.*) But time loses us. It's very boring, always putting on the shirt first and the pants over it and going to bed at night and crawling out again in the morning and always putting one foot before the other—there's no hope that it will ever be any different. It's all very sad . . . and millions have done it this way and millions will keep on doing it—and, above all, we're made up of two parts which do the same thing so that everything happens twice. That's very sad.

Camille.
You sound like a child.

Danton.
The dying often become childish.

Lacroix.
Your hesitation is dragging you down to destruction, and you're taking all your friends with you. Let the cowards know that it's time to gather around you. Call to the Plain and to the Mountain. Cry out against the tyranny of the decemvirs, speak of daggers, call on Brutus—then you will frighten the tribunes and even gather up those who are denounced as accomplices of Hébert. Give way to your anger! At least don't let us die defenseless and humiliated like that disgraceful Hébert.

Danton.
You have a bad memory. You called me a dead saint.

43

You were right—even more so than you thought. I was at the Section meetings—they were respectful but like undertakers. I am a relic and relics are thrown into the street. You were right.

Lacroix.

Why did you let it come to that?

Danton.

To that? Yes, in fact, I was finally bored with it all. Always walking around in the same coat and making the same face. That's pitiful. To be such a wretched instrument, whose string always sounds the same tone. I can't bear it. I wanted to make it easy for myself. I was successful: the Revolution is letting me retire, but in another way than I expected. Besides, what can we rely on? Our whores could still compete with the devoted sisters of the guillotine; that's all I can think of. I can count it all off on my fingers: the Jacobins have announced that virtue is now the order of the day, the Cordeliers call me Hébert's executioner, the Commune does penance, the Convention—that might still be a way! But there'd be a 31st of May, they wouldn't obligingly withdraw. Robespierre is the dogma of the Revolution which cannot be erased. That wouldn't work either. We haven't made the Revolution; the Revolution has made us. And even if it worked—I would rather be guillotined than guillotine others. I'm sick of it. Why should we human beings fight each other? We should sit down with each other in peace. A mistake was made when we were created—something is missing. I have no name for it. We won't rip it out of each other's intestines, so why should we break open each other's bodies? Oh, we are miserable alchemists.

Camille.

To say it in a more sublime way: how long should humanity devour its own limbs in eternal hunger? Or: how long should we, stranded on a wreck, suck blood out of each other's veins in unquenchable thirst? Or: how long should we algebraists of the flesh write our calculations with tattered limbs while searching for the unknown, eternally withheld X?

Danton.

You are a strong echo.

Camille.

Yes, a pistol shot resounds as loudly as a thunderclap, doesn't it? So much the better for you, you should always have me with you.

Philippeau.

And France is left with her executioners?

Danton.

What's the difference? The people are very happy with them. The people are not well off. Can one ask more in order to be moved, noble, virtuous, or witty—or not to be bored at all? What's the difference if they die under the guillotine or from a fever or from old age? As long as they can walk offstage nimbly and can make pretty gestures and hear the audience clap as they exit. That's very nice—and it's fitting for us. We're always on the stage, even if we're finally stabbed in earnest. It's a good thing that our life span is being shortened a little. The coat was too long, our bodies couldn't fill it out. Life becomes an epigram—that's not so bad. Whoever has enough breath and spirit for an epic poem in fifty or sixty cantos? It's time that we drink that little bit of essence not out of tubs but out of liqueur glasses. That will still fill our mouths. In the past we could hardly get a few drops to run together in that bulky container. Finally—I ought to cry out, but that's too much trouble. Life isn't worth the effort we make to maintain it.

Paris.

So escape, Danton!

Danton.

Do we take our homeland along on the soles of our shoes? And finally—and that's the main point: they won't dare. (*To* CAMILLE.) Come, my boy, I tell you, they won't dare. Good-bye. Good-bye!

(DANTON *and* CAMILLE *exit.*)

Philippeau.

There he goes.

Lacroix.

And he doesn't believe a word he's said. Nothing but laziness! He would rather let himself be guillotined than make a speech.

Paris.

What do we do now?

Lacroix.

We'll go home and think like Lucretia about an honorable death.

2

A promenade.

PASSERSBY.

A Citizen.

My good Jacqueline—I mean, Corn . . . uh, Cor . . .

Simon.

Cornelia, citizen, Cornelia.

Citizen.

My good Cornelia has blessed me with a son.

Simon.

Has borne a son for the Republic.

Citizen.

. . . for the Republic—that's too general. One might say . . .

Simon.

That's just it, the part must succumb to the whole . . .

Citizen.

Oh, yes, my wife says the same thing.

Balladeer.

> Tell me, tell me everyone,
> What's man's joy, what's his fun?

Citizen.

Oh, but his name, I just can't think of anything.

Simon.

Call him Pike, Marat.

Balladeer.

> With sorrow and with care he's worn,
> Working from the early morn,
> Till the day is done.

Citizen.

Three'd be better, there's something about the number

46

Three—now, something useful and something just. I've got it: Plow Robespierre. And then the third?

Simon.

Pike.

Citizen.

Thank you, neighbor. Pike Plow Robespierre, those are pretty names, that'll be nice.

Simon.

I tell you, the breast of your Cornelia will be like the udder of the Roman she-wolf—no, that won't do—Romulus was a tyrant, that won't do. (*They pass on.*)

A Beggar.

> A handful of earth
> And a little bit of moss . . .

Dear sirs, kind ladies!

First Gentleman.

Go and work, you dog, you look very well fed.

Second Gentleman.

There! (*He gives him money.*) His hand's like velvet. What impudence!

Beggar.

Sir, how did you get that coat of yours?

Second Gentleman.

Work, work! You could have one just like it. I'll give you a job. Call on me—I live at . . .

Beggar.

Sir, why did you work?

Second Gentleman.

So I could have the coat, idiot.

Beggar.

You tortured yourself for a piece of pleasure. A coat like that's a pleasure . . . so's a rag.

Second Gentleman.

Certainly, otherwise you can't have it.

Beggar.

If I were such a fool! It all balances out. The sun's shining warmly on the corner and that's easy to have. (*Sings.*)

> A handful of earth
> And a little bit of moss . . .

Rosalie.

(*To* ADELAIDE.) Hurry up, there come the soldiers. We haven't had anything warm in our bodies since yesterday.

Beggar.

> . . . Is all I'll have left
> When I lie beneath the cross!

Gentlemen, ladies!

Soldier.

Wait! Where are you off to, my dears? (*To* ROSALIE.) How old are you?

Rosalie.

As old as my pinkie.

Soldier.

You're very sharp.

Rosalie.

You're very blunt.

Soldier.

So I'll have to whet myself on you. (*He sings.*)

> Christina, O Christina dear,
> Does the pain make you sore, make you sore,
> Make you sore, make you sore?

Rosalie.

(*Sings.*)

> Oh no, dear soldiers,
> All I say is: give me more, give me more,
> Give me more, give me more!

(DANTON *and* CAMILLE *enter.*)

Danton.

Isn't that a laugh! I sense something in the atmosphere. It's as if the sun were hatching out lechery. Don't you feel like jumping into the middle of it, tearing off your pants and copulating over someone's ass like dogs in the street? (*They go past.*)

Young Gentleman.

Ah, Madame, the tolling of a bell, twilight on the treetops, a twinkling star . . .

Madame.

A flower's scent! These natural pleasures, this pure enjoyment of nature! (*To her daughter.*) You see, Eugénie, only virtue has eyes for such things.

Eugénie.

(*Kisses her mother's hand.*) Oh, Mama, I see only you!

Madame.

Good girl!

Young Gentleman.

(*Whispers into* EUGÉNIE'*s ear.*) Do you see that pretty lady over there with the old gentleman?

Eugénie.

I know her.

Young Gentleman.

They say her hairdresser gave her a special treatment.

Eugénie.

(*Laughs.*) Naughty tongues.

Young Gentleman.

The old gentleman walks with her, he sees the little bud swelling and takes it for a walk in the sun, thinking he was the thundershower that made it grow.

Eugénie.

How shameful! I almost feel like blushing.

Young Gentleman.

That could make me turn pale. (*They exit.*)

Danton.

(*To* CAMILLE.) Don't expect me to be serious. I can't understand why people don't stop on the street and laugh in each other's faces. I'd think they'd have to laugh out of the windows and out of the graves, and the heavens would burst and the earth would be convulsed with laughter. (*They exit.*)

First Gentleman.

An extraordinary discovery, I assure you. All the technical arts will acquire a new look. The human race is making giant strides toward its great destiny.

Second Gentleman.

Have you seen the new play? A Tower of Babylon! A maze of arches, stairways, halls—and it's all blown up with the greatest of ease. You get dizzy at every step. A bizarre idea! (*He stops in embarrassment.*)

First Gentleman.

What's the matter?

Second Gentleman.

Oh, nothing! Your arm, sir . . . it's the puddle—there. Thank you. I barely managed it—that could have been dangerous!

First Gentleman.

You weren't afraid?

Second Gentleman.

Yes, the earth is a thin crust. I always think I'll fall through a hole like that. You have to walk carefully— you might break through. But go to the theater—take my advice.

3

A room.

DANTON. CAMILLE. LUCILE.

Camille.

I tell you, if they aren't given everything in wooden copies, scattered about in theaters, concerts, and art exhibits, they'll have neither eyes nor ears for it. Let someone whittle a marionette where the strings pulling it are plainly visible and whose joints crack at every step in iambic pentameter: what a character! What consistency! Let someone take a little bit of feeling, an aphorism, a concept, and clothe it in a coat and pants, give it hands and feet, color its face and let the thing torment itself through three acts until it finally marries or shoots itself: an ideal! Let someone fiddle an opera which reflects the twists and turns of the human spirit the way a clay pipe with water imitates a nightingale: oh, art! Take people out of the theater and put them in the street: oh, miserable reality! They forget their Creator because of His poor imitators. They see and hear nothing of Creation, which renews itself every moment in and around them, glowing, rushing, luminous. They go to the theater, read poetry and novels, make faces like the masks they find there, and say to God's creatures: how ordinary! The Greeks knew what they were saying when they said that Pygmalion's statue did in fact come to life but never had any children.

Danton.

And the artists treat nature like David, who cold-bloodedly sketched those murdered in September, when they were thrown out of the Force Prison onto the streets, saying: I am capturing the last spasms of life in these villains. (DANTON *is called out.*)

Camille.
What do you think, Lucile?

Lucile.
Nothing, I like to watch you talk.

Camille.
Do you listen to what I say, too?

Lucile.
Yes, of course.

Camille.
Was I right? Did you understand what I said?

Lucile.
No—not at all. (DANTON *returns.*)

Camille.
What's the matter?

Danton.
The Committee of Public Safety has decided to arrest me. I've been warned and offered a place of refuge. They're after my head—so what? I'm sick of all this bungling. Let them have it. What will it matter? I'll know how to die bravely—that's easier than living.

Camille.
Danton, there's still time.

Danton.
Impossible . . . but I wouldn't have thought . . .

Camille.
Your laziness!

Danton.
I'm not lazy, just tired. The soles of my feet are on fire.

Camille.
Where will you go?

Danton.
Yes, if I only knew.

Camille.
Seriously, where?

Danton.
For a walk, my boy, for a walk. (*He goes.*)

Lucile.
Oh, Camille!

Camille.
Don't worry, my dear.

Lucile.
When I think that this head—Camille! That's nonsense, right? Am I crazy to think it?

Camille.
Don't worry. Danton and I are not the same person.

Lucile.
The world is large and there're many things on it—why just this one—who would take this from me? That would be awful. What good would it do them?

Camille.
I'm telling you, it'll be all right. Yesterday I talked to Robespierre—he was friendly. Things are a little strained, that's true—differing opinions, that's all.

Lucile.
Go look for him.

Camille.
We sat next to each other in school. He was always gloomy and aloof. I was the only one who went to him and made him laugh sometimes. He's always showed me great affection. I'll go.

Lucile.
Off so fast, my friend? Go ahead . . . come here! Just that (*She kisses him.*) and that! Go! Go! (CAMILLE *exits.*) These are terrible times. But that's the way it is. Who can change it? You have to live with it. (*Sings.*)

> Oh, parting, oh parting, oh parting,
> Whoever invented parting?

Why did I just think of *that?* That's not good, if it simply comes out by itself that way. When he left it seemed as if he could never turn back and had to go farther and farther away from me, farther and farther away. The room's so empty, the windows are open, as if a dead man had been lying here. I can't stand it up here. (*She leaves.*)

4

Open field.

Danton.
I won't go on. I don't like to break this silence with my clattering footsteps and my panting breath. (*He sits. After*

a pause.) I've heard of a sickness that makes one lose one's memory. Death, they say, is like that. Then I hope sometimes that death would be even stronger and make one lose everything. If only that were so! Then I'd run like a Christian to save my enemy—that is, my memory. That place[8] is supposed to be safe. Maybe for my memory, but not for me—the grave would be safer. At least it would make me forget. It would kill my memory. But there my memory will live on and kill me. It or I? The answer is easy. (*He rises and turns around.*) I'm flirting with death. It's pleasant to ogle him like this through an eyeglass from a distance. Actually, the whole affair makes me laugh. There's a feeling of permanence in me which says that tomorrow will be the same as today, and the day after and all the days to come will be alike. It's all a lot of empty noise. They want to scare me. They won't dare. (*Exit.*)

5

A room. Night.

DANTON. JULIE.

Danton.

(*At the window.*) Won't it ever stop? Won't the light ever fade, the sound die away? Won't it ever become quiet and dark so that we don't hear and see each other's ugly sins? —September!—

Julie.

(*Calls from inside.*) Danton! Danton!

Danton.

Yes?

Julie.

(*Enters.*) What did you shout?

Danton.

Did I shout?

Julie.

You talked of ugly sins and then you moaned, "September!"

---

[8] The place to which he is fleeing.

Danton.

Did I? No, I didn't say it. I hardly thought it. Those were just very quiet secret thoughts.

Julie.

You're trembling, Danton.

Danton.

And shouldn't I tremble when the walls begin to talk? When my body is so shattered that my uncertain, wavering thoughts speak with the lips of stones? That's strange.

Julie.

Georges, my Georges!

Danton.

Yes, Julie, that's very strange. I'd like to stop thinking when such talking is going on. There are thoughts, Julie, for which there shouldn't be any ears. It's not good that they scream at birth like children. That's not good.

Julie.

May God keep you in your right mind, Georges. Georges, do you recognize me?

Danton.

Oh, why not? You are a human being, a woman, and specifically my wife; the earth has five continents, Europe, Asia, Africa, America, Australia; and two times two is four. I haven't lost my senses, you see. Didn't something scream "September"? Isn't that what you said?

Julie.

Yes, Danton, I heard it through all the rooms.

Danton.

As I came to the window—(*He looks out.*) the city is quiet, the lights are out . . .

Julie.

A child is crying nearby.

Danton.

As I came to the window—through all the streets it cried and shrieked—"September!"

Julie.

You were dreaming, Danton. Get hold of yourself.

Danton.

Dreaming? Yes, I was dreaming—but it was different— I'll tell you right away, my poor head is weak—right away! There—now I've got it! Beneath me the globe was panting in its flight, I had seized it like a wild horse, with immense limbs I rooted in its mane and pressed its ribs, with my head bent down, my hair streaming out over the abyss. I was being dragged along. I screamed in fear and awoke. I went to the window—and that's when I heard it, Julie. What does that word want from me? Why just that, what do I have to do with that? Why does it stretch out its bloody hands toward me? I didn't strike it down. Oh, help me, Julie, my senses are dull. Wasn't it in September, Julie?

Julie.

The kings were just forty hours from Paris . . .

Danton.

The defenses had fallen, the aristocrats were in the city . . .

Julie.

The Republic was lost.

Danton.

Yes, lost. We couldn't ignore the enemy at our backs. We would have been fools—two enemies at once. We or they —the stronger strikes down the weaker, isn't that reasonable?

Julie.

Yes, yes.

Danton.

We killed them. That was not murder, that was internal war.

Julie.

You saved the country.

Danton.

Yes, I did. It was self-defense, we had to. The Man on the Cross made it easy for Himself: "It must needs be that offenses come, but woe to that man by whom the offense cometh." It must—it was this "must." Who would curse the hand on which the curse of "must" has fallen? Who has determined this "must," who? What is it in us that whores, lies, steals, and murders? We are nothing but puppets, our strings are pulled by unknown forces, we ourselves are nothing, nothing! Swords that spirits fight with—you just don't see any hands, like in a fairy tale. Now I'm calm.

Julie.

Completely calm, dear?

Danton.
Yes, Julie, come to bed.

6

Street in front of DANTON's *house.*

SIMON. CIVILIAN TROOPS.

Simon.
How far into the night?
First Citizen.
What into the night?
Simon.
How far are we into the night?
First Citizen.
As far as between sunset and sunrise.
Simon.
Idiot, what time is it?
First Citizen.
Look on your dial. It's the time when perpendiculars rise up under the bed sheets.
Simon.
Let's go up. Onward, citizens! We'll vouch for it with our heads. Dead or alive! He's very strong. I'll go first, citizens. Make way for freedom. Look to my wife! I'll leave her a wreath of laurels.
First Citizen.
A wreath of balls? Enough balls fall into her lap every day.
Simon.
Onward, citizens! The country will be grateful for your service!
Second Citizen.
I wish the country would serve *us*. With all those holes we make in other people's bodies, not a single one in our pants has been mended.
First Citizen.
Do you want your fly sewed up? Heh, heh, heh!
The Others.
Heh, heh, heh!

Simon.
Let's go, let's go! (*They force their way into* DANTON's *house.*)

7

The National Convention.

A group of DEPUTIES.

Legendre.
When will this slaughtering of deputies stop? Who is safe if Danton falls?

A Deputy.
What can we do?

Another Deputy.
He must be heard before the Convention. It's bound to work. How can they compete against his voice?

Another Deputy.
Impossible. A decree prohibits it.

Legendre.
It must be repealed or an exception must be granted. I'll make the motion. I'm counting on your support.

President.
The session is opened.

Legendre.
(*Ascends the tribune.*) Four members of the National Convention were arrested last night. I know that Danton is one of them; I do not know the names of the others. Whoever they may be, I demand that they be heard here. Citizens, I declare Danton to be as innocent as myself, and I believe my record to be beyond reproach. I do not wish to accuse any member of the Committees of Public Safety or of General Security, but for well-founded reasons I fear that personal enmity and emotion could deprive freedom of such men who have served it well. The man who through his exertions saved France in 1792 deserves to be heard. He must be allowed to account for himself when he is accused of high treason. (*Great commotion.*)

Several Voices.

We support Legendre's motion.

A Deputy.

We are here in the name of the people. We cannot be deprived of our seats without the will of the electorate.

Another Deputy.

Your words smell of corpses. They come from the mouths of the Girondists. Are you asking for privileges? The ax of the law hangs over *all* heads.

Another Deputy.

We cannot allow our committees to send our legislators from the immunity of the law to the guillotine.

Another Deputy.

Crime knows no immunity. Only royal crimes find it on the throne.

Another.

Only scoundrels appeal to the right of immunity.

Another.

Only murderers refuse to recognize it.

Robespierre.

Such disorder, unknown in this assembly for a long time, proves that weighty matters are at stake. It shall be decided today whether a few men will stand as victors over the country. How can you compromise your principles to such an extent that you grant a few individuals today that which you refused Chabot, Delaunai, and Fabre yesterday? Why should these few men be treated differently? What do I care about the eulogies one makes for oneself and for one's friends? Only too many experiences have shown us what to think of that. We do not ask whether a man has performed this or that patriotic act; we inquire about his entire political career. Legendre does not appear to know the names of those who were arrested. The entire Convention knows them. His friend Lacroix is among them. Why does Legendre appear not to know that? Because he knows that only impudence can defend Lacroix. He named only Danton because he believes that this name demands special privileges. No, we want no privileges, we want no idols! (*Applause.*) What distinguishes Danton from Lafayette, from Dumouriez, from Brissot, Fabre, Chabot, Hébert? What was said about them that you could not also say about him? Did you spare them?

Why should he be preferred to his fellow citizens? Possibly because a few deceived individuals and others who did not let themselves be deceived gathered around him in order to rush into the arms of fortune and power as his followers? The more he has deceived patriots who trusted him, the more forcefully he must feel the severity of the friends of freedom. They want to intimidate you against the misuse of power which you yourselves have practiced. They cry out against the despotism of the committees as if the trust which the people have placed in you and which you have delegated to these committees were not a certain guarantee of patriotism. They pretend to tremble. But I say that whoever trembles at this moment is guilty, for innocence never trembles before the watchful eye of the public. (*General applause.*) They tried to intimidate me: I was led to understand that the danger which threatens Danton might extend to me. They wrote me that Danton's friends had besieged me in the opinion that a memory of old ties, a blind belief in simulated virtues could resolve me to moderate my zeal and passion for freedom. Thus I declare that nothing shall stop me, even if I should be faced with the danger Danton is in. We all need some courage and magnanimity. Only criminals and base souls fear to see their allies fall at their side, for when they are no longer hidden by a crowd of accomplices, they are exposed to the light of truth. Yet if there are such souls in this assembly, there are also heroic ones here. The villains are not great in number. We need only strike down a few heads, and the country is saved. (*Applause.*) I demand that Legendre's motion be rejected. (*The* DEPUTIES *rise together as a sign of universal approval.*)

St. Just.

There appear to be in this assembly a number of sensitive ears which cannot endure the word "blood." May a few general observations convince them that we are no crueler than nature or time. Nature follows its laws serenely and irresistibly; man is destroyed when he comes in conflict with them. A change in the elements of the atmosphere, an eruption of tellurian fires, a fluctuation in the balance of a body of water, a plague, a volcanic eruption, a flood bury thousands. What is the result? A generally insignificant, hardly noticeable change of physical nature that would have passed almost without a trace, were not corpses lying on its path. I ask you now: should *moral* nature in its revolutions take greater consideration than physical nature? Should not an idea be permitted to destroy its opposition just as well as a law of physics? Should any event whatsoever which transforms the shape of moral nature—that is, humanity—not be permitted to shed blood? The world spirit makes use of our arms in the sphere of the intellect just as in the physical sphere it generates volcanic eruptions or floods. What does it matter if men die from a plague or a revolution? The strides of humanity are slow, they can only be counted in centuries. Behind each stride rise the graves of generations. The achievement of the simplest inventions or principles has cost the lives of millions who died along the way. Is it then not obvious that at a time when the course of history accelerates, more people lose their breath? We will conclude quickly and simply: since everyone was created under the same conditions, all men are therefore equal, aside from the differences nature itself has caused. This is to the advantage of all, yet no one may therefore enjoy prerogatives, neither an individual nor a smaller nor a greater class of individuals. Every portion of our proposition, applied in reality, has killed its human beings. The 14th of July, the 10th of August, the 31st of May are its punctuation marks. It needed four years to be realized in the physical world. Under normal conditions it would have required a century and would have been punctuated with generations. Is it therefore so surprising that the flow of the revolution throws out its corpses at every dip, at every new turn? We have yet to add several conclusions to our proposition: shall a few hundred corpses prevent us from making them? Moses led his people through the Red Sea and into the desert until the old decadent generation had destroyed itself before he founded a new state. Legislators! We have neither a Red Sea nor a desert, but we have the war and the guillotine. The Revolution is like the daughters of Pelias: it cuts humanity in pieces to rejuvenate it. Humanity will rise up with mighty limbs out of this cauldron of blood, like the earth out of the waters of the Flood, as if it had been

newly created. (*Long, sustained applause. Several* DEPU-
TIES *rise with enthusiasm.*) We summon all secret
enemies of tyranny, who in Europe and in the entire
world carry the dagger of Brutus beneath their cloaks, to
share with us this sublime hour! (*The spectators and the*
DEPUTIES *begin the* Marseillaise.)

ACT THREE

1

The Luxembourg prison. A room with prisoners.

CHAUMETTE. PAYNE. MERCIER. HÉRAULT-SÉCHELLES.
Other prisoners.

Chaumette.
(*Tugs at* PAYNE'S *sleeve.*) Listen, Payne, it could be that
way after all. Something came over me a while ago.
Today I have a headache. Help me a little with your
syllogisms, I feel very peculiar.

Payne.
Come then, philosopher Anaxagoras, I will catechize you.
There is no God, because: either God created the world
or He did not. If He did not, then the world has its basis
of existence within itself and there is no God, since God
only becomes God in that He contains the root of all
existence. However, God cannot have created the world,
for Creation is either eternal like God or it has a beginning. If the latter be true, then God must have brought
it into being at a specific moment. Thus, having been idle
for an eternity, God must have become active at a certain
point; He must therefore have experienced a change
within Himself, which subjects Him to the concept of
time. Both these points contradict the nature of God. God
therefore cannot have created the world. Since we know

61

very well, however, that the world or at least our own self exists, and, according to the above, must contain the basis of its existence within itself or within something that is not God, God therefore cannot exist. *Quod erat demonstrandum*.

Chaumette.

Yes, indeed, that makes it all very clear again. Thank you, thank you.

Mercier.

Just a moment, Payne. What if Creation is eternal?

Payne.

Then it is no longer Creation. Then it is one with God or an attribute of God, as Spinoza says. Then God is in everything, in you, my dear friend, in the philosopher Anaxagoras here, and in me. That would not be so objectionable, but you must admit that the Heavenly Majesty wouldn't come to much if our dear Lord were to suffer a toothache, get the clap, or be buried alive along with each of us—or at least experience the very unpleasant conceptions of these miseries.

Mercier.

But a cause must exist.

Payne.

Who denies that? But who can claim that this cause is that which we think to be God, for example, perfection? Do you consider the world to be perfect?

Mercier.

No.

Payne.

Then how can you postulate a perfect cause from an imperfect effect? Voltaire dared to spoil things with God as little as with the monarchs, that's why *he* did it. He who has nothing but his reason and doesn't even know or dare to use it consistently is a blunderer.

Mercier.

To that I ask: can a perfect cause have a perfect effect—that is, can perfection create perfection? Isn't that impossible because the created object can never have the basis of existence within itself, which, however, as you said, is a part of perfection?

Chaumette.

Be quiet! Be quiet!

Payne.

Calm yourself, philosopher. You are right; but if God were once to create and could only create imperfection, He had better forget about it entirely. Isn't it very human to be able to think of God only as a Creator? Because we always have to stretch and shake ourselves only in order to say, "We exist." Must we attribute this miserable necessity also to God? When our spirit becomes absorbed in the essence of an everlasting bliss, harmoniously at rest within itself, must we immediately assume that it has to stretch out its fingers and knead little men of dough on the table? It's because of a boundless need of love, as we secretly whisper into each other's ears. Must we do this only to make ourselves sons of God? I am satisfied with a lesser father. At least, I won't be able to say of him that he raised me beneath his station in pigsties or in the galleys. Eliminate imperfection; only then can you demonstrate God. Spinoza tried it. One may deny evil but not pain; only reason can prove the existence of God, our feelings rebel against it. Note this, Anaxagoras: why do I suffer? That is the rock of atheism. The smallest twinge of pain—and may it stir only in a single atom—makes a rent in Creation from top to bottom.

Mercier.

And what of morality?

Payne.

First you prove God from morality and then morality from God. What do you want with your morality? I don't know if in fact good or evil exist, and for that reason I certainly don't have to change my way of acting. I act according to my nature. Whatever is in keeping with it is good for me and I do it, and whatever is not is evil and I don't do it, and I protect myself against it when it comes in my way. One can remain virtuous, as they say, and defend oneself against so-called vice without having to despise one's opponents for that—which is really a sad feeling.

Chaumette.

True, very true!

Hérault.

Oh, philosopher Anaxagoras, one could also say that if God were to be all things, He would also have to be His own opposite—that is, perfect and imperfect, evil and good, blissful and suffering. The result would certainly equal zero, it would negate itself. We would come to nothing. Be happy—you'll get through all right. You can go on worshiping in Madame Momoro a masterpiece of nature. At least she has left her rosary in your groin.

Chaumette.

I thank you very much, gentlemen. (*Exits.*)

Payne.

He still doesn't believe it. In the end he'll take extreme unction, turn his feet toward Mecca, and get circumcised so he doesn't miss a chance.

(DANTON, LACROIX, CAMILLE, PHILIPPEAU *are led in.*)

Hérault.

(*Goes up to* DANTON *and embraces him.*) Good morning. Good night, I should say. I cannot ask how you've slept. How will you sleep?

Danton.

Well. One has to go to bed laughing.

Mercier.

(*To* PAYNE.) This hound with dove's wings! He's the evil genius of the Revolution, he dared to turn on his mother, but she was stronger than he.

Payne.

His life and his death are equally unfortunate.

Lacroix.

(*To* DANTON.) I didn't think that they would come so quickly.

Danton.

I knew it, I had been warned.

Lacroix.

And you said nothing?

Danton.

What for? A stroke is the best death. Would you rather be sick before it? And—I didn't believe they would dare. (*To* HÉRAULT.) It's better to lie down in the earth than to get corns walking on it. I'd rather have it as a pillow than as a footstool.

Hérault.

At least we won't stroke the cheeks of the fair Lady Decay with callused fingers.

Camille.

(*To* DANTON.) Don't trouble yourself. You can hang your tongue out as far as you like and you still won't be able to lick the sweat of death from your brow. Oh, Lucile! It's a great pity.

(*The prisoners crowd around the new arrivals.*)

Danton.

(*To* PAYNE.) What you have done for the good of your country I have tried to do for mine. I wasn't as lucky. They're sending me to the scaffold. So what, I won't stumble.

Mercier.

(*To* DANTON.) The blood of the twenty-two is drowning you.

A Prisoner.

(*To* HÉRAULT.) The power of the people and the power of reason are one.[9]

Another.

(*To* CAMILLE.) Now, Attorney General of the Lamppost, your improvement of street lighting hasn't made things any brighter in France.

Another.

Let him be! Those are the lips which spoke the word "mercy." (*He embraces* CAMILLE. *Several prisoners follow his example.*)

Philippeau.

We are priests who have prayed with the dying; we have been infected and will die of the same plague.

Several Voices.

The blow that strikes you kills us all.

Camille.

Gentlemen, I'm very sorry that our efforts were so fruitless. I go to the scaffold because my eyes became moist at the fate of a few unfortunates.

---

9 The prisoner taunts Hérault with his own words.

A room.

FOUQUIER-TINVILLE. HERMAN.

Fouquier.
Is everything ready?

Herman.
It'll be hard to make it stick. If Danton weren't among them, it would be easy.

Fouquier.
He must be made to lead the dance.

Herman.
He'll frighten the jury. He's the scarecrow of the Revolution.

Fouquier.
The jury will have to will it.

Herman.
I know of a way, but it would violate legal formality.

Fouquier.
Go ahead.

Herman.
We won't draw lots, but we'll pick out the reliable ones.

Fouquier.
That will have to work. We'll have a nice shooting gallery. There are nineteen of them, a cleverly mixed group. The four Forgers, then a few Bankers and Foreigners. A spicy meal—the masses need things like that. So we'll need dependable people. Who, for instance?

Herman.
Leroi—he's deaf and won't hear a word from the defendants. Danton can shout himself hoarse at him.

Fouquier.
Very good. Go on.

Herman.
Vilatte and Lumière. The one's always sitting in a tavern and the other's always asleep. They only open their mouths to say the word "guilty." Girard maintains that no one who has been brought before the Tribunal may go free. Renaudin . . .

Fouquier.

He, too? He once spared a few priests.

Herman.

Don't worry—he came to me a few days ago demanding that all who are to be executed should be bled beforehand to weaken them, because their usually defiant attitude annoys him.

Fouquier.

Oh, very good. Then I'll count on you.

Herman.

Leave it up to me.

3

The Conciergerie. A corridor.

(LACROIX, DANTON, MERCIER, *and other prisoners are walking up and down.*)

Lacroix.

(*To a prisoner.*) What, are there so many unfortunates, and in such miserable condition?

Prisoner.

Didn't the guillotine carts ever tell you that Paris is a slaughterhouse?

Mercier.

That's true, Lacroix. Equality swings its sickle over all our heads, the lava of the Revolution flows on, the guillotine creates a republic! The galleries clap and the Romans rub their hands, but they don't hear that each of these words is the death rattle of a victim. Try following your rhetoric to the point where it becomes reality. Look around you: all this you have spoken; here is a translation of your words in pantomime. These wretches, their hangmen, and the guillotine are the realization of your speeches. You built your systems, like Bajazet his pyramids, out of skulls.

Danton.

You're right. These days everything is worked in human flesh. That's the curse of our times. Now my body will be used up, too. A year ago I created the Revolutionary

Tribunal. I ask God and mankind to pardon me for that; I wanted to avoid new September massacres, I hoped to save the innocent, but this gradual murder with its formalities is more horrible and just as inevitable. Gentlemen, I hoped to help you leave this place.

Mercier.

Oh, we'll leave all right.

Danton.

Now I'm here with you. Heaven knows how this will end.

4

The Revolutionary Tribunal.

HERMAN. DANTON.

Herman.

(*To* DANTON.) Your name, citizen.

Danton.

The Revolution calls out my name. My residence will soon be in nothingness and my name in the Pantheon of history.

Herman.

Danton, the Convention accuses you of having conspired with Mirabeau, with Dumouriez, with Orléans, with the Girondists, with foreigners, and with the faction of Louis XVII.

Danton.

My voice, which has so often rung out on behalf of the people, will easily refute this slander. Let the wretches who accuse me appear here and I will cover them with disgrace. Let the committees appear; I will only answer before them. I need them as accusers and witnesses. Let them show themselves! Besides, why should I care about you or your judgment? I have already told you: nothingness will soon be my abode—life is a burden. Let them tear it from me; I long to shake it off.

Herman.

Danton, audacity suits a crime, calmness reflects innocence.

Danton.

Personal audacity certainly deserves reproach, but national audacity, which I have shown so often, with which I have so often fought for freedom, is the worthiest of all virtues. *This* is my audacity. I use it here for the sake of the Republic against my wretched accusers. Can I control myself when I see myself slandered in such a base way? One cannot expect a cold defense from a revolutionary such as I. Men of my sort are invaluable in revolutions, on our brows hovers the spirit of freedom. (*Signs of applause among the spectators.*) They accuse me of conspiring with Mirabeau, with Dumouriez, with Orléans; of crawling to the feet of wretched despots. They challenge me to answer before inescapable, unbending justice. You, miserable St. Just, will be responsible to posterity for this slander!

Herman.

I demand that you answer calmly. Think of Marat—he appeared before his judges with reverence.

Danton.

They have laid hands on my whole life, so let it arise and confront them. I will bury them under the weight of my every deed. I am not proud of this. Fate guides our arm, but only powerful natures are its organs. On the Field of Mars I declared war on the monarchy: I defeated it on the 10th of August, I killed it on the 21st of January and threw a king's head down as a gauntlet before all monarchs. (*Repeated signs of applause. He takes the papers of accusation.*) When I glance at these slanderous words, I feel my whole being tremble. Who are they, who had to force Danton to appear on that memorable day, the 10th of August? Who are the privileged beings, from whom he borrowed his energy? Let my accusers come forth! This is a most reasonable demand. I will unmask these vulgar rascals and hurl them back into the nothingness out of which they never should have crept.

Herman.

(*Rings a bell.*) Don't you hear the bell?

Danton.

The voice of a man who defends his honor and his life will cry down your bell. In September I gorged the young brood of the Revolution with the dismembered corpses of the aristocrats. My voice forged weapons for the masses out of the gold of the aristocrats and the rich. My voice was the typhoon which buried the satellites of despotism under waves of bayonets. (*Loud applause.*)

Herman.
Danton, your voice is worn out, you are far too emotional. At the next sitting you will conclude your defense. You are in need of rest. The session is adjourned.

Danton.
Now you know Danton. In a few hours he will fall asleep in the arms of glory.

5

The Luxembourg prison. A cell.

DILLON. LAFLOTTE. *A* JAILER.

Dillon.
Hey, stop shining your nose in my face. Heh, heh, heh!

Laflotte.
Keep your mouth shut—your moon has a halo. Heh, heh, heh!

Jailer.
Heh, heh, heh! Sir, do you think you could read by its light? (*Points to a paper in his hand.*)

Dillon.
Give it here!

Jailer.
Sir, my moon's brought on a low tide.

Laflotte.
From the looks of your pants I'd say a *high* tide.

Jailer.
No, my moon attracts water. (*To* DILLON.) It's hidden itself away from your sun, sir. You'll have to give me something to fire it up again if you want to read by its light.

Dillon.
Here, take this! Now get out. (*He gives him money. Exit* JAILER. DILLON *reads.*) Danton has frightened the Tri-

bunal, the jury wavers, the spectators were grumbling. The crowds were enormous. The people massed around the Palace of Justice out to the bridges. A handful of money, a willing arm—hm, hm! (*He walks back and forth, drinking out of a bottle from time to time.*) If only I had one foot in the street. I won't let myself be slaughtered like this. Yes, just one foot in the street!

Laflotte.
And on the guillotine cart, it's all the same.

Dillon.
You think so? There'd still be a few steps in between, long enough to measure with the corpses of the decemvirs.—It's high time that the honest people raise their heads.

Laflotte.
(*To himself.*) So much the better, that makes it easier to cut them off. Keep it up, old man, a few more glasses and my ship will be afloat.

Dillon.
The rascals, the fools! They'll guillotine each other in the end. (*He walks up and down.*)

Laflotte.
(*Aside.*) I could really love life again, like my own child, if I give it back to myself. It doesn't happen often that I can commit incest with chance and become my own father. Father and child in one. A pleasant Oedipus!

Dillon.
The people can't be fed with corpses. Danton's and Camille's wives ought to throw money to them, that's better than heads.

Laflotte.
(*Aside.*) But I wouldn't tear out my eyes afterward. I might need them to mourn for the good general.

Dillon.
Laying their hands on Danton! Who is still safe? Fear will unite them.

Laflotte.
(*Aside.*) He's lost anyway. What does it matter if I step on a corpse in order to climb out of the grave?

Dillon.
Just one foot in the street! I'll find enough people, old

soldiers, Girondists, former noblemen. We'll storm the prisons; we must unite with the prisoners.

Laflotte.

(*Aside.*) Well, yes, it smells a little like villainy. So what? I feel like trying *that* for once. Up to now I was too one-sided. I'll have conscience pangs, but that's a change too. It's not so unpleasant to smell one's own stink. The prospect of the guillotine has gotten boring. To have to wait for it so long! I've experienced it in my mind twenty times already. It's not even enticing anymore; it's gotten quite ordinary.

Dillon.

We must send a letter to Danton's wife.

Laflotte.

(*Aside.*) And then—I'm not afraid of death, but of pain. It could hurt—who is to answer for that? They say it's only for an instant, but pain measures time more finely, it splits a sixtieth of a second. No! pain is the only sin and suffering the only vice. I'll remain virtuous.

Dillon.

Listen, Laflotte, where did that fellow go? I've got money, that'll have to work. We must strike while the iron is hot, my plan is complete.

Laflotte.

Right away, right away. I know the jailer, I'll speak to him. You can count on me, general. We'll get out of this hole (*To himself as he leaves.*) and enter into another, I into the largest, the world; he into the smallest, the grave.

6

The Committee of Public Safety.

ST. JUST. BARÈRE. COLLOT D'HERBOIS. BILLAUD-VARENNES.

Barère.

What did Fouquier write?

St. Just.

The second hearing is over. The prisoners demand the appearance of several members of the Convention and of

72

the Committee of Public Safety. They appeal to the people because they are being denied witnesses. The excitement among the people is said to be indescribable. Danton parodied Jupiter and shook his locks.

Collot.

All the more easily will Samson grasp hold of them.

Barère.

We dare not show ourselves. The fishwives and the ragpickers wouldn't find us as imposing.

Billaud.

The masses have an instinct for letting themselves be stepped upon, even if only with a glance. They love insolent faces such as his. Such brows are worse than a noble coat of arms. The refined aristocratic scorn of humanity sits upon them. Everyone who dislikes being looked down on should help smash them in.

Barère.

He's like the horn-skinned Siegfried—the blood of the September massacres has made him invulnerable. What does Robespierre say?

St. Just.

He acts as if he had something to say. The jury must declare itself to be sufficiently informed and close the debates.

Barère.

Impossible, that won't work.

St. Just.

They must be taken care of at all costs, even if we have to strangle them with our own hands. "Dare!" Let it not be said that Danton taught us this word in vain. The Revolution will not trip over their bodies; but if Danton remains alive, he will catch it by the robe, and he has something about him that could ravish freedom itself. (ST. JUST *is called out.*)

(*A* JAILER *enters.*)

Jailer.

In St. Pelagie prisoners are dying, they are calling for a doctor.

Billaud.

That's unnecessary. Less work for the executioner.

Jailer.

There are pregnant women among them.

Billaud.

So much the better; their children won't need a coffin.

Barère.

A consumptive aristocrat saves the Revolutionary Tribunal a sitting. Any medical help would be counter-revolutionary.

Collot.

(*Takes a paper.*) A petition, a woman's name!

Barère.

Probably one of those who would like to be forced to choose between the board of the guillotine and the bed of a Jacobin. They die like Lucretia after being dishonored, but a little later than the Roman—namely, in childbirth, or from cancer or old age. It might not be so unpleasant to drive a Tarquin out of the virtuous republic of a virgin.

Collot.

She is too old. Madame demands death, she knows how to express herself—the prison rests upon her like the lid of a coffin. She's only been there four weeks. The answer is easy. (*He writes and reads.*) "Citizen, you have not wished for death long enough."

(JAILER *leaves.*)

Barère.

Well said. But Collot, it's not good if the guillotine begins to laugh. The people will no longer fear it. One shouldn't be so familiar.

(ST. JUST *returns.*)

St. Just.

I've just received a denunciation. There's a conspiracy in the prisons. A young man named Laflotte discovered it all. He sat in the same room with Dillon. Dillon was drinking and chattering.

Barère.

He cuts off his head with his bottle, that's happened before.

St. Just.

The wives of Danton and Camille are to throw money

74

among the people, Dillon is to escape, the prisoners will be set free, the Convention blown up.

Barère.

Those are fairy tales.

St. Just.

We will put them to sleep with this fairy tale. The denunciation I have right here; then the impudence of the accused, the unrest among the people, the consternation of the jury ... I'll make a report.

Barère.

Yes, go, St. Just, and spin your phrases, where each comma is a swordstroke and each period a decapitated head.

St. Just.

The Convention must decree that the Tribunal should continue the trial without interruption and may exclude from debate any of the accused who infringes upon the respect due to the court or creates a disturbance.

Barère.

You have a revolutionary instinct. That sounds very moderate, but it will have its effect. They cannot remain silent; Danton will have to shout.

St. Just.

I will count on your support. There are people in the Convention who are as sick as Danton and are afraid of getting a similar cure. They have taken courage again, they will scream about infraction of regulations ...

Barère.

(*Interrupting him.*) I will tell them: in Rome the consul who had discovered the Catiline conspiracy and had executed the criminals on the spot was accused of violating regulations. Who were his accusers?

Collot.

(*With pathos.*) Go, St. Just. The lava of the Revolution is flowing. Freedom will strangle in its embraces those weaklings who intended to fertilize its enormous womb; the majesty of the people will appear to them in thunder and lightning like Jupiter to Semele and transform them to ashes. Go, St. Just, we will help you hurl the thunderbolt upon the heads of the cowards. (ST. JUST *exits.*)

Barère.

Did you hear the word "cure"? They'll manage to make

the guillotine into medication against venereal disease. They're not fighting the moderates, they're fighting vice.

Billaud.

Up to now the two have followed the same path.

Barère.

Robespierre wants to use the Revolution as a lecture hall for morality and the guillotine as a pulpit.

Billaud.

Or as a praying stool.

Collot.

On which he'll eventually lie rather than kneel.

Barère.

That will be easy. The world would have to be standing on its head if the so-called rascals are to be hanged by the so-called righteous people.

Collot.

(*To* BARÈRE.) When will you come again to Clichy?

Barère.

When the doctor stops coming to me.

Collot.

Yes, indeed, there's a comet over that place whose scorching rays dry out your spinal fluid.

Billaud.

Soon the pretty fingers of the charming Demaly will pull it out of its case and make it hang down over his back like a braid.

Barère.

(*Shrugs his shoulders.*) Shh! The Incorruptible must not know about that.

Billaud.

He is an impotent Mohammed. (BILLAUD *and* COLLOT *leave.*)

Barère.

(*Alone.*) The monsters! "You have not wished for death long enough!" Those words should have withered the tongue that spoke them. And what about me? When the September murderers forced their way into the prisons, a prisoner grabbed his knife, and, mingling among the killers, plunged it into the breast of a priest—and he was saved! Who can object to that? Now what if I mingle with the killers or join the Committee of Public Safety? What

76

if I use a guillotine blade or a pocketknife? The situation remains the same, only with somewhat more complicated circumstances. The basic principles are alike. And if he could murder one—what about two, or three, or more? Where does it stop? Here come the barleycorns—are two a pile, three, four—how many then? Come, conscience, come, my little chicken. Come, cluck, cluck, cluck— here's food for you. And yet—was I ever a prisoner? I was suspect, that's the same thing. Death was certain. (*Exits.*)

7

The Conciergerie.

LACROIX. DANTON. PHILIPPEAU. CAMILLE.

Lacroix.
Well roared, Danton. If you had worried like that about your life a little sooner, things would be different now. It's bad, isn't it, when death comes so shamefully close and its breath stinks and it becomes ever more insistent?

Camille.
If only it would ravish us and tear its prey from our hot limbs in a fierce fight! But with all these formalities, it's like marrying an old woman, with the contracts drawn up, the witnesses called, Amen said, and then the bed sheets are raised and she crawls in with her cold limbs.

Danton.
If only it were a fight with hands and teeth! But I feel as if I've fallen into a mill and my limbs were slowly, systematically being screwed off by cold physical force. To be killed so mechanically!

Camille.
To lie there alone, cold, stiff, in the rotting dampness. It's possible that death slowly tortures life out of our fibers, perhaps to rot away consciously.

Philippeau.
Be calm, my friends. We are like the autumn crocus which only blooms after winter is over. We differ from

transplanted flowers only in that we stink a little from the experiment. Is that so bad?

Danton.

A pleasant prospect! From one dungheap to another. Isn't it just like the divine theory of classes? From first grade to second, from second to third, and so on? I'm sick of school benches, I've gotten calluses on my backside like a monkey from sitting on them.

Philippeau.

Then what do you want?

Danton.

Peace.

Philippeau.

Peace is in God.

Danton.

In nothingness. Try to immerse yourself in something more peaceful than nothingness, and if God is the greatest peace, isn't nothingness God? But I'm an atheist. Those cursed words: something cannot become nothing! And I am something, that's the pity of it. Creation has spread itself out so far that nothing is empty, it's all a jumble. Nothingness has killed itself, Creation is its wound, we are its drops of blood, the world is the grave in which it rots. That sounds crazy, but there's some truth to it.

Camille.

The world is the Wandering Jew, nothingness is death, but death is impossible. Oh, that I cannot die, that I cannot die, as the song says.

Danton.

We are all buried alive and entombed like kings in triple or quadruple coffins—under the sky, in our houses, in our coats and shirts. For fifty years we scratch on the lid of the coffin. Oh, to believe in obliteration—that would help. There's no hope in death; it's only a simpler—and life a more complicated—form of decay; that's the only difference! But I just happen to be used to this kind of decay. The devil only knows how I could adjust to another. Oh, Julie! If I had to go alone! If she would abandon me! And if I decomposed entirely, dissolved completely—I'd be a handful of tormented dust. Each of

my atoms could find peace only with her. I can't die, no,
I cannot die. We must cry out; they will have to tear out
every drop of life from my limbs.

8

A room.

FOUQUIER. AMAR. VOULAND.

Fouquier.
I no longer know how to answer. They demand a commission.

Amar.
We've got the rascals. Here's what you need. (*He gives*
FOUQUIER *a paper.*)

Vouland.
That will satisfy them.

Fouquier.
You're right, we needed that.

Amar.
Now go to work, so all of us can get this thing off our
necks.

9

The Revolutionary Tribunal.

DANTON. HERMAN. CAMILLE. OTHERS.

Danton.
The Republic is in danger and he (*Pointing to* HERMAN.)
has no instructions! We appeal to the people. My voice is
still strong enough to hold a funeral oration for the
decemvirs. I repeat: we demand a commission; we have
important revelations to make. I will withdraw into the
citadel of reason, I will burst forth with the cannon of
truth and crush my enemies. (*Signs of applause.*)

(FOUQUIER, AMAR, VOULAND *enter.*)

Fouquier.

Peace in the name of the Republic, reverence before the law! The Convention has resolved: whereas signs of mutiny are evident in the prisons; whereas the wives of Danton and Camille are throwing money to the people and General Dillon is to escape. and become the leader of the insurgents in order to free the accused; whereas the latter have acted in a disorderly fashion and have endeavored to insult the Tribunal, the Tribunal is hereby authorized to continue the investigation without interruption and bar from debate any of the accused who neglects the respect due to the law.

Danton.

I ask those present if we have libeled the Tribunal, the people, or the National Convention?

Many Voices.

No! No!

Camille.

The wretches, they want to murder my Lucile!

Danton.

Someday the truth will come to light. I see great misfortune coming over France. This is dictatorship—it has torn off its veil, it carries its head high, it strides over our corpses. (*Pointing to* AMAR *and* VOULAND.) Look there at the cowardly murderers, look at the scavengers of the Committee of Public Safety! I accuse Robespierre, St. Just, and their hangmen of high treason. They want to choke the Republic in blood. The tracks of the guillotine carts are the highways upon which the foreign powers will force their way into the heart of the fatherland. How much longer should the footprints of freedom be graves? You want bread and they throw you heads. You are thirsty and they make you lick the blood from the steps of the guillotine. (*Great agitation among the spectators, shouts of approval.*)

Many Voices.

Long live Danton, down with the decemvirs! (*The prisoners are forcibly led away.*)

10

Square before the Palace of Justice.

A crowd of people.

Several Voices.
Down with the decemvirs! Long live Danton!

First Citizen.
Yes, that's right, heads instead of bread, blood instead of wine.

Several Women.
The guillotine is a bad mill and Samson is a bad baker's boy. We want bread, bread!

Second Citizen.
Danton gobbled up your bread. His head will give bread to all of you again. He was right.

First Citizen.
Danton was with us on the 10th of August, Danton was with us in September. Where were those who accused him?

Second Citizen.
And Lafayette was with you at Versailles and was a traitor anyway.

First Citizen.
Who says Danton is a traitor?

Second Citizen.
Robespierre.

First Citizen.
And Robespierre is a traitor.

Second Citizen.
Who says that?

First Citizen.
Danton.

Second Citizen.
Danton has fancy clothes, Danton has a nice house, Danton has a beautiful wife, he bathes in Burgundy wine, eats venison from silver plates, and sleeps with your wives and daughters when he's drunk. Danton was poor like you. Where did he get all this? The Veto bought it

for him to save the crown. The duke of Orléans gave it to him so Danton would steal the crown for him. That foreigner[10] gave it to him so he would betray you all. What does Robespierre have? The virtuous Robespierre. You all know him.

All.
Long live Robespierre! Down with Danton! Down with the traitor!

ACT FOUR

1

A room.

JULIE. *A* BOY.

Julie.
It's all over. They were trembling before him. They'll kill him out of fear. Go! I've seen him for the last time—tell him I couldn't see him this way. (*She gives the* BOY *a lock of her hair.*) There, bring him that and tell him he won't go alone. He'll understand. Then come back quickly. I want to read his looks in your eyes.

2

A street.

DUMAS. *A* CITIZEN.

Citizen.
How can they condemn so many innocent people to death after such a trial?

---

[10] Probably William Pitt the Younger, with whom Danton is alleged to have conspired.

Dumas.
That is unusual, to be sure, but the men of the Revolution have an instinct which is lacking in other men, and this instinct never deceives them.
Citizen.
That is the instinct of a tiger.—You have a wife.
Dumas.
I will soon have had one.
Citizen.
So it's true!
Dumas.
The Revolutionary Tribunal will announce our divorce, the guillotine will separate us from bed and board.
Citizen.
You are a monster!
Dumas.
Idiot! You admire Brutus?
Citizen.
With all my heart.
Dumas.
Must one be a Roman consul and cover his head with a toga in order to sacrifice his beloved to the fatherland? I will wipe my eyes with the sleeve of my red coat, that's the only difference.
Citizen.
That's horrible.
Dumas.
Go on, you don't understand me. (*They exit.*)

3

The Conciergerie.

LACROIX, HÉRAULT *on a bed.* DANTON, CAMILLE
on another.

Lacroix.
It's really shameful how one's hair and nails grow here.
Hérault.
Watch out—you're sneezing sand into my face.

Lacroix.

And please don't you step on my feet like that, friend, I've got corns.

Hérault.

You've got lice besides.

Lacroix.

Oh, if I could only get rid of the worms.

Hérault.

Well, sleep well. We'll have to see how we can work this out—we've got little space. Don't scratch me with your fingernails while you sleep. There! Don't tug at our shroud, it's cold down there.

Danton.

Yes, Camille, tomorrow we'll be worn-out shoes which are thrown into the lap of that beggar, earth.

Camille.

We are the cowhide from which, according to Plato, the angels cut out slippers to grope around on the earth. No wonder things are so bad. My Lucile!

Danton.

Calm down, my boy.

Camille.

Can I calm down? Do you really think so, Danton? Can I? They won't dare lay a hand on her. The beautiful radiance which streams from her body is inextinguishable. Impossible! Look, the earth wouldn't dare bury her, it would arch around her. The mist of the grave would sparkle on her eyelashes like dew, crystals would sprout around her limbs like flowers, and bright springs would lull her to sleep.

Danton.

Sleep, my boy, sleep.

Camille.

Listen, Danton, between you and me—it's so miserable to have to die. It's of no use either. I want to steal the last glances from life's beautiful eyes; I want *my* eyes to be open.

Danton.

They'll stay open on their own. Samson won't close them for us. Sleep is kinder. Sleep, my boy, sleep.

Camille.

Lucile, your kisses are dreaming on my lips. Every kiss

becomes a dream, my eyes sink down and enclose it tightly.

Danton.

Why doesn't the clock stop? With every tick it moves the walls closer around me until they're as tight as a coffin. I once read a story like that as a child; my hair stood on end. Yes—as a child! Was it worth the trouble to let me grow up and keep me warm? Just more work for the gravedigger! It's as if I'm smelling already. My dear body, I'll hold my nose and imagine that you're a woman, sweating and stinking after the dance, and pay you compliments. We've often passed the time with each other already. Tomorrow you'll be a shattered violin; the melody is played out. Tomorrow you'll be an empty bottle; the wine has been drunk, but it hasn't made *me* drunk and I'll go to bed sober. Happy are they who can still get drunk. Tomorrow you'll be a worn-out pair of pants. You'll be thrown into the closet and you'll be eaten by moths—you can stink as much as you like. Oh, that doesn't help. Yes, it's so miserable to have to die. Death apes birth: dying we're just as helpless and naked as newborn children. Indeed, our shroud is our diaper. How will that help? We can whimper in the grave as well as in the cradle. Camille! He's asleep. (*Bending over him.*) A dream is dancing under his eyelashes. I won't brush the golden dew of sleep from his eyes. (*He gets up and goes to the window.*) I won't go alone—thank you, Julie. And yet I'd have liked to die in another way, as effortlessly as a falling star, as an expiring tone kissing itself dead with its own lips, as a ray of light burying itself in clear waters.—The stars are scattered over the sky like shimmering tears. There must be deep sorrow in the eye from which they trickled.

Camille.

Oh! (*He has gotten up and is reaching toward the ceiling.*)

Danton.

What's the matter, Camille?

Camille.

Oh, oh!

Danton.

(*Shakes him.*) Do you want to tear down the ceiling?

Camille.

Oh, you, you . . . oh, hold me—say something, Danton!

Danton.

You're trembling all over, there's sweat on your brow.

Camille.

That's you—this is me—there! This is my hand! Yes, now I remember. Oh, Danton, that was terrifying.

Danton.

What was?

Camille.

I was half dreaming, half awake. The ceiling disappeared and the moon sank down very near, very close, my hand seized it. The sky with its lights had come down, I beat against it, I touched the stars, I reeled like a man drowning under a layer of ice. That was terrifying, Danton.

Danton.

The lamp is throwing a round beam at the ceiling, that's what you saw.

Camille.

For all I care—you don't need much to lose the little bit of reason you have. Insanity grabbed me by the hair. (*He gets up.*) I don't want to sleep anymore, I don't want to go mad. (*He reaches for a book.*)

Danton.

What are you reading?

Camille.

The *Night Thoughts*.

Danton.

Do you want to die prematurely? I'll read the *Pucelle*. I don't want to slip out of life from a praying stool but from the bed of a sister of mercy. Life's a whore, it fornicates with the whole world.

4

Square in front of the Conciergerie.

A JAILER. *Two* DRIVERS *with carts. Women.*

Jailer.

Who called you here?

First Driver.
I'm not called Here, that's a funny name.
Jailer.
Stupid, who gave you the order to come?
First Driver.
I don't get any ordure, just ten sous a head.
Second Driver.
That rascal will take the bread out of my mouth.
First Driver.
What do you call *your* bread? (*Pointing to the prison windows.*) There's food for worms.
Second Driver.
My kids are worms too and they want their share. Oh, things are bad in our profession, and yet we're the best drivers.
First Driver.
How's that?
Second Driver.
Who is the best driver?
First Driver.
Whoever drives farthest and quickest.
Second Driver.
Now, you ass, who drives farther than a man who drives someone out of this world, and who's quicker than the man who does it in fifteen minutes? It's exactly fifteen minutes from here to the Square of the Revolution.
Jailer.
Hurry up, you bums! Closer to the gate! Make room, girls!
First Driver.
Leave your room where it is! You don't drive around a girl, but always right through the middle.
Second Driver.
Yeah, I'll believe that. you can drive in with cart and horse, you'll find good tracks, but when you come out, you'll have to go into quarantine.

(*They drive up.*)

Second Driver.
(*To the women.*) What are you staring at?
A Woman.
We're waiting for old customers.

87

Second Driver.

You think my cart is a whorehouse? It's a respectable cart—it's carried the king and all the elegant men of Paris to the blade.

Lucile.

(*Enters. She sits on a rock under the prison windows.*) Camille, Camille! (CAMILLE *appears at a window.*) Say, Camille, you make me laugh with your long coat of stone and your iron mask over your face. Can't you bend down? Where are your arms? I want to lure you down, dear bird. (*Sings.*)

Two little stars shine in the sky
Shining brighter than the moon,
The one shines on my dear love's window,
The other at her chamber door.

Come, come, my friend! Up the steps, quietly—they're all asleep. The moon helps me in my long wait. But you can't get through the gate, that's an unbearable costume you have. It's too nasty for a joke, please stop it. But you aren't moving. Why don't you say anything? You're making me afraid. Listen! People say you have to die, and they make such serious faces. Die! The faces make me laugh. "Die!" What kind of a word is that? Tell me, Camille. Die. I'll think about it. There—there it is. I want to run after it, come, sweet friend, help me catch it, come, come! (*She runs off.*)

Camille.

(*Calls out.*) Lucile! Lucile!

5

The Conciergerie.

DANTON *at a window which opens into the next room.*
CAMILLE. PHILIPPEAU. LACROIX. HÉRAULT.

Danton.

You're quiet now, Fabre.

A Voice.

(*From inside.*) Dying.

Danton.

Do you know what we'll do now?

The Voice.

Well?

Danton.

What you did all your life—*des vers.*[11]

Camille.

(*To himself.*) Insanity lurked behind her eyes. She isn't the first to go insane, that's the way of the world. What can we do about it? We wash our hands of it. It's better that way.

Danton.

I'm leaving everything behind in terrible confusion. No one knows how to rule. Things might still work out if I left Robespierre my whores and Couthon my legs.

Lacroix.

We would have made a whore out of freedom.

Danton.

What's the difference? Whores and freedom are the most cosmopolitan things under the sun. Freedom will now respectably prostitute herself in the marriage bed of the lawyer of Arras. But I imagine she'll play Clytemnestra to him. I don't give him six months. I'm dragging him down with me.

Camille.

(*To himself.*) May heaven help her to a comfortable delusion. The usual delusions we call sound reason are unbearably dull. The happiest of all men was the one who could imagine he was God the Father, the Son, and the Holy Ghost.

Lacroix.

The asses will yell "Long live the Republic!" as we go by.

Danton.

What does it matter? The flood of the Revolution can discharge our corpses wherever it wants; they'll still be able to beat in the skulls of all kings with our fossilized bones.

Hérault.

Yes, if a Samson turns up for our jawbones.

---

[11] Verses or worms.

89

Danton.

They are brothers of Cain.

Lacroix.

There's no better proof that Robespierre is a Nero than the fact that he was never friendlier to Camille than he was two days before Camille's arrest. Isn't that so, Camille?

Camille.

If you like—what does it matter to me? (*To himself.*) What a beautiful child she has borne of insanity. Why must I leave now? We would have laughed with it, cradled it, kissed it.

Danton.

If history ever opens its graves, despotism can still suffocate from the stench of our dead bodies.

Hérault.

We stank well enough while alive. This is all rhetoric for posterity, isn't it, Danton? It means nothing to us.

Camille.

He's making a face as if it should turn to stone to be dug up by posterity as an antique. Is that worth the trouble of putting on false smiles and rouge and speaking with a good accent? We ought to take the masks off for once: as in a room with mirrors we would see everywhere only the same age-old, countless, indestructible muttonhead, no more, no less. The differences aren't so great. We're all villains and angels, fools and geniuses—and all that in one. These four things find enough space in the same body, they aren't as expansive as one thinks. Sleeping, digesting, making children—that's what we all do. All other things are merely variations in different keys on the same theme. Is that why we stand on our toes and make faces? Is that why we're self-conscious about each other? We've all eaten ourselves sick at the same table and have a stomachache. Why are you holding your napkins in front of your faces? Scream and whine as it suits you. Just don't make such virtuous and witty and heroic and intelligent faces—we know each other, after all. Save yourselves the trouble.

Hérault.

Yes, Camille, we'll sit down together and cry out. There's

nothing more stupid than to press one's lips together when something hurts. Greeks and gods cried out, Romans and Stoics put on a heroic front.

Danton.
But they were just as good Epicureans as the Greeks. They worked out for themselves a very comfortable feeling of self-satisfaction. It's not such a bad idea to drape yourself in a toga and look around to see if you throw a long shadow. Why should we be at odds? Does it matter if we cover our shame with laurel leaves, rose wreaths, or vine leaves, or if we carry the ugly thing openly and let the dogs lick at it?

Philippeau.
My friends, one needn't stand very far above the earth to see nothing more of all this confused vacillation and flickering and to have one's eyes filled with a small number of great, divine forms. There is an ear for which cacophony and deafening outcries are a stream of har monies.

Danton.
But we are the poor musicians and our bodies the instruments. Are those horrible sounds they scratch out only there to rise up higher and higher and finally die away as a sensual breath in heavenly ears?

Hérault.
Are we like young pigs that are beaten to death with rods for royal dinners so that their meat is tastier?

Danton.
Are we children who are roasted in the glowing Moloch arms of this world and are tickled with light rays so that the gods amuse themselves with the children's laughter?

Camille.
Is the ether with its golden eyes a bowl of golden carp, which stands at the table of the blessed gods, and the blessed gods laugh eternally and the fish die eternally and the gods eternally enjoy the iridescence of the death battle?

Danton.
The world is chaos. Nothingness is the world-god yet to be born.

(*The* JAILER *enters.*)

Jailer.

Gentlemen, you may depart. The carts are waiting at the door.

Philippeau.

Good night, my friends. Let us pull the great blanket over ourselves under which all hearts stop beating and all eyes fall shut. (*They embrace each other.*)

Hérault.

(*Takes* CAMILLE's *arm.*) Be happy, Camille, the night will be beautiful. The clouds hang in the quiet evening sky like a dying Olympus with fading, sinking, godlike forms. (*They exit.*)

6

A room.

Julie.

The people were running through the streets, now all is quiet. I don't want to let him wait for a moment. (*She takes out a phial.*) Come, dearest priest, your amen makes us go to sleep. (*She goes to the window.*) Parting is so pleasant; I just have to close the door behind me. (*She drinks.*) I'd like to stand here like this forever. The sun has set. The lines of the earth were so sharply drawn in its light, but now her face is as still and serious as that of a dying person. How beautifully the evening light plays on her forehead and cheeks. She's becoming ever paler; she's sinking like a corpse into the flood of the ether. Isn't there an arm to catch her by her golden locks and pull her from the stream and bury her? I'll leave her quietly. I won't kiss her, so that no breath, no sigh will wake her from her slumber. Sleep, sleep. (*She dies.*)

7

The Square of the Revolution.

The carts drive up and stop before the guillotine. Men and women sing and dance to the carmagnole. The prisoners begin the Marseillaise.

A Woman with children.
Make room! Make room! The children are crying, they're hungry. I have to let them look, so they'll be quiet. Make room!

A Woman.
Hey, Danton, now you can fornicate with the worms.

Another Woman.
Hérault, I'll have a wig made out of your pretty hair.

Hérault.
I don't have enough foliage for such a barren mound of Venus.

Camille.
Damned witches! You'll be screaming, "Fall upon us, you mountains!"

A Woman.
The mountain's already on you, or rather you fell from it.

Danton.
(*To* CAMILLE.) Easy, my boy, you've screamed yourself hoarse.

Camille.
(*Gives the driver money.*) There, old Charon, your cart is a good serving tray. Gentlemen, I'll serve myself first. This is a classic meal: we'll lie in our places and shed a little blood as a libation. Adieu, Danton. (*He ascends the scaffold. The prisoners follow him one after the other.* DANTON *is the last to ascend.*)

Lacroix.
(*To the people.*) You kill us on the day when you have lost your reason; you'll kill *them* on the day when you've regained it.

Several Voices.
We've heard that before. How dull!

Lacroix.

The tyrants will break their necks on our graves.

Hérault.

(*To* DANTON.) He thinks his body's a hotbed of freedom.

Philippeau.

(*On the scaffold.*) I forgive you. I hope that your last hour be no more bitter than mine.

Hérault.

I thought so. Once again he has to bare his chest to show the people down there that he has clean linen.

Fabre.

Farewell, Danton. I'm dying twice.

Danton.

Adieu, my friend. The guillotine is the best doctor.

Hérault.

(*Tries to embrace* DANTON.) Oh, Danton, I can't even make a joke anymore. Then it's time. (*An* EXECUTIONER *pushes him back.*)

Danton.

(*To the* EXECUTIONER.) Do you want to be more cruel than death? Can you prevent our heads from kissing at the bottom of the basket?

8

A street.

Lucile.

There seems to be something serious about it. I'll have to think about that. I'm beginning to understand. To die —to die . . . Everything may live, everything, the little gnat there, the bird. Why not he? The stream of life ought to stop short if that one drop were spilled. The earth ought to be wounded from the blow. Everything moves, clocks tick, bells ring, people walk around, water runs—it all keeps going up to that point—no! It mustn't happen, no—I'll sit on the ground and scream so that everything will stop moving out of fright—everything will stand still, nothing will move. (*She sits down, covers her eyes and screams. After a pause she arises.*) It doesn't help—it's all still the same, the houses, the street, the wind blows, the clouds move—I suppose we must bear it.

(*Several women come down the street.*)

First Woman.
A good-looking man, that Hérault.

Second Woman.
When he stood at the Arch of Triumph during the Constitutional Celebration, I thought, "He'll look good next to the guillotine, he will." That was sort of a hunch.

Third Woman.
Yes, you got to see people in all kinds of situations. It's good that dying's being made public now. (*They go past.*)

Lucile.
My Camille! Where should I look for you now?

9

The Square of the Revolution.

Two EXECUTIONERS *busy at the guillotine.*

First Executioner.
(*Stands on the guillotine and sings.*)
    And when I'm off to bed,
    The moon shines on my head . . .

Second Executioner.
Hey! You! Finished soon?

First Executioner.
Right away, take it easy. (*Sings.*)
    My grandpa says when I come,
    "Been with the whores, ya bum?"
Come on! Give me my jacket! (*They go off singing.*)
    And when I'm off to bed,
    The moon shines on my head.

Lucile.
(*Enters and sits on the steps of the guillotine.*) I'm sitting in your lap, you silent angel of death. (*She sings.*)

95

> I know a reaper, Death's his name,
> His might is from the Lord God's flame.

You dear cradle, you lulled my Camille to sleep, you strangled him under your roses. You death knell, you sang him to the grave with your sweet tongue. (*She sings.*)

> A hundred thousand, big and small,
> His sickle always makes them fall.

(*A patrol appears.*)

A Citizen.

Hey—who's there?

Lucile.

Long live the king!

Citizen.

In the name of the Republic! (*She is surrounded by the watch and is led off.*)

GLOSSARY

(See also "The Historical Background of *Danton's Death*.")

Adonis: figure of Greek mythology. In his *Metamorphoses,* Ovid tells of Venus's love for the young man. After he was killed by a wild boar, Venus caused a flower to spring from his blood.

Alcibiades: (c. 450–404 B.C.), Athenian statesman and general, a devoted friend of Socrates.

Amar: Jean Baptiste André Amar (1755–1816), a lawyer who greatly admired Robespierre.

Anaxagoras: Chaumette called himself "Anaxagoras" after the Greek philosopher (c. 500–428 B.C.) who was forced to flee from Athens after being charged with atheism and blasphemy.

Appius Claudius: see **Virginius.**

Arch of Triumph: not the *Arc de Triomphe de l'Étoile,* which was built to commemorate Napoleon's victories, but probably an arch glorifying the achievements of the French Revolution.

Aristides: (c. 530–468 B.C.), Athenian statesman and general, known for his rectitude as "Aristides the Just."

August 10, 1792: the Tuileries were stormed, King Louis XVI was taken captive, and his Swiss Guard massacred.

bacchantes: also called "maenads," female worshipers of the god Dionysus or Bacchus. Their rites were performed in frenzied ecstasy.

Bajazet: Bajazet I (1347–1403), Ottoman sultan, known as a fierce warrior and a merciless conqueror.

Barère: Bertrand Barère de Vieuzac (1755–1841), a prominent radical who turned against Robespierre soon after Danton's execution. Barère was later by turns an agent of Napoleon and a royalist. He was eventually granted a pension by Louis Philippe.

Baucis: figure of Greek mythology. She and her husband Philemon, both aged and poor, showed hospitality to the gods Zeus and Hermes. Philemon and Baucis typify marital devotion, since they wished to die together.

Billaud-Varennes: Jacques Nicolas Billaud-Varennes (1756–1819), like Barère, a radical antimonarchist who eventually denounced his former ally Robespierre, calling him a "moderate" and a Dantonist. Billaud-Varennes was subsequently arrested and deported.

Brissot: Jacques Pierre Brissot de Warville (1754–1793), editor of the Girondist paper *Patriote français* and a popular Girondist leader. The Jacobins brought about his execution.

Brutus: Lucius Junius Brutus, one of the first consuls of Rome (c. 509 B.C.). He sentenced his sons to death for conspiring against him.

carmagnole: a coat popular with the Revolutionaries; also a Revolutionary dance and song that often accompanied the executions.

Catiline: Lucius Sergius Catilina (c. 108–62 B.C.). Sallust describes Catiline's attempt to seize the Roman consulship by force. His plans were thwarted by Cicero.

Cato's dagger: Cato the Younger or Cato of Utica (95–46 B.C.) committed suicide after an unsuccessful attempt to oppose Julius Caesar.

such pompous Catonians: Cato of Utica (see above) was known as an austere, stoic politician.

Chabot: François Chabot (1757–1794), a Forger (see below).

Chalier: Joseph Chalier (1747–1793), Jacobin leader in Lyons. After an unsuccessful attempt to purge the city of royalists, he was executed by them. The Jacobins regarded him as a martyr.

Charon: in Greek mythology, the boatman who carried the souls of the dead across the river Styx to Hades.

Chaumette: Pierre Gaspard Chaumette (1763–1794), a member of the Cordeliers and procurator of the Paris Commune. He promoted with Hébert the worship of Reason. His sympathy for the Hébertists led to his arrest and execution.

Clichy: a town northwest of Paris where Jacobin leaders kept women.

Clytemnestra: murdered her husband, Agamemnon, when he returned from the Trojan War.

Collot d'Herbois: Jean Marie Collot d'Herbois (1750–1796), originally an actor and playwright. As an ally of Robespierre, he was a president of the National Convention and a member of the Committee of Public Safety. His suppression of the counterrevolutionary movement in Lyons resulted in a bloodbath. After helping to overthrow Robespierre, he was deported along with Billaud-Varennes and Barère.

Committee of Clemency: proposed in December 1793 by Camille Desmoulins as a measure to reduce the excesses of the "Reign of Terror."

Committee of General Security: established in 1792, it had unlimited powers to prosecute "crimes against the state."

Committee of Public Safety: created from the Committee of General Defense. The ten members of the Committee of Public Safety were the supreme authority in France from 1793 until Robespierre's fall. The Committee was responsible for national defense, and it was empowered to carry out whatever measures it considered necessary to protect the country.

Conciergerie: a royal palace that was converted into a prison.

Constitutional Celebration: held on August 10, 1793, in honor of the Constitution.

Convention: see **National Convention.**

Cordeliers: a political club named after its original meeting place, the monastery of the Cordeliers (Franciscan Recollects). Founded in 1790, its first leaders were Danton and Desmoulins, but it became more extremist under Marat and Hébert. After Hébert's fall it was dissolved.

Couthon: Georges Auguste Couthon (1755?–1794), partially paralyzed. He was a member of the Committee of Public Safety and a close associate of Robespierre, with whom he was guillotined.

Danton, Georges: Georges Jacques Danton (1759–1794). At the start of the French Revolution, Danton was active as a lawyer and as a leader of the Cordeliers club. The Cordeliers championed the cause of the lower classes, calling for radical measures against the monarchy. Danton was their most popular spokesman. A robust, impulsive man of great intelligence and energy, he was probably the most imposing orator of the entire Revolution. August 10, 1792, was a significant date in his political career: he helped to instigate the attack on the Tuileries, which resulted in the overthrow of the monarchy and the establishment of a republic. He was immediately appointed minister of justice. He was not directly responsible for the September massacres, but he did not intervene, perhaps thinking that violence might calm the panic brought about by the threat of foreign invasion. In 1793 he helped found the Revolutionary Tribunal and the Committee of Public Safety. His opposition to the Girondists was dictated by practical considerations: the revolutionary spirit in France was too strong, the dangers too great, to permit a moderate, decentralized government as the Girondists wished. On the other hand, he deplored Hébert's "anarchism" and the terror tactics of numerous Jacobins. Hoping to overcome factionalism in France and strengthen the nation, he and Camille Desmoulins called for a cessation of wanton executions. Robespierre was too powerful, however. Despite warnings, Danton did not act to strengthen his position until after his arrest. He was executed on April 5, 1794.

Danton, Julie: actually Sébastienne-Louise Danton, née Gély, Danton's second wife, whom he married six months before his death. She did not commit suicide; in fact, she remarried three years after Danton's death and outlived even Georg Büchner.

David: Jacques Louis David (1748–1825), court painter to Louis XVI. After 1789 he was an ardent Revolutionary and sat in the National Convention. He was the foremost painter of Revolutionary events and themes, which he executed in a rigidly classical style. Napoleon later appointed him as his leading artist.

decemvirs: F. A. Mignet called the Committee of Public Safety *les décemvirs* from the Latin *decemviri*—committee of ten.

Delaunai: a Forger (see below).

Demaly: an actress.

Desmoulins, Camille: Lucie Simplice Camille Benoît Desmoulins (1760–1794). He and Robespierre were fellow students in the Collège Louis-le-Grand in Paris. Like Danton, he began his career as a lawyer, but he was to make his mark as a radical pamphleteer and journalist. On July 12, 1789, hearing of the dismissal of the finance minister Necker, he raised an impromptu and impassioned call to arms in the streets of Paris. This agitation resulted in the storming of the Bastille two days later. Desmoulins soon acquired much notoriety and many enemies with his bitingly critical extremist publications. As Danton's secretary he began to voice more moderate views, calling in his journal *Le Vieux Cordelier* for a Committee of Clemency. After the arrest of the Dantonists, Desmoulins' courage turned to abject terror when he knew he was to be guillotined.

Desmoulins, Lucile: née Duplessis. Camille and Lucile were married in 1790. They had one child. Lucile did not willingly surrender to the authorities; she was guillotined eight days after her husband because of Laflotte's denunciation.

Dictionary of the Academy: the standard dictionary of the French language, first published in 1694 by the French Academy.

Dillon: Arthur Dillon (1750–1794), general of the army of the Ardennes in 1792. He was arrested for complicity with the royalists. His attempt to help Danton was used by Robespierre as proof of a Dantonist conspiracy.

Dumas: René François Dumas (1758–1794). Dumas' enthusiasm for the Revolution led Robespierre to appoint him president of the Revolutionary Tribunal. He tried to prevent Robespierre's downfall and was therefore executed with him.

Dumouriez: Charles François Dumouriez (1739–1823), French general who became commander of the army in August 1792. After initial victories he was defeated by the Austrians. He deserted, finally settling in England.

Epicurus: (341–270 B.C.), Greek philosopher who taught that pleasure is the highest good that man can achieve. Epicurus's concept of pleasure, based on self-control, implied serenity in the absence of pain. Epicureanism later came to be associated with indulgent hedonism.

Fabre d'Églantine: Philippe François Nazaire Fabre d'-

Églantine (1755–1794), a dramatist; arrested and executed as a Forger (see below).

Fabricius: Gaius Fabricius Luscinus (died 250 B.C.), Roman general and statesman noted for his honesty.

Field of Mars: on July 17, 1791, on the *Champs de Mars*, Danton incited Parisians to sign petitions calling for the abolition of the monarchy.

Force Prison: the building in which it was housed originally belonged to the de la Force family.

Foreigners: a group arrested for financial speculation. They and the Forgers were tried and executed together with the Dantonists to give the appearance of mutual complicity.

Forgers: a group of Jacobins, including Chabot, Delaunai, and Fabre d'Églantine, who forged for personal profit a document relating to the liquidation of the India Company.

Fouquier-Tinville: Antoine Quentin Fouquier-Tinville (1746–1795), from March 1793 to July 1794 public prosecutor of the Revolutionary Tribunal. As coldly ruthless as Robespierre, he seldom failed to secure a conviction. After Robespierre's fall he was brought to trial and executed in May 1795.

Gaillard: an actor and Hébertist who committed suicide.

Girondists: a moderate political group, so named because many of its leaders came from the Gironde department. Sometimes called Brissotins after J. P. Brissot, they originally were allies of the Jacobins, but their allegiance to the middle classes rather than to the poor soon caused them to clash with the Jacobin radicals. When twenty-two Girondist leaders were executed in 1793, others fled to the provinces and attempted to stir up a civil war. Marat's assassination added to their unpopularity, and they were expunged from the government, only to be formally reinstated in 1795.

grisettes: working girls who usually dressed in gray (*gris*). Some supplemented their income by catering to the pleasures of the rich bourgeoisie and the aristocracy, and the term came to mean "high-class whore."

Hébert: Jacques René Hébert (1757–1794), journalist, prominent member of the Cordeliers. He and Chaumette founded the cult of the worship of Reason. As deputy procurator of the powerful Paris Commune (which was the political voice of the people of Paris) he challenged the authority of Robespierre, who seized on the opportunity to suppress the atheistic Hébertists.

Hérault-Séchelles: Marie Jean Hérault de Séchelles (1759–1794), originally a lawyer, popular for his good looks and elegant manners. He was from the beginning an ardent reformer, eventually allying himself with Danton. He served several times as president of the National Convention. He was executed with Danton.

Herman: Martial Joseph Armand Herman (1749–1795), formerly president of the criminal court of Calais, appointed by Robespierre to the presidency of the Revolutionary Tribunal. The Tribunal condemned him to death after Robespierre's fall.

Jacobins: a political club founded in 1789. Its members first assembled in the unused monastery of the Jacobins (Dominicans) in Paris. Affiliated clubs sprang up all over France. In 1791 the public was admitted to the political debates at the club. The Jacobins supported universal social equality, a welfare system for the poor, and a centralized national government. Under the leadership of Marat and Robespierre, the Jacobins became the dominant force in the National Convention, overcoming all those who disagreed with them. After Robespierre's downfall the club was closed.

January 21, 1793: date of the execution of King Louis XVI.

July 14, 1789: date of the fall of the Bastille.

Lacroix: actually Jean François Delacroix (1754–1794), a lawyer, ally of Danton. He and Danton were sent to the Netherlands in 1792 to assist the French army. He was executed with Danton.

Lafayette: Marie Joseph Paul Yves Roch Gilbert du Motier, Marquis de Lafayette (1757–1834). Of noble birth, he was attracted to the American Revolution and joined George Washington's army in 1777. He was highly respected by the reformers in the early days of the French Revolution, but when the radicals seized power he fled from France and was imprisoned in Austria. Reinstated by Napoleon, he lived to take part in the Revolution of 1830.

Legendre: Louis Legendre (1752–1797). Originally a butcher, he joined the Jacobins and helped found the Cordelier Club. He played a prominent role in the major events of the Revolution. When Danton was brought to trial, Legendre at first defended him, but he soon became intimidated and allowed events to run their course. After Robespierre's fall, Legendre became a reactionary and was elected president of the Convention.

Louis XVII: proclaimed king by the royalists after the execution of Louis XVI. It is assumed that he died in prison in 1795, aged ten.

Lucretia: Roman matron who committed suicide after being raped by Sextus Tarquinius.

Luxembourg prison: the state prison, formerly a palace.

Marat: Jean Paul Marat (1743–1793). In 1789 he founded the radical journal *L'Ami du peuple;* in 1790 he suggested "executing 500 royalists in order to save the lives of 500,000 innocent citizens." A foe of the Girondists, he was brought to trial while they were still in power, but he was acquitted. His assassination by Charlotte Corday prompted the Jacobins to take reprisals against the Girondists.

Marseillaise: French national anthem, composed in 1792 by Claude Joseph Rouget de Lisle. Originally known as *Chant de guerre pour l'armée du Rhin,* it was sung by men from Marseilles as they marched on the Tuileries on August 10, 1792.

May 31, 1793: the beginning of the Jacobin insurrection against the Girondists.

Medea: in Greek mythology, princess of Colchis. When she fled from Colchis with Jason, she murdered her brother Absyrtus and scattered parts of his body, delaying her pursuing father.

Mercier: Louis-Sébastien Mercier (1740–1814), dramatist and essayist. Politically he was a moderate (Girondist), which led to his arrest in 1793. He was set free after Robespierre's execution. His *Le Nouveau Paris* (1799), a description of the Revolution, was one of Büchner's sources for *Danton's Death.*

Minotaur: born of a woman and a bull, this monster lived in King Minos's labyrinth in Crete. It devoured youths and maidens, who were sacrificed to it.

Mirabeau: Honoré Gabriel Riquetti, comte de Mirabeau (1749–1791). Although one of the most effective Revolutionary leaders in 1789, he was secretly allied to the court of Louis XVI. To avoid the excesses of the "Terror," which he foresaw, he hoped to create a constitutional kingdom like that of England. He was nevertheless still popular with the masses at the time of his death in 1791.

Moloch: Canaanitish god of fire to whom children were sacrificed.

Momoro, Madame: an actress who represented the Goddess of Reason in Chaumette's Festival of Reason in 1793.

the Mountain: see the Plain.

National Convention: created in September 1792, replacing the Legislative Assembly. France thereby became a republic. The Convention was dominated by the Jacobins; its power was centralized in its committees.

Night Thoughts: *Night Thoughts on Life, Death, and Immortality,* a blank-verse poem in nine books written between 1742 and 1745 by Edward Young (1683–1765). Translated into many languages, the work influenced many European sentimental and Romantic poets.

The Old Franciscan: *Le Vieux Cordelier,* edited by Camille Desmoulins. The journal voiced his and Danton's desire to bring an end to the "Reign of Terror."

Orléans: Louis Philippe Joseph, duc d'Orléans (1747–1793). Although an aristocrat, he championed the cause of the lower classes and helped the Jacobins to power. As "Citizen Égalité" he even voted for the execution of Louis XVI. He was nevertheless charged with aspiring to the crown and plotting with Dumouriez, for which he was executed. His son became King Louis Philippe.

Paetus: when Caecina Paetus was sentenced to die, his wife Arria stabbed herself, then handed him the dagger, saying, "Paete, non dolet."

Palais Royal: formerly the property of the duc d'Orléans, it contained shops, cafés, and gambling casinos. It was frequented by politicians and prostitutes.

Panthéon: named after the Pantheon in Rome, the French

Panthéon was dedicated to the memory of the great men of France.

Paris: ("Fabricius"), a member of the Revolutionary Tribunal who warned Danton of his impending arrest.

Payne: Thomas Paine (1737–1809), political theorist and author. Born in England, Paine went to America in 1774 at Benjamin Franklin's urging. In 1776 he published the pamphlet *Common Sense,* calling for the establishment of a republic. During the Revolutionary War his *The American Crisis* bolstered the morale of the colonists. Returning to Europe, he countered Edmund Burke's negative appraisal of the French Revolution with *The Rights of Man* (1791, 1792). Indicted for treason, he fled from England to France, where he was elected to the National Convention. Robespierre had him arrested for opposition to the Jacobins, but after Robespierre's fall, Paine was released. In 1802 he returned to America. His religious views were expressed in *The Age of Reason* (1794, 1795); they are not those of an atheist, as Büchner indicates, but those of a deist, who rejects organized religion in favor of a moral code founded on natural religion.

Pelias: Pelias stole the kingdom Iolcus from his brother and sent his nephew Jason in search of the Golden Fleece. In revenge, Medea advised his daughters to cut their father to pieces and boil him in a cauldron to restore his youth. Contrary to St. Just's implication, Pelias was not restored to life.

Philippeau: Pierre Philippeaux (1754–1794), a lawyer and a member of the National Convention. He was a Dantonist, but he did not share the Dantonists' libertinism.

Pitt: William Pitt (1759–1806), prime minister of England who launched a blockade against the ports of France in 1793.

the Plain and the Mountain: Jacobin and Girondist delegates sat separated during meetings of the National Convention. The Jacobins took the highest seats on the left and were therefore known as "the Mountain." The Girondists were on the right, and the other delegates sat in the middle, in "the Plain."

Portia: daughter of Cato of Utica, wife of Marcus Brutus. She killed herself when her husband, having taken part in the assassination of Julius Caesar, was defeated by Marc Antony and Octavian.

Pucelle: a satire of Joan of Arc by Voltaire.

Pygmalion: in Greek mythology, king of Cyprus. His marble sculpture of Galatea was so beautiful that he prayed to Aphrodite for a wife like it. The goddess made the statue come to life and Pygmalion married Galatea.

red caps: the symbol of the Jacobins.

Revolutionary Tribunal: created by Danton, it tried all crimes against the state without appeal. The jury voted openly.

Robespierre: Maximilien François Marie Isidore de Robespierre (1758–1794). A scholarship enabled the young and impoverished Robespierre to study law at the Collège Louis-le-Grand in Paris. Afterward he returned to his native Arras to practice. He resigned from a judgeship in Arras because he disapproved of capital punishment. He returned to Paris as a representative from his native district, soon distinguishing himself as a radical reformer. He was intensely devoted to the philosophy of Rousseau, espousing deism, utopian democracy, and a rigid moral ethos, for which he received the nickname "the Incorruptible." Unlike the Girondists, he was opposed to a war against Austria, fearing a resurgence of militarism in France. Having tried in vain to prevent the September massacres, he called for the execution of Louis XVI. The Girondists, unwilling to form a coalition with the Jacobins, were eventually defeated, and Robespierre was elected to the Committee of Public Safety. He was fundamentally opposed to the communism of the Hébertists and the libertinism of the Dantonists, and he helped eradicate both factions. On May 7, 1794, he officially inaugurated the worship of the Supreme Being. On June 10 the Revolutionary Tribunal (with Robespierre's connivance) was granted completely arbitrary powers in its sentencing, since witnesses were no longer allowed to testify. On July 26, he called for the removal of certain members of the Committees of Public Safety and of General Security in order to secure his position as absolute dictator of France, but on the following day the National Convention turned against him, ordering his arrest. That night he was freed by members of the Paris Commune; but the next day, July 28, he was guillotined with several followers.

Romulus: the legendary founder of Rome. He and his twin brother, Remus, were abandoned at birth and suckled by a she-wolf. Romulus eventually killed his brother during a quarrel.

Ronsin: commandant of the Revolutionary army. A follower of Hébert, he was executed in 1794 with his leader.

St. Denis: first bishop of Paris, patron saint of France, who died a martyr. He is generally represented carrying his own head.

Saint Jacob: the Jacobin club, which originally met in the monastery of the Jacobins (Dominicans).

St. Just: Louis Antoine Léon de Richebourg de Saint-Just (1767–1794), a worshipful adherent of Robespierre who shared his idol's idealism. He supervised the military operations at the Rhône which drove the allies out of France. Upon his return to Paris he was appointed president of the National Convention. Robespierre arranged his appointment to the Committee of Public Safety, where he ruthlessly eliminated enemy factions. He called for the automatic execution of deserters and defeated generals and proposed a dictatorship for the sake of France's salvation. On July 27, 1794, he attempted to defend Robespierre before the Convention but was shouted down. He went to the guillotine with Robespierre on the following day.

St. Pelagie: a cloister used as a prison.

Sallust: Gaius Sallustius Crispus (86–34 B.C.), Roman historian. His major work describes the Catiline conspiracy.

Samson: actually Henri Sanson (1767–1840), chief executioner during the "Reign of Terror."

sansculottes: lower-class Frenchmen wore long trousers instead of the aristocratic knee breeches (*culottes*). Revolutionaries who wished to be identified with this class often adopted this form of dress.

Saturn: Roman equivalent of the Greek god Kronos, who

swallowed his children to prevent them from overthowing him.

Sections: Paris was divided into forty-eight sections by the Municipal Law of 1790.

Semele: figure in Greek mythology. Semele was loved by Zeus. His jealous wife, Hera, convinced her to ask Zeus to appear before her in his magnificence as a god. Zeus was bound by oath to comply, and Semele was consumed by his lightning.

September 7, 1792: the culmination of the September massacres. Armed volunteers entered Paris prisons and murdered a great number of inmates.

Siegfried: in Germanic mythology Siegfried killed a dragon and bathed in its blood, making him invulnerable except for a spot between his shoulders where a leaf had fallen.

Spinoza: Baruch Spinoza (1632–1677), Dutch philosopher. His *Ethics* reflects a radically pantheistic concept of God. Free will and chance are denied since they are part of God's will.

sublimate baptism: corrosive sublimate or mercuric chloride was often used to treat venereal disease. Büchner creates a double pun on "sublimate" and "baptism."

Tacitus: Publius Cornelius Tacitus (c. 55–117), Roman historian. In his *Annals* he criticizes the tyranny of the emperor Tiberius and the corruption of Rome. Camille Desmoulins quoted Tacitus in his *Le Vieux Cordelier* with obvious reference to Robespierre.

Tarpeian Rock: cliff on the Capitoline Hill from which the Romans threw criminals and traitors.

Tarquin: see **Lucretia.**

the twenty-two: on October 31, 1793, twenty-two Girondists were executed.

Venus with the beautiful backside: the Callipygian Venus (Greek *kallipygos*, "beautiful buttocks").

vestal virgins: Roman girls of noble birth who tended the temple of the goddess Vesta. They swore an oath of obedience and chastity.

the Veto: King Louis XVI was called "the Veto" because he had the right of veto in the Legislative Assembly.

Virginius: a Roman centurion who stabbed his daughter

Virginia to protect her from the lust of the decemvir Appius Claudius Crassus.

the Wandering Jew: according to legend, a Jew who taunted Jesus on the way to Calvary. The Jew was condemned to wander on earth until Judgment Day.

LENZ

1* On the 20th[1] Lenz went through the mountains. The peaks and high slopes covered with snow, gray rock down into the valleys, green fields, boulders, and pine trees. It was cold and damp, water trickled down the rocks and leaped over the path. Pine branches hung down heavily in the moist air. Gray clouds moved across the sky, but everything so dense, and then the fog steamed up, oppressive and damp, trailing through the bushes, so sluggish, so shapeless. He went on indifferently, the path did not matter to him, up or down. He felt no fatigue, but at times he was irritated that he could not walk on his head. At first he felt tension in his chest when stones jumped away, when the gray forest shivered beneath him, when at times the fog enveloped these shapes or partly revealed the powerful branches; he felt an urge, he searched for something, as though for lost dreams, but he found nothing. Everything seemed so small to him, so close, so wet, he would have liked to set the earth behind the stove, he could not understand why he needed so much time to climb down a steep slope, to reach a distant point; he felt he should be able to cover any distance in a few steps. Only at times when the storm hurled the clouds into the valley, and they steamed up through the forest, and voices awakened on the rocks, often like thunder echoing in the distance and then raging up violently, as if they wanted to celebrate the earth in their wild rejoicing, and the clouds galloped along like wild neighing horses, and sunshine pierced through them

* Paragraph numbers refer to "Structural Parallels in *Lenz*," pp. 328–31.
1 January 20, 1778.

and emerged and drew its flashing sword along the snowy slopes, so that a bright, blinding light cut across the peaks down into the valleys; or when the storm forced the clouds downward and tore a light blue sea into them, and then the wind died down, humming up like a lullaby and chiming bells from deep within the ravines, from the tops of the pine trees, and when a soft red glow arose against the deep blue, and tiny clouds fled by on silver wings, and all the mountain peaks, sharp and firm, gleamed and flashed far across the countryside: then pain tore through his chest, he stood panting, his body bent forward, eyes and mouth wide open, he thought he must draw the storm into himself, contain all within him, he stretched out and lay over the earth, he burrowed into the cosmos, it was a pleasure that hurt him; or he stood still and rested his head on the moss and half-closed his eyes, and then it all moved far away from him, the earth receded below him, it became small like a wandering star and plunged into a rushing river flowing limpidly beneath him. But these were only moments, and then he rose, calm, steady, quiet, as if phantoms had passed before him, he remembered nothing. Toward evening he came to the mountain ridge, to the snowfield from which one descended to the plain in the west, he sat down at the top. It had become more peaceful toward evening; the clouds hung firm and motionless against the sky, nothing but the mountaintops as far as the eye could see, with broad slopes leading down, and all so quiet, gray, in twilight; he became terribly lonely, he was alone, all alone, he wanted to talk to himself but he could not, he hardly dared breathe, the creak of his foot below him sounded like thunder, he had to sit down; a nameless fear seized him in this nothingness, he was in a void, he jumped up and raced down the slope. It had grown dark, heaven and earth melted together. It seemed as if something were following him, as if something horrible would overtake him, something that man cannot endure, as if insanity were pursuing him on horseback. At last he heard voices, he saw lights, he was relieved, he was told it was another half hour to Waldbach. He went through the village, lights shone through the windows, he looked in as he passed by, children at the table, old women, girls, all calm, quiet faces, it seemed to him as if the light must radiate from them, he felt at ease, he was soon in the parsonage at Waldbach. They were sitting at the table, he went in; his blond locks hung around his pale face, his eyes and mouth twitched, his clothes were torn. Oberlin welcomed him, he took him for a laborer. "Welcome, although I don't know you."—"I am a friend of +++[2] and bring you greetings from him."—"Your name, if you please?"—"Lenz."— "Ha, ha, ha, hasn't it appeared in print? Haven't I read several dramas ascribed to a man of that name?"—"Yes, but I beg you not to judge me by them." They continued talking, he searched for words and spoke rapidly but in torment; gradually he became calm, the cozy room and the quiet faces emerging from the shadows, the child's bright face on which all light seemed to rest, looking up curiously, trustingly, finally the mother, sitting quietly back in the shadow like an angel. He began to tell of his homeland; he drew all sorts of costumes, they gathered around him with interest, he felt right at home, his pale child's face, smiling now, his lively narration; he grew calm, it seemed to him as if old forms, forgotten faces were stepping out of the dark once again, old songs awoke, he was far, far away. Finally it was time to leave, he was led across the street, the parsonage was too small, he was given a room in the schoolhouse. He went upstairs, it was cold up there, a large room, empty, a high bed in the background, he placed the lamp on the table and walked up and down, he recalled the day just past, how he had come here, where he was, the room in the parsonage with its lights and dear faces, it was like a shadow to him, a dream, and he felt empty as he had on the mountain, but he could no longer fill the void with anything, the light was out, darkness swallowed everything; an inexpressible fear seized him, he jumped up, he ran through the room, down the stairs, in front of the house; but in vain, all was dark, nothing, he felt himself to be a dream, isolated thoughts flitted by, he held them fast, he felt he

---

[2] Christoph Kaufmann (1753–1795), called the "Apostle of Genius" because of his friendship with many of the major authors of the Storm and Stress period. He had known Lenz for two years and had taken him into his house a few months before Lenz's visit to Oberlin.

had to keep saying "Our Father"; he could no longer find himself, an obscure instinct urged him to save himself, he beat against the stones, he tore at himself with his fingernails, the pain began to restore him to consciousness, he threw himself into the basin of the fountain, but the water was not deep, he splashed around in it. Then people came, they had heard this, they called out to him. Oberlin came running; Lenz had come to his senses again, he was fully aware of his situation, he was at ease again, now he was ashamed and sorry to have given these good people cause for fright, he told them he was used to taking cold baths and went back up; exhaustion finally allowed him to rest.

2   The next day went well. With Oberlin through the valley on horseback; broad mountain slopes contracting from a great height into a narrow, winding valley that led high up into the mountains in many directions, large masses of rock, spreading out toward the base, few woods, but all in a gray, somber hue, a view toward the west into the country and to the mountain range running straight from south to north, immense, grave, silent peaks standing like a dusky dream. Huge masses of light gushing at times from the valleys like a golden river, then clouds again, hanging on the highest peak, then climbing down the forest slowly into the valley or sinking and rising in the sunbeams like a flying silvery web; not a sound, no movement, no birds, nothing but the wind, sometimes near, sometimes far. Dots also appeared, skeletons of huts, boards covered with straw, a somber black in color. People, silent and grave, as though not daring to disturb the peace of their valley, greeted them quietly as they rode past. In the huts it was lively, they crowded around Oberlin, he instructed, gave advice, consoled; everywhere trusting glances, prayer. People told of dreams, premonitions. Then quickly to practical affairs, laying roads, digging canals, visiting the school. Oberlin was tireless, Lenz his constant companion, at times conversing, attending to business, absorbed in nature. It all had a beneficial and soothing effect on him, he often had to look into Oberlin's eyes, and the immense peace that comes upon us in nature at rest, in the deep forest, in moonlit, melting summer nights seemed even nearer to

him in these calm eyes, this noble, serious face. He was shy, but he made remarks, he spoke, Oberlin enjoyed his conversation and Lenz's charming child's face delighted him. But he could bear it only as long as the light remained in the valley; toward evening a strange fear came over him, he felt like chasing after the sun; as objects gradually became more shadowy, everything seemed so dreamlike, so abhorrent, he felt the fear of a child sleeping in the dark; he seemed to be going blind; now it grew, the demon of insanity sat at his feet, the hopeless thought that all was but a dream gaped before him, he clung to all objects, shapes rushed past him, he pressed up against them, they were shadows, life drained from him, and his limbs were quite rigid. He spoke, he sang, he recited passages from Shakespeare, he clutched at everything that used to make his blood run faster, he tried everything, but cold, cold. Then he had to go out into the open, when his eyes had gotten used to the dark, the weak light diffused through the night restored him, he threw himself into the fountain, the harsh effect of the water restored him, he also secretly hoped to fall ill, he now bathed with less noise. Yet the more he accustomed himself to this way of life, the calmer he became, he assisted Oberlin, drew, read the Bible; old, long gone hopes reawakened in him; the New Testament was so near to him here, and [. . .][3] When Oberlin told him how an invisible hand had stopped him on the bridge, how a dazzling light on a hill had blinded his eyes, how he had heard a voice, how it had spoken to him at night, and how God had entered into him so completely that he took his Bible verses[4] from his pocket like a child in order to know what to do—this faith, this eternal Heaven in life, this being in God; now for the first time he comprehended the Scriptures. How close nature came to these people, all in heavenly mystery; yet not overpoweringly majestic, but still familiar!—One morning he went out, snow had fallen that night, bright sunshine lay in the valley, but farther off the landscape partly in fog. He soon left the path, up a gradual slope, no sign of footprints,

---

[3] Gap in the text.

[4] The pietistic Herrenhuter sect regularly published collections of verses from the Scriptures for each day of the year; Oberlin presumably had a devotional handbook of this sort.

past a pine forest, the sun formed crystals, the snow was light and fluffy, here and there on the snow light traces of game leading up into the mountains. No movement in the air besides a soft breeze, the rustle of a bird lightly dusting snowflakes from its tail. All so quiet, and into the distance, trees with swaying white feathers in the deep blue air. Gradually it all began to seem comfortable to him, hidden were those massive, uniform planes and lines that at times seemed to be speaking to him in mighty sounds, a comfortable Christmas spirit crept over him, sometimes he thought his mother would step out from behind a tree, tall, and tell him she had presented all this to him; as he went down he saw that a rainbow of rays surrounded his shadow, something seemed to have touched his forehead, the Being spoke to him. He came back down. Oberlin was in the room, Lenz went up to him cheerfully, saying he would like to give a sermon sometime. "Are you a theologian?"—"Yes!"—"Good, then next Sunday."

3   Lenz went happily to his room, he thought about a text for his sermon and grew pensive, and his nights became peaceful. Sunday morning came, a thaw had set in. Clouds streaming by, blue in between, the church stood on a rise next to the mountain, the churchyard around it. Lenz stood up above as the church bell rang, and the congregation came from various directions up and down the narrow paths among the rocks, women and girls in their somber black dresses, folded white handkerchief on the hymnal and a sprig of rosemary. Patches of sunshine appeared at times over the valley, the warm air moved slowly, the landscape swam in a haze, distant church bells, it seemed as if everything were dissolving into one harmonious wave.

4   The snow had disappeared from the little churchyard, dark moss under the black crosses, a late rosebush leaned against the churchyard wall, late flowers coming up through the moss, sometimes sunshine, then darkness again. The service began, voices joined in clear, bright sound; an effect like looking into a pure mountain spring. The singing died away, Lenz spoke, he was shy, the music had calmed his convulsions entirely, all his pain awakened now and settled in his heart. A sweet feeling of endless well-being crept over him. He spoke simply to the people,

they all suffered with him, and it was a comfort to him when he could bring sleep to several eyes tired from crying, bring peace to tortured hearts, direct toward Heaven this existence tortured by material needs, these weighty afflictions. He had grown more confident toward the end, then the voices began again:

> Burst, o divine woe,
> The floodgates of my soul;
> May pain be my reward,
> Through pain I love my Lord.[5]

5   The emotion in him, the music, the pain shattered him. For him the universe was wounded; it caused him deep, nameless grief. Now, another existence, divine, twitching lips bent down over him and sucked on his lips; he went up to his lonely room. He was alone, alone! Then the spring rushed forth, torrents broke from his eyes, his body convulsed, his limbs twitched, he felt as if he must dissolve, he could find no end to this ecstasy; finally his mind cleared, he felt a quiet, deep pity for himself, he cried over himself, his head sank on his chest, he fell asleep, the full moon hung in the sky, his locks fell over his temples and his face, tears hung on his eyelashes and dried on his cheeks, so he lay there alone, and all was calm and silent and cold, and the moon shone all night and hung over the mountains.

6   Next morning he came down, he told Oberlin quite calmly how during the night his mother had appeared to him; she had stepped out from the dark churchyard wall in a white dress with a white and a red rose on her breast; then she had sunk down in a corner, and the roses had slowly grown over her, she was surely dead; he was quite calm about it. Then Oberlin told him how he had been alone on a field at his father's death and had heard a voice, so that he knew his father was dead, and when he came home it was so. That led them further, Oberlin spoke about the people in the mountains, about girls who sensed water and metals under the earth, about men who had been seized on certain mountaintops and wrestled with a spirit; he told him too how in the mountains he had fallen into a kind of somnambulism by looking into a clear deep

---

[5] See *Woyzeck*, Scene 4,17.

mountain pool. Lenz said that the spirit of the water had come over him, that he had at that moment sensed something of his unique being. He continued: the simplest, purest character was closest to elemental nature, the more sophisticated a man's intellectual feelings and life, the duller is this elemental sense; he did not consider it to be an elevated state of being, it was not independent enough, but he believed it must be boundless ecstasy to be touched in this way by the unique life of every form; to commune with rocks, metals, water, and plants; to assimilate each being in nature as in a dream, as flowers take in air with the waxing and waning of the moon.

7 He continued to speak his mind, how in all things there was an inexpressible harmony, a tone, a blissfulness that in higher forms of life reaches out, resounds, comprehends with more organs but was consequently far more sensitive, whereas in the lower forms everything was more repressed, limited but was consequently far more at peace with itself. He continued this further. Oberlin broke it off, it led too far from his simple ways. Another time Oberlin showed him color charts, telling him the relationship of each color with human beings, he brought out twelve Apostles, each represented by a color. Lenz understood, he carried the idea further, came to have frightening dreams and began to read the Apocalypse like Stilling[6] and read much in the Bible.

8 Around this time Kaufmann came to the Steintal[7] with his bride. At first Lenz was irritated by the encounter, he had created a small place for himself, that little bit of peace was so valuable to him, and now someone was coming who reminded him of so much, with whom he had to speak, converse, who knew of his situation. Oberlin knew nothing of all this; he had taken him in, taken care of him; he saw this as the will of God, who had sent him this unfortunate one, he loved him dearly. Besides, it was necessary to everyone that he was there, he belonged to them as though he had been there for a long time, and no one asked where he came from and where he would go. At table

---

[6] Johann Heinrich Jung-Stilling (1740–1817), a Pietist, wrote an interpretation of Revelation. He was best known for his autobiographical novel *Heinrich Stilling's Youth* (1777).

[7] "Stone valley" in which Waldbach is located.

Lenz was in a good mood again, they talked about literature, he was in his element; the idealistic period was beginning then, Kaufmann was one of its supporters, Lenz
disagreed vigorously. He said: the poets who supposedly
give us reality actually have no idea of it, yet they are
still more bearable than those who wish to transfigure it.
He said: the good Lord has certainly made the world as
it should be, and we surely cannot scrawl out anything
better, our only goal should be to imitate Him a little. In
all things I demand—life, the possibility of existence, and
then all is well; we must not ask whether it is beautiful or
ugly, the feeling that the work of art has life stands above
these two qualities and is the sole criterion of art. Moreover, we encounter it rarely, we find it in Shakespeare, and
it resounds fully in folk songs, sometimes in Goethe. All
the rest can be thrown in the fire. Those people cannot
even draw a doghouse. They wanted idealistic figures, but all
I have seen of them are wooden puppets. This idealism is the
most disgraceful mockery of human nature. They ought to
try immersing themselves for once in the life of the most insignificant person and reproduce its palpitations, its intima-
tions, its most subtle, scarcely perceptible gestures; he had
attempted this in *The Tutor* and *The Soldiers*.[8] These are
the most prosaic people under the sun; but the vein of
sensitivity is alike in nearly all men, all that varies is the
thickness of the crust through which it must break. One
need only have eyes and ears for it. As I went by the
valley yesterday, I saw two girls sitting on a rock, one was
putting up her hair, the other was helping her; and the
golden hair hung down, and a serious, pale face, and yet
so young, and the black dress, and the other one working
so carefully. The most beautiful, most profound paintings
of the Old German School barely give you an idea of it.
At times one would like to be a Medusa's head to transform such a group into stone and summon everyone to
see it. They stood up, the beautiful group was destroyed;
but as they climbed down among the rocks they formed
another picture. The most beautiful pictures, the richest
sounds group and dissolve. Only one thing remains: an
endless beauty moving from one form to another, eter-

8 See Notes, pp. 325–26.

nally unfolding, changing, it is true one cannot always hold it fast and put it into museums and write it out in notes and summon young and old and let boys and old men rave about it and go into raptures. One must love mankind in order to penetrate into the unique essence of each individual, no one can be too low or too ugly, only then can you understand mankind; the most insignificant face makes a deeper impression than the mere sensation of beauty, and one can let the figures come to life without copying anything into them from the outside, where no life, no pulse, no muscles swell and beat. Kaufmann objected that he would find no prototype in reality for an Apollo of Belvedere or a Raphael Madonna. What does it matter, he answered, I must admit they make me feel lifeless. If I delve into myself, I may indeed feel something, but then I do most of the work. I prefer the poet or painter who makes nature most real to me, so that I respond to his portrayal, everything else disturbs me. I prefer the Dutch painters to the Italians, they alone are intelligible; I know of only two paintings, by Dutchmen, which gave me the same impression as the New Testament; one is "Christ and the Disciples at Emmaus,"[9] I don't know by whom. When you read how the disciples went forth, all nature is in those few words. It's a gloomy, dusky evening, a straight red streak on the horizon, the street half dark, a stranger comes to them, they talk, he breaks bread, then they recognize him in a simple, human way, and his divine, suffering features speak distinctly to them, and they are afraid because it has gotten dark, and something incomprehensible has neared them, but it is no spectral terror; it is as though a beloved dead man had come to them in his accustomed way at twilight, that's what the painting is like, with its uniform, brown mood, the gloomy, quiet evening. Then the other. A woman sits in her room holding a prayer book. Everything is cleaned up for Sunday, the sand strewn on the floor, so comfortably clean and warm. The woman was unable to go to church, and she performs her devotions at home, the window is open, she sits turned toward it, and it seems as if the sound of the bells from the village were floating over

[9] Luke 24:13–49.

the wide, flat landscape into the window, and from the church the singing of the nearby congregation were drifting over to her, and the woman is following the text.—He continued in this manner, the others listened attentively, much was to the point, his face had flushed from speaking, and often smiling, often serious, he shook his blond locks. He had completely forgotten himself. After the meal Kaufmann took him aside. He had received letters from Lenz's father, his son should return, should support him. Kaufmann told him how he was throwing away his life here, wasting it fruitlessly, he should set a goal for himself, and more of the same. Lenz snapped at him: "Away from here, away! Go home? Go mad there? You know I can't stand it anywhere but here, in this area; if I couldn't go up a mountain and see the scenery and then back into the house, walk through the garden and look in through the window—I'd go mad! Mad! Leave me in peace! Just a little peace, now that I'm beginning to feel a little better! Away from here? I don't understand that, with those three words the world is ruined. Everyone needs something; if he can rest, what more could he want! Always climbing, struggling, and thereby eternally throwing away all that the moment can offer and always starving just to enjoy something for once; thirsting while bright springs leap across your path. I can bear it now, and I want to stay here; why? Why? Because I feel comfortable here; what does my father want? Can he give me more? Impossible! Leave me in peace." He became vehement, Kaufmann left, Lenz was upset.

9 Kaufmann wanted to leave on the following day, he convinced Oberlin to accompany him to Switzerland. He was persuaded by the desire to meet Lavater[10] in person, whom he had known for a long time through correspondence. He agreed to go. Preparations kept them waiting an extra day. Lenz was struck to the heart, he had anxiously clung to everything to be rid of his endless torment; at certain moments he felt deeply how he was deceiving himself; he treated himself like a sick child, he rid himself of certain thoughts, powerful feelings only in the greatest fear,

10 Johann Caspar Lavater (1741–1801), Swiss theologian noted for his *Physiognomic Fragments* (1775–1778), composed of investigations of human character based on facial features.

then he was driven back to them again with boundless force, he trembled, his hair almost stood on end, until he conquered it with incredible strain. He found refuge in an image that always floated before his eyes, and in Oberlin; his words, his face did him a world of good. So he was apprehensive about his departure.

10 Lenz now found it intolerable to remain in the house alone. The weather had become mild, he decided to accompany Oberlin into the mountains. On the other side where the valleys smooth out into a plain, they parted. He went back alone. He wandered through the mountains in various directions, broad slopes led down into the valleys, few woods, nothing but mighty lines, and farther out the broad, smoking plain, a strong wind, not a trace of people except for an occasional deserted hut resting against the slopes where shepherds spent the summer. He grew still, perhaps almost dreaming, everything seemed to melt into a single line like a rising and falling wave between heaven and earth, it seemed as though he were lying by an endless sea that gently rose and fell. Sometimes he sat, then he went on again, but slowly, dreaming. He did not look for a path. It was dark when he came to an inhabited hut on a slope toward the Steintal. The door was locked, he went to the window, through which faint light came. A lamp illuminated little more than one spot, its light fell on the pale face of a girl resting behind it, eyes half open, softly moving her lips. Farther off an old woman sat in the dark, singing from a hymnal in a droning voice. After much knocking she opened; she was partly deaf, she served Lenz some food and showed him to a place to sleep, singing her song continuously. The girl had not moved. A little later a man entered, he was tall and thin, traces of gray hair, with a restless, perplexed face. He approached the girl, she gave a start and became restless. He took a dried herb from the wall and put the leaves on her hand so she would become calm, and she crooned intelligible words in sustained, piercing tones. He told of hearing a voice in the mountains and then seeing sheet lightning over the valleys, it had seized him too, and he had wrestled with it like Jacob. He dropped to his knees and prayed softly with fervor while the sick girl sang in a sustained, softly lingering tone. Then he went to sleep.

11   Lenz fell asleep dreaming, and then he heard the clock ticking in his sleep. The rushing wind often sounded near, often far through the girl's soft singing and the old woman's voice, and the moon, now bright, now hidden, cast its changing light like a dream into the room. At one point the sounds grew louder, the girl spoke intelligibly and decisively, she said that a church stood on the cliff opposite. Lenz looked up and she was sitting upright behind the table with her eyes wide open, and the moon cast its quiet light on her features which seemed to radiate an uncanny glow, while the old woman droned on, and during this changing and sinking of light, tones, and voices, Lenz fell at last into a deep sleep.

12   He awoke early, everyone was asleep in the dim room, even the girl had become quiet, she was leaning back, hands folded under her left cheek; the ghostly look had vanished from her features, she now had an expression of indescribable suffering. He went to the window and opened it, the cold morning air struck him. The house lay at the end of a narrow, deep valley open toward the east, red rays shot through the gray morning sky into the half-lit valley lying in white mist, they sparkled on gray rocks and shone through the windows of the huts. The man awoke, his eyes met a sunlit picture on the wall, he stared at it fixedly, then began to move his lips and pray softly, then ever louder. Meanwhile people entered the hut, they dropped to their knees in silence. The girl was in convulsions, the old woman droned her song and chatted with the neighbors. The people told Lenz that the man had come into the region a long time ago, no one knew from where; he was said to be a saint, he could see water underground and conjure up spirits, and people made pilgrimages to him. At the same time Lenz discovered that he had strayed farther away from the Steintal. he left with several woodsmen going in that direction. It did him good to find company; he felt ill at ease with that powerful man who seemed at times to be speaking in horrendous tones. Besides, he was afraid of himself when he was alone.

13   He came home. Yet the past night had left a powerful impression. The world had seemed bright to him, and within himself he felt a stirring and crawling toward an abyss to which an inexorable power was drawing him. Now

123

he was burrowing within himself. He ate little; half the night spent in prayer and feverish dreams. A powerful urge, then beaten back in exhaustion; he lay bathed in the hottest tears, and then suddenly strength returned and he rose cold and indifferent, his tears were like ice then, he had to laugh. The higher he raised himself up, the deeper he fell. Everything streamed together again. Visions of his former state flashed through his mind and threw search-lights into the wild chaos of his spirit. During the day he usually sat in the room downstairs, Madame Oberlin went back and forth, he drew, painted, read, clutched at every diversion. Always hastily from one thing to another. Now he attached himself to Madame Oberlin, especially when she sat there, her black hymnal before her, next to a plant grown in the room, her youngest child between her knees; he also spent much time with the child. Once when he was sitting there he grew anxious, jumped up, paced back and forth. The door ajar, he heard the maid singing, first unintelligibly, then the words came:

In all this world no joy for me,
I have a love, far off is he.

14 This crushed him, he almost dissolved from the sound. Madame Oberlin looked at him. He steeled himself, he could no longer remain silent, he had to talk about it. "Dearest Madame Oberlin, can't you tell me how the lady[11] is, whose fate lies like a hundredweight on my heart?"—"But Mr. Lenz, I know nothing about it."

15 He fell silent again and paced hastily back and forth in the room; then he began again: "You see, I want to leave; God, you are the only people with whom I can bear to live, and yet—yet I must go, to *her*—but I can't, I must not." He was highly agitated and went out.

16 Toward evening Lenz returned, the room was in twi-light; he sat down beside Madame Oberlin. "You see," he began again, "when she used to walk through the room sing-ing half to herself, and each step was music, there was such happiness in her, and it overflowed into me, I was always at peace when I looked at her or when she leaned her head against me like this, and—God! God—I haven't been at peace for a long time [. . .] Completely like a child: it was

---

[11] Friederike Brion; see Notes, p. 319.

as if the world were too vast for her, she withdrew into herself so, she looked for the smallest place in the whole house, and there she sat as if all her happiness were focused on one little spot, and then I felt that way too; then I could have played like a child. Now I feel so confined, so confined, you see, sometimes it's as if my hands were hitting the sky; oh, I'm suffocating! Sometimes I feel as if I'm in physical pain, here on the left side, in the arm that used to embrace her. But I can't visualize her anymore, the image escapes me, and that torments me, only sometimes when my mind is completely clear do I feel much better." He often spoke about this afterwards with Madame Oberlin, but mostly in fragmented sentences; she could say only little in response, but it did him good.

17   Meanwhile his religious torments continued. The emptier, the colder, the deader he felt inwardly, the more he felt urged to ignite a blaze within himself, he remembered the times when everything seethed within him, when he panted under the weight of all his sensations; and now so dead. He despaired of himself, then he threw himself down, he wrung his hands, he stirred up everything inside him; but dead! Dead! Then he begged God for a sign, then he burrowed within himself, fasted, lay dreaming on the floor. On the third of February he heard that a child had died in Fouday,[12] he took this up like an obsession. He retired to his room and fasted for a day. On the fourth he suddenly entered the room where Madame Oberlin was, he had smeared his face with ashes and demanded an old sack; she was alarmed, he was given what he wanted. He wrapped the sack around himself like a penitent and set out for Fouday. The people in the valley were already used to him; they told all sorts of strange stories about him. He came into the house where the child lay. The people went about their business indifferently; they showed him to a room, the child lay in a nightgown on straw, on a wooden table.

18   Lenz shuddered as he touched the cold limbs and saw the half-opened, glassy eyes. The child seemed so abandoned, and he so alone and lonely; he threw himself on the

---

[12] Oberlin mentions in his diary that the child was named Friederike.

corpse; death frightened him, violent pain seized him, these features, this quiet face must decay, he dropped to his knees, he prayed in all the misery of despair that God should grant him a sign and revive the child, how weak and unhappy he was; then he sank into himself completely and concentrated all of his willpower on one point, he sat rigidly like this for a long time. Then he rose and grasped the child's hands and said loudly and firmly: "Arise and walk!" But the echo from the sober walls seemed to mock him, and the corpse remained cold. He collapsed, half insane, then he was driven up, out into the mountains. Clouds moved swiftly across the moon; at times all was dark, at times in the moonlight the landscape was revealed, vanishing as in a fog. He ran up and down. Hell's song of triumph was in his breast. The wind sounded like a song of titans, he felt as if he could thrust a gigantic fist up into Heaven and tear God down and drag Him through His clouds; as if he could grind up the world in his teeth and spit it into the Creator's face; he swore, he blasphemed. So he came to the crest of the mountain ridge, and the uncertain light spread down to the white masses of stone, and the sky was a stupid blue eye and the moon hung in it most ludicrously, foolishly. Lenz had to laugh out loud, and in that laughter atheism seized and held him quite securely and calmly and firmly. He no longer knew what had disturbed him so before, he was freezing, he thought he would go to bed now, and he went coldly and stolidly through the uncanny darkness—all seemed empty and hollow, he had to run and went to bed.

19 The following day he felt great horror because of his state the day before, he was now standing at the abyss, where a mad desire urged him to look down into it again and again and to relive this torment. Then his fear increased, the sin against the Holy Ghost loomed before him.

20 A few days later Oberlin returned from Switzerland, much earlier than expected. This disturbed Lenz. But he cheered up when Oberlin told him about his friends in Alsace. Oberlin went back and forth in the room meanwhile, unpacked, put things away. He talked about Pffeffel[13]

---

[13] Gottlieb Konrad Pfeffel (1736–1809), blind poet and author of fables, active in educational and religious enterprises.

praising the happy life of a country pastor. He admonished him to comply with his father's wishes, to live in keeping with his profession, to return home. He told him: "Honor your father and mother" and more of the same. During the conversation Lenz grew highly agitated; he sighed deeply, tears welled from his eyes, he spoke disjointedly. "Yes, but I won't be able to bear it; do you want to turn me out? In you alone is the way to God. But it's all over with me! I have sinned. I'm damned for eternity, I'm the Wandering Jew." Oberlin told him Christ had died for that, he should turn to Him fervently and he would partake of His grace.

21 Lenz raised his head, wrung his hands and said: "Ah! Ah! Divine consolation." Then suddenly he asked affably how the lady was. Oberlin said he knew nothing about this, yet he would help and advise him in all things, but he must tell him the place, circumstances, and the name. He answered only in broken words: "Ah, she's dead! Is she still alive? You angel, she loved me—I loved her, she was worthy of it, oh, you angel. Damned jealousy, I sacrificed her—she still loved another—I loved her, she was worthy of it—oh, good mother, she loved me too. I'm a murderer." Oberlin answered: perhaps all these people were still alive, perhaps content; be that as it may, if he would turn to God, then God could and would do them so much good that the benefit they would gain through Lenz's prayers and tears would perhaps far outweigh the injury he had inflicted upon them. He gradually grew quieter and went back to his painting.

22 He returned in the afternoon with a piece of fur on his left shoulder and a bundle of rods in his hand, which had been given to Oberlin along with a letter for Lenz. He handed Oberlin the rods with the request that he should beat him with them. Oberlin took the rods from his hand, pressed several kisses on his mouth and said: these are the blows he had to give him, he should be calm, settle his affairs alone with God, no amount of blows would erase a single sin; Jesus had seen to that, to Him should he turn. He went away.

23 At supper he was somewhat pensive as usual. Yet he talked about all sorts of things, but in anxious haste. At midnight Oberlin was awakened by a noise. Lenz was run-

ning through the yard, calling out the name Friederike in a
hollow, harsh voice with extreme rapidity, confusion, and
despair, then he threw himself into the basin of the fountain, splashed around, out again and up to his room, down
again into the basin, and so on several times, finally he
grew quiet. The maids who slept in the nursery below him
said they had often—but especially that night—heard a
droning sound that they could compare only to the sound
of a shepherd's pipe.[14] Perhaps it was his whining in a
hollow, ghastly, despairing voice.

24 Next morning Lenz did not appear for a long time.
Finally Oberlin went up to his room, he was lying quietly
and motionless in bed. Oberlin questioned him repeatedly
before he received an answer; at last he said: "Yes,
Pastor, you see, boredom! Boredom! Oh! So boring, I no
longer know what to say, I've already drawn all sorts of
figures on the wall." Oberlin told him to turn to God; he
laughed at that and said: "Yes, if I were as happy as you
to have found such a comforting pastime, yes, one could
indeed spend one's time that way. All out of boredom.
For most people pray out of boredom; others fall in love
out of boredom, a third group is virtuous, a fourth corrupt, and I'm nothing, nothing at all, I don't even want to
kill myself: it's too boring![15]

> O God, Thy waves of radiant light,
> Thy glowing midday shining bright,
> Have made my watchful eyes so sore,
> Will not the night come evermore?"

Oberlin looked at him angrily and started to go. Lenz
rushed after him and, looking at him with haunted eyes:
"You see, now I've finally thought of something, if I could
only determine whether I'm dreaming or awake: you see,
that's very important, we must look into it—" then he
rushed back into bed. That afternoon Oberlin wanted to
pay a visit nearby; his wife had already left; he was just
about to leave when there was a knock at his door and

---

[14] Büchner's editors may have misread this word (*Haberpfeife*).
Oberlin used *Habergeise*, which meant either "snipe" (the cack-
ling call of a snipe caused it to be associated with hobgoblins
and night phantoms) or "humming top," a large toy with a
droning sound.

[15] See *Leonce and Lena*, Act I, Scene 1, p. 138.

Lenz entered, his body bent forward, his head hanging down, ashes all over his face and here and there on his clothes, holding his left arm with his right hand. He asked Oberlin to pull on his arm, he had sprained it, he had thrown himself from the window, but since no one had seen it, he did not want to tell anyone. Oberlin was seriously alarmed, but he said nothing, he did what Lenz asked, and immediately wrote to the schoolmaster at Bellefosse, asking him to come down and giving him directions. Then he rode off. The man came. Lenz had already seen him often and had grown attached to him. He pretended he had wanted to discuss something with Oberlin, then started to leave again. Lenz asked him to stay, and so they remained together. Lenz suggested a walk to Fouday. He visited the grave of the child he had tried to resurrect, knelt down several times, kissed the earth on the grave, seemed to be praying, though in great confusion, tore off part of the bouquet of flowers on the grave as a souvenir, returned to Waldbach, turned back again, Sebastian[16] with him. At times he walked slowly and complained about great weakness in his limbs, then he walked in desperate haste, the landscape frightened him, it was so confining that he was afraid of bumping into everything. An indescribable feeling of discomfort came over him, his companion finally got on his nerves, he probably guessed his purpose and looked for a way to be rid of him. Sebastian appeared to give in to him but secretly found a way to inform his brother of the danger, and now Lenz had two guardians instead of one. He continued to lead them around, finally he returned to Waldbach, and as they neared the village he turned like a flash and ran like a deer back toward Fouday. The men chased after him. While they were looking for him in Fouday, two shopkeepers came and told them that a stranger who called himself a murderer had been tied up in a house, but he could not possibly be a murderer. They ran into the house and found it was so. A young man had been frightened into tying him up at his vehement insistence. They untied him and brought him safely to Waldbach, where Oberlin had since returned with his wife. He looked con-

---

[16] Sebastian Scheidecker, the schoolmaster.

fused, but when he noticed he was received with kindness and friendship, he took courage, his expression changed for the better, he thanked his two companions affably and tenderly and the evening passed quietly. Oberlin implored him not to take any more baths, to spend the night quietly in bed, and if he could not sleep, to converse with God. He promised and did so that night, the maids heard him praying almost all night long.—Next morning he came to Oberlin's room looking cheerful. After they had discussed various things, he said with exceptional friendliness: "Dear Pastor, the lady I was telling you about has died, yes, died, the angel."—"How do you know that?"—"Hieroglyphics, hieroglyphics—" and then looking up to heaven, and again: "yes, died—hieroglyphics." Then nothing else could be gotten out of him. He sat down and wrote several letters and gave them to Oberlin, asking him to add a few lines. See the letters.[17]

25 Meanwhile his condition had become ever bleaker, all the peace he had derived from Oberlin's nearness and the valley's stillness was gone; the world he had wished to serve had a gigantic crack, he felt no hate, no love, no hope, he felt a terrible void and yet a tormenting anxiety to fill it. He had *nothing*. Whatever he did, he did consciously and yet an inner instinct drove him on. Whenever he was alone, he was so horribly lonely that he constantly talked out loud to himself, called out, and then he was startled again, and it seemed as if a strange voice had spoken to him. He often stammered in conversation, an indescribable fear came over him, he had lost the end of his sentence; then he thought he ought to hold on to the last word spoken and keep repeating it, only with great effort did he suppress these desires. The good people were deeply concerned when at times he was sitting with them in quiet moments and speaking freely, and then he would stammer and an unspeakable fear would come over his

---

[17] Büchner's uncharacteristic directive to the reader (or to himself, for an eventual revision of the manuscript?) refers to letters that no longer exist. Oberlin writes that he looked at them briefly; one was to "a noble lady in W." (Weimar?), in which Lenz compared himself to a figure in Klopstock's epic *The Messiah* who is damned and yearns to enter the gates of Heaven. The second was to Friederike's mother. He could only say, he wrote, that Friederike was now an angel and would "receive satisfaction."

features, he would convulsively seize the arms of those sitting closest to him and only gradually come to his senses. When he was alone or reading it was even worse, at times all his mental activity would catch on one thought; if he thought about or visualized another person vividly, it seemed as if he were becoming that person, he became utterly confused, and at the same time he had a boundless urge to internalize everything around him arbitrarily; nature, people, Oberlin alone excepted, everything dreamlike, cold; he amused himself by standing houses on their roofs, dressing and undressing people, concocting the maddest pranks imaginable. At times he felt an irresistible urge to carry out whatever he just happened to have in mind, and then he made horrible faces. Once he was sitting next to Oberlin, the cat was lying on a chair opposite, suddenly his eyes became fixed, he held them riveted on the animal, then he slipped slowly off the chair, so did the cat, as if transfixed by his gaze, it grew terribly frightened, it bristled with fear, Lenz making the same sounds with a horribly distorted face, they threw themselves at each other as though in desperation, then finally Madame Oberlin rose to separate them. Once again he was deeply ashamed. The incidents during the night increased to a dreadful state. He fell asleep only with the greatest effort after attempting to fill the dreadful void. Then, between sleep and waking, he entered into a horrifying state; he bumped against something hideous, horrible, insanity seized him, he started up with terrible screams, drenched in sweat, and only gradually found himself again. He then had to begin with the simplest things in order to come to his senses. It was actually not he who did this but a powerful instinct of self-preservation, it seemed as if he were double and one part were trying to save the other, calling out to itself; he told stories, he recited poems in the most acute fear until he came to his senses.

26 These attacks occurred also during the day, then they were even more appalling; previously daylight had protected him from them. Then he seemed to be existing alone, as if the world were merely in his imagination, as if there were nothing besides him, he was the eternally damned, he was Satan; alone with his tormenting fantasies. He rushed with blinding speed through his past life and

131

then he said: "consistent, consistent"; when someone said something: "inconsistent, inconsistent"; it was the abyss of incurable insanity, an insanity throughout eternity. The instinct of preserving his sanity aroused him; he flung himself into Oberlin's arms, he clung to him as if he wanted to force himself into him, he was the only being alive to him and through whom life was revealed to him. Gradually Oberlin's words brought him to his senses, he knelt before Oberlin, his hands in Oberlin's hands, his face drenched in cold sweat in his lap, his whole body trembling and shivering. Oberlin felt boundless compassion, the family knelt and prayed for the unfortunate one, the maids fled and thought he was possessed. And when he calmed down it was like a child's misery, he sobbed, he felt deep, deep pity for himself; these were his happiest moments. Oberlin talked to him about God. Lenz quietly drew away and looked at him with an expression of unending suffering and finally said: "But I, if I were almighty, you see, if I were, I couldn't bear this suffering, I would save, save, I just want nothing but peace, peace, just a little peace and to be able to sleep." Oberlin said this was blasphemy. Lenz shook his head dejectedly. His half-hearted suicide attempts that he undertook regularly were not wholly serious, it was less a wish to die, for him there was after all no peace nor hope in death; it was more an attempt to bring himself to his senses through physical pain in moments of most terrifying fear or of apathetic inactivity bordering on non-existence. Those moments when his mind seemed to be riding on some sort of insane idea were still the happiest ones. That provided at least some peace, and his wild look was not as terrible as that fear thirsting for salvation, the eternal torment of anxiety! He often beat his head against the wall or inflicted violent physical pain on himself in other ways.

27 On the morning of the 8th he remained in bed, Oberlin went up; he was lying in bed nearly naked and was violently agitated. Oberlin wanted to cover him, but he complained much about how heavy everything was, so heavy, he doubted greatly he could walk, now at last he felt the immense weight of the air. Oberlin urged him to take courage. But he remained in this condition for most of the day, and he ate nothing. Toward evening Oberlin was

called to visit a sick person in Bellefosse. The weather was mild, there was moonlight. On the way back Lenz met him. He seemed quite rational and spoke calmly and affably with Oberlin. Oberlin begged him not to go too far, he promised; walking away, he suddenly turned and came up close to Oberlin and said quickly: "You see, Pastor, if only I didn't have to hear that anymore, that would do me good."—"Hear what, my dear friend?"—"Don't you hear anything, don't you hear the terrible voice, usually called silence, screaming around the entire horizon? Ever since I've been in this silent valley I always hear it, it won't let me sleep, yes, Pastor, if only I could sleep once again." He went away shaking his head. Oberlin went back to Waldbach and was about to send someone after him when he heard him going upstairs to his room. A moment later something crashed in the yard with such a loud noise that Oberlin thought it could not possibly have been caused by a falling human body. The nursemaid came, deathly pale and trembling all over [. . .][18]

28   In cold resignation he sat in the coach as they rode out of the valley toward the west. He did not care where they were taking him; several times when the coach was endangered by the bad road he remained sitting quite calmly; he was totally indifferent. In this state he traveled through the mountains. Toward evening they were in the Rhine valley. Gradually they left the mountains behind, which now rose up like a deep blue crystal wave into the sunset, and on its warm flood the red rays of evening played; above the plain at the foot of the mountains lay a shimmering, bluish web. It grew darker as they approached Strasbourg; a high full moon, all distant objects in the dark, only the mountain nearby formed a sharp line, the earth was like a golden bowl from which the foaming golden waves of the moon overflowed. Lenz stared out quietly, no perception, no impulse; only a dull fear grew in him the more things became lost in darkness. They had to stop for the night; again he made several attempts on his life but he was too closely watched. Next morning he arrived in Strasbourg in dreary, rainy weather. He seemed quite ra-

[18] The events omitted by Büchner are described in the excerpt from Oberlin's diary on pp. 331–35.

tional, spoke with people; he acted like everyone else, yet there was a terrible void inside him, he no longer felt any fear, any desire; his existence was a necessary burden.—So he lived on.

LEONCE AND LENA

A Comedy

PROLOGUE

Alfieri: "E la fama?"
Gozzi: "E la fame?"

CHARACTERS

King Peter of the Kingdom of Popo
Prince Leonce, his son, engaged to
Princess Lena of the Kingdom of Peepee
Valerio
The Governess
The Tutor
The Master of Ceremonies
The President of the State Council
The Court Chaplain
The District Magistrate
The Schoolmaster
Rosetta
Servants, Councillors, Peasants, etc.

ACT ONE

O that I were a fool!
I am ambitious for a motley coat.
As You Like It

1

A garden.

LEONCE *reclining on a bench. The* TUTOR.

Leonce.
Sir, what do you want from me? To prepare me for my profession? I have my hands full, work has me at my wit's end. Look: first I have to spit on this stone here three hundred sixty-five times in a row. Have you ever tried it? Do it, it's uniquely entertaining. Then—you see this handful of sand?—(*He picks up some sand, throws it in the air and catches it on the back of his hand.*)— Now I throw it in the air. Shall we bet? How many grains on the back of my hand? Odd or even?—What? You don't want to bet? Are you a heathen? Do you believe in God? I usually bet with myself and can keep it up for days. If you could find me someone who would like to bet with me, I'd be much obliged. Then—I must figure out how I could manage to see the top of my head.—Oh, if only a man could see the top of his head for once! That's one of my ideals. That would do me good. And then—and then more of the same, endlessly.— Am I an idler? Don't I have anything to do?—Yes, it's sad . . .

Tutor.
Very sad, Your Highness.

Leonce.

. . . that the clouds have been moving from west to east for three weeks. It's making me quite melancholy.

Tutor.

A very well-founded melancholy.

Leonce.

Why don't you contradict me, man? You're in a hurry, aren't you? I'm sorry I've detained you so long. (*The* TUTOR *exits with a deep bow.*) Sir, I congratulate you on the beautiful parentheses your legs make when you bow. (*Alone,* LEONCE *stretches out on the bench.*) The bees sit so slothfully on the flowers, and the sunshine lies so lazily on the ground. A horrible idleness prevails.— Idleness is the root of all vice.—What people won't do out of boredom! They study out of boredom, they pray out of boredom, they fall in love, marry, and multiply out of boredom and finally die out of boredom, and—and that's the humor in it—they do everything with the most serious faces, without realizing why and with God knows what intentions. All these heroes, these geniuses, these idiots, these saints, these sinners, these fathers of families are basically nothing but refined idlers.—Why must *I* be the one to know this? Why can't I take myself seriously and dress this poor puppet in tails and put an umbrella in its hand so that it will become very proper and very useful and very moral? That man who just left me—I envied him, I could have beaten him out of envy. Oh, to be someone else for once! Just for a minute.— (VALERIO, *half drunk, comes running in.*) How that man runs! If only I knew of one thing under the sun that could still make me run.

Valerio.

(*Stands close to* LEONCE, *puts a finger next to his nose and stares at him.*) Yes!

Leonce.

(*Does the same.*) Correct!

Valerio.

You understand?

Leonce.

Perfectly.

Valerio.

Then let's change the subject. (*He lies down in the*

grass.) Meanwhile I'll lie in the grass and let my nose bloom through the blades and inhale romantic sensations when the bees and butterflies sway on it as on a rose.

Leonce.

But don't sniff so hard, my dear fellow, or the bees and butterflies will starve because you're inhaling immense pinches of pollen from the flowers.

Valerio.

Ah, my Lord, what a feeling I have for nature! The grass looks so beautiful that I wish I were an ox so I could eat it, and then a man again to eat the ox that has eaten such grass.

Leonce.

Unhappy man, you too seem to be suffering from ideals.

Valerio.

What a pity. You can't jump off a church steeple without breaking your neck. You can't eat four pounds of cherries with the pits without getting a stomachache. Look, my Lord, I could sit in a corner and sing from morning to night: "Hey, there's a fly on the wall! Fly on the wall! Fly on the wall!" and so on for the rest of my life.

Leonce.

Shut up with your song, it could turn a man into a fool.

Valerio.

Then at least he'd be something. A fool! A fool! Who will trade his folly for my reason? Ha, I'm Alexander the Great! Look how the sun shines a golden crown in my hair, how my uniform glitters! Generalissimo Grasshopper, let the troops advance! Finance Minister Spider, I need money! Dear Lady Dragonfly, how is my beloved wife, Beanstalk? Ah, dear Royal Physician Spanish Fly, I need an heir to the throne. And on top of these delicious fantasies you get good soup, good meat, good bread, a good bed, and a free haircut—in the madhouse, that is— while I with my sound mind could at best hire myself out to a cherry tree as a promoter of ripening in order to —well?—in order to?

Leonce.

In order to make the cherries red with shame at the holes in your pants. But, noblest sir, your trade, your profession, your occupation, your rank, your art?

Valerio.

(*With dignity.*) My Lord, I have the great occupation of being idle, I am incredibly skilled in doing nothing, I have an enormous capacity for laziness. No callus desecrates my hands, the earth has not drunk a drop of sweat from my brow. As for work, I'm a virgin—and if it weren't too much trouble, I would take the trouble to expound on these merits in greater detail.

Leonce.

(*With comic enthusiasm.*) Come to my bosom! Are you one of those godlike beings who wander effortlessly with a clear brow through sweat and dust down the highway of life and enter Olympus with gleaming feet and glowing bodies like the blessed gods? Come! Come!

Valerio.

(*Sings as he leaves.*) Hey! There's a fly on the wall! Fly on the wall! Fly on the wall! (*They go off arm in arm.*)

2

A room.

KING PETER *is being dressed by two valets.*

King Peter.

(*While being dressed.*) Man must think, and I must think for my subjects, for they do not think, they do not think.—The substance is the thing-in-itself, that is I. (*He runs around the room almost naked.*) Understood? "In-itself" is "in-itself," you understand? Now for my attributes, modifications, affections, and accessories: where is my shirt, my pants?—Stop! Ugh! Free will is wide open here in front. Where is morality—where are my cuffs? The categories are in the most scandalous disorder, two buttons too many have been buttoned, the snuffbox is in the right-hand pocket. My whole system is ruined.—Ha, what is the meaning of this knot in my handkerchief? Fellow, what does the knot mean, what did I want to remind myself of?

First Valet.

When Your Majesty deigned to tie this knot in your handkerchief, you wanted . . .

King Peter.

Well?

First Valet.

To remind yourself of something.

King Peter.

A complicated answer!—My! Well, what do *you* think?

Second Valet.

Your Majesty wanted to remind yourself of something when you deigned to tie this knot in your handkerchief.

King Peter.

(*Runs up and down.*) What? What? These people mix me up, I am utterly confused. I am at my wit's end. (*A servant enters.*)

Servant.

Your Majesty, the State Council is assembled.

King Peter.

(*Happily.*) Yes, that's it, that's it.—I wanted to remind myself of my people! Come, gentlemen! Walk symmetrically. Isn't it very hot? Take your handkerchiefs and wipe your faces. I am always so embarrassed when I have to speak in public. (*All go off.*)

KING PETER. *The State Council.*

King Peter.

My dear and faithful subjects, I wish you to know by these presents, to know by these presents—because either my son marries or not (*Puts a finger next to his nose.*) —either, or—you understand, of course? There is no third possibility. Man must think. (*Stands musing for a while.*) When I speak out loud like that, I don't know who it really is—I or someone else: that frightens me. (*After long reflection.*) I am I.—What do you think of that, President?

President.

(*Slowly, with gravity.*) Your Majesty, perhaps it is so, but perhaps it is also not so.

The State Council.

(*In chorus.*) Yes, perhaps it is so, but perhaps it is also not so.

King Peter.

(*Emotionally.*) Oh, my wise men!—Now what were we talking about? What did I want to say? President, how can you have such a short memory on such a solemn occasion? The meeting is adjourned. (*He leaves solemnly, the State Council follows him.*)

3

A richly decorated hall with burning candles.

LEONCE *with several servants.*

Leonce.

Are all the shutters closed? Light the candles! Away with day! I want night, deep, ambrosial night. Put the lamps under crystal shades among the oleanders, so that they peer out dreamily like girls' eyes under leafy lashes. Bring the roses nearer, so that the wine sparkles on their petals like dewdrops. Music! Where are the violins? Where is Rosetta? Away! Everybody out! (*The servants go off.* LEONCE *stretches out on a couch.* ROSETTA *enters, prettily dressed. Music in the distance.*)

Rosetta.

(*Approaches coquettishly.*) Leonce!

Leonce.

Rosetta!

Rosetta.

Leonce!

Leonce.

Rosetta!

Rosetta.

Your lips are lazy. From kissing?

Leonce.

From yawning!

Rosetta.

Oh!

Leonce.

Ah, Rosetta, I have the terrible task . . .

Rosetta.

Well?

142

Leonce.

Of doing nothing . . .

Rosetta.

Besides loving?

Leonce.

That's certainly a task!

Rosetta.

(*Insulted.*) Leonce!

Leonce.

Or an occupation.

Rosetta.

Or idleness.

Leonce.

You're right as usual. You're a clever girl, and I admire your keenness.

Rosetta.

So you love me out of boredom?

Leonce.

No, I'm bored because I love you. But I love my boredom as I love you. You are one and the same. *O dolce far niente!*[1] I dream over your eyes as over magic springs, deep and hidden; your caressing lips lull me to sleep like murmuring waves. (*He embraces her.*) Come, dear boredom, your kisses are sensual yawns and your steps a delicate hiatus.

Rosetta.

You love me, Leonce?

Leonce.

Why not?

Rosetta.

And forever?

Leonce.

That's a long word: forever! Now if I love you for five thousand years and seven months, is that enough? It's far less than forever, of course, but it's still a considerable length of time, and we can take time to love each other.

Rosetta.

Or time can take love from us.

---

[1] "Oh, delightful idleness!"

143

Leonce.

Or love can take time from us. Dance, Rosetta, dance—
let time pass to the beat of your dainty feet!

Rosetta.

My feet would rather pass out of time. (*She dances and
sings.*)

> O tired feet, why must you dance
> In shoes so bright?
> You'd rather lie, so deep, so deep
> In earth's dark night.

> O fiery cheeks, why must you burn
> In wild delight?
> You'd rather bloom, not roses red,
> But roses white.

> O poor dear eyes, why must you gleam
> In candle's glow?
> You'd rather sleep, until is gone
> All pain and woe.

Leonce.

(*Dreamily to himself meanwhile.*) Oh, a dying love is
more beautiful than a growing one. I'm a Roman—for
dessert at our lavish banquet golden fish play in their
death's colors. How her red cheeks fade, how softly her
eyes dim, how gently her swaying limbs rise and fall!
Addio, addio, my love, I shall love your corpse. (ROSETTA
approaches him again.) Tears, Rosetta? A fine Epicureanism—to be able to cry. Go stand in the sun and let the
precious drops crystallize, they'll be magnificent diamonds.
You can have a necklace made of them.

Rosetta.

Yes, diamonds. They're cutting my eyes. Oh, Leonce!
(*Tries to embrace him.*)

Leonce.

Careful! My head! I've buried our love in it. Look into
the windows of my eyes. Do you see how nice and dead
the poor thing is? Do you see the two white roses on its
cheeks and the two red ones on its breast? Don't nudge
me, or a little arm might break off, that would be a pity.
I must carry my head straight on my shoulders, like a
mourning woman with a child's coffin.

Rosetta.

(*Jokingly.*) Fool!

Leonce.

Rosetta! (ROSETTA *makes a face.*) Thank God! (*Covers his eyes.*)

Rosetta.

(*Frightened.*) Leonce, look at me.

Leonce.

Not for the world!

Rosetta.

Just one look!

Leonce.

None! Are you crying? The slightest thing would bring my beloved love to life again. I'm happy to have buried it. I'll retain the impression.

Rosetta.

(*Goes off sadly and slowly, singing.*)

> I'm a poor orphan girl,
> Afraid and all alone.
> Ah, sorrow, dear,
> Will you not see me home?

Leonce.

(*Alone.*) Love is a peculiar thing. You lie half-asleep in bed for a year, then one fine morning you wake up, drink a glass of water, get dressed, and run your hand across your forehead and come to your senses—and come to your senses.—My God, how many women does one need to sing up and down the scale of love? One woman is scarcely enough for a single note. Why is the mist above the earth a prism that breaks the white-hot ray of love into a rainbow?—(*He drinks.*) Which bottle has the wine that will make me drunk today? Can't I even get that far anymore? It's as if I were sitting under a vacuum pump. The air so sharp and thin, I'm cold —it's like going ice skating in cotton pants.—Gentlemen, gentlemen, do you know what Caligula and Nero were? I know.—Come, Leonce, let's have a soliloquy, I'll listen. My life yawns at me like a large white sheet of paper that I have to fill, but I can't write a single letter. My head is an empty dance hall, a few withered roses and crumpled ribbons on the floor, broken violins in the corner, the last dancers have taken off their masks and look at each other with dead-tired eyes. I turn myself inside out twenty-four times a day, like a glove. Oh, I know myself, I know what I'll be thinking and dreaming in a quarter of an hour, in a week, in a year. God, what have I done that you make me recite my lesson so often like a schoolboy?—Bravo, Leonce! Bravo! (*He applauds.*) It does me good to cheer for myself like this. Hey! Leonce! Leonce!

Valerio.

(*From under a table.*) Your Highness really seems to be well on the way to becoming a genuine fool.

Leonce.

Yes, seen in that light it looks the same to me.

Valerio.

Wait, we'll discuss this in detail in a minute. I just have to finish a piece of roast beef I stole from the kitchen, and some wine I stole from your table. I'm almost through.

Leonce.

How he smacks his lips. That fellow brings on the most idyllic feelings; I could begin again with the simplest things, I could eat cheese, drink beer, smoke tobacco. Hurry up, don't grunt like that with your snout and don't rattle your tusks.

Valerio.

Most worthy Adonis, do you fear for your thighs? Don't worry, I'm neither a broommaker nor a schoolmaster. I need no twigs for my rods.

Leonce.

You're never at a loss.

Valerio.

I wish it were the same with you, my Lord.

Leonce.

So that you'll get a thrashing, you mean? Are you so concerned about your education?

Valerio.

Oh heavens, procreation is easier to come by than education. It's a pity that propagation can cause such a sorry situation! What labor have I known since my mother was in labor! What good have I received from being conceived?

146

Leonce.
Concerning your conception, its exceptional perfection deserves repression. Improve your expression, or you'll experience a most unpleasant impression of my negative reception.

Valerio.
When my mother sailed around the Cape of Good Hope . . .

Leonce.
And your father was shipwrecked on Cape Horn . . .

Valerio.
Right, for he was a nightwatchman. But he didn't put the horn to his lips as often as the fathers of well-born sons to their foreheads.

Leonce.
Man, your impertinence is sublime. I feel a certain desire to become more closely acquainted with it. I have a passion to thrash you.

Valerio.
That is a striking response and an impressive proof.

Leonce.
(*Goes after him.*) Or you are a stricken response. Because you'll be struck for your response.

Valerio.
(*Runs away.* LEONCE *trips and falls.*) And you are a proof that remains to be proven, because it trips over its own legs which are fundamentally unproven as yet. These are highly improbable calves and very problematic thighs. (*The State Council enters.* LEONCE *remains seated on the floor.*)

President.
Pardon me, Your Highness . . .

Leonce.
As I pardon myself! As I pardon myself—for being kind enough to listen to you. Won't you take a seat, gentlemen?—What faces people make when they hear the word "seat"! Just sit on the ground and make yourselves at home. That's the last seat you'll ever have, but it's of no value to anyone besides the gravedigger.

President.
(*Snapping his fingers in embarrassment.*) May it please Your Highness . . .

147

Leonce.

But don't snap your fingers like that, unless you want to make a murderer out of me.

President.

(*Snapping ever more violently.*) If you would most graciously consider . . .

Leonce.

My God, put your hands in your pockets or sit on them. He's ready to burst. Pull yourself together.

Valerio.

Children must not be interrupted while they are pissing, or they'll become repressed.

Leonce.

Control yourself, man. Think of your family and the state. You'll risk a stroke if you hold back your speech.

President.

(*Pulls a piece of paper from his pocket.*) May it please Your Highness . . .

Leonce.

What, you can read? Well now . . .

President.

His Royal Majesty desires to inform Your Highness that the awaited arrival of Your Highness's betrothed, Her Most Serene Princess Lena of Peepee, is to take place tomorrow.

Leonce.

If my betrothed awaits me, then I'll do as she wishes and let her wait. I saw her last night in a dream, her eyes were so large that my Rosetta's dancing shoes could have been her eyebrows, and on her cheeks instead of dimples there were drainage canals for her laughter. I believe in dreams. Do you ever dream, President? Do you have premonitions?

Valerio.

Of course. Every night before a roast for His Majesty's table burns, a capon drops dead, or His Royal Majesty gets a stomachache.

Leonce.

Apropos, didn't you have something else on the tip of your tongue? Go ahead, relieve yourself of everything.

President.

On the wedding day it is the intention of the Highest Will

to transmit the exalted disposition of His Will to Your Highness's hands.

Leonce.

Tell the Highest Will that I shall do anything except that which I forbear to do, which, however, shall in any case not be as much as if it were twice as much.—Gentlemen, you will excuse me if I do not see you out—right now I have a passion for sitting, but my goodwill is so great that I can't possibly measure it with my legs. (*He spreads his legs.*) President, measure this so you can remind me of it later. Valerio, bring the gentlemen out.

Valerio.

Ring them out? Shall I hang a bell on the President? Shall I direct them as if they could not walk erect?

Leonce.

Man, you are nothing more than a bad pun. You have neither father nor mother—the five vowels gave birth to you.

Valerio.

And you, Prince, are a book without words, with nothing but dashes. Come, gentlemen! It's a pity about the word "come": if you want an income, you must steal; you won't come up in the world except when you're hanged; your only accommodation is a comedown to the grave; and a shortcoming is the lack of an accomplished comeback, when one is completely at a loss for words, as I am now, and as you are *before* you commence to speak. Discomfited by such a comeuppance, you are commanded to come away. (*The State Council and* VALERIO *go off.*)

Leonce.

(*Alone.*) How vilely I played the cavalier to those poor devils! And yet there's a kind of pleasure in a certain kind of vileness. Hm! To marry! In other words, to drink a well dry. Oh, Shandy, old Shandy, if only I had your clock![2] (VALERIO *returns.*) Ah, Valerio, did you hear that?

---

[2] "My father . . . was, I believe, one of the most regular men in everything he did, whether 'twas matter of business, or matter of amusement, that ever lived. As a small specimen of this extreme exactness of his, to which he was in truth a slave,—he had made it a rule for many years of his life,—on the first *Sunday-night* of every month throughout the whole year,—as certain as ever the *Sunday-night* came,—to wind up a large house-clock, which we had

149

Valerio.

Well, you're to be king—that's a lot of fun. You can ride around all day and make people wear out their hats because they have to take them off all the time; you can carve decent soldiers out of decent people, so that will become the natural order of things; you can turn black tails and white ties into state officials, and when you die every shiny button will tarnish and the bell-ropes will tear like threads from all that tolling. Isn't that entertaining?

Leonce.

Valerio! Valerio! We've got to find something else to do. Think!

Valerio.

Ah, science, science! Let's be scholars! *A priori?* Or *a posteriori?*[3]

Leonce.

A priori you can learn from my father, and *a posteriori* always begins like an old fairy tale—once upon a time!

Valerio.

Then let's be heroes. (*He marches up and down trumpeting and drumming.*) Trara-ta-ta!

Leonce.

But heroism stinks terribly of liquor and gets hospital fever and can't exist without lieutenants and recruits. Get away with your Alexander and Napoleon romanticism!

Valerio.

Then let's be geniuses.

Leonce.

The nightingale of poetry warbles over our heads all day long, but the best of it goes to the devil until we tear out its feathers and dip them into ink or paint.

Valerio.

Then let's be useful members of human society.

---

standing on the backstairs head, with his own hands:—And being somewhere between fifty and sixty years of age at the time . . . he had likewise gradually brought some other little family concernments to the same period, in order . . . to get them all out of the way at one time, and be no more plagued and pestered with them the rest of the month."—Laurence Sterne, *The Life and Opinions of Tristram Shandy, Gentleman,* Book I, Chapter 4.

[3] Deductive versus inductive reasoning.

Leonce.

I'd rather resign from the human race.

Valerio.

Then let's go to the devil.

Leonce.

Oh, the devil exists only for the sake of contrast, so that we believe there's something to the idea of Heaven. (*Jumping up.*) Ah, Valerio, Valerio, now I've got it! Don't you feel the breeze from the south? Don't you feel the surging, deep blue, glowing ether, the light flashing from the golden, sunny earth, from the holy salt sea and the marble columns and statues? Great Pan sleeps, and in the shade above the deep, rushing waves, bronze figures dream of the old magician Virgil, of tarantellas and tambourines and dark, wild nights, full of masks, torches, and guitars. A *lazzarone!*[4] Valerio! A *lazzarone!* We're going to Italy.

4

A garden.

PRINCESS LENA *in bridal clothes. The* GOVERNESS.

Lena.

Yes, now! Here it is. Up to now I didn't think about anything. Time passed, and suddenly *that* day looms before me. The bridal wreath is in my hair—and the bells, the bells! (*She leans back and shuts her eyes.*) Look, I wish the grass would grow over me and the bees would hum above me. Look, now I'm all dressed and have rosemary in my hair. Isn't there an old song:

> In the earth I'd lay my head,
> Like a child in its bed. . . .

Governess.

Poor child, how pale you are under your glittering jewels.

Lena.

Oh God, I could love, why not? We walk all alone and reach out for a hand to hold until the undertaker sepa-

---

4 A Neapolitan idler.

rates the hands and folds them over our breasts. But why drive a nail through two hands that weren't searching for each other? What has my poor hand done? (*She draws a ring from her finger.*) This ring stings me like an adder.

Governess.

And yet—they say he's a real Don Carlos.

Lena.

But—a man—

Governess.

Well?

Lena.

Whom I don't love. (*She rises.*) Bah! You see, I'm ashamed.—Tomorrow I'll be stripped of all fragrance and luster. Am I like a poor, helpless stream whose quiet depths must reflect every image that bends over it? Flowers open and shut to the morning sun and evening breeze as they please. Is a king's daughter less than a flower?

Governess.

(*Weeping.*) Dear angel, you're really like a lamb to the slaughter.

Lena.

Yes—and the priest is already raising his knife.—My God, my God, is it true that we must redeem ourselves through pain? Is it true that the world is a crucified Savior, the sun its crown of thorns, and the stars the nails and spears in its feet and sides?

Governess.

My child, my child! I can't bear to see you like this. This can't go on, it will kill you. Perhaps, who knows! I've got an idea. We'll see. Come! (*She leads the* PRINCESS *away.*)

ACT TWO

Did not once a voice resound
Deep within me,
And instantly within me drowned
All my memory.
                                    —Adelbert von Chamisso[5]

1

Open field. An inn in the background.

Enter LEONCE and VALERIO, carrying a pack.

Valerio.
(*Panting.*) On my honor, Prince, the world is an incredibly spacious building.

Leonce.
Not at all! Not at all! I hardly dare stretch out my hands, as if I were in a narrow room of mirrors, afraid of bumping against everything—then the beautiful figures would lie in fragments on the floor and I'd be standing before the bare, naked wall.

Valerio.
I'm lost.

Leonce.
That's a loss only to the man who finds you.

Valerio.
Soon I'll stand in the shadow of my shadow.

Leonce.
You're evaporating in the sun. Do you see that pretty cloud up there? At least a quarter of it is from you. It's

---

[5] A Romantic poet (1781–1838); altered stanza from his *"Die Blinde"* ("The Blind Girl"), published in 1834.

looking down contentedly at your grosser material substance.

Valerio.

That cloud would do your head no harm if your head were shaved and the cloud were to drip on it, drop by drop.—A delightful thought. We've walked through a dozen principalities, half a dozen grand duchies, and several kingdoms with the greatest haste in half a day, and why? Because you're to become king and marry a beautiful princess. And in such a situation you're still alive? I can't understand your resignation. I can't understand why you haven't taken arsenic, climbed on a parapet of a church steeple, and put a bullet through your head, just to be on the safe side.

Leonce.

But Valerio, my ideals! I have the ideal woman in my mind, and I must search for her. She's infinitely beautiful and infinitely stupid. Her beauty is so helpless, so touching—like a newborn child. The contrast is delicious. Those gloriously stupid eyes, that divinely simple mouth, that mutton-headed Greek profile, that spiritual death in that spiritual body.

Valerio.

Damn! Here we're at a border again. This country is like an onion, nothing but skins—or like boxes, one inside another: in the largest there's nothing but boxes and in the smallest, nothing at all. (*He throws down his pack.*) Shall this pack be my tombstone? Look, Prince, I'm getting philosophical—an image of human existence: I haul this pack with sore feet through frost and broiling sun because I want to put on a clean shirt in the evening, and when the evening finally comes, my brow is wrinkled, my cheeks are hollow, my eye is dim, and I just have enough time to put on my shirt as a shroud. Now wouldn't it have been smarter to take my bundle off its stick and sell it in the nearest bar, get drunk and sleep in the shade till evening—without sweating and getting corns on my feet? And now, Prince, the practical application: out of pure modesty we shall now clothe the inner man and put on a coat and pants internally. (*Both go toward the inn.*) Hey, you dear pack, what a delicious aroma, what scents of wine and roast beef! Hey, you

dear pants, how you root in the earth and turn green and
bloom—and the long, heavy grapes hang into my mouth,
and the must ferments in the wine-press. (*They go off.*)

(PRINCESS LENA *and the* GOVERNESS *enter.*)

Governess.
The day must be bewitched. The sun won't set, and it's
been an eternity since we ran off.

Lena.
Not at all, my dear. The flowers I picked as we left the
garden have hardly wilted.

Governess.
And where will we sleep? We haven't come across a
thing. No convent, no hermit, no shepherd.

Lena.
I guess we dreamed things differently behind our garden
wall with our books among the myrtles and oleanders.

Governess.
Oh, the world is horrible! We can't begin to think about
a stray prince.

Lena.
Oh, the world is beautiful and so vast, so infinitely vast.
I'd like to go on like this day and night. Nothing is stirring. Look how the red glow from the orchids plays over
the meadow and the distant mountains lie on the earth
like resting clouds.

Governess.
Jesus, what will people say? And yet, it's all so delicate
and feminine. It's a renunciation. It's like the flight of
Saint Odilia.[6] But we must look for shelter. Night is
coming!

Lena.
Yes, the plants are closing their leaves in sleep and the
sunbeams are swaying on blades of grass like tired drag-
onflies.

---

[6] Patron saint of Alsace. Born blind, she fled with her nurse from
her father, who intended to have her killed. She eventually gained
her sight and founded a convent.

The inn on a hill beside a river. Extensive view. The garden in front of the inn.

VALERIO. LEONCE.

Valerio.

Well, Prince, don't your pants provide a delicious drink? Don't your boots slide down your throat with the greatest of ease?

Leonce.

Look at those old trees, the hedges, the flowers. They all have their legends—dear, secret legends. Look at the old, friendly faces under the vines at the front door. How they sit holding hands, afraid because they're so old and the world is still so young. Oh, Valerio, and I'm so young, and the world is so old. Sometimes I'm afraid for myself and could sit in a corner and weep hot tears in self-pity.

Valerio.

(*Gives him a glass.*) Take this bell, this diving-bell, and immerse yourself in the sea of wine till bubbles foam over you. Look how the elves float over the flowers of the wine-bouquet, in golden shoes, clashing cymbals.

Leonce.

(*Jumping up.*) Come, Valerio, we've got to do something, do something. Let's busy ourselves with profound thoughts: let's investigate why a stool stands on three legs but not on two, why we blow our noses with our hands and not with our feet as flies do. Come, let's dissect ants, count flower filaments. I'll manage to find some kind of princely hobby yet. I'll find a child's rattle that will only fall from my hand when I'm woolgathering and plucking at the blanket on my deathbed. I still have a certain dose of enthusiasm to use up, but when I've warmed everything up, it takes me an eternity to find a spoon for the meal, and it goes stale.

Valerio.

Ergo bibamus.[7] This bottle is not a mistress, not an idea,

---

[7] "Therefore, let's drink!"

it causes no labor pains, it won't be boring or unfaithful —it stays the same from the first to the last drop. You break the seal and all the dreams slumbering inside bubble out at you.

Leonce.

Oh God! I'll spend half my life in prayer if I only could have a blade of straw on which to ride as on a splendid steed, until I lie on the straw myself.—What an uncanny evening! Down there everything is quiet, and up there the clouds change and drift and the sunshine comes and goes. Look what strange shapes chase each other up there, look at the long white shadows with horribly skinny legs and bats' wings—and all so swift, so chaotic, and down there not a leaf, not a blade of grass is stirring. The earth has curled up like a frightened child, and ghosts stalk over its cradle.

Valerio.

I don't know what you're after—I feel very comfortable. The sun looks like the sign of an inn and the fiery clouds over it like the inscription: "Inn of the Golden Sun." The earth and the water down there are like wine spilled on a table, and we lie on it like playing cards, and God and the Devil are having a game with us out of boredom, and you're the king and I'm the jack, and all we need is a queen, a beautiful queen with a large gingerbread heart on her breast, her nose sinking sentimentally into a giant tulip . . . (*The* GOVERNESS *and the* PRINCESS *enter.*) . . . and—by God, there she is! But it's not really a tulip but a pinch of snuff, and it's not really a nose but a trunk. (*To the* GOVERNESS.) Why do you walk so fast, gracious lady, that one can see your former calves up to your respectable garters?

Governess.

(*Very angry, stops.*) Why do you, most honorable sir, open your mouth so wide that you tear a hole in the landscape?

Valerio.

So that you, most honorable madam, won't bloody your nose on the horizon. Thy nose is as the tower of Lebanon which looketh toward Damascus.[8]

---

[8] Song of Solomon 7:5.

Lena.

(*To the* GOVERNESS.) My dear, is the way so long?

Leonce.

(*Musing to himself.*) Oh, every way is long! The ticking of the death-watch beetle in our breast is slow, and each drop of blood measures its time, and our life is a lingering fever. For tired feet every way is too long . . .

Lena.

(*Listening to him anxiously, pensively.*) And for tired eyes every light is too bright and for tired lips every breath too difficult, (*Smiling.*) and for tired ears every word too much. (*She enters the inn with the* GOVERNESS.)

Leonce.

Oh, dear Valerio! Couldn't I, too, say: "Would not this and a forest of feathers with two Provincial roses on my razed shoes—"?[9] I think I said it quite melancholically. Thank God I'm beginning to come down with melancholy. The air isn't so clear and cold anymore, the glowing sky is sinking down closely around me, and heavy drops are falling.—Oh, that voice: "Is the way so long?" Many voices talk about the world, and we think they're speaking of other things, but this voice I understood. It rests on me like the Spirit moving upon the face of the waters before there was light. What ferment in the depths, what growth in me, how the voice pours through space! —"Is the way so long?" (*Exit.*)

Valerio.

No. The way to the madhouse is not so long. It's easy to find; I know every footpath, every highway and byway leading to it. I can see him now: going there down a broad avenue on an icy winter day, his hat under his arm, standing in the long shadows under the bare trees, fanning himself with his handkerchief.—He's a fool! (*Follows him.*)

---

[9] *Hamlet*, Act III, Scene 2: "Would not this, sir, and a forest of feathers—if the rest of my fortunes turn Turk with me—with two Provincial roses on my razed shoes, get me a fellowship in a cry of players, sir?" The feathers, roses, and shoes were traditionally part of an actor's costume.

3

A room.

LENA. *The* GOVERNESS.

Governess.
Don't think about him.

Lena.
He was so old under his blond hair. Spring on his cheeks and winter in his heart. That's sad. A tired body finds a pillow everywhere, but when the spirit is tired, where shall it rest? I've just had a horrible thought: I think there are people who are unhappy, incurable, just because they *exist.* (*She rises.*)

Governess.
Where are you off to, my child?

Lena.
I want to go down to the garden.

Governess.
But . . .

Lena.
But, dear mother—I should have been placed in a flower-pot, you know. I need dew and night air, like flowers. Do you hear the evening harmonies? How the crickets sing the day to sleep and the violets lull it with their fragrance! I can't stay in this room. The walls are falling in on me.

4

The garden. Night and moonlight.

LENA *is sitting on the grass.*

Valerio.
(*At a certain distance.*) Nature is a pleasant thing, but it would be even more pleasant if there weren't any gnats, if the beds in the inn were a little cleaner, and the death-watch beetles wouldn't tick so in the walls. Inside, people

snore, and outside, frogs croak; inside, house crickets chirp, and outside, it's the field crickets. Dear ground, this is a well-grounded decision. (*He lies down on the grass.*)

Leonce.

(*Enters.*) O night, balmy as the first that descended on Paradise. (*He notices the* PRINCESS *and approaches her quietly.*)

Lena.

(*To herself.*) The warbler chirped in its dreams, the night sleeps more deeply, its cheeks grow paler and its breath calmer. The moon is like a sleeping child, its golden locks have fallen over its dear face.—Oh, its sleep is death. Look how the dead angel rests on its dark pillow and the stars burn around it like candles. Poor child, are the bogeymen coming to get you soon? Where is your mother? Doesn't she want to kiss you once more? Ah, it's sad, dead and so alone.

Leonce.

Arise in your white dress and follow the corpse through the night and sing its requiem.

Lena.

Who said that?

Leonce.

A dream.

Lena.

Dreams are blessed.

Leonce.

Then dream yourself blessed and let me be your blessed dream.

Lena.

Death is the most blessed dream.

Leonce.

Then let me be your angel of death. Let my lips sink like its wings onto your eyes. (*He kisses her.*) Dear corpse, you rest so beautifully on the black pall of night that nature begins to hate life and falls in love with death.

Lena.

No, let me be. (*She jumps up and rushes off.*)

Leonce.

Too much! Too much! My whole being is in that one

160

moment. Now die. More is impossible. How Creation struggles out of chaos toward me, breathing freshly, glowing beautifully! The earth is a bowl of dark gold—how the light foams in it and overflows and the stars bubble out brightly. My lips suck their fill; this one drop of bliss makes me a priceless vessel. Down with you, holy chalice! (*He tries to throw himself into the river.*)

Valerio.

(*Jumps up and grabs him.*) Stop, my Serene Highness!

Leonce.

Let me be!

Valerio.

I'll let you be as soon as you let yourself be calm and promise to let the water be.

Leonce.

Idiot!

Valerio.

Hasn't Your Highness outgrown that lieutenants' romanticism yet—throwing the glass out of the window after you've drunk to your sweetheart's health?

Leonce.

I almost think you're right.

Valerio.

Console yourself. Even if you won't sleep *under* the grass tonight, at least you'll sleep *on* it. It would be an equally suicidal venture to sleep on one of those beds. You lie on the straw like a dead man and the fleas bite you like a living one.

Leonce.

All right. (*He lies down in the grass.*) Man, you ruined a most beautiful suicide. I'll never find such a marvelous moment for it again in my whole life, and the weather is so perfect. Now I'm not in the mood anymore. That fellow with his yellow vest and his sky-blue pants[10] spoiled everything for me.—Heaven grant me a good and healthy, solid sleep.

Valerio.

Amen.—And I've saved a human life, and I'll keep myself warm tonight with my good conscience. To your health. Valerio!

---

[10] The costume of Goethe's Werther (*The Sorrows of Young Werther*, 1774), who committed suicide out of rejected love.

ACT THREE

1

LEONCE. VALERIO.

Valerio.

Marriage? Since when has Your Highness decided to be bound by a perpetual calendar?

Leonce.

Do you know, Valerio, that even the most insignificant human being is so great that life is far too short to love him? And yet I can say to those people who imagine that nothing is so beautiful and holy that they can't make it even more beautiful and holier: go ahead and enjoy yourselves. There's a certain pleasure in this sweet arrogance. Why shouldn't I indulge them?

Valerio.

Very humane and philobestial. But does she know who you are?

Leonce.

She knows only that she loves me.

Valerio.

And does Your Highness know who she is?

Leonce.

Idiot! Try asking a carnation and a dewdrop what their names are.

Valerio.

That is, assuming she's anything at all, if that isn't already too indelicate and smacks of personal description. —But what then? Hm!—Prince, will I be your Minister of State when you are joined today before your father in holy matrimony with the unspeakable, nameless one? Your word on that?

Leonce.

I give you my word.

Valerio.
The poor devil Valerio takes his leave of His Excellency the Minister of State, Valerio of Valerianshire.—"What does the fellow want? I do not know him. Off with you, rascal!" (*He runs off,* LEONCE *follows.*)

2

Open square before KING PETER'*s palace.*

The DISTRICT MAGISTRATE. *The* SCHOOLMASTER. *Peasants in Sunday clothes, holding pine branches.*

Magistrate.
How are your people holding up, schoolmaster?
Schoolmaster.
They're holding up so well in their suffering that for quite a while they've been holding on to each other. They're downing a lot of liquor, otherwise they couldn't possibly hold out in this heat. Courage, people! Hold your branches out straight, so they'll think you're a pine forest and your noses the strawberries and your three-cornered hats the antlers and your leather pants the moonlight in it, and remember: the last one always walks ahead of the first, so it looks as if you'd been squared.
Magistrate.
And you, schoolmaster, stand for sobriety.
Schoolmaster.
That's understood. I'm so sober I can hardly stand.
Magistrate.
Pay attention, people. The program states: "All subjects shall voluntarily assemble along the highway, neatly dressed, well fed, and with contented faces." Don't give us a bad name!
Schoolmaster.
Stand firm! Don't scratch behind your ears and don't blow your noses with your fingers while the royal couple rides past, and show proper emotion, or we'll use emotive means on you. Look what we're doing for you: we've placed you so the breeze from the kitchen passes over

163

you, and for once in your life you'll smell a roast. Do you still know your lesson? Hey? Vi!

Peasants.
Vi!

Schoolmaster.
Vat!

Peasants.
Vat!

Schoolmaster.
Vivat!

Peasants.
Vivat!

Schoolmaster.
There, Mr. Magistrate. You see how intelligence is on the upswing. Just think, it's *Latin*. Besides, tonight we'll hold a transparent ball thanks to the holes in our jackets and pants, and we'll beat rosettes onto our heads with our fists.

3

Large hall.

Well-dressed gentlemen and ladies, carefully arranged in groups. The MASTER OF CEREMONIES *with several servants in the foreground.*

Master of Ceremonies.
What a shame! Everything's going to pot. The roasts are drying up. Congratulations are going stale. Stand-up collars are all bending over like melancholy pigs' ears. The peasants' nails and beards are growing again. The soldiers' curls are drooping. Among the twelve bridesmaids there is none who wouldn't prefer a horizontal position to a vertical one. In their white dresses they look like exhausted Angora rabbits, and the Court Poet grunts around them like a distressed guinea pig. The officers are going limp. (*To a servant.*) Go tell our private tutor to let his boys make water.—The poor Court Chaplain! His coat is hanging its tails most dejectedly. I think he has

164

ideals and is changing all the chamberlains into chamber stools. He's tired of standing.

First Servant.

All meat spoils from standing. The Court Chaplain is at a stale standstill too, after standing up this morning.

Master of Ceremonies.

The ladies-in-waiting stand there like saltworks, the salt crystallizes on their necklaces.

Second Servant.

At least they're taking it easy. You can't accuse them of bearing a weight on their shoulders. If they aren't exactly openhearted, at least they're open down to the heart.

Master of Ceremonies.

Yes, they're good maps of the Turkish Empire—you can see the Dardanelles and the Sea of Marmara. Out, you rascals! To the windows! Here comes His Majesty! (KING PETER *and the State Council enter.*)

King Peter.

So the Princess has disappeared as well? Has no trace been found of our beloved Crown Prince? Have my orders been carried out? Are the borders being watched?

Master of Ceremonies.

Yes, Your Majesty. The view from this hall allows us the strictest surveillance. (*To the* FIRST SERVANT.) What have you seen?

First Servant.

A dog ran through the kingdom looking for its master.

Master of Ceremonies.

(*To another.*) And you?

Second Servant.

Someone is taking a walk on the northern border, but it's not the Prince—I'd recognize him.

Master of Ceremonies.

And you?

Third Servant.

Begging your pardon, nothing.

Master of Ceremonies.

That's very little. And you?

Fourth Servant.

Nothing either.

Master of Ceremonies.
That's even less. .

King Peter.
But Council, have I not resolved that My Royal Majesty shall rejoice today and that the wedding shall be celebrated? Was this not our most solemn resolution?

President.
Yes, Your Majesty, it is so registered and recorded.

King Peter.
And would I not compromise myself, if I did not carry out my resolution?

President.
If it were possible for Your Majesty to otherwise compromise yourself, this would be an instance in which this might be so.

King Peter.
Have I not given my Royal Word? Yes, I shall carry out my resolution immediately: I shall rejoice. (*He rubs his hands.*) Oh, I am exceptionally happy!

President.
We join in sharing Your Majesty's emotion, insofar as it is possible and proper for subjects to do so.

King Peter.
Oh, I am beside myself with joy. I shall have red coats made for my chamberlains, I shall promote some cadets to lieutenants, I shall permit my subjects to . . . but . . . but, the wedding? Does not the other half of the resolution state that the wedding shall be celebrated?

President.
Yes, Your Majesty.

King Peter.
Yes, but if the Prince does not come and neither does the Princess?

President.
Yes, if the Prince does not come and neither does the Princess, then . . . then . . .

King Peter.
Then, then?

President.
Then indeed they cannot get married.

166

King Peter.

Wait, is the conclusion logical? If . . . then.—Correct! But my Word, my Royal Word!

President.

Take comfort, Your Majesty, with other majesties. A Royal Word is a thing . . . a thing . . . a thing . . . of nothing.

King Peter.

(*To the servants.*) Do you see anything yet?

Servants.

Nothing, Your Majesty, nothing at all.

King Peter.

And I had resolved to be so happy. I wanted to begin at the stroke of twelve and wanted to rejoice a full twelve hours. I am becoming quite melancholy.

President.

All subjects are commanded to share the feelings of His Majesty.

Master of Ceremonies.

For the sake of decorum, those who carry no hand-kerchiefs are forbidden to cry.

First Servant.

Wait! I see something! It's something like a projection, like a nose—the rest is not over the border yet—and now I see another man and two people of the opposite sex.

Master of Ceremonies.

In which direction?

First Servant.

They're coming closer. They're approaching the palace. Here they are. (VALERIO, LEONCE, *the* GOVERNESS, *and the* PRINCESS *enter, masked.*)

King Peter.

Who are you?

Valerio.

Do I know? (*He slowly takes off several masks, one after another.*) Am I this? Or this? Or this? I'm truly afraid I could pare and peel myself away completely like this.

King Peter.

(*Confused.*) But . . . but you must be something, after all?

Valerio.

If Your Majesty commands it. But gentlemen, then turn

167

the mirrors around and hide your shiny buttons somewhat and don't look at me so that I'm mirrored in your
eyes, or I'll really no longer know who I actually am.

King Peter.

This man makes me confused, desperate. I am thoroughly
mixed up.

Valerio.

But I actually wanted to announce to this exalted and
honored company that the two world-famous automatons
have arrived, and that I'm perhaps the third and most
peculiar of them all, if only I really knew who I am,
which by the way shouldn't surprise you, since I myself
don't know what I'm talking about—in fact, I don't even
know that I don't know it, so that it's highly probable
that I'm merely being *allowed* to speak, and it's actually
nothing but cylinders and air hoses that are saying all
this. (*In a strident voice.*) Ladies and gentlemen, here
you see two persons of opposite sexes, a little man and a
little woman, a gentleman and a lady. Nothing but art
and machinery, nothing but cardboard and watchsprings.
Each one has a tiny, tiny ruby spring under the nail of
the little toe of the right foot—press on it gently and the
mechanism runs a full fifty years. These persons are so
perfectly constructed that one couldn't distinguish them
from other people if one didn't know that they're simply
cardboard; you could actually make them members of
human society. They are very noble: they speak the
Queen's English. They are very moral: they get up
punctually, eat lunch punctually, and go to bed punctually; they also have a good digestion, which proves they
have a good conscience. They have a fine sense of
propriety: the lady has no word for the concept "pants,"
and it is absolutely impossible for the gentleman to follow
a lady going upstairs or to precede her downstairs. They
are highly educated: the lady sings all the new operas
and the gentleman wears cuffs. Take note, ladies and
gentlemen: they are now in an interesting state. The
mechanism of love is beginning to function—the gentleman has already carried the lady's shawl several times,
the lady has turned her eyes up to heaven. Both have
whispered more than once: "Belief, love, hope!" Both

168

already appear to be completely in accord; all that is lacking is the tiny word "amen."

King Peter.

(*Puts a finger next to his nose.*) In effigy? In effigy? President, if you hang a man in effigy, isn't that just as good as hanging him properly?

President.

Begging Your Majesty's pardon, it's very much better, because no harm comes to him, yet he is hanged nevertheless.

King Peter.

Now I've got it. We shall celebrate the wedding in effigy. (*Pointing to* LEONCE *and* LENA.) This is the Prince, this is the Princess. I shall carry out my resolution—I shall rejoice. Let the bells ring, prepare your congratulations! Quickly, Court Chaplain! (*The* COURT CHAPLAIN *steps forward, clears his throat, looks toward heaven several times.*)

Valerio.

Begin! Leave thy damnable faces, and begin![11] Come on!

Court Chaplain.

(*In the greatest confusion.*) When we . . . or . . . but . . .

Valerio.

Whereas and because . . .

Court Chaplain.

For . . .

Valerio.

It was before the creation of the world . . .

Court Chaplain.

That . . .

Valerio.

God was bored . . .

King Peter.

Just make it short, my good man.

Court Chaplain.

(*Composing himself.*) May it please Your Highness Prince Leonce from the Kingdom of Popo and may it please Your Highness Princess Lena from the Kingdom of Peepee, and may it please Your Highnesses mutually to

---

[11] *Hamlet*, Act III, Scene 2.

169

want each other respectively, then say a loud and audible "yes."

Lena and Leonce.

Yes.

Court Chaplain.

Then I say amen.

Valerio.

Well done, short and to the point—thus man and woman are created and all the animals of paradise surround them. (LEONCE *takes off his mask.*)

All.

The Prince!

King Peter.

The Prince! My son! I'm lost, I've been deceived! (*He runs over to the* PRINCESS.) Who is this person? I shall declare everything invalid.

Governess.

(*Takes off the* PRINCESS's *mask, triumphantly.*) The Princess!

Leonce.

Lena?

Lena.

Leonce?

Leonce.

Why Lena, I think that was an escape into paradise. I've been deceived.

Lena.

I've been deceived.

Leonce.

Oh, Fortune!

Lena.

Oh, Providence!

Valerio.

I can't help laughing, I can't help laughing. Fate has certainly been fortuitous for the two of you. I hope Your Highnesses will be so fortunate as to find favor with each other forthwith.

Governess.

That my old eyes could see this! A wandering prince! Now I can die in peace.

King Peter.
My children, I am deeply moved, I am almost beside myself with emotion. I am the happiest of all men! I shall now, however, most solemnly place the kingdom in your hands, my son, and shall immediately begin to do nothing but think without interruption. My son, you will leave me these wise men (*He points to the State Council.*), so they can support me in my efforts. Come, gentlemen, we must think, think without interruption. (*He leaves with the State Council.*) That person confused me before—I must find my way out again.

Leonce.
(*To those present.*) Gentlemen, my wife and I are terribly sorry that you have had to attend us for so long today. Your deportment is so tenuous that we do not intend to test your tenacity any longer. Go home now, but don't forget your speeches, sermons, and verses, because tomorrow, in peace and leisure, we'll begin the game all over again. Good-bye! (*All leave except* LEONCE, LENA, VALERIO, *and the* GOVERNESS.)

Leonce.
Well, Lena, now do you see how our pockets are full of dolls and toys? What shall we do with them? Shall we give them beards and hang swords on them? Or shall we dress them up in tails and let them play at protozoan politics and diplomacy and watch them through a microscope? Or would you prefer a barrel organ on which milk-white aesthetic shrews are scurrying about? Shall we build a theater? (LENA *leans against him and shakes her head*.) But I know what you really want: we'll have all the clocks smashed, all calendars prohibited, and we'll count hours and months only by flower-clocks, only by blossoms and fruit. And then we'll surround the country with heat reflectors so there'll be no more winter, and in the summer we'll distill ourselves up to Ischia and Capri, and we'll spend the whole year among roses and violets, among oranges and laurels.

Valerio.
And I'll be Minister of State, and it shall be decreed that whoever gets calluses on his hands shall be placed in custody, that whoever works himself sick shall be criminally prosecuted, that anyone who boasts of eating his

bread in the sweat of his face[12] shall be declared insane and dangerous to human society, and then we'll lie in the shade and ask God for macaroni, melons, and figs, for musical voices, classical bodies, and a comfortable religion!

[12] Genesis 3:19.

VARIANT TO ACT ONE, SCENE 1

1

. . . [*The beginning of the variant is almost identical to the later version on pages 137–39.*]

Valerio.
Ah, my Lord, what a feeling I have for nature! The grass looks so beautiful that I wish I were an ox so I could eat it, and then a man again to eat the ox that has eaten such grass.

Leonce.
Unhappy man, you too seem to be suffering from ideals.

Valerio.
Oh God! For a week I've been running after an ideal roast beef without finding it anywhere in reality. (*He sings.*)

> Our hostess has a pretty maid,
> She's in her garden night and day,
> She sits inside her garden,
> Until the bells have all struck twelve
> And stares at all the soo-ooldiers.[1]

(*He sits on the ground.*) Look at these ants, dear children —it's amazing what instinct is in these little creatures— order, diligence . . . My Lord, there are only four ways a man can earn money: find it, win it in a lottery, inherit it, or steal it in God's name, if you're clever enough not to suffer any conscience pangs.

Leonce.
You've grown rather old on these principles without dying of hunger or on the gallows.

Valerio.
(*Always staring at him.*) Yes, my Lord, and I maintain

---

[1] Eventually incorporated into *Woyzeck*, Scene 4,10.

that whoever earns money in any other way is a scoundrel.

Leonce.

Because one who works is a subtle suicide, and a suicide
is a criminal, and a criminal is a scoundrel: therefore
whoever works is a scoundrel.

Valerio.

Yes.—However: ants are most useful pests, but they'd be
even more useful if they didn't do any damage. Nevertheless, most honored vermin, I can't deny myself the pleasure of kicking a few of you in the ass with my heel,
blowing your noses and cutting your nails. (*Two police-
men enter.*)[2]

First Policeman.

Halt—where's the rascal?

Second Policeman.

There are two over there.

First Policeman.

Check if either of them is running away.

Second Policeman.

I don't think anyone is running away.

First Policeman.

Then we'll have to interrogate them both.—Gentlemen,
we're looking for someone—a subject, an individual, a
person, a delinquent, a suspect, a rascal. (*To the other
policeman.*) Check if either of them is blushing.

Second Policeman.

Nobody blushed.

First Policeman.

Then we'll have to try something else. Where's the war-
rant, the description, the certificate? (*The* SECOND POLICE-
MAN *takes a paper out of his pocket and hands it over.*)
Inspect the subjects as I read: a human being . . .

Second Policeman.

Doesn't match, there are two of them.

First Policeman.

Idiot! . . . walks on two feet, has two arms; in addition, a

---

[2] If the following episode is to be used in a production of the
play, it would seem more appropriate to place it into Act II, after
Leonce and Valerio have fled, perhaps before the entrance of Lena
and the Governess in Scene 1.

mouth, a nose, two eyes, two ears. Distinguishing characteristics: is a highly dangerous individual.

Second Policeman.

That fits both. Shall I arrest them both?

First Policeman.

Two . . . that's dangerous . . . there are only two of us. But I'll make a report. It's a case of highly criminal complexity or highly complex criminality. For if I get drunk and lie down in bed, that's my affair and doesn't concern anyone, but if I squander my bed on drink, whose affair is that, you rogue?

Second Policeman.

Well . . . I don't know.

First Policeman.

Well . . . I don't know either, but that's the point. (*They go off.*)

Valerio.

Just try to deny destiny. Look what one can accomplish with a flea. If it hadn't crawled over me last night, I wouldn't have carried my bed into the sun this morning, and if I hadn't carried it into the sun, I wouldn't have ended up with it next to the Inn of the Moon, and if sun and moon hadn't shone on it, I couldn't have pressed any wine out of my straw mattress and gotten drunk from it—and if all that hadn't happened I wouldn't be in your company now, most honored ants, letting you strip me to a skeleton and being dried up by the sun, but I'd be carving up a piece of meat and drying up a bottle of wine —in the hospital, namely.

Leonce.

A pleasant way of life.

Valerio.

I have a racy way of life. Because only my racing in the course of the war saved me from receiving a round of rifle bullets in my ribs. As a result of this rescue, I got a rasping cough, and the doctor resolved that my racing had become a galloping and that I had galloping consumption. But since I realized I had nothing to consume, I fell into or rather upon a consuming fever, during which I was required to eat good soup, good beef, good bread and drink good wine every day in order to sustain a defender of the Fatherland.

Leonce.

But, noblest sir, your trade, your métier, your profession, your occupation, your rank, your art?

Valerio.

My Lord, I have the great occupation of being idle, I am incredibly skilled in doing nothing, I have an enormous capacity for laziness.

WOYZECK: A RECONSTRUCTION

[consisting of Büchner's incomplete revision (Fourth Draft) and scenes from the First Draft]

CHARACTERS

Franz Woyzeck
Marie
Captain
Doctor
Drum Major
Sergeant
Andres
Margret
Barker
Announcer
Old Man
Child
Jew
Innkeeper
First Apprentice
Second Apprentice
Karl, an idiot
Katey
Grandmother
First Child
Second Child
First Person
Second Person
Court Clerk
Judge
Soldiers, Students, Young Men, Girls, Children

Open field. The town in the distance.

WOYZECK *and* ANDRES *are cutting branches in the bushes.*

Woyzeck.
Hey, Andres! That streak across the grass—that's where heads roll at night. Once somebody picked one up, thought it was a hedgehog. Three days and three nights, and he was lying in a coffin. (*Softly.*) Andres, it was the Freemasons. That's it—the Freemasons! Shh!

Andres.
(*Sings.*)
> I saw two big rabbits
> Chewing up the green, green grass . . .

Woyzeck.
Shh! Something's moving!

Andres.
> Chewing up the green, green grass
> Till it all was gone.

Woyzeck.
Something's moving behind me—under me. (*Stamps on the ground.*) Hollow! You hear that? It's all hollow down there. The Freemasons!

Andres.
I'm scared.

Woyzeck.
It's so quiet—that's strange. You feel like holding your breath. Andres!

Andres.
What?

Woyzeck.
Say something! (*Stares off into the distance.*) Andres!

Look how bright it is! There's fire raging around the sky, and a noise is coming down like trumpets. It's coming closer! Let's go! Don't look back! (*Drags him into the bushes.*)

Andres.

(*After a pause.*) Woyzeck! Do you still hear it?

Woyzeck.

Quiet, everything's quiet, like the world was dead.

Andres.

Listen! They're drumming. We've got to get back.

4,2.

[*The town.*][1]

MARIE *with her* CHILD *at the window.* MARGRET. *A parade goes by, the* DRUM MAJOR *leading.*

Marie.

(*Rocking the* CHILD *in her arms.*) Hey, boy! Ta-ra-ra-ra! You hear it? They're coming.

Margret.

What a man, like a tree!

Marie.

He stands on his feet like a lion. (*The* DRUM MAJOR *greets them.*)

Margret.

Say, what a friendly look you gave him, neighbor. We're not used to that from you.

Marie.

(*Sings.*)

A soldier is a handsome fellow . . .

Margret.

Your eyes are still shining.

Marie.

So what? Why don't you take *your* eyes to the Jew and have them polished—maybe they'll shine enough to sell as two buttons.

---

1 Brackets indicate additions to the text (as in this case) or doubtful readings.

Margret.

What? Why, Mrs. Virgin! I'm a decent woman, but you
—you can stare through seven pairs of leather pants!

Marie.

Bitch! (*Slams the window shut.*) Come on, boy. What do
they want from us, anyway? You're only the son of a
whore, and you make your mother happy with your
bastard face. Ta-ta! (*Sings.*)

> Maiden, now what's to be done?
> You've got no ring, you've a son.
> Oh, why worry my head,
> I'll sing here at your bed:
> Rockabye baby, my baby are you,
> Nobody cares what I do.
>
> Johnny, hitch up your six horses fleet,
> Go bring them something to eat.
> From oats they will turn,
> From water they'll turn,
> Only cool wine will be fine, hooray!
> Only cool wine will be fine.

(*A knock at the window.*)

Marie.

Who's that? Is that you, Franz? Come on in!

Woyzeck.

I can't. Have to go to roll call.

Marie.

What's the matter with you, Franz?

Woyzeck.

(*Mysteriously.*) Marie, there was something out there
again—a lot. Isn't it written: "And lo, the smoke of the
country went up as the smoke of a furnace"?

Marie.

Franz . . .

Woyzeck.

It followed me until I reached town. What's going to
happen?

Marie.

Franz!

Woyzeck.

I've got to go. (*He leaves.*)

Marie.

That man! He's seeing things. He didn't even look at his own child. He'll go crazy with those thoughts of his. Why are you so quiet, son? Are you scared? It's getting so dark, you'd think you were blind. Usually there's a light shining in. I can't stand it. It frightens me. (*Goes off.*)

4,3.

Fair booths. Lights. People.[2]

Old Man. Dancing Child.

> How long we live, just time will tell,
> We all have got to die,
> We know that very well!

Barker.

(*In front of a booth.*) Ladies and gentlemen, here is to be seen the astronomical horse and the little cannery-birds[3] —they're favorites of all potentates of Europe and members of all learned societies. They'll tell you everything: how old you are, how many children you have, what kind of illnesses. [*Points to a monkey.*] He shoots a pistol, stands on one leg. It's all education; he has merely a beastly reason, or rather a very reasonable beastliness— he's no dumb individual like a lot of people, present company excepted. Enter! The presentation will begin. The commencement of the beginning will start immediately. Observe the progress of civilization. Everything progresses—a horse, a monkey, a cannery-bird! The monkey is already a soldier. That's not much—it's the lowest level of the human race!

(SERGEANT. DRUM MAJOR. [MARIE. WOYZECK.])

Sergeant.

Hold it! Over there. Look at her! What a piece!

2 In his revision, Büchner wrote only this title and left one and a half pages blank. The scene has been reconstructed from earlier drafts.

3 The Barker says *Canaillevogel* instead of *Kanarienvögel*, which means "canaries." *Canaille* means "rascal."

Drum Major.
Goddamn! Good enough for the propagation of cavalry regiments and the breeding of drum majors!

Sergeant.
Look how she holds her head—you'd think that black hair would pull her down like a weight. And those eyes, black . . .

Drum Major.
It's like looking down a well or a chimney. Come on, after her!

Marie.
Those lights!

Woyzeck.
Yeah, like black cats with fiery eyes. Hey, what a night!

(*Inside the booth.*)

Announcer.
[*Presenting a horse.*] Show your talent! Show your beastly wisdom. Put human society to shame. Gentlemen, this animal that you see here, with a tail on his body, with his four hoofs, is a member of all learned societies, is a professor at our university with whom the students learn to ride and fight. That was simple comprehension. Now think with double *raison*. What do you do when you think with double *raison?* Is there in the learned *société* an ass? (*The horse shakes its head.*) Now you understand double *raison?* That is beastiognomy.[4] Yes, that is no dumb animal, that's a person! A human being, a beastly human being, but still an animal, *une bête*. (*The horse behaves improperly.*) That's right, put *société* to shame. You see, the beast is still nature, unideal nature. Take a lesson from him. Go ask the doctor, it's very unhealthy.[5] All this means: Man, be natural. You were created from dust, sand, dirt. Do you want to be more than dust, sand, dirt? Observe his reason: he can add, but he can't count on his fingers. How come? He simply can't express himself, explain himself. He's a transformed person! Tell the gentlemen what time it is. Does anyone have a watch—a watch?

---

4 *Viehsionomik:* a pun on "beast" and "physiognomy."
5 Meaning "to hold it in."

Sergeant.
A watch! (*Slowly and grandly he pulls a watch out of his pocket.*) There you are.
Marie.
This I've got to see. (*She climbs into the first row. The* SERGEANT *helps her.*)

4,4.

[*Room.*]

MARIE *sits with her* CHILD *on her lap, a piece of mirror in her hand.*

Marie.
(*Looks at herself in the mirror.*) These stones really sparkle! What kind are they? What did he say?—Go to sleep, son! Shut your eyes tight. (*The* CHILD *covers his eyes with his hands.*) Tighter—stay quiet or he'll come get you. (*Sings.*)

> Close up your shop, fair maid,
> A gypsy boy's in the glade.
> He'll lead you by the hand
> Off into gypsyland.

(*Looks in the mirror again.*) It must be gold. The likes of us only have a little corner in the world and a little piece of mirror, but my mouth is just as red as the great ladies with their mirrors from top to toe and their handsome lords who kiss their hands. I'm just a poor woman. (*The* CHILD *sits up.*) Shh, son, eyes shut! Look, the sandman! He's running along the wall. (*She flashes with the mirror.*) Eyes shut, or he'll look into them, and you'll go blind.

(WOYZECK *enters behind her. She jumps up with her hands over her ears.*)

Woyzeck.
What's that you got there?
Marie.
Nothing.

184

Woyzeck.
Something's shining under your fingers.
Marie.
An earring. I found it.
Woyzeck.
I've never found anything like that. Two at once.
Marie.
What am I—a whore?
Woyzeck.
It's all right, Marie. Look, the boy's asleep. Lift him up under his arms, the chair's hurting him. Those shiny drops on his forehead; everything under the sun is work. Sweat, even in our sleep. Us poor people! Here's some more money, Marie, my pay and some from my captain.
Marie.
Bless you, Franz.
Woyzeck.
I have to go. See you tonight, Marie. Bye.
Marie.
(*Alone, after a pause.*) What a bitch I am. I could stab myself. Oh, what a world! Everything goes to hell anyhow, man and woman alike.

4,5.

The CAPTAIN. WOYZECK.

The CAPTAIN *in a chair,* WOYZECK *shaves him.*

Captain.
Take it easy, Woyzeck, take it easy. One thing at a time. You're making me dizzy. You're going to finish early today—what am I supposed to do with the extra ten minutes? Woyzeck, just think, you've still got a good thirty years to live, thirty years! That's 360 months, and days, hours, minutes! What are you going to do with that ungodly amount of time? Get organized, Woyzeck.
Woyzeck.
Yes, Cap'n.
Captain.
I fear for the world when I think about eternity. Activ-

ity, Woyzeck, activity! Eternal—that's eternal—that is—eternal—you realize that, of course. But then again it's not eternal, it's only a moment, yes, a moment. Woyzeck, it frightens me to think that the earth rotates in one day. What a waste of time! What will come of that? Woyzeck, I can't look at a mill wheel anymore or I get melancholy.

Woyzeck.
Yes, Cap'n.

Captain.
Woyzeck, you always look so upset. A good man doesn't act like that, a good man with a good conscience. Say something, Woyzeck. What's the weather like?

Woyzeck.
It's bad, Cap'n, bad—wind.

Captain.
I can feel it, there's something rapid out there. A wind like that reminds me of a mouse. (*Cunningly.*) I believe it's coming from the south-north.

Woyzeck.
Yes, Cap'n.

Captain.
Ha-ha-ha! South-north! Ha-ha-ha! Oh, are you stupid, terribly stupid! (*Sentimentally.*) Woyzeck, you're a good man, a good man—(*With dignity.*) but Woyzeck, you've got no morality. Morality—that's when you are moral, you understand. It's a good word. You have a child without the blessing of the church, as our Reverend Chaplain says, without the blessing of the church. *I* didn't make that up.

Woyzeck.
Cap'n, the good Lord isn't going to look at a poor worm only because amen was said over it before it was created. The Lord said: "Suffer little children to come unto me."

Captain.
What's that you're saying? What kind of a crazy answer is that? You're getting me all confused with your answer. When I say *you*, I mean you—you!

Woyzeck.
Us poor people. You see, Cap'n—money, money. If you don't have money . . . Just try to raise your own kind on morality in this world. After all, we're flesh and blood. The likes of us are unhappy in this world and in the next.

I guess if we ever got to Heaven, we'd have to help with the thunder.

Captain.
Woyzeck, you have no virtue. You're not a virtuous person. Flesh and blood? When I'm lying at the window after it has rained, and I watch the white stockings as they go tripping down the street—damn it, Woyzeck, then love comes all over me. I've got flesh and blood, too. But Woyzeck, virtue, virtue! How else could I make time go by? I always say to myself: you're a virtuous man, (*Sentimentally.*) a good man, a good man.

Woyzeck.
Yes, Cap'n, virtue! I haven't figured it out yet. You see, us common people, we don't have virtue. We act like nature tells us. But if I was a gentleman, and had a hat and a watch and a topcoat and could talk refined, then I'd be virtuous, too. Virtue must be nice, Cap'n. But I'm just a poor guy.

Captain.
That's fine, Woyzeck. You're a good man, a good man. But you think too much, that's unhealthy. You always look so upset. This discussion has really worn me out. You can go now—and don't run like that! Slowly, nice and slow down the street.

4,6.

MARIE. DRUM MAJOR.

Drum Major.
Marie!
Marie.
(*Looking at him expressively.*) Go march up and down for me. A chest like a bull and a beard like a lion. Nobody else is like that. No woman is prouder than me.
Drum Major.
Sundays when I have my plumed helmet and my white gloves—goddamn, Marie! The prince always says: man, you're quite a guy!

Marie.

(*Mockingly.*) Aw, go on! (*Goes up to him.*) What a man!

Drum Major.

What a woman! Hell, let's breed a race of drum majors, hey? (*He embraces her.*)

Marie.

(*Moody.*) Leave me alone!

Drum Major.

You wildcat!

Marie.

(*Violently.*) Just try to touch me!

Drum Major.

You've got the devil in your eyes.

Marie.

For all I care. What does it matter?

4,7.

MARIE. WOYZECK.

Woyzeck.

(*Stares at her, shakes his head.*) Hm! I don't see anything, I don't see anything. Oh, I should be able to see it; I should be able to grab it with my fists.

Marie.

(*Intimidated.*) What's the matter, Franz? You're out of your mind, Franz.

Woyzeck.

A sin so fat and so wide—it stinks enough to smoke the angels out of Heaven. You've got a red mouth, Marie. No blister on it? Good-bye, Marie. You're as beautiful as sin. Can mortal sin be so beautiful?

Marie.

Franz, you're delirious.

Woyzeck.

Damn it! Was he standing here like this, like this?

Marie.

As the day is long and the world is old, lots of people can stand on one spot, one after another.

Woyzeck.
I saw him.
Marie.
You can see all sort of things if you've got two eyes and aren't blind, and the sun is shining.
Woyzeck.
[With my own eyes!]
Marie.
(*Fresh.*) So what!

4,8.

WOYZECK. *The* DOCTOR.

Doctor.
What's this I hear, Woyzeck? A man of his word!
Woyzeck.
What is it, Doctor?
Doctor.
I saw it, Woyzeck. You pissed on the street, you pissed on the wall like a dog. And you get two cents a day. Woyzeck, that's bad. The world's getting bad, very bad.
Woyzeck.
But Doctor, the call of nature . . .
Doctor.
The call of nature, the call of nature! Nature! Haven't I proved that the *musculus constrictor vesicae* is subject to the will? Nature! Woyzeck, man is free. In man alone is individuality exalted to freedom. Couldn't hold it in! (*Shakes his head, puts his hands behind his back, and paces back and forth.*) Did you eat your peas already, Woyzeck? I'm revolutionizing science, I'll blow it sky-high. Urea ten per cent, ammonium chloride, hyperoxidic. Woyzeck, try pissing again. Go in there and try.
Woyzeck.
I can't, Doctor.
Doctor.
(*With emotion.*) But pissing on the wall! I have it in writing. Here's the contract. I saw it all—saw it with my

own eyes. I was just holding my nose out the window, letting the sun's rays hit it, so as to examine the process of sneezing. (*Goes up to him.*) No, Woyzeck, I'm not getting angry. Anger is unhealthy, unscientific. I am calm, perfectly calm. My pulse is beating at its usual sixty, and I tell you this in all cold-bloodedness. Now, who would get excited about a human being, a human being? If it were a Proteus that were dying—! But you shouldn't have pissed on the wall . . .

Woyzeck.

You see, Doctor, sometimes you've got a certain character, a certain structure. But with nature, that's something else, you see, with nature. (*He cracks his knuckles.*) That's like—how should I put it—for example . . .

Doctor.

Woyzeck, you're philosophizing again.

Woyzeck.

(*Confidingly.*) Doctor, have you ever seen anything of double nature? When the sun's standing high at noon and the world seems to be going up in flames, I've heard a terrible voice talking to me!

Doctor.

Woyzeck, you've got an *aberratio!*

Woyzeck.

(*Puts his finger to his nose.*) The toadstools, Doctor. There—that's where it is. Have you seen how they grow in patterns? If only someone could read that.

Doctor.

Woyzeck, you've got a marvelous *aberratio mentalis partialis*, second species, beautifully developed. Woyzeck, you're getting a raise. Second species: fixed idea with a generally rational condition. You're doing everything as usual? Shaving your captain?

Woyzeck.

Yes, sir.

Doctor.

Eating your peas?

Woyzeck.

Same as ever, Doctor. My wife gets the money for the household.

Doctor.

Going on duty?

Woyzeck.
Yes, sir.
Doctor.
You're an interesting case. Subject Woyzeck, you're getting a raise. Now behave yourself. Show me your pulse!
Yes.

4,9.

CAPTAIN. DOCTOR.

Captain.
Doctor, I feel sorry for horses when I think that the poor beasts have to go everywhere on foot. Don't run like that! Don't wave your cane around in the air like that! You'll run yourself to death that way. A good man with a good conscience doesn't go so fast. A good man . . . (*He catches the* DOCTOR *by the coat.*) Doctor, allow me to save a human life. You're racing . . . Doctor, I'm so melancholy. I get so emotional. I always start crying when I see my coat hanging on the wall—there it is.
Doctor.
Hm! Bloated, fat, thick neck, apoplectic constitution. Yes, Captain, you might be stricken by an *apoplexia cerebralis*. But you might get it just on one side and be half paralyzed, or—best of all—you might become mentally affected and just vegetate from then on. Those are approximately your prospects for the next four weeks. Moreover, I can assure you that you will be a most interesting case, and if, God willing, your tongue is partially paralyzed, we'll make immortal experiments.
Captain.
Doctor, don't frighten me! People have been known to die of fright, of pure, sheer fright. I can see them now, with flowers in their hands—but they'll say, he was a good man, a good man. You damn coffin nail!
Doctor.
[*Holds out his hat.*] What's this, Captain? That's brainless!

Captain.

(*Makes a crease.*) What's this, Doctor? That's in-crease!

Doctor.

I take my leave, most honorable Mr. Drillprick.

Captain.

Likewise, dearest Mr. Coffin Nail.

4,10.

The guardroom.

WOYZECK. ANDRES.

Andres.

(*Sings.*)

> Our hostess has a pretty maid,
> She's in her garden night and day,
> She sits inside her garden. . . .

Woyzeck.

Andres!

Andres.

Huh?

Woyzeck.

Nice weather.

Andres.

Sunday weather. There's music outside town. All the broads are out there already, everybody's sweating—it's really moving along.

Woyzeck.

(*Restlessly.*) A dance, Andres. They're dancing.

Andres.

Yeah, at the Horse and at the Star.

Woyzeck.

Dancing, dancing.

Andres.

Big deal. (*Sings.*)

> She sits inside her garden,
> Until the bells have all struck twelve,
> And stares at all the soldiers.

Woyzeck.

Andres, I can't keep still.

Andres.

Stupid!

Woyzeck.

I've got to get out of here. Everything's spinning before my eyes. Dancing. Dancing. With their hot hands. Damn it, Andres!

Andres.

What do you want?

Woyzeck.

I've got to go.

Andres.

With that whore.

Woyzeck.

I've got to get out. It's so hot in here.

4,11.

Inn.

The windows are open, a dance. Benches in front of the house. APPRENTICES.

First Apprentice.

       This shirt I've got, I don't know whose,
       My soul it stinks like booze . . .

Second Apprentice.

Brother, shall I in friendship bore a hole in your nature? I want to bore a hole in your nature. I'm quite a guy, too, you know. I'm going to kill all the fleas on his body.

First Apprentice.

My soul, my soul it stinks like booze. Even money must eventually decay. Forget-me-not! Oh, is this world beautiful! Brother, I could cry a rain barrel full of tears. I wish our noses were two bottles and we could pour them down each other's throats.

Others.

(*In chorus.*)

       A hunter from the west
       Once went riding through the woods.
       Hip-hip, hooray! A hunter has a merry life,

O'er meadow and o'er stream,
Oh, hunting is my dream!

(WOYZECK *stands at the window.* MARIE *and the* DRUM MAJOR *dance past without seeing him.*)

Marie.
(*Dancing by.*) On! and on, on and on!
Woyzeck.
(*Chokes.*) On and on! On and on! (*Jumps up violently and sinks back on the bench.*) On and on, on and on. (*Beats his hands together.*) Spin around, roll around. Why doesn't God blow out the sun so that everything can roll around in lust, man and woman, man and beast. They'll do it in broad daylight, they'll do it on our hands, like flies. Woman! That woman is hot, hot! On and on, on and on. (*Jumps up.*) The bastard! Look how he's grabbing her, grabbing her body! He—he's got her now, [like I used to have her!][6]
First Apprentice.
(*Preaches on the table.*) Yet when a wanderer stands leaning against the stream of time and/or gives answer in the wisdom of God, asking himself: Why does Man exist? Why does Man exist? But verily I say unto you: how could the farmer, the cooper, the shoemaker, the doctor exist if God hadn't created man? How could the tailor exist if God hadn't given man a feeling of shame? How could the soldier exist, if men didn't feel the necessity of killing one another? Therefore, do not ye despair, yes, yes, it is lovely and fine, yet all that is earthly is passing, even money must eventually decay. In conclusion, my dear friends, let us piss crosswise so that a Jew will die.

4,12.

Open field.

Woyzeck.
On and on! On and on! Shh! Music! (*Stretches out on*

---

[6] Or: "like it always is at the beginning!"

the ground.) Ha—what—what are you saying? Louder, louder . . . stab—stab the bitch to death? Stab—stab the bitch to death. Should I? Must I? Do I hear it over there, is the wind saying it too? It goes on and on—stab her to death . . . to death.

4,13.

Night.

ANDRES *and* WOYZECK *in a bed.*

Woyzeck.
(*Shakes* ANDRES.) Andres! Andres! I can't sleep. When I close my eyes, everything starts spinning, and I hear the fiddles, on and on, on and on, and then there's a voice from the wall. Don't you hear anything?

Andres.
Oh, yeah. Let them dance! God bless us, amen. (*Falls asleep again.*)

Woyzeck.
And it floats between my eyes like a knife.

Andres.
Drink some brandy with a painkiller in it. That'll cut your fever.

4,14.

Inn.

DRUM MAJOR. WOYZECK. ONLOOKERS.

Drum Major.
I'm a man! (*Pounds his chest.*) A man, you hear? Who wants to start something? If you're not drunk as a lord, stay away from me. I'll shove your nose up your ass. I'll . . . (*To* WOYZECK.) Man, have a drink. A man gotta drink. I wish the world was booze, booze.

Woyzeck.
(*Whistles.*)

Drum Major.
You bastard, you want me to pull your tongue out of your throat and wrap it around you? (*They wrestle,* WOYZECK *loses.*) Shall I leave you as much breath as an old woman's fart? Shall I?

(WOYZECK *sits on the bench, exhausted and trembling.*)

Drum Major.
He thinks he's so great. Ha!
> Oh, brandy, that's my life,
> Oh, brandy gives me courage!

An Onlooker.
He sure got his.
Another.
He's bleeding.
Woyzeck.
One thing after another.

4,15.

WOYZECK. *The* JEW.

Woyzeck.
The pistol costs too much.
Jew.
Well, do you want it or don't you?
Woyzeck.
How much is the knife?
Jew.
It's good and straight. You want to cut your throat with it? Well, how about it? I'll give it to you as cheap as anybody else. Your death'll be cheap—but not for nothing. How about it? You'll have an economical death.
Woyzeck.
That can cut more than just bread.
Jew.
Two cents.
Woyzeck.
There! (*Goes off.*)
Jew.
There! Like it was nothing. But it's money! The dog.

[MARIE. KARL, *the idiot.* CHILD.]

Marie.
(*Leafs through the Bible.*) "And no guile is found in his mouth" . . . My God! My God! Don't look at me. (*Pages further.*) "And the scribes and Pharisees brought unto him a woman taken in adultery, and set her in the midst . . . And Jesus said unto her, 'Neither do I condemn thee: go, and sin no more.'" (*Clasps her hands together.*) My God! My God, I can't. God, just give me enough strength to pray. (*The* CHILD *snuggles up to her.*) The boy is like a knife in my heart. [Karl! He's sunning himself.]

Karl.
(*Lies on the ground and tells himself fairy tales on his fingers.*) This one has a golden crown—he's a king. Tomorrow I'll go get the queen's child. Blood sausage says, come on, liver sausage! (*He takes the* CHILD *and is quiet.*)

[Marie.]
Franz hasn't come, not yesterday, not today. It's getting hot in here. (*She opens the window.*) "And stood at his feet weeping, and began to wash his feet with tears, and did wipe them with the hairs of her head, and kissed his feet, and anointed them with ointment." (*Beats her breast.*) It's all dead! Savior, Savior, I wish I could anoint your feet.

4,17.

ANDRES. WOYZECK *rummages through his things.*

Woyzeck.
This jacket isn't part of the uniform, Andres. You can use it, Andres. The crucifix is my sister's—so's the little ring. I've got an icon, too—two hearts in beautiful gold. It was in my mother's Bible, and it says:
> May pain be my reward,
> Through pain I love my Lord.

> Lord, like Thy body, red and sore,
> So be my heart forevermore.

My mother can only feel the sun shining on her hands now. That doesn't matter.

Andres.

(*Blankly, answers to everything.*) Yeah.

Woyzeck.

(*Pulls out a piece of paper.*) Friedrich Johann Franz Woyzeck, soldier, rifleman in the second regiment, second battalion, fourth company, born . . . Today[7] I'm thirty years, seven months, and twelve days old.

Andres.

Franz, you better go to the hospital. You poor guy—drink brandy with a painkiller in it. That'll kill the fever.

Woyzeck.

You know, Andres, when the carpenter nails those boards together, nobody knows who'll be laying his head on them.

[End of Büchner's revision.]

[Scenes from the First Draft:]

1,14.

[*Street.*]

MARIE *with little girls in front of the house door.*
[GRANDMOTHER. *Then* WOYZECK.]

Girls.

> How bright the sun on Candlemas Day,
> On fields of golden grain.
> As two by two they marched along
> Down the country lane.
> The pipers up in front,
> The fiddlers in a chain.
> Their red socks . . .

---

[7] Büchner inserted here: "on the Feast of the Annunciation, the 20th of July" (actually March 25).

First Child.
I don't like it!
Second Child.
What do you want, anyway?
Why'd you start it?

Yeah, why?

I can't.

Because!

Who's going to sing—?

Why because?

Marie, you sing to us.
Marie.
Come, you little crabs.
  ([*Children's games:*] "Ring-around-a-rosy" and "King
  Herod.")
Grandmother, tell a story.
Grandmother.
Once upon a time there was a poor little child with no
father and no mother, everything was dead, and no one
was left in the whole world. Everything was dead, and it
went and searched day and night. And since nobody was
left on the earth, it wanted to go up to the heavens, and
the moon was looking at it so friendly, and when it
finally got to the moon, the moon was a piece of rotten
wood and then it went to the sun and when it got there,
the sun was a wilted sunflower and when it got to the
stars, they were little golden flies stuck up there like the
shrike sticks 'em on the blackthorn and when it wanted
to go back down to the earth, the earth was an upset pot
and was all alone and it sat down and cried and there
it sits to this day, all alone.
Woyzeck.[8]
Marie!
Marie.
(*Startled.*) What is it?
Woyzeck.
Marie, we have to go. It's time.
Marie.
Where to?

---

[8] Actually, Woyzeck is named "Louis" and Marie is "Margret" in
this draft.

Woyzeck.
How do I know?

1,15.

MARIE *and* WOYZECK.

Marie.
That must be the town back there. It's dark.
Woyzeck.
Stay here. Come on, sit down.
Marie.
But I have to get back.
Woyzeck.
You won't get sore feet.
Marie.
What's gotten into you!
Woyzeck.
Do you know how long it's been, Marie?
Marie.
Two years since Pentecost.
Woyzeck.
Do you know how long it's going to be?
Marie.
I've got to go make supper.
Woyzeck.
Are you freezing, Marie? But you're warm. How hot
your lips are! Hot—the hot breath of a whore—but I'd
give heaven and earth to kiss them once more. Once
you're cold, you don't freeze anymore. The morning dew
won't make you freeze.
Marie.
What are you talking about?
Woyzeck.
Nothing. (*Silence.*)
Marie.
Look how red the moon is.
Woyzeck.
Like a bloody blade.

Marie.
What are you up to? Franz, you're so pale. (*He pulls out the knife.*) Franz—wait! For God's sake—help!

Woyzeck.
Take that and that! Can't you die? There! There! Ah—she's still twitching. Not yet? Not yet? Still alive? (*Keeps on stabbing.*) Are you dead? Dead! Dead! (*People approach, he runs off.*)

1,16.

Two people.

First Person.
Wait!

Second Person.
You hear it? Shh! Over there!

First Person.
Ooh! There! What a sound!

Second Person.
That's the water. it's calling. Nobody has drowned for a long time. Let's go. It's bad to hear things like that.

First Person.
Ooh! There it is again. Like someone dying.

Second Person.
It's weird. It's so foggy—gray mist everywhere and the beetles humming like broken bells. Let's get out of here!

First Person.
No—it's too clear. too loud. Up this way. Come on.

1,17.

The inn.

[WOYZECK. KATEY. KARL. INNKEEPER. *People.*]

Woyzeck.
Dance, all of you, on and on. Sweat and stink. He'll get you all in the end. (*Sings.*)

Our hostess has a pretty maid,
She's in her garden night and day,
She sits inside her garden,
Until the bells have all struck twelve,
And stares at all the soldiers.

(*He dances.*) Come on, Katey! Sit down! I'm hot, hot.
(*He takes off his jacket.*) That's the way it is: the devil
takes one and lets the other go. Katey, you're hot! Why?
Katey, you'll be cold someday, too. Be reasonable. Can't
you sing something?

[**Katey.**][9]

For Swabian hills I do not yearn,
And flowing gowns I always spurn,
For flowing gowns and pointed shoes
A servant girl should never choose.

[**Woyzeck.**]

No, no shoes. You can go to hell without shoes, too.

[**Katey.**]

For shame, my love, I'm not your own,
Just keep your money and sleep alone.

[**Woyzeck.**]

Yes, that's right! I don't want to make myself bloody.

Katey.

But what's that on your hand?

Woyzeck.

Who? Me?

Katey.

Red . . . blood! (*People gather around.*)

Woyzeck.

Blood? Blood.

Innkeeper.

Ooh. Blood.

Woyzeck.

I guess I must have cut myself on my right hand.

Innkeeper.

But how'd it get on your elbow?

Woyzeck.

I wiped it off.

---

[9] It is unclear whether Katey or Woyzeck sings this song.

Innkeeper.
What! With your right hand on your right elbow? You're talented.

Karl.
And then the giant said: I smell, I smell, I smell human flesh. Phew! That stinks already.

Woyzeck.
Damn it, what do you want? What do you care? Get away, or the first one who . . . God damn it! You think I killed someone? Am I a murderer? What are you staring at? Look at yourselves! Out of my way! (*He runs out.*)

1,18.

Children.

First Child.
Come on! Marie!

Second Child.
What's wrong?

First Child.
Don't you know? Everybody's gone out there already. Someone's lying there!

Second Child.
Where?

First Child.
To the left through the trench, near that red cross.

Second Child.
Let's go, so we can still see something. Otherwise they'll carry her away.

1,19.

WOYZECK *alone.*

Woyzeck.
The knife? Where's the knife? Here's where I left it. It'll give me away! Closer, still closer! What kind of a place

is this? What's that I hear? Something's moving. Shh!
Over there. Marie? Ah—Marie! Quiet. Everything's quiet!
You're so pale, Marie. Why is that red thread around
your neck? Who helped you earn that for your sins? They
made you black, black! Now I've made you white. Your
black hair looks so wild. Didn't you do your braids today? Something's lying over there! Cold, wet, still. Got
to get away from here. The knife, the knife—is that it?
There! People—over there. (*He runs off.*)

1,20.

WOYZECK *at a pond.*

Woyzeck.
Down it goes! (*He throws the knife in.*) It sinks like a
stone in the dark water. The moon is like a bloody blade.
Is the whole world going to give me away? No—it's too
far in front—when people go swimming—(*He goes into
the pond and throws it far out.*) All right, now—but in
the summer, when they go diving for shells . . . Oh, it'll
rust. Who'll recognize it? I wish I'd smashed it! Am I
still bloody? I better wash myself. There's a spot—and
there's another.

1,21.

COURT CLERK. BARBER. DOCTOR. JUDGE.

[Clerk.]
A good murder, a real murder, a beautiful murder. As
good a murder as you'd ever want to see. We haven't
had one like this for a long time.

WOYZECK: THE DRAFTS

FIRST DRAFT

1,1. *Booths. People.*

Announcer.
(*In front of a booth.*) Gentlemen! Gentlemen! Look at
this creature, as God made it—he's nothing, nothing at
all. Now see the effect of art: he walks upright, wears
coat and pants, carries a sword! Ho! Take a bow! Presto
—you're a baron. Give me a kiss! (*He trumpets.*) The
little fellow is musical. Ladies and gentlemen, here is to
be seen the astronomical horse and the little cannery-
birds—they're favorites of all crowned heads. The presentation will begin! The beginning of the beginning! The
commencement of the commencement!

[Woyzeck.]
Want to?

Margret.[1]
All right. It ought to be good. Look at his tassels—and
the woman's got pants on!

1,2. *Inside the booth.*

Announcer.
Show your talent! Show your beastly wisdom! Put human

[1] I.e., Marie.

society to shame! Gentlemen, this animal that you see here, with a tail on his body, with his four hoofs, is a member of all learned societies, is a professor at our university with whom the students learn to ride and fight. That was simple comprehension. Now think with double *raison*. What do you do when you think with double *raison?* Is there in the learned *société* an ass? (*The horse shakes its head.*) Now you understand double *raison?* That is beastiognomy. Yes, that is no dumb animal, that's a person! A human being, a beastly human being, but still an animal, *une bête.* (*The horse behaves improperly.*) That's right, put *société* to shame. You see, the beast is still nature, unideal nature! Take a lesson from him. Go ask the doctor, it's very unhealthy. All this means: Man, be natural. You were created from dust, sand, dirt. Do you want to be more than dust, sand, dirt? Observe his reason: he can add but he can't count on his fingers. How come? He simply can't express himself, explain himself. He's a transformed person! Tell the gentlemen what time it is. Does anyone have a watch—a watch?

Sergeant.
A watch! (*Slowly and grandly he pulls a watch out of his pocket.*) There you are . . . What a piece! She can stare through seven layers of leather pants!

Margret.
This I've got to see. (*She climbs into the first row. The* SERGEANT *helps her.*)

Sergeant.

———

1,3. MARGRET *alone.**2

Margret.
The other one gave him an order and he had to go. Ha! What a man!

———
2 An asterisk indicates that Büchner crossed out the scene while he was revising the play.

1,4. *The barrack square.**

ANDRES. LOUIS.[3]

Andres.
(*Sings.*)

> Our hostess has a pretty maid,
> She's in her garden night and day,
> She sits inside her garden,
> Until the bells have all struck twelve,
> And stares at all the soldiers.

Louis.
Hey, Andres, I can't keep still.
Andres.
Stupid!
Louis.
What are you talking about? So say something!
Andres.
Well?
Louis.
Why do you think I'm here?
Andres.
'Cause it's nice weather and they're dancing today.
Louis.
I got to get out there, got to see it!
Andres.
What do you want?
Louis.
To get out there!
Andres.
You worrywart, because of that whore?
Louis.
I got to get out.

---

[3] I.e., Woyzeck.

1,5. *Inn.**

The windows are open. People are dancing. On the bench in front of the house LOUIS *looks through the window.*

Louis.
It's him—with her! Hell! (*He sits down, shivering. He looks, goes to the window.*) They're really moving! Yeah, roll around on each other! Look at her—on! and on, on and on.

Idiot.
Phew! That stinks!

Louis.
Yeah, that stinks! She's got red, red cheeks, but why does she stink already? Karl, what's on your mind?

Idiot.
I smell, I smell blood.

Louis.
Blood? Why is everything turning red in front of my eyes? It's like they were rolling around in a sea of blood, all of them together! Ha! a red sea!

1,6. *Open field.**

Louis.
On! and on! On and on! Shssh, shssh, that's how the fiddles and flutes go. On and on! On and on! What's that talking down there? There—out of the earth, very softly. What? What? (*He stoops down.*) Stab! Stab! Stab the Woyzeck woman to death. Stab! Stab the Woyzeck woman to death. The Woyzeck woman—on and on! It's hissing and rumbling and thundering.

1,7. A room.*

LOUIS. ANDRES.

Andres.
Hey!
Louis.
Andres!
Andres.
(*Mumbles in his sleep.*)
Louis.
Hey, Andres!
Andres.
Well, what is it?
Louis.
I can't keep still. I keep hearing it, the fiddling and the jumping, on and on! On and on! And then when I shut my eyes, I see flashes, and there's a big broad knife lying on a table by the window. It's in a dark, narrow alley and an old man is sitting there. And the knife's always between my eyes.
Andres.
Go to sleep, you fool!

1,8. The barrack square.

Louis.
Didn't you hear anything?
Andres.
He's still there with a friend.
Louis.
He said something.
Andres.
How do you know? How shall I say it? Well, he laughed, and then he said: What a piece! She's got thighs—and it's all so firm!
Louis.
(*Very coldly.*) So that's what he said? . . . What was I

209

dreaming about last night? Wasn't it about a knife? What stupid dreams we get.

Andres.

Where're you going, friend?

Louis.

To get wine for my officer . . . But Andres, she was one in a million.

Andres.

Who was?

Louis.

Never mind. See you around.

1,9. *The* OFFICER. LOUIS.*

Louis.

(*Alone.*) What did he say? Well, don't count your chickens.

1,10. *An inn.**

BARBER. SERGEANT.

Barber.

> Oh daughter, dear daughter,
> What's got into you?
> You took up with coachmen
> And stablemen too!

What is it that God can't do, huh? Undo what's been done, that's what. Heh heh heh! But that's the way it is, and that's the way it should be. But better is better. (*Sings.*)

> Booze, that's my life,
> Booze gives me courage.

And a decent man loves life, and a man who loves life has no courage, a virtuous man has no courage. Whoever's got courage is a dog.

Sergeant.

(*With dignity.*) You're forgetting yourself in the presence of a brave man.

Barber.
I'm not referring to anybody in particular, like the French do, and it was nice of you. But whoever's got courage is a dog!

Sergeant.
Damn you! You broken shaving basin, you stale soapsuds! I'll make you drink your piss and swallow your razor!

Barber.
Sir, you're wronging yourself! Was I talking about you? Did I say that you had courage? Sir, leave me alone! I am science. Every week I get half a dollar for my scientific self. Don't break me apart or I'll go hungry. I am a *spinosa pericyclyda*. I have a Latin backbone. I'm a living skeleton. All mankind studies me. What is man? Bones! Dust, sand, dirt. What is nature? Dust, sand, dirt. But those stupid people, those stupid people. Let's be friends. If you didn't have courage, there wouldn't be any science. Only nature, no amputation. What's this? A leg, an arm, flesh, bones, veins? What's this? Dirt? When will it be dirt? So should I cut my arm off? No. Man is egoistic, but he hits, shoots, stabs, goes whoring. (*He sobs.*) We must. Friends, I'm touched. Look, I wish our noses were two bottles and we could pour them down each other's throats. Oh, how beautiful the world is! Friend! A friend! The world! (*Moved.*) Look how the sun's coming out of the clouds, like a bedpan emptying out. (*He cries.*)

1,11. *The inn.*

LOUIS *sits in front of the inn. People go out.* ANDRES.

Andres.
What are you doing there?

Louis.
What time is it?

Andres.
———

Louis.
Isn't it later than that? I thought it would go faster. I wish it was the day after tomorrow.

211

Andres.
Why?
Louis.
Then it'd be over.
Andres.
What?
Louis.
Scram.

[Andres.]
Why're you sitting there in front of the door?
Louis.
I'm all right sitting here, and I know it, but lots of people sit in front of a door and they *don't* know it: a lot get carried out the door feet first!
[Andres.]
Come on, let's go!
[Louis.]
I'm all right sitting here, and I'd be even better lying here. If everybody knew what time it is, they'd get undressed and put on a silk shirt and have their coffin measured.
[Andres.]
He's drunk.
Louis.
What's that lying over there? It's flashing. It's always floating between my eyes. Look how it's shining. I got to have it.

1,12. *Open field.*

Louis.
(*Lays the knife in a hole.*) Thou shalt not kill. Stay there! Got to get out of here! (*He runs off quickly.*)

1,13. *Night. Moonlight.*

ANDRES *and* LOUIS *in a bed.*

Louis.
(*Softly.*) Andres!
Andres.
(*Dreams.*) There—wait! Yes . . .
Louis.
Hey, Andres!
Andres.
What?
Louis.
I can't keep still! Andres.
Andres.
You had a nightmare?
Louis.
Something's lying out there, in the earth. They're always pointing to it. You hear that—and that? How they're knocking inside the walls? One of them just looked in at the window. Don't you hear it? I hear it all day long. On and on. Stab, stab the Woyzeck woman.
Andres.
Lie down, Louis. You better go to the hospital. Drink some brandy with a painkiller in it; that'll cut the fever.

[For 1,14 to 1,21[4]: see Reconstruction, pages 198–204.]

---

[4] Note to Scene 1,21: after the Clerk's words, this fragment contains the following: *"Barber. Tall, haggard, cowardly."*

SECOND DRAFT

2,1. *Open field. The town in the distance.**

WOYZECK. ANDRES. *They are cutting branches in the bushes.*

Andres.

(*Whistles and sings.*)

> A hunter's life for me,
> A hunter's always free;
> Where I can hunt
> That's where I'll go.
>
> One day a rabbit I did see,
> "Are you a hunter?" he asked me.
> A hunter I used to be,
> But shooting I can't do.

Woyzeck.

Yeah, Andres, it really is—this place is haunted. You see that shining streak there across the grass, where the toadstools are growing? That's where heads roll at night. Somebody picked one up once, thought it was a hedgehog. Three days and three nights, and he went crazy and died. (*Softly.*) It was the Freemasons, that's it.

Andres.

It's getting dark. You're almost making me scared. (*He sings.*)

Woyzeck.

(*Grabs him.*) You hear it, Andres? Do you hear it next to us, under us? Let's go—the ground's swaying under our feet! The Freemasons! How they're swirling around! (*He drags him away.*)

Andres.

Leave me alone! Are you crazy? Damn it!

Woyzeck.

Are you a mole? Are your ears full of sand? Don't you

214

hear that terrible noise in the sky? Over the town. It's all glowing! Don't look back! Look how it's shooting up, and everything's thundering.

Andres.
You scare me.

Woyzeck.
Don't look back. (*They hide in the bushes.*)

Andres.
Woyzeck, I can't hear anything anymore.

Woyzeck.
Quiet, all quiet, like death.

Andres.
They're drumming. We've got to get back.

2,2. *The town.**

LOUISE.[1] MARGRET *at the window. Parade goes by, the* DRUM MAJOR *leading.*

Louise.
Hey, son! They're coming.

Margret.
What a man!

Louise.
Like a tree. (*The* DRUM MAJOR *greets them.*)

Margret.
Say, what a friendly look you gave him, neighbor. We're not used to that from you.

Louise.
A soldier is a handsome fellow . . .

Margret.
Your eyes are still shining.

Louise.
What's it to you? Why don't you take your eyes to the Jew and have them polished—maybe they'll shine enough to sell as two buttons.

Margret.
Why, Mrs. Virgin! I'm a decent woman, but you—every-

---

[1] I.e., Marie.

body knows you can stare through seven pairs of leather pants!

Louise.

Bitch! (*Slams the window shut.*) Come on, my boy. Shall I sing you something? What do they want from us, anyway? You're only the son of a whore, and you make your mother happy with your bastard face.

> Johnny, hitch up your six horses fleet,
> Go bring them something to eat.
> From oats they will turn,
> From water they'll turn,
> Only cool wine will be fine, hooray!
> Only cool wine will be fine.
>
> Maiden, now what's to be done?
> You've got no ring, you've a son.
> Oh, why worry my head,
> I'll sing here at your bed:
> Rockabye baby, my baby are you,
> Nobody cares what I do.

(*A knock at the window.*)

Is that you, Franz? Come on in.

Woyzeck.

I can't. Have to go to roll call.

Louise.

Did you cut wood for the major?

Woyzeck.

Yes, Louise.

Louise.

What's the matter with you, Franz? You look so upset.

Woyzeck.

Shh! Quiet! I've got it! The Freemasons! There was a terrible noise in the sky and everything was glowing! I'm on the track of something! Something big!

Louise.

Franz!

Woyzeck.

Don't you think so? Look around! Everything's rigid, hard, dark. Something's moving behind it all. Something that we don't understand. It moves quietly, and it can drive us insane, but I figured it out. I got to go.

216

Louise.

And your child?

Woyzeck.

Oh, the boy! Tonight—at the fair. I saved something up again. (*Goes off.*)

Louise.

That man'll go crazy. He frightened me. It's eerie. I don't like to stay around when it gets dark, I think I'm going blind, I catch it from him. Usually there's a light shining in. Oh, us poor people. (*She sings.*)

Rockabye baby, on the treetop,
When the wind blows, your cradle will rock.

(*She goes off.*)

2,3. *Open square. Booths. Lights.*

Old Man. Dancing Child.

How long we live, just time will tell,
We all have got to die,
We know that very well!

Hey! Whee! Poor man, old man! Poor child! Little child! Cares and fairs! Hey, Louise . . . Beautiful world!

Barker.

(*In front of a booth.*) Ladies and gentlemen, here is to be seen the astronomical horse and the little cannery-birds—they're favorites of all potentates of Europe and members of all learned societies. They'll tell you everything: how old you are, how many children you have, what kind of illnesses. He shoots a pistol, stands on one leg. It's all education. He has merely a beastly reason, or rather a very reasonable beastliness—he's no dumb individual like a lot of people, present company excepted. Enter! The presentation will begin. The commencement of the beginning will start immediately.

Observe the progress of civilization. Everything progresses—a horse, a monkey, a cannery-bird! The monkey is already a soldier. That's not much—it's the lowest level of the human race!

A Man.

Grotesque! Very grotesque!

Student.

Are you an atheist, too? I'm a dogmatic atheist.

———.

Is it grotesque? I'm a friend of the grotesque. You see that? What a grotesque effect.

———.

I'm a dogmatic atheist. Grotesque!

2,4. APPRENTICES.*

[An Apprentice.]

Brother! Forget-me-not! Friendship! I could cry a rain barrel full, out of sadness. If I only had one! It only stinks, it only smells. Why is this world so beautiful? If I close one eye and look out over my nose, then everything's red as a rose. Brandy, that's my life.

Another.

He sees everything red as a rose, when he looks backward over his nose.

[An Apprentice.]

It's all out of order! Why did the street-lamp cleaner forget to sweep out my eyes—it's all dark. May God go to the devil! I'm lying in my own way and have to jump over myself. What happened to my shadow? There's no safety in this stable anymore. Somebody shine the moon between my legs to see if I've still got my shadow.

> Chewing up the green, green grass,
> Chewing up the green, green grass
> Till all the grass was go-o-ne.

Shooting star, I have to blow the noses of all the stars.

[Another.]

Don't make a hole in nature.

[An Apprentice.]

Why did God create man? That has its reasons. What would the farmer, the shoemaker, the tailor do, if he couldn't make shoes or pants for people? Why did God give man a feeling of shame? So that the tailor can exist. Yes! Yes! So there! That's why! For that reason!

Therefore! Or, on the other hand, if He hadn't done it—
but in that we see His wisdom, that the animals He
created would be respected by man, because mankind
would otherwise have eaten up the animals. This infant,
this weak, helpless creature, this infant . . . Now let's piss
crosswise so that a Jew will die.

> Brandy, that's my life,
> Brandy gives me courage.

2,5. SERGEANT. DRUM MAJOR.

Sergeant.
Hold it! Over there. Look at her! What a piece!
Drum Major.
Damn! Good enough for the propagation of cavalry
regiments and the breeding of drum majors!
Sergeant.
Look how she holds her head—you'd think that black
hair would pull her down like a weight. And those eyes,
black . . .
Drum Major.
It's like looking down a well or a chimney. Come on,
after her!
Louise.
Those lights!
Franz.
Yeah, like black cats with fiery eyes. Hey, what a night!

2,6. WOYZECK. DOCTOR.*

Doctor.
What's this I hear, Woyzeck? A man of his word? You!
you! you!
Woyzeck.
What is it, Doctor?
Doctor.
I saw it, Woyzeck. You pissed on the street like a dog.

For that I give you three cents and board every day? The world's getting bad, very bad, bad, I say. Oh! Woyzeck, that's bad.

Woyzeck.

But Doctor, when you can't help it?

Doctor.

Can't help it, can't help it. Superstition, horrible superstition! Haven't I proved that the *musculus constrictor vesicae* is subject to the will? Woyzeck, man is free. In man individuality is exalted to freedom. Couldn't hold it in? That's cheating, Woyzeck. Did you eat your peas already? Nothing but peas, nothing but legumes, *cruciferae* —remember that. Then next week we'll start on mutton. Don't you have to go to the toilet? Go ahead. I'm telling you to. I'm revolutionizing science. A revolution! According to yesterday's report: ten per cent urine, and ammonium chloride . . . But I saw how you pissed on the wall! I was just holding my head outside . . . Did you catch some frogs for me? Got any fish eggs? No freshwater polyps? no hydra? *vestillae? cristatellae?* Don't bump into my microscope. I've just got the left molar of a protozoon under it. I'll blow them sky-high, all of them together. Woyzeck, no spiders' eggs, no toads? But pissing against the wall! I saw it. (*Goes up to him.*) No, Woyzeck, I'm not getting angry. Anger is unhealthy, unscientific. I am calm, perfectly calm, and I tell you this in all cold-bloodedness. Now, who would get excited about a human being, a human being? If it were a Proteus that were dying—! But you shouldn't have pissed on the wall.

Woyzeck.

Yes, nature, Doctor, when nature has run out.

Doctor.

What's that when nature has run out?

Woyzeck.

When nature has run out, that's when nature has run out! When the world gets so dark that you have to feel your way around it with your hands, and you think it'll dissolve into spiderwebs! That's when something is and yet isn't. When everything is dark and there's only a red glow in the west, like from a furnace. When . . . (*Paces up and down in the room.*)

Doctor.
Man, you're tapping around with your feet like a spider.
Woyzeck.
(*Stands rigidly.*) Have you seen the rings of toadstools on the ground yet? Long lines, crooked circles, figures. That's where it is! There! If only someone could read that. When the sun's standing high and bright at noon and the world seems to be going up in flames. Don't you hear anything? I think then when the world speaks, you see, the long lines, and it's like someone's talking with a terrible voice.
Doctor.
Woyzeck! You're going to the insane asylum. You've got a beautiful fixed idea, a marvelous *alienatio mentis*. Look at me. Now what are you supposed to do? Eat your peas, then eat your mutton, polish your rifle; you know all that. And then the fixed ideas. That's good, Woyzeck! You'll get a raise of one cent a week. My theory, my new theory—brave, eternally youthful. Woyzeck, I'll be immortal. Show me your pulse. I have to feel your pulse mornings and evenings.

2,7. Street.[2]

CAPTAIN. DOCTOR. *The* CAPTAIN *comes panting down the street, stops, pants, looks around.*

Captain.
Where to so fast, most honorable Mr. Coffin Nail?
Doctor.
Where to so slowly, most honorable Mr. Drillprick?
Captain.
Take your time, honorable tombstone.
Doctor.
I don't waste my time like you, honorable . . .

Captain.
Don't run like that, Doctor. A good man doesn't go so

---

[2] Büchner wrote three alternate beginnings to this scene.

fast, sir, a good man. (*Pants.*) A good man. You'll run yourself to death that way. You're really frightening me.

Doctor.

I'm in a hurry, Captain, I'm in a hurry.

Captain.

Mr. Coffin Nail, you're wearing out your little legs on the pavement. Don't ride off in the air on your cane.

Doctor.

She'll be dead in four weeks. She's in her seventh month —I've had twenty patients like that already. In four weeks—you can count on that.

Captain.

Doctor, don't frighten me—people have been known to die of fright, of pure, sheer fright!

Doctor.

In four weeks, the stupid beast. She'll make an interesting preparation. I'm telling you, four . . .

Captain.

May you get struck by lightning! I'll hold you back, Mr. Rascal, I won't let you go, you devil. Four weeks? Doctor, coffin nail, shroud, I'll [live] as long as I exist. Four weeks—and the people with flowers in their hands, but they'll say, he was a good man, a good man.

Doctor.

Say, good morning, Captain. (*Swinging his hat and cane.*) Cock-a-doodle-doo! My pleasure! My pleasure! (*Holds out his hat.*) What's this, Captain? That's brain-less. Ha?

Captain.

(*Makes a crease.*) What's this, Doctor? That's an in-crease! Ha-ha-ha! No harm meant. I'm a good man— but I can when I want to, Doctor, ha-ha-ha, when I want to.

[WOYZECK *comes running down the street.*]

Captain.

Hey, Woyzeck, why are you running past us like that? Stay here, Woyzeck. You're running around like an open razor blade. You might cut someone! You're running like you had to shave a regiment of castrates and would be

hanged by the last hair. But about those long beards—
what was I going to say? Woyzeck—those long beards . . .

Doctor.
A long beard on the chin. Pliny speaks of it. Soldiers
should be made to give them up.

Captain.
(*Continues.*) Hey? What about those long beards? Say,
Woyzeck, haven't you found a hair from a beard in your
soup bowl yet? Hey? You understand of course, a human
hair, from the beard of an engineer, a sergeant, a—a
drum major? Hey, Woyzeck? But you've got a decent
wife. Not like others.

Woyzeck.
Yes, sir! What are you trying to say, Cap'n?

Captain.
Look at the face he's making! Now, it doesn't necessarily
have to be in the soup, but if you hurry around the
corner, you might find one on a pair of lips—a pair of
lips, Woyzeck. I know what love is, too, Woyzeck. Say!
You're as white as chalk!

Woyzeck.
Cap'n, I'm just a poor devil—and that's all I have in the
world. Cap'n, if you're joking . . .

Captain.
Joking? Me? Who do you think you are?

Doctor.
Your pulse, Woyzeck, your pulse—short, hard, skipping,
irregular.

Woyzeck.
Cap'n, the earth is hot as hell—for me it's ice cold! Ice
cold—hell is cold, I'll bet. It can't be! God! God! It can't
be!

Captain.
Listen, fellow, how'd you like to be shot, how'd you like
to have a couple of bullets in your head? You're looking
daggers at me; but I only mean well, because you're a
good man, Woyzeck, a good man.

Doctor.
Facial muscles rigid, tense, occasionally twitching. Posture
tense.

Woyzeck.
I'm going. A lot is possible. A man! A lot is possible. The

weather's nice, Cap'n. Look: such a beautiful, hard, gray sky—you'd almost feel like pounding a block of wood into it and hanging yourself on it, only because of the hyphen between yes, and yes again—and no. Cap'n, yes and no? Is no to blame for yes, or yes for no? I'll have to think about that. (*Goes off with long strides, first slowly, then ever faster.*)

Doctor.

(*Races after him.*) A phenomenon! Woyzeck! A raise!

Captain.

These people make me dizzy. Look at them go—that tall rascal takes off like the shadow before a spider, and the short one—he's trotting along. The tall one is lightning and the short one is thunder. Ha-ha! After them. I don't like that! A good man loves life, a good man has no courage! A dog has courage! I just went to war to strengthen my love for life. Grotesque! Grotesque!

2,8. WOYZECK. LOUISE.*

Louise.

Hello, Franz.

Franz.

(*Looking at her.*) Oh, it's you! Well, well, what do you know! No, I don't see anything. I should be able to see it! Louise, you're beautiful!

Louise.

Why are you looking at me like that, Franz? I'm scared.

Franz.

What a nice street. You can get corns walking on it. But it's good to stand on the street, and good to be in society.

Louise.

Society?

Franz.

Lots of people go through the streets, don't they? And you can talk to anyone you want; that's none of my business. Was he standing here like this? Like this? Close to you like this? I wish I'd been him.

Louise.
What "he"? I can't tell anybody to stay off the streets or leave their mouths at home when they go past.

Franz.
Or their lips at home. That'd be a shame—they're so beautiful. But wasps like to sit on them.

Louise.
And what kind of a wasp stung you? You look as crazy as a cow chased by hornets.

Franz.
Whore! (*Goes after her.*)

Louise.
Don't you touch me, Franz! I'd rather have a knife in my body than your hand on mine. When I was ten years old, my father didn't dare touch me when I looked at him.

Franz.
Woman! No, it should show on you! Everyone's a chasm. You get dizzy when you look down into it. It could be! She looks like Miss Innocence herself. Now, Innocence, you have a mark on you. Do I know it? Do I know it? Who can tell?

2,9. LOUISE *alone. Prayer.*

Louise.
And no guile is found in his mouth. My God![3]

---

[3] Above these words Büchner wrote in French: "The corruption of our age has reached the point that in order to preserve morality . . ."

THIRD DRAFT: SCATTERED SCENES

3,1. *The* PROFESSOR's *courtyard.*

STUDENTS *below, the* PROFESSOR *at the attic window.*

[Professor.]
Gentlemen, I am on the roof like David when he saw Bathsheba, but all I see are panties hanging in the garden of the girls' boarding house. Gentlemen, we are dealing with the important question of the relationship of subject to object. If we take only one of the things in which the organic self-affirmation of the Divine manifests itself to such a high degree, and examine its relationship to space, to the earth, to the planetary system . . . gentlemen, if I throw this cat out of the window, how will it relate to the *centrum gravitationis* and to its own instinct? Hey, Woyzeck. (*Shouts.*) Woyzeck! [PROFESSOR *comes down.*]
Woyzeck.
Professor, it bites!
Professor.
The fellow holds the beast so tenderly, like it was his own grandmother!
Woyzeck.
Doctor, I've got the shivers.
Doctor. [*sic*]
(*Elated.*) Say, that's wonderful, Woyzeck! (*Rubs his hands. He takes the cat.*) What's this, gentlemen—a new species of rabbit louse, a beautiful species, quite different, deep in the fur. (*He pulls out a magnifying glass.*) Ricinus, gentlemen! (*The cat runs off.*) Gentlemen, that animal has no scientific instinct. Ricinus—the best examples—bring your fur collars. Gentlemen, instead of that you can see something else. Take note of this man —for a quarter of a year he hasn't eaten anything but

peas. Notice the result. Feel how uneven his pulse is. There—and the eyes.

Woyzeck.

Doctor, everything's getting black. (*He sits down.*)

Doctor.

Courage! Just a few more days, Woyzeck, and then it'll be all over. Feel him, gentlemen, feel him. (STUDENTS *feel his temples, pulse, and chest.*) Apropos, Woyzeck, wiggle your ears for the gentlemen. I meant to show it to you before. He uses two muscles. Come on, hop to it!

Woyzeck.

Oh, Doctor!

Doctor.

You dog, do I have to wiggle them for you? Are you going to act like the cat? This, gentlemen, represents a transition to the donkey, frequently resulting from being brought up by women and from the use of the mother tongue. How much hair has your mother pulled out for a tender memory? It's gotten very thin in the last few days. Yes, the peas, gentlemen.

3,2. [KARL,] *the idiot. The* CHILD. WOYZECK.

Karl.

(*Holds the* CHILD *on his lap.*) He fell in the water, he fell in the water, he fell in the water.

Woyzeck.

Son—Christian!

Karl.

(*Stares at him.*) He fell in the water.

Woyzeck.

(*Wants to caress the* CHILD, *who turns away and screams.*) My God!

Karl.

He fell in the water.

Woyzeck.

Christian, you'll get a hobbyhorse. Da-da! (*The* CHILD *resists. To* KARL.) Here, go buy the boy a hobbyhorse.

Karl.

(*Stares at him.*)

Woyzeck.
  Hop-hop! Horsey!
Karl.
  (*Cheers.*) Hop-hop! Horsey! Horsey! (*Runs off with the* CHILD.)

FOURTH DRAFT: THE REVISION

[See Scenes 4,1–17 of the Reconstruction.]

SYNOPSIS:

CORRESPONDENCES AMONG DRAFTS

PART TWO

NOTES AND DOCUMENTARY MATERIAL

*All unsigned material written or translated by
Henry J. Schmidt.*

GEORG BÜCHNER'S LIFE

1813   October 17: Karl Georg Büchner born in God-
delau, a small town in the Grand Duchy
of Hesse-Darmstadt, to Ernst and Caroline
Büchner. Other children:
Mathilde (1815–1888).
Wilhelm (1816–1892), chemist, owner of a dye
factory, politician.
Louise (1821–1877), writer, campaigner for
women's rights.
Ludwig (1824–1899), doctor, author of the in-
fluential work *Power and Matter*.
Alexander (1827–1904), writer, activist in the
Revolution of 1848, professor of literature in
France.

1816   Family moves to Darmstadt.

1825–31   Georg a student at the Ludwig-Georg-Gym-
nasium in Darmstadt.

1830   Delivers a speech in defense of Cato's suicide
during a ceremony at the Gymnasium.

1831   Enrolls in the medical school of the University
of Strasbourg.

1832   Delivers a speech to the student organization
"Eugenia" on political conditions in Germany.

1833   Becomes secretly engaged to Wilhelmine
(Minna) Jaeglé (1810–1880). Leaves Strasbourg and enrolls at the University of Giessen, continuing his medical studies. Returns
to Darmstadt in November to recover from
an attack of meningitis.

1834	Returns to Giessen. Becomes acquainted with Pastor Friedrich Ludwig Weidig. Büchner founds a "Society for the Rights of Man" based on French model. Writes *The Hessian Messenger*, which Weidig edits. Travels to Darmstadt and Strasbourg. *The Hessian Messenger* is seized by the authorities; Büchner goes to Offenbach and Frankfurt to warn his friends. Returns to Darmstadt.
1835	January–February: writes *Danton's Death*, which he sends to the writer Karl Gutzkow for eventual publication. March: flees to Strasbourg. Authorities issue a warrant for his arrest. July: a censored version of *Danton's Death* is published. He translates *Lucretia Borgia* and *Maria Tudor* (Victor Hugo) for Gutzkow. Writes the prose fragment *Lenz*. Begins dissertation on the nervous system of fish.
1836	Completes dissertation, which he reads before the Society of Natural Sciences in Strasbourg. Writes *Leonce and Lena*. September: the University of Zurich grants him a doctorate and invites him to join the faculty, which he does in November, after an introductory lecture on the cranial nerves of fish. Begins *Woyzeck*.
1837	February: becomes ill with typhus. Dies on February 19.
1838	Gutzkow publishes scenes from *Leonce and Lena* in *Telegraph für Deutschland*.
1839	*Lenz* appears in the same periodical.
1850	Publication of Büchner's works (but without *Woyzeck*), edited by his brother Ludwig.
1875	Karl Emil Franzos's reconstruction of *Wozzeck* (*sic*) appears in the Viennese newspaper *Neue Freie Presse*.
1879	Publication of Franzos's edition of Büchner's collected works.

(Continued on page 404.)

"MEMORIES OF BÜCHNER"

Ludwig Wilhelm Luck

. . . Perhaps the most important, independent, and active man in our circle was Georg Büchner, who was as old as I. It was not in his character to devote himself to others recklessly or without reflection; he was rather a quiet, meticulous, reserved observer. Yet where he found that someone was searching for "real life," he could become warm, even enthusiastic. . . . Already early in life Büchner concentrated directly upon that which he recognized to be the essence of things—in science, especially in philosophy, as well as in the political necessities of the masses as he saw them. His overall principle was freedom. He was not in favor of using the ignorance of the masses to cheat them or to make them into tools, nor did he want to turn his own talent to lucrative speculation. . . .

Completely independent . . . in his thoughts and actions, no outward authority or worthless pretense could impress him. The awareness of his intellectual attainments compelled him constantly to criticize unmercifully whatever claimed sole authority for itself in human society, philosophy, or art. . . . He scorned most deeply those who nourished themselves or others with trivial formulas instead of searching for the lifeblood of truth and passing it on . . . looking at his forehead, his eyes, his lips, one noticed that he practiced this criticism in his private thoughts even when he was silent. . . .

Once in a friend's room he apostrophized laconically: "Luck, how many gods do you believe in?" Answer: "Only one." "How many states should we have in Germany and how many princes?"—Silence on both sides.

"GEORG BÜCHNER'S OBITUARY"

Karl Gutzkow[1]

Frankfurter Telegraf, June 1837

During the last days of February 1835—a somewhat stormy year in the history of our modern literature—I had invited a congenial circle of friends of art and truth. . . . Just before the arrival of the expected guests I received a manuscript and a letter from Darmstadt. The letter read: [Büchner's first letter to Gutzkow, pages 311–12]. I print it in order to reveal the personality whose memory we are celebrating. I print it without regard for his well-to-do parents, who are still living, because we shall soon explain the slight affectation and the *unnecessary* poverty of which it speaks. The letter enticed me to read the manuscript immediately. It was a drama: *Danton's Death.* One could see from its appearance how hurriedly it had been thrown together. Its subject was arbitrarily chosen and over-worked in its realization. Scenes and words followed each other rapidly, stormily. It was the frightened language of a pursued man who had to conclude something in haste and then find his safety in flight. Yet this haste did not hinder this genius from revealing his talent in short, sharp outlines, quickly, as in passing.

Every motif and elaboration in this loosely constructed drama grew out of his personality and talent. His personality did not allow his talent to develop itself broadly and at leisure, and his talent, on the other hand, prevented his personality from merely formulating feelings and hyperboles without at least a hasty attempt at smoothing out scenes and those bright and lively words flowing out of the most priceless spring of nature. *Danton's Death* was pub-

---

[1] See Introduction to "Correspondence on *Danton's Death,*" p. 309.

lished. The first scenes I read secured him the gracious, friendly interest of the publisher Sauerländer on that same evening. A recitation of selected scenes aroused admiration for the talent of the youthful author, although now and then someone interrupted with the statement that this or that stood word for word in Thiers.

Georg Büchner had hardly received an answer when we discovered that he was on the way to Strasbourg. An arrest warrant in the *Frankfurter Journal* followed on his heels. He had lived in hiding in Darmstadt . . . for he feared at any moment to be called in for an interrogation. He was involved in that unfortunate political confusion which has undermined the peace of so many families, robbing so many fathers of their sons and wives of their husbands. I do not know whether he was merely under suspicion or had been accused. . . . At any rate it became clear that he was *happy* to flee. He was engaged to a young woman in Strasbourg; exile, for others a torment, was for him a blessing. He admitted to me that his desperate actions were taxing the concern of his (probably loyal) parents to the utmost, and he did not have the courage to prolong this. He felt the urge to make his own way toward a bourgeois existence and to derive all possible advantages from his talents. This explains the despair of the accompanying letter to *Danton*, the pistol and the innocent words of a bandit: your money or your life!

Several of Büchner's letters from Strasbourg addressed to me no longer exist. I had great difficulty with his *Danton*, since such expressions as Büchner had permitted himself to cast about cannot be printed today. *Sansculotte* atmosphere pervaded the work; the Declaration of the Rights of Man roamed about in it, covered with roses, but naked. The symbol that held the whole work together was the red cap. Büchner studied medicine. His imagination played with that human misery which sickness incurs; indeed, the sicknesses of levity had to serve as the foil to his wit. The poetic vegetation of his book consisted of field blossoms and buds of mercury. His imagination disseminated the former, his cocky satire the latter. To deprive the censor of the pleasure of deleting, I assumed this office myself and pruned the drama's proliferating liberalism with the scissors of precensorship. I realized that the discarded parts, which had to be sacrificed to our customs and circumstances, were the best, the most individualistic and characteristic aspects of the whole. Long, off-color dialogues in the folk scenes, bubbling with wit and inspiration, had to be cut. Puns had to be blunted or bent awry, replaced by stupid figures of speech. Büchner's *true Danton* did *not* appear. What came of it was an impoverished remnant, the ruin of a devastation that caused me great reluctance.

In the summer [actually March] of 1835 Büchner wrote:

Honored Sir: You may have read about my departure from Darmstadt in an arrest warrant in the *Frankfurter Journal*. For the last few days I have been here in Strasbourg. I don't know whether I'll stay; that depends on various circumstances. I suppose my manuscript has been secretly making the rounds.

My future is so problematic that it's even beginning to interest *me*, and that's saying a lot. I can't easily decide to commit a subtle suicide by working. I hope to extend my laziness another three months and then I'll take a handout either from the Jesuits in the service of Maria or from the St. Simonists in the service of the *femme libre*—or I'll die with my sweetheart. We'll see. Maybe I'll be around when the Strasbourg Cathedral puts on a Jacobin cap. What do you say to that? It's only a joke. But you will see what a German will do when he's hungry. I wish the entire nation were in my place. If we only had a bad year where only hangman's hemp would thrive! That would be fun—we would soon weave it into a boa constrictor. For the time being my Danton is a silk thread and my muse a disguised Samson.

The wild spirit in this letter is the afterbirth of *Danton*. The young poet must rid himself of Thiers and Mignet, he is using up the remnants of his palette from which he had painted those dramatic scenes from the French Reign of Terror. The manner of expression is more important to him than the subject. Revolutionary phraseology impels him to search for ideal foundations. He will soon express other opinions and free himself of that uneasiness which one always feels when one has just stepped from a coach, when the pulse beats more often every minute than one has thoughts for each beat. Büchner soon stopped dreaming of violent upheavals. The increasing material prosperity of the populace seemed to him to be postponing the revolution. As the former increases, the prospect of the latter disappears. He wrote to me among other things:

The whole revolution has already divided itself into liberals and absolutists, and it has to be eaten up by the uneducated and poor classes. The relationship between the poor and the rich is the only revolutionary element in the world, hunger alone can become the goddess of freedom, and only a Moses, who set the seven Egyptian plagues on our necks, could become a Messiah. Fatten the peasants and the revolution will have a stroke. A chicken in the pot of every peasant will kill the Gallic rooster.

. . . Since Büchner was devoting all his efforts toward preparing for an academic appointment, he could devote his leisure time only to lighter tasks. For the series of Victor Hugo's works he translated *Maria Tudor* and *Lucretia Borgia* with poetic affinity for the originals. I cannot locate one of his letters where he appraised Hugo's weaknesses with a critical eye. He was attracted to Alfred de Musset, but he did not know how he could "chew his way through V. Hugo"; Hugo only created "suspenseful incidents," de Musset, on the other hand, created "characters, even though they are cutouts." Although he was hardly able to write—he explained that during the rapid genesis of *Danton* "the Darmstadt police were his muses"—he was nevertheless occcupied with a novella on the playwright J. M. R. Lenz. He claimed to have discovered new and unusual information about this friend of the young Goethe and about Friederike [Brion] and her later acquaintanceship with Lenz.

Büchner's later letters deal mainly with his plans for the future. His heart was captivated; he searched for an existence as the forger of his own good fortune. He had abandoned medicine and had plunged into abstract philos-

239

ophy. . . . His postdoctoral work kept him inordinately busy. I did not insist on news, for I hoped that his settling in Zurich would have good results. Meanwhile Büchner fell sick and died. . . .

THE HESSIAN MESSENGER

Georg Büchner's birthplace, the Grand Duchy of Hesse-Darmstadt, was far less imposing than its name would suggest. It was a small, agrarian country with a virtually stagnant economy and a feudal social structure. Its inhabitants were mostly peasants and laborers who, despite the abolition of serfdom in 1820, still adhered to the practices of their medieval ancestors. Plagued by persistent crop failure, the peasants were taxed both by their landowners and by the state; whatever they managed to produce for export was subject to high tariffs, which effectively strangled Hesse's domestic industry. While the Industrial Revolution flourished in the centralized societies of England and France, Hesse remained a European backwater. Like their colleagues elsewhere in the German Confederation, Hesse's rulers lived in splendor, draining the financial resources of their already impoverished subjects and leaving administrative matters to their ministers. The bourgeoisie, as a whole, did not threaten their dominance. During the eighteenth century, the German middle classes had gained considerable independence and prominence in the cultural sphere, fostering an intellectual spirit that glorified individuality but neglected larger social issues. Thus, while France was crowning Louis Philippe, its "citizen-king," the states within the German Confederation remained in the grip of the aristocracy.

Yet even the aristocrats could not afford to ignore the liberal sentiment sweeping Europe in the wake of the American and French Revolutions. Napoleon's defeat had raised German hopes for political and cultural unification, for greater equality and individual liberties. As a consequence, the Hessian government was one of several that grudgingly agreed to establish a constitution and a representative legislature—a "reform" that in fact still left most Hessians without any voice whatsoever in government affairs. The aristocracy was not about to establish voluntarily a threat to its power, so it saw to it that the legislature would remain appropriately impotent, and that dissidents would be kept out of the government through extremely complex and selective election laws. Only highly propertied individuals could be elected to the "representative" assembly; in 1820 only 985 citizens from a population of 700,000 could qualify, and consequently two-thirds of the legislature consisted of high government officials. The legislature could approve but not deny taxation measures, and it could be dissolved at any time by the Grand Duke. Nevertheless, protests soon arrived from the governments of Prussia and Austria: Hesse's reforms were too dangerously liberal.

Prussia and Austria were, after all, merely reasserting the doctrine of European political stability that had been formulated by the Congress of Vienna. Any weakening of the status quo was considered a threat to the balance of power. Open or clandestine opposition, nationalistic sentiment, even among monarchists—these were sparks that might lead to a conflagration. Prince Metternich of Austria kept a watchful eye on such activities within the German Confederation. He found provocations enough: in 1817 numerous student organizations (*Burschenschaften*) demonstrated in favor of national unity and against military oppression; the liberal opposition was making itself heard in the press and at the universities; in 1819 the reactionary dramatist August von Kotzebue was murdered by Karl Ludwig Sand, a theology student and a member of a *Burschenschaft*. At Metternich's urging, the German Confederation reacted quickly and passed the Carlsbad Decrees, which increased press censorship, prohibited the formation of unauthorized political organizations, suppressed freedom of speech at the universities, and dissolved the *Burschenschaften*. To be sure, the Decrees could not hope to eradicate subversive activity entirely, but they established a pattern that was to recur for decades to come: any demonstration or radical action, no matter how ineffective or foolhardy it might have been (such as the Frankfurt Putsch in 1833), was immediately countered by increasingly severe repressive measures.

The year 1830 was an unsettling one for the protectors of the status quo. Revolutions in France, Belgium, and Poland—all neighbors of the Confederation—compelled the German dissidents to ask themselves: Why not here? The revolutionary fever even reached the Hessian peasants. Upper Hesse had suffered greatly from heavy taxation and restrictive tariffs, and in September 1830 the peasants revolted, destroying several customshouses, ransacking offices, and burning documents. They dispersed as soon as they heard that government troops—including a large number of university students, their supposed allies—were approaching. The troops entered the village of Södel, where they found only onlookers, but a disturbance occurred and two people were shot. This was the "bloodbath at Södel," a bitter memory for the Hessians, upon which Büchner later tried to capitalize in *The Hessian Messenger*.

The euphoria of 1830 dissipated quickly. Life had not improved for the growing European proletariat; the bourgeois *juste milieu* of Louis Philippe's regime was a bitter disappointment to the working classes. The Polish revolution was crushed. German dissidents had not even managed to begin a revolution, and the aftermath of 1830 only increased their frustration. Ludwig Börne, a prominent "Young German" journalist and critic, cynically enumerated the consequences of the year of revolutions for Germany:

1. Cholera. 2. In Brunswick there used to be a prince who at least didn't side with the nobility; now there's one whom the nobility leads around by the nose. 3. The Saxons now have two princes instead of one. 4. The Hessians now have, instead of the prince's old mistress, a young one. 5. In Baden one used to be able to publish a newspaper without a security deposit, now it must be paid. 6. Whoever insulted the Bavarian king formerly had to apologize before his oil portrait; now the offender spends five years in jail. So at least you know where you stand.

As a result, Germany remained "Europe's ghetto," enjoying "the peace of a cemetery" (Börne).

When Georg Büchner arrived in Strasbourg in 1831 to study medicine, he left Hessian provincialism behind and entered a rich intellectual climate, a melting pot of French and German culture where the legacy of Robespierre coexisted with that of Herder and Goethe. It is not surprising that Büchner's father, proud of his service in Napoleon's "Old Guard," sent his son there to study. Strasbourg's effect on young Georg eventually exceeded his father's expectations, however, for he absorbed not only the intellectual traditions of the past but the political realities of the present. During this postrevolutionary era, the city sheltered a multitude of factions. The bourgeoisie was divided over the success of the July Revolution. Political opposition ranged from moderately liberal critics of the regime to secret radical societies that advocated the teachings of Robespierre, Saint-Just, and Babeuf. Followers of Saint-Simon's "socialized Christianity" intermingled with devotees of German Romanticism. Strasbourg's medical students were at that time in the front ranks of the liberal opposition. When refugees from the Polish revolution began arriving, students would often spite French authorities to give them a public welcome. Although Büchner participated in these demonstrations, he stood apart from the enthusiasm they generated. His earliest extant letters to his parents reveal an independent, somewhat cynical observer. (After describing a reception for the Polish general Ramorino, he concluded, "The comedy is over.") His unaffected attitude soon gave way to vehement protests against social injustice, which in turn led to thoughts about revolution. At times his letters anticipated the savage prose of *The Hessian Messenger*:

My opinion is this: if anything can help in these times, it is force. We know what to expect from our princes. All they have granted us has been forced from them by necessity. And even their concessions were thrown at our feet like a favor we had begged for, like a wretched child's toy, to make that eternal simpleton, the masses, forget his too tightly wrapped swaddling clothes. Only a German could indulge in the absurdity of playing soldier with a tin rifle and a wooden sword. Our legislatures are a satire against good sense . . . . Young people are accused of using force. But aren't we in an eternal state of force? Because we were born and raised in a prison, we no longer realize that we're sticking in a hole with fettered hands and feet and with gags in our mouths. What do you call a lawful state? A law that transforms the great masses of citizens into toiling cattle in order to satisfy the unnatural needs of an unimportant and decadent minority? Supported by raw military might and by the stupid conniving of its agents, this law is eternal, brute force, insulting justice and good sense, and I will fight tooth and nail against it wherever I can.   [April 1833]

Similarly, to his friend August Stöber:

The political situation could drive me insane. The poor people patiently draw the cart upon which the princes and the liberals play their comedy of apes. Every night I pray to the hangman's hemp and the lampposts.   [December 9, 1833]

In June of that year, he announced to his parents the fundamental premise of his impending revolutionary activity:

I shall always act according to my principles, but I have recently learned that only the essential needs of the masses can bring about change, that all activity and shouting by individuals is vain folly. They write but are not read; they shout but are not heard; they act but are not helped.

A mature, differentiated political stance is already evident in these early letters. His outrage against inequitable social conditions was tempered by a keen, realistic understanding of existing economic and political relationships. He was as unlikely to go tilting against windmills as to support the bourgeois status quo. To be sure, his repeated

245

assurances to his parents that he was not about to become involved in subversion do not appear to be entirely sincere, considering his subsequent activities in Giessen. He could mollify his parents without wholly betraying his principles by writing:

If I do not take part in whatever has happened or might happen, I do so neither out of disapproval nor out of fear, but only because at the present time I regard any revolutionary movement as a futile undertaking, and I do not share the delusion of those who see in the Germans a people ready to fight for its rights. [April 1833]

In little more than a year, he was to discover how accurate this assessment of the German situation was. As a resident of Hesse, he was obliged by law to transfer to the University of Giessen to continue his studies. He left Strasbourg reluctantly, assuring his parents, "You can imagine that I shall not get involved in clandestine politics and revolutionary children's pranks in Giessen." This was probably a deliberate deception, for he had learned two important lessons in Strasbourg: only a total social revolution that rejects vague liberal idealism and focuses on the "essential needs of the masses" is meaningful; mass revolution is best achieved by secret, well-organized cadres that concentrate on action, not rhetoric. His model was the *Société des droits de l'homme et du citoyen* ("Society for the Rights of Man and the Citizen"). Büchner was not long in Giessen before he founded a German equivalent: *Die Gesellschaft der Menschenrechte.*

Setting up a subversive organization in Hesse was certainly no "children's prank." One observer of social conditions there was Wilhelm Grimm, and his description was anything but a fairy tale:

Hesse 1832. Freedom had gradually sunk to a point so low that it is inconceivable to anyone who has not experienced it. Every candid remark, not to mention freedom of speech, was suppressed. The police—public and secret, authorized and voluntary—penetrated into all matters and poisoned the privacy of social life.

All the supports of a society—religion, justice, respect for morality and the law—were demolished or severely shaken. Only one thing remained: any contradiction of the express will of the government, spoken directly or indirectly, was a crime.

In January 1834, Büchner met a man whom the Hessian police had tried in vain to convict as a dangerous subversive: Friedrich Ludwig Weidig, pastor and school principal, forty-three years old, married, two children. He had been involved in illegal political activities since 1820, publishing and distributing pamphlets, establishing contacts with radicals and the liberal opposition. When Büchner met him, he stood at the vortex of all conspiratorial activity in Hesse. At the outset, their collaboration appeared to be of mutual benefit: Büchner valued Weidig's experience and contacts; Weidig could put Büchner's penetrating intellect and forceful style to good use. Both were convinced of the need to make the masses understand the system oppressing them as a prelude to revolutionary change, knowing that it is the awareness of injustice, not injustice itself, that leads to revolt. Büchner organized a small number of students and laborers into a revolutionary action group, as he had learned in Strasbourg, while Weidig cultivated his loose coalition of liberals and published an antigovernment *Illuminator for Hesse*. These activities during the early months of 1834 already indicated, however, that Büchner and Weidig were traveling on separate paths. Their collaboration soon proved to be a marriage of quite incompatible partners.

Both were idealists; their differences stemmed from the antithetical sources of their idealism. Weidig was above all a devout Christian, schooled in the ethics of Classicism, sharing with the Romantics a yearning for a Christian Empire. In a sense, his battle against tyranny and corruption was a religious crusade, a battle of good against evil. He envisioned a German nation united culturally and spiritually under a liberal government. As long as basic freedoms could be guaranteed, he did not consider it necessary to speculate further on the nature of postrevolutionary society. As a tactician, however, he was a pragmatist. Knowing the strength of his oppressors and the weakness of his allies, he concentrated on gradual reform, building as broad a coalition of like-minded dissidents as possible. A "grand coalition" could succeed only if the goals were moderate, which in Hesse meant: constitutional reform, freedom of speech, freedom of the press, and, above all, freedom from arbitrary oppression. The natural leaders of such a reform movement were middle-class intellectuals, and he indeed found his most valuable support among university professors, doctors, and lawyers.

Where Weidig saw a battle between God and the Devil, Büchner saw a struggle between rich and poor. Büchner's social idealism derived from the great secular upheaval of the eighteenth century, the French Revolution. His political activity in Giessen was nothing less than an attempt to establish Jacobin radicalism on Hessian soil. He was influenced as well by the socialistic theories of Gracchus Babeuf and, to a degree, by Johann Gottlieb Fichte, who maintained that class distinctions based on the possession of property could be abolished only if society were reoriented toward the principle that no one has the right to eat if one does not perform one's share of work. (Few Jacobins, it should be added, were willing to consider *égalité* an absolute principle that would challenge the sacred rights of property.) "I believe," wrote Büchner in 1836, "that in social affairs one must proceed from an absolute legal principle, striving for the formation of a new life of the spirit among the masses and letting effete modern society go to the devil. Why should a thing like this walk around between heaven and earth? Its whole life consists only of attempts to dissipate its most horrifying boredom. Let it die out: that is the only new thing it can still experience." Small wonder that he scorned the moderation of Weidig's collaborators; they were people, Büchner is reported to have said, "who let themselves be frightened by the French Revolution like children by a nursery tale, who are afraid that they might see in every village a Paris with a guillotine." He saw compromise—that is, concessions to the material interests of the bourgeoisie—as the most dangerous enemy of mass revolution. Social reforms that lessened the polarization between exploiters and the exploited would undermine any possibility of success, be it in France or Germany:

. . . the relationship between poor and rich is the only revolutionary element in the world, hunger alone can become the goddess of freedom, and only a Moses, who set the seven Egyptian plagues on our necks, could become a Messiah. Fatten the peasants and the revolution will have a stroke. A chicken in the pot of every peasant will kill the Gallic rooster.

[1835]

He believed that the peasants would rather eat well than fight for their rights, that the aristocrats could, if they wished, manipulate the material needs of the masses to suit their purposes. The revolutionary leader's duty was therefore to overcome the ignorance, indifference, and self-centered materialism of the masses before they would arise to overthrow the princes. He did not consider literary journalism, written by and for the middle classes, to be an effective means to this end:

I do not in any way belong to the literary party of Gutzkow and Heine. Only a complete misunderstanding of our social conditions could make those people believe that a complete transformation of our religious and social ideas would be possible through our current literature.   [to his family, January 1, 1836]

He soon confronted Gutzkow directly on this issue:

In all honesty it seems to me that you and your friends did not take the most sensible path. Reform society through ideas, through the educated classes? Impossible! Our times are purely materialistic; if you had ever worked along more directly political lines, you soon would have come to the point where reform would have stopped on its own. You will never bridge the chasm between educated and uneducated classes.

I am convinced that the educated and prosperous minority, as many concessions as it might desire for itself from the authorities, will never want to give up its antagonistic attitude toward the masses. And the masses themselves? For them there are only two levers: material poverty and religious fanaticism. Any

249

party that knows how to operate these levers will conquer. Our times demand iron and bread—and then a cross or something like that.   [1836]

The tone is cynical; a scant two years earlier, however, he had been sufficiently idealistic to set to work with Weidig to "reveal the truth to the State of Hesse," despite the threat of legal reprisals.

Emulating the tactics of French activists, he believed that hard economic facts could best incite the masses to action. After collecting statistics, he drafted an essay and sent it to Weidig, who recognized its potential as anti-government propaganda but objected to passages that would alienate his allies. According to Büchner's friend August Becker, Weidig eliminated Büchner's attacks against the bourgeoisie, blunting his socialistic premise by focusing on the aristocrats as the sole perpetrators of social injustice. Thus Büchner's references to "the rich" were altered to "the elegant." Weidig added lengthy passages of his own, numerous quotations from the Bible, and provided a preface and a title: *The Hessian Messenger*.

Since the original is lost, it is impossible to distinguish Weidig's words from Büchner's with absolute certainty, but their differing attitudes and styles are relatively easy to detect. Büchner, the medical student, dissects Hessian society with his rhetorical scalpel, laying bare its seamy interior. His analytical argumentation is vivid, direct, mercilessly logical, and devastatingly sarcastic. Besides the material on Hesse, he probably also wrote the passage summarizing the fruitless struggles of the French against their monarchs. Weidig, the theologian, interprets historical development in terms of divine intervention and sermonizes about the resurrection of the German Empire as a "paradise." He attempts throughout to establish the primacy of human rights upon a synthesis of enlightened reason and Holy Writ. The pamphlet's style and content are certainly inconsistent, yet it is unfair to say, as many critics have done, that Weidig "ruined" Büchner's essay. That the *Messenger* expressed more than one political viewpoint, that it was in fact a duet of discordant voices, was merely another instance of Weidig's coalition politics. It was designed to appeal to as broad a public as possible. If a reader

were alienated by the tone of one portion of the pamphlet,
he might be attracted and convinced by another portion.

Despite his objections to the final draft, Büchner agreed
to help publish the *Messenger*. He brought the manuscript
to the town of Offenbach, where approximately three hundred copies were printed on a press hidden in a cellar. On
July 31, Karl Minnigerode and two other friends of
Büchner's picked up the pamphlets, but Minnigerode was
arrested as he returned to Giessen. The enterprise had
been betrayed by a man from Weidig's circle. Hearing of
the arrest, Büchner went off to warn his friends. Meanwhile, his papers and belongings were searched by the
police, but no incriminating evidence was found. Weidig
was transferred to a remote village, but otherwise the
authorities left the two authors of the treasonous pamphlet
alone. Weidig was not to be stopped by a mere transfer. In
the following months he published another number of his
Illuminator for Hesse and a second edition of the *Messenger*, to which he added passages concerning the up-
coming legislative elections. That a second edition was
published seems to speak for the effectiveness of the first.
True, many copies had been turned over to the police, but
Weidig knew of peasants who claimed that the *Messenger*
had impressed them deeply. He also organized an attempt
to free Minnigerode from prison, but his interrogation had
been so brutal that he was too weak to flee. He was
released from prison in 1837 because of poor health,
emigrated to America, and eventually became an Episcopal
bishop and a friend of Jefferson Davis.

Eventually a second informer provided the police with
enough information to proceed against Weidig and Büchner. Weidig, who could not bring himself to flee, was
"detained for interrogation" . . . for two years. An acquaintance of Büchner's named Carl Vogt recalled the
methods and consequences of such detention in his memoirs:

I have known people who were driven from their
houses and from thriving businesses, compelled to
struggle for their bread in a foreign country, only
because a spy had found a package of the hated
journal [not the *Messenger*] under their front gate,

251

placed there by a stranger. I have known others who were held in the most bitter solitary confinement for years, where any activity, even manual work, was prohibited with clever cruelty, and who were then released from detention, which had brought absolutely nothing to light, and were pardoned from that time on, broken in spirit.

Büchner himself was outraged that "in Bavaria two young people, after being kept in close confinement for almost *four years*, were recently released and proclaimed *innocent!*" (Strasbourg, 1836). Weidig's interrogator was a brutal alcoholic named Georgi, who had earlier ordered an illegal search of Büchner's quarters in Giessen. Weidig was subjected to horrible torture, but admitted nothing. On February 23, 1837, he slashed his wrists and wrote in blood on his cell wall: "Since my enemy denies me any defense, I freely choose a shameful death." Prison officials delayed sending for a doctor, and Weidig bled to death.

Büchner had chosen flight over martyrdom. He went from Giessen to Darmstadt, where he lived with his parents until March 1835; when his arrest seemed imminent, he fled to Strasbourg. During the next eighteen months, he wrote a dissertation on the nervous system of fish, worked on several literary projects, and read extensively in philosophy. His dissertation earned him an appointment at the University of Zurich, where he delivered a highly praised inaugural address and began lecturing on anatomy. On the verge of a brilliant career in medicine, he suddenly contracted typhus. In less than three weeks after the onset of the disease he was dead . . . on February 19, 1837, four days before Weidig committed suicide in his cell.

The Hessian Messenger had had little meaningful impact upon the uneducated and intimidated peasantry; to the contrary, it had demonstrated once again the effectiveness of governmental repression. Besides eliminating the Weidig circle, the regime was soon able to gain a ruling majority in the legislature, stifling the voice of opposition for more than a decade. Büchner watched these developments from afar, "going [his] own way and remaining in the field of drama, which has nothing to do with all of these controversial questions." His letters from Strasbourg after March 1835 indicate his disillusionment about continued political resistance:

> I would not tell you [Wilhelm Büchner] this, if I could believe in any way at all in the hope of a political upheaval at this time. For the last six months I have been convinced that nothing is to be done and that everyone who sacrifices himself right now is doing so at his own risk like a fool. I can't tell you anything more specific, but I know the situation; I know how weak, how insignificant, how fragmented the liberal party is. I know that purposeful, unified action is impossible and that every attempt doesn't have the slightest result.
>
> A close acquaintance with the activities of German revolutionaries outside Germany has convinced me that nothing is to be hoped from them either. They are in a state of tremendous confusion which will never be resolved. Let's hope for times to come!

To the last, he did not forget his friends and allies suffering in German jails. Wilhelm Schulz reported that during his terminal illness Büchner "spoke . . . about the abominable treatment of political victims who are kept in detention for years according to regulation and with the appearance of leniency, until their minds are driven insane and their bodies are tortured to death. 'During that French Revolution,' he exclaimed, 'so often condemned for its brutality, they were more merciful than now. They chopped off their opponents' heads. Good! But they didn't let them waste away for years and die.' " Nevertheless, after the *Messenger*, Büchner no longer agitated directly for social reform. Unlike his contemporaries Heinrich Heine and Ludwig Börne, who polemicized openly against political repression in Germany even while in exile, he continued to reject any political alliance with middle-class liberals. His uncompromising stance was perhaps more farsighted than that of his "Young German" colleagues—ideologically he was part of the radical stream that culminated in the *Communist Manifesto* of 1848—yet as a political refugee just beginning to establish himself at the University of Zurich, he remained aloof from the immediate ills of his time, unwilling to risk his career for the sake of social agitation. Neither political insight nor self-preservation, however, explains his aloofness sufficiently. A month or two before he prepared his draft of the *Messenger,* he wrote these lines to his fiancée:

I studied the history of the Revolution. I felt as if I were crushed under the terrible fatalism of history. I find in human nature a horrifying sameness, in the human condition an inescapable force, granted to all and to no one. The individual merely foam on the waves, greatness sheer chance, the mastery of genius a puppet play, a ludicrous struggle against an iron law: to recognize it is our utmost achievement, to control it is impossible. I no longer intend to bow down to the parade horses and cornerstones of history. I accustomed myself to the sight of blood. But I am no guillotine blade. The word *must* is one of the curses with which man has been baptized. The dictum, "It must needs be that offenses come; but woe to that man by whom the offense cometh," is terrifying. What is it within us that lies, murders, steals? I no longer care to pursue the thought.

But the thought pursued him persistently. While at Giessen he was often ill (largely due to overwork), lonely, numb ("I am an automaton, my soul has been stolen"), suffering from melancholia that did not appear to dissipate until he was forced to flee to Strasbourg. Moreover, his goal-oriented, "extroverted" idealism was gradually being undermined by the insights gained from his studies of philosophy as well as history. The Fichtean dictum that there is no reality beyond the ego itself seemed literally to de-moralize him, causing him to experience within himself the destruction of enlightened rationalism initiated by Kant and his followers. Another great iconoclastic German dramatist had undergone a similar crisis about thirty years earlier: Heinrich von Kleist. Neither he nor Büchner was able to find solace in the theoretical systems and abstract categories offered by philosophy. Both dwelt on the unclassifiable uniqueness of the individual and came to no solutions; Kleist, in fact, committed suicide. Their dramas question the possibility of human contact, of bridging the abyss between the self and the outside world. *Danton's Death* begins on this note:

Julie.
Do you believe in me?
Danton.
How do I know? We know little about each other. We're all thick-skinned. We stretch out our hands toward each other, but it's all in vain, we just rub the rough leather off . . . we are very lonely.
Julie.
You know me, Danton.
Danton.
Yes, whatever "knowing" means. You have dark eyes and curly hair and a nice complexion and you always say to me: dear Georges. But (*He points to her forehead and eyes.*) there—there: what's behind that? No, our senses are coarse. Know each other? We'd have to break open our skulls and pull each other's thoughts out of the brain fibers.

Danton, who dominates the play, reflects the ambivalence of Büchner's *Weltanschauung*: still committed to the goals of the Revolution, Danton has nevertheless recognized and succumbed to the "fatalism of history." He senses the dreadful, inescapable curse of the word *must*, protesting eloquently and heroically against injustice, resisting escape into self-denying ideology while retaining his sense of moral responsibility, yet going to his death without an answer. There is, however, a clear line of demarcation between Danton and Büchner. We cannot forget that Büchner's protagonist is a member of that class with which he refused to compromise. Danton is a self-indulgent, pleasure-seeking liberal, an aesthete whose love of beauty is genuine but who lives in pseudoaristocratic luxury. Politically, Büchner stood closer to the teachings of Danton's antagonist Robespierre—yet in *Danton's Death* he, too, experiences the agonizing conflict between revolutionary idealism and self-questioning isolation.

Among German and French radicals of the 1830's, the speeches and writings of Maximilien de Robespierre were still quite influential. Büchner's "Society for the Rights of Man" and his contribution to *The Hessian Messenger* bore Robespierre's imprint, yet the Robespierre of *Danton's Death* is a demagogue rather than a lodestar. Although he speaks in rhetorical abstractions and is therefore suspect as a distorter of reality, his orations before the masses and the National Convention are invariably effective. In these scenes, Büchner seems to admit the need for such rhetoric while he simultaneously criticizes the gullibility of those who applaud it. In Act I, Danton has withdrawn from active leadership into disillusioned resignation, while Robespierre remains at the helm, devising ever more drastic measures to protect the Revolution against its enemies. But after a confrontation with Danton, Robespierre lets his mask fall to reveal a man plagued by guilt and—more important—by doubt in the efficacy of any rational action:

> I can't tell what part of me is deceiving the other. (*He steps to the window.*) Night snores over the earth and wallows in wild dreams. Thoughts, hardly perceived wishes, confused and formless, having crept shyly from daylight, now take shape and steal into the silent house of dreams. They open doors, they look out of windows, they become almost flesh, their limbs stretch out in sleep, their lips murmur . . . And isn't our waking a more lucid dream? Aren't we sleepwalkers? Aren't our actions dreamlike, only clearer, more certain, more complete? Who can reproach us for that? The mind accomplishes in one hour more acts of thought than the sluggish organism of our body can carry out in years. The sin is in our thoughts. Whether thought becomes action, whether the body carries it out—that is pure chance.

He suffers the "agony of the executioner," the "Messiah of Blood who sacrifices and is not sacrificed." His isolation is absolute in a cosmic sense, and the Jacobin resorts to Christian imagery to express it: "Truly the Son of Man is crucified in each of us, we all struggle in bloody sweat in the Garden of Gethsemane, but not one of us redeems the other with his wounds . . . —all is desolate and empty—I am alone." He has two alternatives: Danton's therapeutic abreaction and the abandonment of concrete political commitment, or self-denial and repression of his doubts for the sake of social progress. He chooses the latter and wills himself back into his demagogic role, but this turns out to be futile as well in the face of the "iron law," the ignorance of the masses, and the corruption of their leaders, for he is destined to fall soon after Danton.

Danton's Death exudes the pessimistic *Weltanschauung* of the alienated nineteenth-century intellectual, which Büchner undeniably was. He savagely attacked "intellectual aristocrats," disparaging the attempt to reform German society through the educated minority, yet he felt no inner solidarity with the masses he yearned to liberate. In fact, he could not help but criticize their shortcomings. Increasingly, his sphere of activity centered on anatomical research and, shortly before his death, teaching. Literature was the tool with which he could "pursue the thought" further, stimulated by contradiction, giving full rein to his extraordinary talent for creating and analyzing states of being in their most profound complexity. Left as he was to his own devices, frustrated by the failure of *The Hessian Messenger,* he was driven to answer questions for himself which he apparently considered to be more basic to human existence than social reform, unable from his vantage point in history to establish a meaningful connection between the two. Between his first and last plays, he investigated symptoms of alienation: insanity in *Lenz,* boredom and self-delusion in *Leonce and Lena*. Only in *Woyzeck* did he approach a synthesis of sociological analysis and philosophical speculation, depicting with restrained eloquence the suffering of an oppressed lower-class individual.

"FROM OLD PAPERS"

August Becker

[Born in 1814 in Hochweissel in der Wetterau, August Becker studied theology in Giessen during the early 1830's. Like his close friend Georg Büchner, he took part in subversive political activities; arrested in 1835, he was imprisoned for four years, enduring beatings, torture, and solitary confinement. Released after his confession in 1839, he settled in Switzerland as a writer of political essays (e.g., *What Do the Communists Want?*). He returned to his native Hesse during the Revolution of 1848 and eventually became a representative in the state legislature. The failure of the revolution caused him to emigrate to America in 1852, where he worked as a journalist and editor for German newspapers in Baltimore, Cincinnati, and New York. During the Civil War he served in a regiment as military chaplain, returning to Cincinnati in 1865. From 1869 to 1871 he was the editor of the *Cincinnati Courier*. He died in March 1871.

This selection, written in 1845 and published in German in the *Courier* on December 19, 1869, relates his experiences during the Hessian peasant rebellion of 1830.]

The second half of the year 1830 was a wildly exciting time: first the July Revolution in France, then the dynastic revolution in Brunswick, then the Hessian revolution and finally at the end of November the violent Polish revolution. I shall not discuss here the impact of these events on my revolutionary friends but shall merely relate how these friends participated in—or rather against—the revolt called the "Vogelsberger riot" or the "Volgelsberger potato-war," of considerable significance to Hessian history. The riot or war broke out in Hesse-Darmstadt toward the end of the

258

potato harvest during that year. Who had begun it? Who were the leaders of the rebellion? What were their goals?

Even today there are no sufficient answers to these questions. Revolutionary fever was in the air, like cholera. In Hanau, rioters who had not been paid by their employers destroyed customshouses in nearby Hesse, Frankfurt, and Nassau, breaking down the frontier barriers established by German dynastic rulers to oppress the poor and rich. From there the crowd surged through Hesse-Darmstadt to Schotten, swelling to 15,000–20,000 peasants, without leadership or plan, cheering and drinking, destroying customshouses, offices, tax bureaus and rent collection agencies, burning tax forms and legal documents. A few hours away from Schotten, the masses separated into two groups, one of which went toward the north almost to the Thuringian border, the other entered Schotten and suddenly disappeared. The rebellion had already made considerable progress by the time the mail-coach, travelling only twice weekly into the hinterlands, brought news of it to the paper mill where I was vacationing with relatives. The news made my young blood run fast, disturbing my sleep and peace of mind. Not so the peasants in the village near the mill. They were unaffected by the news. I asked them what they would do when the rebels came.

"Just let them come," they answered, "we'll show them their place." But they smiled and winked, so I wasn't sure whether their threat was to be taken seriously. My fat cousin, who had always been complaining about the government, said the same thing. He pointed to his imposing collection of weapons, saying that if he barricaded himself in the mill, he and his assistants could take on a whole regiment of such bums. And the assistants nodded in agreement and laughed at me for my different opinion.

That annoyed and frightened me. I wanted to leave, but my cousin held me back with the assurance that the next mail would announce the end of the whole spectacle. Then a fresh packet of newspapers arrived. The rebels had forced their way into the province of Upper Hesse; Prince Emil, the Generalissimo, had placed himself at the head of the Hesse-Darmstadt army in order to rout the rebels; students had hurried back from vacation to Giessen to defend the threatened muses against the vandals, etc. Now my good cousin couldn't let me dangle any longer, but he refused to lend me a gun from his collection. Instead, he gave me some money, with which I bought an old flintlock in a neighboring town. Lacking a permit, I secured the safety catch to be able to transport it unhindered. Before daybreak I set out for Giessen, ten hours away. Passing through a village, I saw Prince Emil's proclamation to the good citizens of Upper Hesse smeared with dirt. I increased my pace. Ah, I thought, if only the student brigade hasn't already defected to the rebels before you arrive.

I arrived in Giessen in good time. At the gate in front of the tobacco factory I met the student Carl Strack, called Stückli. (He eventually emigrated to Missouri.) He wore a broadsword and had spurs on his boots. "Ah," he called to me before I could greet him, "ah, are you with the infantry? Why aren't you with the cavalry on foot? I'm with the cavalry. A terrific unit, the cavalry. Brrr! Brrr! Beat 'em down!" And he stamped his feet like a parade horse and looked around to see if a pretty girl were watching from a window.

"Damn it all," I yelled at the idiot, "I'm not with the infantry nor the cavalry, but I've come as fast as I could from vacation to see what's going on. Where are the rebels?"

"What, you don't know that? Well, you're really behind the times. The fun's over. The rebels had bad luck. Too bad that they took off. A terrific unit, the riding cavalry on foot. Should have been there. Terrific maneuvers—always in gallop! Forward! Beat 'em down! Brrr!" There was nothing to be learned from him and I had to search elsewhere for information. . . .

The news of the rebels' attack in Upper Hesse had spread holy terror among the good inhabitants of Giessen. . . . It was not known that the rebels had laid hands on private property—leaving untouched, however, the furniture of the hated officials. But had the "heartless Turks" . . . "who didn't spare the child at its mother's breast" invaded the country, the panic could not have been greater. Everyone, including the gentlest civil servant, university student, or baker's apprentice, suddenly felt himself to be a scourge of the peasants, and they all said to themselves, "You dog, defend yourself!"

What had been said about the cavalry was true: it consisted mostly of students. Many of them, led by the members of the *Burschenschaften,* had indeed rushed back from vacation to Giessen and joined it. It was supposed to defend the flanks of the civil guard and charge at the enemy. Its loyalty and bravery could be relied upon. For my part, I had counted on what I thought to be the *Burschenschaften*'s sympathy for the rebels. There I had badly miscalculated. No one burned with a prouder lust for battle, with nobler rage against the "peasant rabble" than they, and they would have attacked "the blockheads" for certain. . . .

Soon the happy news came to Giessen that the rebels had dispersed, and not only the good citizens but all the so-called scourges of the peasants—some of whom had been badly beaten up by the rebels—breathed a sigh of relief and joy was everywhere. "In consideration of these events," the most wise Magistrate of the provincial capital of Giessen had decreed a banquet for the brave cavalry on foot, in thanks for its help in the hour of danger. . . .

[However, when the innkeeper served the students his customary mixture of water and sulfur instead of wine, they rioted and beat up the innkeeper, the city officials, and the members of the banquet committee, fought among themselves, and stole the silverware. Becker ends this chapter of his memoirs with the statement that a "political idea" had motivated the potato-war: the peasants had hoped to elect a well-known liberal as King of Hesse, which would have been possible only if the *Burschenschaften,* who believed that a revolution in Germany could be initiated solely by the "intelligent classes," had joined them.]

"AUGUST BECKER'S TESTIMONY
ABOUT BÜCHNER'S AND WEIDIG'S
POLITICAL ACTIVITIES"

(September to November 1837,
transcribed by Dr. Friedrich Noellner)

Concerning the *Messenger*, I shall take the liberty to let its author, Georg Büchner, speak in his own words, which I still recall quite well. . . . Previous attempts to alter conditions in Germany, he said, were based on thoroughly naive calculations: if the anticipated war had actually come about, there would have been only a handful of undisciplined liberals to confront the German governments and their armies. If a revolution is ever to be successful, it can and must come solely from the masses, who will crush the soldiers by the weight of their numerical superiority. It is therefore essential to win them over, which at this time can only be done with pamphlets.

The earlier pamphlets of this sort were unsuitable. They spoke of the Congress of Vienna, freedom of the press, legislative ordinances, etc.—things which don't interest the peasants in the least . . . as long as they remain preoccupied with material needs. For obvious reasons, these people have no feeling whatsoever for their country's honor and freedom, no idea about the rights of man, etc. They are indifferent to all that, and in this apathy rests their alleged loyalty to their princes and their unconcern about current liberal activities. Nevertheless, they appear to be discontented, and with good cause: their meager earnings extracted from their hard work, so necessary to improve their condition, are claimed as taxes. Therefore, in all partiality one cannot help but admit that they have a relatively primitive outlook, and sad to say, they are accessible only through their purse. You must realize this if you want to free them from oppression; you must show them through statistics that they belong to a state which they support in great measure while others benefit from them, that most of the taxes are drawn from their property

—hard to maintain in any case—while the capitalists go scot-free, that the laws controlling their lives and property lie in the hands of the nobility, the rich, and the state officials, etc. This instrument to win over the masses, Büchner continued, must be employed while there is still time. Were it to occur to the princes to improve the material conditions of the people, were they to reduce the size of their court (which must discomfort them anyway) and their expensive standing armies (which might well be superfluous), were they to reduce to simpler principles their governmental machinery, that artificial organism which costs so much to maintain—then, if the heavens are not merciful, the revolutionary cause is forever lost in Germany. Look at the Austrians, they are well fed and content! Prince Metternich, the cleverest of all, has permanently smothered in their own fat whatever revolutionary spirit might arise. . . .

The pamphlet [*The Hessian Messenger*] hoped to join the materialistic concerns of the masses with those of the revolution. . . . Büchner often said that materialistic oppression of a large number of Germans was just as wretched and disgraceful as intellectual oppression; in his eyes it was not nearly so distressing that this or that liberal could not publish his thoughts as that many thousand families were unable to eat fat with their potatoes.

. . . Weidig said [after reading Büchner's draft of the *Messenger*] that such principles would alienate from us all honest men (he meant the liberals). . . . In all things, Weidig was Büchner's opposite; Weidig maintained that one must gather up even the smallest revolutionary spark if a conflagration were to occur. He was republican among the Republicans and constitutional among the Constitutionalists. Büchner was most dissatisfied with Weidig's remark, saying it was easy to be an honest man if one is able to eat soup, vegetables, and meat every day. Weidig nevertheless could not refrain from praising the pamphlet, saying it would render a great service if it were altered. . . . He eliminated whatever was said against the so-called Liberal party, replacing it with comments about the effectiveness of the constitution, whereby the character of the document became even more malevolent. The original manuscript could have been read as a fanatical, documented sermon against Mammon, wherever he was to be found—but not the revision. . . . Büchner was extremely upset by Weidig's alterations. He no longer wanted to claim it as his, saying that Weidig had deleted all that was most important to him and that justified everything else. . . .

As he often told me, Büchner wanted to determine through this pamphlet to what extent the German people were inclined to take part in a revolution. . . . When he discovered later that the peasants had turned over most of the pamphlets to the police, that even the Patriots [a radical organization?] had spoken out against it, he gave up all hope for political change. He did not believe that the constitutional legislative opposition could bring about truly free social conditions in Germany. He often said that if they were to succeed in overthrowing the German governments and establish a general monarchy or even a republic, we would have a moneyed aristocracy here like in France, and things should rather stay the way they are now. . . . If the attempt with this first pamphlet had been successful, Büchner and his friends in Giessen planned to make sure that similar pamphlets would be distributed in other countries. This did not occur, however, since the enterprise had been so unsuccessful. . . .

I recall that Büchner once had an argument with Weidig about the right to vote. Büchner maintained that in a just republic, like in most of the North American states, everyone should have a vote irrespective of property assets. He said that Weidig, who believed that a dictatorship of the rabble would then arise like in France, was misjudging the conditions of the German people and of our times. Büchner once expressed himself vehemently in Zeuner's presence about Weidig's aristocratism, as he called it, and Zeuner was indiscreet enough to repeat this to Weidig. This led to a disagreement between Weidig and Büchner that I attempted to settle. . . .

DANTON'S DEATH

"THE HISTORICAL BACKGROUND OF
DANTON'S DEATH"

Roy C. Cowen

The French Revolution of 1789 marks the beginning of the modern era in European politics, military science, and many other fields. But it was only the culmination of a development that extended far back into the eighteenth century. The political order in France before the Revolution, the "ancien régime," was essentially that of the Middle Ages, in which the clergy and the nobility enjoyed most privileges and responsibilities. By 1770, however, the position of the privileged classes had come under pressure, first, from the Enlightenment and such French philosophers as Voltaire (1694–1778) who had experienced political freedom outside of France, second, from the "enlightened" monarchs in Sweden and Austria, and third, from the financial situation of France itself, which was now on the verge of bankruptcy.

Revolutionary movements had been arousing the entire world. The most significant one was the American Revolution, which had been supported by the French. Ironically enough, the treaty ending the American Revolution was signed in the city of Paris in 1783, and in 1789, the year Washington assumed office as the first President of the United States, Paris was the scene of the events which mark the actual beginning of the French Revolution. In 1789, Louis XVI summoned the "Estates General," a pseudo-representative body which had not met since 1614. This body was divided into three estates or classes: the clergy, the nobility, and the commoners. Soon after the opening of the "Estates General" on May 5, 1789, however, differences in opinion regarding procedure brought about the secession of the third estate, which then called itself "National Assembly." On June 19, the clergy voted by a narrow margin to join the Assembly, and they were followed by several liberal-minded nobles. When on June 20 the Assembly was locked out of its meeting place, it retired to a tennis court and took an oath, known as the "Tennis Court Oath," that it would not disperse until a new constitution had been enacted. This seemed to be the signal for a rapid breakdown of public order which culminated on July 14, 1789, in the storming of the Bastille, an ancient prison. After this first major act of violence, which is celebrated as the actual start of the Revolution, the threat of anarchy was constantly present on the political scene.

As a conciliatory gesture the King hurriedly reappointed Jacques Necker, the former Minister of Finance. The Marquis de Lafayette, a liberal aristocrat and hero of the American Revolution, was elected commander of the National Guard, which had been formed as the military force of the Third Estate. The Tricolor—representing a compromise between white, the color of the Bourbons, and red and blue, the colors of the city of Paris—was adopted as the new national flag. Many cities, the most prominent of which was Paris, were transformed into communes under the direct supervision of the Assembly. The National Assembly now assumed the responsibility for giving France a new government and constitution. On August 26, it issued the "Declaration of the Rights of Man and of the Citizen," an abstract statement of general principles mostly derived from the philosophies of J.-J. Rousseau (1712–1778) and other intellectuals.

By the end of October 1789, the clergy and the nobility had lost virtually all of their power, and the number of "émigrés," aristocrats who chose to flee France, continued to grow. The King was now a virtual prisoner in Paris, which, because of the breakdown of the feudal order, was to be the center of political activity during the remaining years of the Revolution. The issues themselves were lost, and further control of the government became a conflict of personalities, a conflict for which the nobility proved inadequate. Louis XVI was too weak a monarch when only a strong one could have avoided chaos. Marie Antoinette, the Queen, was vain, shortsighted, and extremely unpopular with the masses, who called her "that Austrian woman." Control of public opinion fell to the radicals such as Jean-Paul Marat, the editor of *L'Ami du Peuple* (The People's Friend).

Officially, the period from October 1789 to September 1790 was known as a constitutional monarchy; but from June 21, 1791, on, this form of government was doomed. That day the King tried to escape from France but was caught not far from the border and returned to Paris as a prisoner. The Assembly closed the borders and assumed full power. For fear of foreign intervention, however, it did not yet depose the King.

On September 14, 1791, the King was forced to accept publicly the Constitution of 1791 as framed by the Assembly. The new constitution provided for a legislative body from which the members of the Assembly at the time were excluded, thus turning all political activity over to groups outside the more experienced and moderate Assembly. These groups included the political clubs, such as the Jacobin Club, and other political organizations like the Paris Commune. The new body created by the constitution, the Legislative Assembly, was from the beginning in a state of deadlock. The political clubs and the Commune now had too much power. Besides the Jacobins there were the Cordeliers, the Feuillants, who were moderate constitutionalists, and the Brissotins, radical followers of J. P. Brissot: all of them felt strong enough to challenge the authority of the Legislative Assembly whenever they did not agree with its decisions. The ministers Narbonne and later Dumouriez pursued a course intended to unite France by means of a foreign war. In April 1792, their plans materialized in a war against Austria. But France was ill-prepared for war. Because of mismanagement of the war, the government soon fell into the hands of radicals such as Robespierre, who had opposed the war from the beginning and now emerged as a man of proven foresight. Internal strife and disagreement, together with dangers from the approaching Austrian army, resulted in virtual chaos that culminated during this period in an order by the Paris Commune to the National Guard to attack the Tuileries Palace, which was set afire. The King and Queen took refuge with the Assembly, which deprived them of all privileges and had them imprisoned.

Of primary interest to us in *Danton's Death* is the subsequent period of the Revolutionary government from September 1792 to July 1794. The Legislative Assembly called for national elections to a National Convention, which for the first time were based on universal suffrage. These elections were held during the end of August and the beginning of September. This new attempt to create an effective government to replace the inefficient National Assembly took place, however, at a time of national turmoil, for on August 17, 1792, General Lafayette had deserted to the Austrians. A series of military defeats followed, and on September 1 the news arrived that Verdun was on the verge of falling to the enemy. Hysteria gripped the masses. From September 1 to September 7, the so-called "September Massacres" took place, during which some 1200 people were murdered. Most of the victims were prisoners; among them the mob suspected Royalists, who were held responsible for the French defeats, but in truth two-thirds of the prisoners had been imprisoned on non-political charges. Danton, the Minister of Justice at the time, showed complete indifference to these murders, possibly because he was so occupied with matters of national defense. Indeed, on September 2, 1792, Danton, with his famous eloquence, rallied the country against the Prussians who had invaded Champagne. The concluding lines of his speech, which are still quoted, are alluded to in Büchner's drama: "To crush them, what is necessary? To dare, to dare again, and always to dare, and France is saved." In *Danton's Death,* however, the "September Massacres" appear over and over again as a great burden on Danton's conscience.

The newly elected National Convention assembled on September 20, 1792. Its first act on September 21 was to abolish the monarchy, and on the following day the new Revolutionary calendar of the French Republic began.

One of the two main parties was the majority Girondins, who held most of the ministerial posts and were largely supported by elements outside of Paris. Their chief rivals were the Jacobins, left-wing radicals led by Danton, Jean-Paul Marat, and Robespierre, who drew their main support from the Paris mobs. The decline of the Girondins was rapid. They engaged in many personal feuds, particularly against Danton, thus alienating any possible left-wing support. Their attempt to overthrow the powerful Commune of Paris gave even more support to the charge that they represented the provinces against the capital (the name of the club came from Gironde, the province from which its most important members came). At first the Girondins, despite public opinion in Paris, opposed a trial of the King for treason, but it was finally held and the King was unanimously declared guilty. A majority of seventy condemned him to death, and on January 21, 1793, he was executed. The Queen, however, was not guillotined until October 16 of that year.

The only bright spot for the Girondins seemed to be the army, which under the leadership of General Dumouriez was successful in the field. But the Girondins pursued such a reckless war policy that soon France was in a state of war against almost all of Europe. William Pitt the Younger, the Prime Minister of England, against whom France had declared war on February 1, 1793, began a blockade of the coast. Shortages caused discontent in France, and there was high feeling against profiteers and speculators which is also reflected in *Danton's Death*. By March there was a crisis on the home front. In addition, Dumouriez was defeated by the Austrians twice within four days of that month. After an armistice had been signed, Dumouriez attempted to overthrow the Convention. After his failure, he fled with his staff on April 5 to Austria.

Because their only claim to success had been military victories, the defeats came as a heavy blow to the Girondins. Dumouriez's treason, however, had even more disastrous consequences, for now the Jacobins, led by Robespierre, accused the Girondins of complicity in the general's treason. Danton demanded a reorganization of the central executive authority, and on April 6, 1793, the Committee of General Defense was converted into the Committee of Public Safety, headed by Danton himself. The Paris Commune joined in denouncing the Girondins, who then unwisely countered by prosecuting Marat, the president of the Jacobin Club, and arrested Jacques Hébert, a leader of the Commune. The extremists then reorganized the Commune in an attempt to attack the Girondins. On June 2, 1793, the Commune surrounded the Convention with forces of the National Guard and forced the Convention to arrest twenty-nine of the Girondin ministers and deputies.

Now in control of the Convention, the Jacobins drew up a new constitution, the "Constitution of the Year I" (1793), which was never really put into effect. In order to regain some support from the provinces, which had sided with the Girondins, the Jacobins instituted land reforms which finally abolished completely feudal practices and tied the peasants for many generations to the cause of the Revolution.

By the end of July 1793, the new government had also experienced military defeats which threatened France's safety. Danton, who headed the Committee of Public Safety and thus had charge of the war effort, was held responsible for these setbacks, and on July 10, 1793, together with six of his colleagues, he was removed from the Committee. On July 28, Robespierre became a member of the Committee of Public Safety, and Danton was made president of the Convention. Soon under pressure from an even more radical element, the "Enragés," followers of Marat, who had been assassinated on July 13, the Committee increased its persecution of hoarders and counterrevolutionaries. The "Enragés" were, however, soon replaced by even more radical extremists led by Hébert and supported by the Commune and the Jacobin Club.

In September 1793, a series of military crises, a bread shortage in Paris, and the discovery of a plot to rescue the still imprisoned Queen led to renewed demands by the Hébertists for more radical controls. On September 17, the period of the "Terror" began with the passage of a law allowing the arrest of suspects by revolutionary committees. On October 10, the newly written "Constitution of the Year I" was put aside and the Committee of Public Safety was empowered to continue as the main government organ until the end of the war.

The main objective of the Committee was the establishment of its central authority, and indeed the name "Terror" is misleading, for the Committee's rule was more a rule by intimidation than a "Reign of Terror." Large numbers of citizens fled the "Terror," and some 40,000 were executed throughout France. Surprisingly enough, no less than seventy per cent of its victims were peasants and laborers, and most of the excesses did not take place in Paris but in La Vendée and Lyon. Nevertheless, the Committee in Paris staged the October trials of the Queen and almost all of the Girondin leaders who were subsequently executed.

Until the spring of 1794 the course of the "Terror" was determined by Danton, Hébert, and Robespierre. Hébert, the most radical of the three, attacked Christianity and tried to establish a "Cult of Reason" as well as a new calendar to break all connections with tradition. But the excesses, together with the obvious political power held by Hébert, led Robespierre to have him and eighteen of his followers arrested. After a summary trial Hébert and his followers were executed.

Büchner's drama begins with the events of March 30, 1794, a week after Hébert's execution on March 24. The drama ends on the day of Danton's execution, April 5, 1794. The events of that week in which Robespierre rids himself of his last major political opponent are more or less faithfully recorded in *Danton's Death*, together with characters and events of Büchner's own invention. To be appreciated as a work of art, Büchner's play must be understood not in terms of its accuracy in giving the real, historical reasons for Danton's downfall, but rather in terms of its effectiveness in presenting reasons which have meaning for all of us. In the week portrayed in the drama, we see Danton, Robespierre, and all the others as Büchner imagined them, and they are part of actions, both real and fictitious, which put their characters in a somewhat different context. I shall therefore omit any description of the historical details of Danton's last week and of the characteristics of the real Danton and Robespierre. Büchner, however, presumes those historical events preceding March 30,

1794, and for that reason they have been briefly summarized above.[1]

Moreover, the entire drama stands under the shadow of what really followed Danton's death, namely Robespierre's own execution. The "Terror" had been justified by the war effort, and, ironically, his own success proved to be Robespierre's undoing. Revitalized by the organizational talent of Lazare Carnot, a member of the Committee, and led by fresh young officers who had gained their positions by merit, the French Republican Army—the first army in Europe raised by conscription—had by the spring of 1794 reached a qualitative and quantitative superiority which eliminated the main cause for the "Terror": the fear of outside forces supported by reactionaries from within. Robespierre's personal tyranny, carried out for patriotic and moral reasons, reached such excesses that the Convention, no longer fearing the dangers which had led to its formation, overthrew the Committee of Public Safety on July 27, 1794. This counterrevolution marked the end of the "Reign of Terror." It became known as the "Thermidorian Reaction," because its date, according to the Revolutionary calendar, was 9 Thermidor. On July 28, just sixteen weeks after Danton's death, Robespierre, Louis de St. Just, and George Couthon were executed. In his play, however, Büchner seems to indicate a further, final irony of the Revolution: only a few years later it was to fall under the dictatorship of an even stronger individual, Napoleon Bonaparte, who called himself a "son of the Revolution."

---

[1] Büchner's main sources of information on the French Revolution were: L. A. Thiers, *Histoire de la Révolution française* (Paris, 1823–1827); F. A. Mignet, *Histoire de la Révolution française* (Paris, 1824); Konrad Friedrich (pseudonym Carl Strahlheim), *Unsere Zeit oder geschichtliche Ubersicht der merkwürdigsten Ereignisse von 1789 bis 1830, nach den vorzüglichsten französischen, englischen und deutschen Werken bearbeitet von einem ehemaligen Offizier der kaiserlichfranzösischen Armee* (Stuttgart, 1826–1830).

"DANTON'S DEATH: ANTIRHETORIC
AND DRAMATIC FORM"*

Herbert Lindenberger

At first glance *Danton's Death* looks like a kind of chronicle play, which in a series of loosely connected scenes details the salient moments of Danton's last weeks, while at the same time providing a good bit of the grim local color appropriate to the period in which it is set. The subtitle which its first publisher (quite to the author's chagrin) attached to it—"Dramatic Scenes of the French Reign of Terror"—gives some indication of how its early readers, what few there were, must have looked at it. At best it was a drama to be read silently, as one would read narrative history. For an audience accustomed to an essentially Aristotelian concept of the drama—and one for whom Schiller's later plays seemed the highest point that German serious theater had yet attained—this work could scarcely be considered a drama in any usual sense. In contrast to works such as Schiller's *Wallenstein, Mary Stuart,* and *The Maid of Orleans, Danton's Death* does not present a hero actively, earnestly wrestling with his fate. Nor can we discern a single, closely controlled line of plot development to which all the elements of the drama—the characters, the philosophical matter, the local color—must be rigorously subordinated. From an Aristotelian point of view *Danton's Death* is sprawling and hopelessly uneconomical. The story of Danton's fate is constantly interrupted by seemingly irrelevant genre scenes. Though a certain line of plot can be made out from the more obvious events of the hero's story, the central emotional crises of the play—if we can even call them that—are not, as in an Aristotelian drama, released through the contrivances of plot structure. Characters such as the prostitute Marion are developed in detail

---

* Passages quoted from *Danton's Death* in this article have been altered to conform to the present translation. Excerpts of Büchner's letters conform to the selections offered in this book; other quotations have been left in their original form and are footnoted.

273

only to be dropped immediately after their first appearance. Lengthy political speeches which are only indirectly related to the hero's fate take up a sizable proportion of pages in the play. The conflict between Danton and Robespierre, which in the first half seems the central action of the play, is quite forgotten once Danton is arrested at the end of Act Two.

Yet Büchner, in this, his first creative effort, developed a mode of dramaturgy as sure and exacting as that of any German writer before him. His essential method, as well as his central themes, are implicit in the first page or two of the play:

> HÉRAULT-SÉCHELLES, *a few women at a card table.*
> DANTON, JULIE *somewhat further off,* DANTON *on a footstool at* JULIE's *feet.*

Danton.
Look at Madame over there—how sweetly she fingers her cards. She knows how, all right—they say her husband always gets a heart, the others a royal flush. You women could even make us fall in love with a lie.

Julie.
Do you believe in me?

Danton.
How do I know? We know little about each other. We're all thick-skinned. We stretch out our hands toward each other, but it's all in vain, we just rub the rough leather off . . . we are very lonely.

Julie.
You know me, Danton.

Danton.
Yes, whatever "knowing" means. You have dark eyes and curly hair and a nice complexion and you always say to me: dear Georges. But (*He points to her forehead and eyes.*) there—there: what's behind that? No, our senses are coarse. Know each other? We'd have to break open our skulls and pull each other's thoughts out of the brain fibers.

A Woman.
(*To* HÉRAULT.) What are you doing with your fingers?

Hérault.

Nothing!

Woman.

Don't twist your thumb under like that! I can't stand
it.

Hérault.

Just look, it has a very peculiar physiognomy.

Danton.

No, Julie, I love you like the grave.

Julie.

(*Turning away*.) Oh!

Danton.

No, listen! They say in the grave there is peace, and
grave and peace are one. If that's so, then in your lap
I'm already lying under the earth. You sweet grave
—your lips are funeral bells, your voice my death
knell, your breasts my burial mound, and your heart
my coffin.

Woman.

You lose!

Hérault.

That was a little adventure of love. It costs money
as they all do.

Woman.

Then you made your declarations with your fingers,
like a deaf-mute.

Hérault.

And why not? Some say that fingers are the easiest
to understand.

The first lines seem about as offhanded as those with
which any tragic drama opens. For the play has no exposition in the conventional sense: we are not given "background details" about the past lives of the main characters,
nor are we prepared in any way for the principal actions
that will take place in the drama. There is nothing com-
parable here to those discussions of a momentous past
which we find between prince and *confident* at the start of
a Racine play, or in the servants' gossip with which so
many Ibsen plays begin. Indeed, the lady whom we see so
intent at her card game is never developed further in the
play. Her function is an altogether temporary one: her

game with Hérault is meant to contrast ironically with the very fundamental matters of life and death which Danton chooses to discuss with his wife. Danton's bittersweet apostrophe about the grave, for instance, is rudely interrupted by the lady's announcement that Hérault has lost at cards. In the space of even this single page Büchner shifts back and forth three times between the two contrasting scenes.

One could speak of a kind of dramatic counterpoint that stands behind Büchner's dramaturgy, just as one speaks of a kind of counterpoint in a scene such as the agricultural fair in *Madame Bovary,* in which two and in a sense three actions, all commenting ironically upon one another, are going on at once.[1] Büchner's manner of shifting contexts from one scene or from one group to another is also reflected from moment to moment in the exchanges of dialogue between his characters. Julie's question to Danton, "Do you believe in me?" is never answered directly by her husband; instead, he shifts the context, as it were, to another area altogether: how can we even talk of believing in each other, he implies, when human beings cannot really know one another? And when Julie responds, "You know me, Danton," he refuses to accept her on her own ground, but begins, instead, to examine the various semantic possibilities of "knowing." Danton's very statement about the impossibility of human communication is, in fact, a reflection of Büchner's dramatic method: the characters in this play do not really confront each other directly, nor do they persuade one another, nor do they even substantially develop the "plot" through their conversations with one another. A simple question such as Julie's does not, from the play's point of view, at least, deserve a simple answer; the question serves principally as a means of opening up new perspectives of discussion for Danton, indeed, of asserting the unreliability of ordinary language for getting at the essential truths of life.

---

[1] I refer to Joseph Frank's well-known discussion of the **fair** scene in *Madame Bovary* in his essay "Spatial Form in Modern Literature," *Sewanee Review,* LIII (1945), 230–32. The "counterpoint" of this scene was a new technique in fiction, though it was a quite traditional technique in drama, at least in farce or in serious drama outside the classical tradition.

This opening passage works in still other ways to reveal the play as a whole. Danton's play on the word *hearts* in his first speech is but the first of innumerable examples of puns that occur throughout this play and *Leonce and Lena*. In fact, the various levels on which we can interpret the word—its reference to the frivolities of card games and faithless women, as well as its ironic reminder, through Julie's reaction, of the possibility of faithfulness and devotion between men and women—anticipate some of the basic human issues which reverberate throughout the play. Büchner's decision to open the play with a scene of card players idling away their time not only provided a significant contrast with the second scene—with its picture of the brute, discontented masses during the Revolution—but it gave him the opportunity to embody one of the play's dominant themes in a concrete image at the start: life, as Danton keeps defining and redefining it throughout the work, is essentially a series of games which we play to pass our time away and to remind us as rarely as possible of the great emptiness that stares at us from behind the surfaces of things. Danton's words about finding peace in the grave introduce the play's most persistent single image, or group of images: for sleep and death are most desirable alternatives to life as Danton conceives it, and he invokes them in a multitude of metaphorical combinations in the course of the drama.

ii

The despair that Danton voices at the difficulty of communication points to one of the central insights that govern the composition of the play: for Büchner the mode of language which a character speaks is intimately related to his whole attitude toward life. The play's more talkative characters can be divided into two groups—those, like Robespierre, St. Just, and the stage-prompter Simon, who, in one way or another, still display a confidence in communicating with the world around them, and those, like Danton and his friends, or the prostitute Marion, who have given up hope in the effectiveness of human action and are thus gloomy about the meaningfulness of communication between people. The characters within the first group generally speak a kind of "set" rhetoric, a rhetoric which, one might say, serves as a sign of their commitment to a fairly rigid system of values. As a recent critic of Büchner has shown, the language used by the drunken Simon in accusing his wife of corrupting their daughter sounds uncomfortably similar to the highly emotive rhetoric often found in the German Classical drama, especially in Schiller.[2] When Simon screams, "Thus I tear thy raiment from thy shoulders,/ Thy naked carcass I cast into the sun," Büchner is not merely parodying the bombast in which Schiller's characters often engage, but he launches into blank verse, which his readers would immediately associate with the heroic world of Classical drama. When Simon starts ranting, "Ha, Lucretia! A knife, give me a knife, Romans! Ha, Appius Claudius!" he attempts to dignify his personal situation by alluding to ancient myth, but unhappily manages to undercut the rhetorical effect by getting the stories of Lucretia and Virginia mixed up.

In parodying the language of an earlier dramatic style, as he does through Simon's speeches, Büchner is using a technique familiar enough in the history of drama, as in Aristophanes' presentation of Aeschylean bombast in *The Frogs,* or Shakespeare's of the old revenge-play fustian in the player's speech about Hecuba in *Hamlet.* But the language which he gives to Robespierre can scarcely be called parody. For Robespierre is a character whom Büchner treats with total seriousness; he is, after all, Danton's chief antagonist (if one may apply such terms from traditional dramatic criticism to so untraditional a play), and through the tone and length of his speeches Büchner is able to portray a world that seems the total antithesis of Danton's. Yet Robespierre's language, by means of this very tone, suggests the grounds on which we must reject the character who speaks it: "Spare the royalists! certain people cry. Spare the wicked? No! Spare the innocent, spare the weak, spare the unfortunate, spare humanity! Only the peaceful citizen deserves the protection of society. In a republic only

[2] Helmut Krapp, *Der Dialog bei Georg Büchner* (Darmstadt, 1958), pp. 15–19.

republicans are citizens, royalists and foreigners are enemies."

Like Flaubert and Joyce after him, Büchner defines and evaluates even those characters whom he takes most seriously through their sins of language, without needing to add his comments through their actions or through other characters. The modern reader of course recognizes the now familiar language of totalitarianism in Robespierre's lines. An early nineteenth-century reader would doubtless have recognized the language as Robespierre's even if it had been quoted out of context. And, indeed, the language *is* Robespierre's and not Büchner's at all: by far the greater portion of Robespierre's public speeches in the play is quoted directly (through somewhat rearranged) from the various histories of the French Revolution which Büchner was using.[3] Büchner, who, soon after completing the play, described his task as dramatic poet "to come as close to history as it actually happened," had no need to invent a language with which to characterize Robespierre; the language was ready-made for him in his sources. The passage quoted above is all Robespierre's except for minor changes in one or two words. . . . If we compare it to any of the lines spoken by Danton in the play, we quickly note the difference between a sensitive, subtle, much-too-inquiring mind such as Danton's and one which can apprehend reality only in black-and-white terms. Robespierre's language, with its absolute assertions, has a heavy, cliché-ridden deadness about it: only a peaceful citizen [and no one else] has a right to the protection of society; only republicans [and no others] can be citizens of a republic; royalists and foreigners [by which he easily disposes of all those who do not fit his definition of republicans] are enemies. Quite in contrast to Danton, who is unable to answer a question directly but must subject it to endless analysis, Robespierre possesses a total, if also a somewhat naïve, certainty about the nature of truth: things are either true or false, as his value system chooses to call them; truth does not admit degrees or shades of meaning. The sentences quoted above are tied to one another by a closely contrived dialectic, a

[3] In his critical edition of *Danton's Death*, Richard Thieberger provides a useful collation of sources and text. See *La Mort de Danton et ses sources* (Paris, 1953), pp. 35–52.

dialectic which can jump boldly from premise to conclusion without having to scruple about the validity of either premises or the argumentative process which binds them together. Throughout the play Robespierre's speeches are dominated by abstractions: *virtue, immorality, terror, innocence, the healthy strength of the people* (*gesunde Volkskraft*), to cite some of the most conspicuous examples.

It is significant that Büchner chooses to present Robespierre largely in his public, speech-making role. By far the greater part of his words are spoken as orations, in three successive speeches, first, to an unruly mob in the second scene of the play, next before the Jacobin Club, and then before the National Convention. In each instance his efforts at persuasion are successful (his very success implies Büchner's attitude toward the groups he has managed to convince). But even when he faces Danton alone, he speaks the same language he had spoken on the rostrum: "Vice must be punished, virtue must rule through terror." At only one moment in the play can we discern another Robespierre —when Danton, after working to strip his pretensions bare, has left him alone in his room. The Robespierre we see at this point, if ever so briefly, is a man plagued by nightmarish fears, one who, for an instant at least, speaks a dimly poetic language totally devoid of the false clarity that characterizes his more public utterances: "Night snores over the earth and wallows in wild dreams. Thoughts, hardly perceived wishes, confused and formless, having crept shyly from daylight, now take shape and steal into the silent house of dreams." By letting his public, rhetorical self master him so fully, he has become, temporarily, a totally opposite self—irrational, confused, the prey of fleeting impressions. And it is in this scene, and here only, that he comes to share a central insight shared also by Danton and his friends—the knowledge of his essential loneliness in a hostile universe. "My Camille!—They're all leaving me," he reflects, directly after his decision to arrest the Dantonists; "all is desolate and empty—I am alone."

In Robespierre Büchner has chosen to give us at least a glimpse of a suffering, introspective self that stands behind the hardened public self. In St. Just, however, he presents an unrelentingly rhetorical being who shows no trace of any private self. St. Just is defined by the language he speaks in public, and by nothing more. His long oration before the Convention, which directly follows Robespierre's, attempts to lift the latter's arguments into a cosmic perspective:

> There appear to be in this assembly a number of sensitive ears which cannot endure the word "blood." May a few general observations convince them that we are no crueler than nature or time. Nature follows its laws serenely and irresistibly; man is destroyed when he comes in conflict with them.

Robespierre's arguments, however abstract his language, had been limited largely to practical politics—to the business of national security, of discerning friends from foes of the state. St. Just's speech seeks a far loftier level of expression: the laws of Nature must be evoked to justify the arrest of Danton and his friends. Büchner drew only a small bit of this speech from his sources; the sources, in fact, indicate that his actual speech on this occasion was probably not much different from Robespierre's. But Büchner, in creating this speech for St. Just, must have felt the necessity of representing still another mode of rhetoric in his play. The idealism it purports to voice about human progress—"Humanity will rise up with mighty limbs out of this cauldron of blood, like the earth out of the waters of the Flood, as if it had been newly created"—seems almost a parody of those lofty expressions about human progress and freedom that mark the dramatic high point of so many German Classical plays: one thinks, for instance, of such tragic figures as Goethe's Egmont, envisioning—with appropriate background music—the benign future which will result from his martyrdom, or of the condemned Marquis Posa, in Schiller's *Don Carlos*, solemnly reminding the hero of that play of the great tasks he must fulfill for the progress of mankind. When seen in the light of such classical moments, the long political speeches in *Danton's Death* seem to voice a hard and bitter skepticism, on Büchner's part, of the validity of rhetoric in voicing any human ideals. "He would rather let himself be guillotined" than make a speech, a character says of Danton at one point;

one feels that Danton's attitude toward speech-making is an attitude which stands behind the drama as a whole.

In obvious contrast to the rhetoric of Robespierre and St. Just is the antirhetoric of characters such as Danton and Marion. Marion's lengthy recital of her history is expressed in simple, natural language that stands at an opposite extreme from the play's political dialectic:

> . . . My mother was a smart woman. She always said chastity was a nice virtue—when people came to the house and started talking about certain things, she told me to leave the room. When I asked what they wanted, she said I ought to be ashamed of myself. When she gave me a book to read, I almost always had to skip over a couple of pages. But I read the Bible whenever I liked—there everything was holy; but there was something in there that I didn't understand, and I didn't want to ask anybody about it—I brooded about myself.

The utter naturalness with which she speaks may not seem extraordinary to the mid-twentieth-century reader, for whom such a mode of speech might well read like a mere literary convention. But a recitation of this sort is something unique in a serious historical drama written in the 1830's. Though Marion has no effect on the plot (in the conventional sense of that term), her speech has an essential dramatic function—a function which becomes clear, I think, if we compare it to Robespierre's speech to the Jacobins, which occurs only two pages before in the text. In striking contrast to Robespierre's inflated arguments and abstractions, Marion's story consists largely of a series of sense impressions, made without comment on her part. Her sentences are built out of simple clauses, usually connected by *and*, without causal connections. When she describes her emotions she states them directly, as though they were simple facts ("I brooded about myself"). Her reference, at the beginning, to her mother's admonition of virtue ironically echoes the word *virtue* (*Tugend*) which had resounded three times in Robespierre's speech. She gains the reader's immediate sympathy, but she is never sentimentalized (it is worth noting that by Büchner's time the sympathetically treated prostitute—who goes back at least to Prévost's Manon Lescaut—had long been a stock character in literature). Our sympathy toward her does not derive from the lowliness of her situation, but from the fact that she speaks to us so directly and unpretentiously as a human being.[4] When she describes the differences between her world and that of ordinary people, Büchner resists the temptation to sentimentalize as surely as any serious modern writer since Hemingway would have done: "Other people have Sundays and working days, they work for six days and pray on the seventh; once a year, on their birthdays, they get sentimental, and every year on New Year's Day they reflect. I don't understand all that. For me there is no stopping, no changing. I'm always the same. . . ."

Marion speaks her lines seated on the floor at Danton's feet. From the nature of her speech one can well imagine that she does not even look at him while she talks: like the other "antirhetorical" characters in the play, she speaks what is essentially a monologue, directed less to her listener than to herself or, for that matter, to no one at all. Her unpretentious acceptance of the isolation imposed by her nature and her role in society is reflected dramatically in the isolation which the monologue form suggests. "That was my nature—who can escape it?"—thus, without either guilt or pride, she explains her first sexual encounters.

Danton, too, puts special emphasis on the fact that he has remained true to himself, most conspicuously perhaps when he tries to lay bare Robespierre's pretensions of virtue. "Each one acts according to his nature, that means he does what is good for him," he tells Robespierre after the latter has solemnly asked him, "You deny virtue?" A character such as Robespierre, who refuses to admit the personal needs that motivate all his thoughts and actions, is forced to adopt an inflated rhetoric to justify these thoughts and actions to others and to himself. Characters such as Danton and Marion, in conscious acceptance of their natures, have no need of pretensions, and the language

---

4 Wolfgang Martens, in his article "Zum Menschenbild Georg Büchners: 'Woyzeck' und die Marionszene in 'Dantons Tod,'" *Wirkendes Wort*, VIII (1957), 13–20, carefully defines Marion's uniqueness as a literary figure and links her to Büchner's thematic preoccupations in *Woyzeck*.

they speak is consequently free of false mannerisms. Danton, of course, speaks a language quite different from Marion's. He is an infinitely more complex character, indeed, one of the most many-sided characters in dramatic literature. Like Hamlet, to whom he has often been compared,[5] one of his functions throughout the play is to subject the assumptions of the other characters to analysis and irony. In the opening scene, he counters even the relatively simple questions of his wife ("You know me, Danton") with a hard-headed, though also well-meaning, analysis of their verbal content. Although the life he leads is an essentially Epicurean one, he is impatient with those who make a fetish of their Epicureanism. His friend Camille Desmoulins at one point waxes eloquent about the new republic which he envisions replacing the reign of Robespierre ("We want naked gods and bacchantes, Olympic games, and from melodic lips the words: 'Ah, uninhibited, wicked love!' "); but when he calls on Danton to help bring the new reign into being ("Danton, you will lead the attack in the Convention."), Danton mocks his words by turning Camille's command into a schoolboy's grammatical exercise: "I will, you will, he will." Epicureanism, like every other way of thinking, has its own form of rhetoric, and Danton is unwilling to fall into the traps imposed by any such form.

But Danton is surely no devil's advocate, no gadfly indiscriminately running about deflating the pretensions of others. Beneath his manner there lies a profoundly held set of convictions—convictions about the uselessness of ambition and endeavor, disillusionment about the Revolution, a sense of the utter absurdity of all human postures and relationships. What separates Danton from most of the other characters is the *way* in which he holds and voices his convictions. For Danton's convictions do not take the form of dogma or ideology. When he voices them, he does so offhandedly, often jokingly. "There's no hope in death," he says in one of the prison scenes; "it's only a simpler— and life a more complicated—form of decay; that's the only difference!"

5 See, for instance, Karl Viëtor's discussion of the relationship of the two characters in *Georg Büchner: Politik, Dichtung, Wissenschaft*, pp. 107–08.

Danton seems so convincing a character for the modern reader through the *tone* with which he speaks. One need only compare him to the character Thomas Payne, who, at the opening of the third act, expounds views not much different from Danton's own.[6] Payne goes to great lengths to demonstrate the nonexistence of God and assert the reality of suffering: like Danton, he makes a point of his hedonism, of "acting according to my nature." But Payne, though generally a sympathetic character in the one scene in which he appears, expresses his views as a dogmatist, passionately and earnestly; indeed, the portrait we have of him in the play corresponds well with our conception of a man of the Enlightenment: *"There is no God,* because: either God created the world or He did not. If He did not, then the world has its basis of existence within itself and there is no God, since God only becomes God in that He contains the root of all existence."

Danton is beyond such argument. In fact, when Danton and his friends are brought into prison in the middle of Payne's Spinozistic disquisition the atmosphere suddenly changes from one of solemnity to one of joking, though of an obviously macabre kind:

Hérault.
   . . . Good morning. Good night, I should say. I cannot ask how you've slept. How will you sleep?
Danton.
   Well. One has to go to bed laughing.

There is nothing of course lightheaded about Danton's attitude: it is the only stance which, given his insights into the nature of things, he can take toward an otherwise unbearable reality. Payne finds consolation by asserting a metaphysic, though a materialistic one, to be sure. Danton, though he declares himself an atheist at one point, can take no metaphysic seriously; his mode of thought undercuts all metaphysics.

In writing of Samuel Beckett, Frederick J. Hoffman

---

[6] One might note that the historical Thomas Paine professed a deistic creed and not the atheism which Büchner's character defends. See Rudolf Majut, "Georg Büchner and Some English Thinkers," *Modern Language Review,* XLVIII (1953), 313–14.

makes the generalization that "the philosophical ground of twentieth-century literature has shifted from metaphysics to epistemology. Characters who were formerly maneuvered within an accepted frame of extraliterary reference are now represented as seeking their own definitions and their own languages."[7] It is precisely in this respect that Büchner, specifically through his character Danton, strikes us as so contemporary. Characters such as Robespierre and Tom Payne assert their views with full and unquestioning metaphysical certainty; through the point of view which Danton provides, these certainties are continually undercut by being placed within an epistemological framework. In one instance after another, as we have seen, Danton insists on breaking down language to its empirical foundations—in the skepticism with which he treats his wife's use of the word *knowing*, in the way he systematically picks up and twists around some of Robespierre's most cherished terms —*conscience, virtue, innocence*—even in his habit of punning, which by its very nature implies a skepticism toward the ability of words to reflect and define a stable reality. The stale rhetoric which certain characters in the play speak is a sign of their all-too-naïve confidence in fixed ways of thought. Danton's antirhetoric is Büchner's way of demonstrating the falseness of this confidence, and, more fundamentally, of laying bare a world of uncertainties which it is the burden of the play to express so poignantly.

iii

A definition of Büchner's mode of dramaturgy in *Danton's Death* must first take into account his conscious deviations from more conventional forms of drama. At the beginning of the second act, when Camille warns Danton to flee—"Hurry, Danton, we have no time to lose"—one would ordinarily expect Danton (if, that is, he were a more traditional sort of tragic hero) either to pick up his coat and leave town before the police arrive, or at least to launch into a solemn statement of his fears, or his regret

[7] *Samuel Beckett: The Language of Self* (Carbondale, Ill., 1962), p. 59.

at leaving. Danton, of course, does no such thing, but instead twists Camille's words around, then loses himself in reflections which have nothing directly to do with the emergency at hand: "But time loses us. It's very boring, always putting on the shirt first and the pants over it and going to bed at night and crawling out again in the morning and always putting one foot before the other . . . That's very sad."

Camille's reply, "You sound like a child," attempts to take us back to the central line of plot, or rather what would seem to be the line of plot. But Danton, just as he confounds the conventional ways of thought of the other characters, also confounds our notions of how a dramatic plot should be developed. One could look at the play as having two lines of action. The first, consisting of Robespierre's actions against Danton and his friends, follows a fairly conventional series of events in political drama: it runs the usual gamut from the initial accusations against a dangerous element within the state through the decision to eliminate the opposition, and the subsequent arrest, trial, appeal, and execution. The second line of action, which consists of the Dantonists' resistance to Robespierre, could better be called a line of inaction, or antiplot. Indeed, there is no real resistance: the progress of the Danton plot consists largely of Danton's quite irrelevant reactions to what is happening to him. Occasionally, as in Camille's lines quoted above, we sense the possibility that the antiplot might tie itself to the Robespierre plot, that Danton might conceivably rise up to a cops-and-robbers game with his opponents. But Danton quickly frustrates any such expectations; his very refusal to resist is Büchner's way of asserting the meaninglessness of the sort of actions we usually associate with dramatic plots.

Not that the horrors of Robespierre's reign are to be interpreted as meaningless. These horrors are painted in very real dramatic terms; but Danton's insights into the nature of things create a perspective so foreign to the one in which the Robespierre plot takes place that he is rendered incapable of coping with these horrors in any effective way. The more conventional tragic hero at least makes an attempt to be "effective," and much of the conventional

287

tragic catharsis results from our admiration at his attempts to act in the face of overwhelming odds. But Danton remains passive and ineffectual from the beginning, at least in terms of the Robespierre plot. In his pioneering study of Büchner, Karl Viëtor has called Danton the first truly passive hero in German drama.[8] Through this passivity, which he betrays in his early speeches, we should be warned from the start not to look at the play in any of the usual Aristotelian ways. Thus, we cannot expect the hero at the end to experience a sudden grand moment of recognition. Danton pronounces essentially the same insights about the burdens of mortality at the beginning of the play as at the end; unlike an Oedipus or a Lear, he is never shown in an initial state of "innocence" from which, as a result of the play's action, he enters the world of "experience." He does not have to wrestle with his fate in order to become aware of the uselessness of action; he is aware of it from the start and, in fact, would prefer to have his fate over with as soon as possible. The increasing anguish of the play resides in the way he must bide his time for so long in full knowledge of what awaits him.

If the larger structure of the play can be defined through the juxtaposition of plot and antiplot, Büchner's mode of composition from moment to moment can be described through his alternation of contrasting scenes. As a very obvious instance, the first scene, with its bored dandies idling away their time with games, contrasts markedly with the second scene, which vividly depicts the discontented mob sweeping through the streets. Moreover, the introspection in which Danton engages so subtly in the first scene finds its opposite in the harsh rhetoric with which Robespierre quiets the crowd in the second. In the last two acts the series of poignant scenes of the Dantonists in prison alternate with scenes of dissident groups in the streets, of St. Just and his committee outdoing one another in exhibiting their talents at callousness, of carters making macabre jokes while waiting to pick up the next batch of victims for the guillotine. Julie's decision to join her husband in death is set next to a scene in which Citizen Dumas self-righteously defends sending his wife to the guillotine.

[8] *Georg Büchner: Politik, Dichtung, Wissenschaft*, p. 152.

The play of contrasts is not confined to the relationships between scenes, but is inherent in the internal organization of individual scenes. In discussing the opening scene, I noted the sustained contrast between the card-game conversation of Hérault and his partner and the more fundamental matters being discussed by Danton and his wife; in a similar way, the solemnity of the Tom Payne scene is contrasted with the joking between Danton and his friends as they are being led into prison. The most obvious function of Büchner's technique is that it enables him to comment ironically on the action without having to introduce characters to argue his own point of view to the reader. To put it another way, the method allows him to treat such seemingly negative characters as Robespierre and St. Just with a high degree of objectivity, even sympathy. St. Just, for instance, though my description may have made him seem direly villainous, would not strike an audience as an ordinary stage Machiavel; indeed, hearing his great oration, one might well feel momentarily persuaded by its resounding arguments. The air of objectivity which Büchner achieves is perhaps the dramatic equivalent of the kind of objectivity which novelists in the Flaubertian tradition were later to seek. By suppressing authorial commentary these novelists developed certain devices similar to Büchner's—ironic juxtapositions, the depiction of a character through the clichés in which he speaks and thinks—to enforce their meanings. And, like many modern novelists, Büchner places much of the burden of interpretation on the spectator. In what seems to me the most penetrating essay on the play yet to appear in English, Lee Baxandall attempts to describe the spectator's role:

What in fact happens here, in this seemingly passive, fragmented, lyrical and monologic play, is that the *spectator* has become the genuine "hero." Situated superior to the events which transpire on the stage, the spectator reflects and makes observations and formulations of what he sees, and he draws conclusions which transcend the knowledge of any of the characters. Deprived of classicism's easy-to-follow causal plot line, and deprived of classicism's summarizing declarations, the spectator assumes the burden of making decisions, a burden formerly reserved to the dramatic hero.[9]

I am none too sure that Danton himself is quite so neutral a hero as Baxandall implies: certainly Danton's comments on the other characters are meant to be taken quite seriously. Yet Danton too is subjected to criticism through Büchner's use of ironic contrasts: when Robespierre succeeds in quieting the crowd in the second scene, Danton's introspections, which had seemed so wise in the first scene, suddenly impress us with their ineffectualness.

To speak of ironic contrasts as the basis of Büchner's technique is perhaps to suggest too much; the word *contrasts* implies opposites, as though each scene reversed the tone and meaning of the preceding one. It would be more accurate to describe Büchner's technique as one of continually shifting perspectives. Just as our perspective upon Danton in the first scene is altered by our view of the street crowds and Robespierre's speech, so our perspective on Robespierre is altered by Marion's speech, with its ironic echo of his favorite word, *virtue;* the word, indeed, re-echoes at various moments in the play, each time creating a somewhat different perspective on Robespierre and his world.

The composition of individual scenes is marked not only by the sharp contrasts I have described, but by frequent, subtle changes of tone. The last of the scenes in the Conciergerie (Act IV, Scene 5), which records the prisoners' last moments together before they are carted through the streets to the guillotine, moves gradually through a series of moods—from the grim punning of the opening:

Danton.
Do you know what we'll do now?
The Voice.
Well?
Danton.
What you did all your life—*des vers.*

9 "Georg Büchner's *Danton's Death*," *Tulane Drama Review*, VI (1962), 148.

through a number of questions in which the prisoners translate their fears into universal terms reminiscent of the most agonized moments of *King Lear:*

Hérault.
Are we like young pigs that are beaten to death with rods for royal dinners so that their meat is tastier?
Danton.
Are we children who are roasted in the glowing Moloch arms of this world and are tickled with light rays so that the gods amuse themselves with the children's laughter?
Camille.
Is the ether with its golden eyes a bowl of golden carp, which stands at the table of the blessed gods, and the blessed gods laugh eternally and the fish die eternally and the gods eternally enjoy the iridescence of the death battle?

while the scene is finally resolved on a serene note:

Hérault.
. . . Be happy, Camille, the night will be beautiful. The clouds hang in the quiet evening sky like a dying Olympus with fading, sinking, godlike forms.

In other scenes the perspective shifts rapidly from moment to moment, most memorably perhaps in the promenade scene (Act II, Scene 2), in which Danton and Camille walk through the streets observing a multitude of little scenes—a whore and a soldier bantering with one another, an elegant lady, with her daughter, spouting polite platitudes, two gentlemen in absurd snatches of meaningless conversation—all woven together into a closely worked fabric.

By refusing to follow the classical pattern of plot development, in which every element would be subordinated to the central dramatic line, Büchner was able to create an expansive and rich texture of persons, atmospheres, and events. Though Danton's fate remains at the center of his vision, Büchner has portrayed the larger historical milieu with a breadth and vigor that still seem remarkable in an age such as ours, which can take for granted the expansive methods of Brechtian epic theater. "The dramatic poet is in my eyes nothing but a writer of history," Büchner wrote in a letter defending his use of "vulgarities" in the play. "He is superior to the latter, however, in that he re-creates history a second time for us. Instead of telling us a dry story, he places us directly into the life of earlier times, giving us characters instead of characteristics and figures instead of descriptions." The directness and objectivity which he sought were possible only by means of the dramatic method he employed.

Still, despite the sudden contrasts and the constant modulations of tone, *Danton's Death* builds steadily in intensity and, in its final scenes, achieves a climax as moving and, in fact, as terrifying as that of any German drama before or after. The comic and absurd moments that alternate with the more somber ones serve not so much to mitigate the tragic effect, but, rather like the gravedigger scene in *Hamlet,* to increase it. The scene of the joking carters is sandwiched between one of the prison scenes and the passage in which Lucile Desmoulins, already close to madness, comes to speak to her husband through the window of the prison. For the hard-headed modern reader Lucile's agitated lines—"Listen! People say you have to die, and they make such serious faces. Die! The faces make me laugh"—these lines seem moving at this point precisely because Büchner has refused to bully the reader into a somber mood; the comedy, rather than undercutting the tragedy, works to validate it and augment it.

Much of the pathos of the final scenes, moreover, comes from the manner in which Büchner has chosen to develop the two grieving women, Lucile and Julie. Julie's death, in fact, has a formality and solemnity about it reminiscent— at least if we look at it out of context—of death scenes in earlier tragedies (for example, that of Shakespeare's Juliet):

. . . I don't want to let him wait for a moment. (*She takes out a phial.*) Come, dearest priest, your amen makes us go to sleep. (*She goes to the window.*) Parting is so pleasant; I just have to close the door behind me.

Julie's lines, not only here but throughout the play, show a purity of expression rare in a work whose more sympathetic characters speak with tough-minded irony and whose unsympathetic characters are exposed to us through the naïveté of their rhetoric.

It is significant that Büchner, despite lifting from his sources innumerable lines spoken by Robespierre and Danton, diverged radically from his sources in his treatment of Julie and Lucile: the real Julie (whose name was Sébastienne-Louise) was a girl who had been married to Danton for only six months at the time of his death and who herself was remarried a few years later, while the real Lucile neither went mad nor died voluntarily, but was executed for attempting to free her husband. But both women, as Büchner created them, were necessary to the design of the play, for both, in their various ways, could express a kind of pathos which their much more Stoic-minded husbands could not have voiced so directly. In the last Conciergerie scene the prisoners admit the uselessness of their Stoicism and ask each other why they cannot "scream and whine as it suits you"; yet they are never able to release their emotions with the unself-conscious force of an Oedipus or a Lear. Even Lucile is unable to purge her emotions through screaming, though she tries to scream on the streets:

. . . I'll sit on the ground and scream so that everything will stop moving out of fright—everything will stand still, nothing will move. (*She sits down, covers her eyes and screams. After a pause she arises.*) It doesn't help—it's all still the same, the houses, the street, the wind blows, the clouds move—I suppose we must bear it.

The uselessness of Lucile's screaming is emblematic, I think, of Büchner's attitude toward older conceptions of tragedy; yet through his honesty in refusing to let her indulge in the rhetoric of a tragic pose, we feel all the more prepared to assent emotionally to the overwhelmingly tragic facts of the play.

Until relatively recent times *Danton's Death* was looked upon as a primarily political drama, and, in particular, as a kind of apology for the French Revolution. For instance, the German historian Treitschke, writing in the late nineteenth century, took it for granted that the play was essentially a reflection of Büchner's radical doctrines:

> Among all his [Büchner's] contemporaries only Carlyle was able to portray the horrors of those days [the Reign of Terror] with such terrifying truth, but while the Scot passionately expressed his moral disgust at these events, the German, in all seriousness, thought of glorifying the Revolution through a work which can only arouse a feeling of abhorrence. One wonders if this, the most talented writer of the era of Young Germany, might perhaps have been able to outgrow his disconsolate materialism.[10]

If a conservative such as Treitschke could attack the play on political grounds, radicals could, by the same token, praise the doctrines which they thought they discerned in it. In 1886, when it was still little known in German, the play was printed in a German-language edition in America in a series entitled the "Socialistic Library," designed for liberal-minded German immigrants.[11] Some of its early German stage productions, most notably the famous Max Reinhardt version in Berlin in 1916, succeeded in continuing this view of the drama by making the Paris mobs seem the play's hero.[12] The distinguished Marxist critic Georg Lukács would have it that Büchner divided his sympathy between Danton, Robespierre and St. Just, and that in Danton he was attempting to depict an essentially eigh-

---

[10] Heinrich von Treitschke, *Deutsche Geschichte im neunzehnten Jahrhundert* (Leipzig, 1907), IV, 434.

[11] See Ralph P. Rosenberg, "Georg Büchner's Early Reception in America," *Journal of English and Germanic Philology*, XLIV (1945), 270–73.

[12] See Ingeborg Strudthoff, *Die Rezeption Georg Büchners durch das deutsche Theater* (Berlin, 1957), pp. 52–55.

teenth-century mind who, in contrast to Robespierre, lacked insight into the nature of the revolutionary process.[13]

All these views of the play, rightist and leftist alike, obviously start from the premise that since Büchner led a revolutionary conspiracy and wrote the inflammatory *Hessian Messenger, ergo* his dramatic work attempted to propound a revolutionary thesis. In the years immediately following the second world war, Büchner's critics sometimes went to an opposite extreme; looking at the play totally from Danton's point of view, and taking some of the more despairing lines—for instance, Danton's "The world is chaos. Nothingness is the world-god yet to be born"—as their prime texts, they often read the play as an essentially nihilist tract.[14] If one must choose between extremes, there is doubtless more truth to the latter interpretation, if only to the extent that Danton's perspective on reality seems more convincing than that of Robespierre or of the crowd. But *Danton's Death,* indeed, all of Büchner's works, stubbornly resist being pigeon-holed into thesis categories: his best German critics of the last few years, moreover, have been at pains to work out the meaning of his plays through detailed analyses of the texts, without preconceptions about any ideologies that might lie beneath them.[15]

Yet I should maintain that *Danton's Death* is a profoundly political drama, though surely not in the old-fashioned sense of the term, which would see such a work as an attempt to propagate a particular political view.

---

[13] "Der faschistisch verfälschte und der wirkliche Georg Büchner," in *Deutsche Realisten des neunzehnten Jahrhunderts* (Berlin, 1952), pp. 75–78. For a more sensitive Marxist interpretation of the play, see Hans Mayer, *Georg Büchner und seine Zeit* (Berlin, 1960), pp. 182–207.

[14] The most extreme nihilist interpretation is that of Robert Mühlher, "Georg Büchner und die Mythologie des Nihilismus," in *Dichtung der Krise* (Vienna, 1951), pp. 97–146. Benno von Wiese's interpretation in *Die deutsche Tragödie von Lessing bis Hebbel,* II, 309–33, also stresses the nihilistic element, but far more moderately and responsibly than Mühlher does.

[15] For instance, Walter Höllerer, in his chapter on *Danton's Death* contributed to *Das deutsche Drama,* ed. Benno von Wiese (Düsseldorf, 1962), II, 65–88; Gerhart Baumann, *Georg Büchner: Die dramatische Ausdruckswelt* (Göttingen, 1961), pp. 9–87; and Wolfgang Martens, "Ideologie und Verzweiflung: Religiöse Motive in Büchners Revolutionsdrama," *Euphorion,* LIV (1960), 83–108.

Rather, *Danton's Death* is political in another, less easily discernible sense: if I may borrow from Irving Howe's definition of the political novel—a definition based on his readings of works such as *The Charterhouse of Parma, The Possessed, The Princess Casamassima*—the play is political through its attempt "to show the relation between theory and experience, between the ideology that has been preconceived and the tangle of feelings and relationships [the author] is trying to represent."[16] Similarly to the political novels which Howe discusses, *Danton's Death* seeks to demonstrate the tragic gap between political ideals and political actualities, to examine, for instance, the paralyzing effect that the political process can have on men of good will such as Danton and his friends. Although the play has much to say about the nature of personal relationships, it is not primarily a drama of private or social experience in the way that the dramas of Chekhov or Strindberg or Beckett are. In *Danton's Death* the political dimension is always discernible; Danton's private despair, for example, gains meaning precisely because we measure it against the smug certainties and optimistic cant of Robespierre.

It is significant that Büchner chose to set his play in the darkest hour of the Revolution, when the great ideals which had once motivated all his characters were put to their most bitter test. The masses at this point are thoroughly disillusioned and can be kept in tow only through the shrewdest demagoguery; the revolutionary leaders can maintain their power only through their systematic annihilation of all conceivable subversion; traditional human relationships—between husband and wife (Danton and Julie, Camille and Lucile), or between life-long friends (Camille and Robespierre had been friends in school)— are threatened at the root. Out of this dramatic image emerge a series of insights into the nature of politics—that ideals, in the face of challenging events, can become hardened into ideology; that the ideology which a man embraces is a consequence of his personal needs, above all, his need to survive; that, in the light of overpowering and uncontrollable forces, the very need to survive is a questionable

---

16 *Politics and the Novel* (New York, 1957), p. 22.

value. The political situation which Büchner depicts is inextricably bound up with the personal situations of his characters, as well as with their metaphysical speculations. Through the techniques which Büchner employs—the ironic contrasts, the air of objectivity with which each of the characters seems to be created—he rarely needs to insist directly on the connections between the political and the personal realms; he does so only at moments, as when Danton attempts to cut down Robespierre's pretensions to his face—"Each one acts according to his nature, that means he does what is good for him." For the most part Büchner lets the play speak for itself; the reader is left to size up Robespierre's pronouncements both on their own rhetorical merits and through the meanings they take on through the context with which they are surrounded.

If we insist on tying the play to the author's biography, we could say it is less Büchner the Revolutionist than Büchner the Scientist who speaks to us in the drama. Indeed, the strong antiteleological bent of Büchner's inaugural lecture in Zurich, above all, his insistence in this lecture that "nature does not exhaust itself through an infinite chain of causes, each determined by the last, but is in all its manifestations sufficient unto itself"[17]—such a statement, though part of a lecture on the cranial nerves, forms a kind of correlative to his dramatic method.

Not that I mean to underestimate the intensity of Büchner's political commitment. But if *Danton's Death* is in certain respects a drama about political disillusionment, one must point out that some of Danton's most despairing lines are echoed by statements that we find in Büchner's letters well before the conspiracy in which he was engaged in 1834. Compare, for instance, these lines written after his meningitis—"O, what miserable, screeching musicians we are! This groaning on our torture-rack, could it be there only that it may pass through the gaps in the clouds and, echoing further and further on its way, die like a breath of melody in celestial ears?"[18] with these lines spoken by Danton in the last scene in the Conciergerie—"But we are

[17] *Georg Büchner: Werke und Briefe*, Fritz Bergemann, ed. (Wiesbaden, 1958), p. 350.
[18] "Some Büchner Letters in Translation," trans. K. W. Maurer, *German Life and Letters*, VIII (1954), 51.

the poor musicians and our bodies the instruments. Are those horrible sounds they scratch out only there to rise up higher and higher and finally die away as a sensual breath in heavenly ears?"

By the same token Büchner's letters after the time of *Danton's Death* show his continued hopes for fundamental changes in the economic and social structure of the German states, though he usually tempers these hopes with skepticism about the immediate means by which these changes might be wrought.[19] Above all, one must not attempt to tie the revolutionary doctrines of the *Hessian Messenger* to those which Büchner attributes to Robespierre and his committee. For one thing, the *Messenger* is a pamphlet directed against tyranny, both economic and political; the revolutionary power at the period he has chosen to set the play has itself become a tyranny of the most uncompromising sort. Moreover, Büchner's prose in the *Messenger* has a concreteness and a liveliness which we never find in the pronouncements of Robespierre and St. Just. The pamphlet is passionate and earthy at once; its very extravagance gives it an appealing quality which we rarely feel in the political rhetoric of the past—

Go to Darmstadt once and see how the lords are amusing themselves there with your money, and then tell your starving wives and children that strangers' stomachs are thriving marvelously on their bread, tell them about the beautiful clothes dyed in their sweat and the dainty ribbons cut from the calluses on their hands, tell them about the stately houses built from the bones of the people; and then crawl into your smoky huts. . . .[20]

I have chosen to quote this passage not only because it exemplifies the flavor that pervades the pamphlet as a whole, but because its idea is echoed at one point in *Danton's Death*, in a speech by a citizen in the mob: "Danton has fancy clothes, Danton has a nice house, Danton has a beautiful wife, he bathes in Burgundy wine, eats venison

---

[19] See, for instance, two of his letters to Gutzkow, in Bergemann, pp. 396, 412. [In this edition, pp. 249–50 and 248.]

[20] *Ibid.*, p. 339.

from silver plates, and sleeps with your wives and daughters when he's drunk. Danton was poor like you." The difference in the effect of the two passages could not be greater. The citizen's speech comes directly after Danton has lost his appeal before the tribunal and forcibly been removed from the courtroom. Our sympathies are unquestionably with Danton at this point, especially so because in the course of this single speech the crowd is shown turning against Danton. Büchner, as we can see, was well aware of the differences between the demands imposed by dogma and drama. He underlined his awareness of this difference in a letter written to his family a year after completing the play; denying his adherence to the doctrines of the literary radicals known as Young Germany (doctrines far less extreme, for that matter, than the ones he had advocated in the *Messenger*), he writes: "I go my own way and remain in the field of drama which has nothing to do with all these controversial issues. I draw my characters in accordance with Nature and History and laugh at those who would like to make me responsible for their morality or immorality."[21]

Still, one can discern a particular mode of commitment, social more than political in nature, which thoroughly pervades all Büchner's works. I refer to his stress on the reality of human suffering. One need not wonder that it is possible for an ingenious stage director to portray the Parisian mob in a favorable light. Although it is not hard for a reader to note that Büchner's mob is every bit as unreliable and fickle as Shakespeare's in *Coriolanus*, Büchner presents their grievances with a real, if also hard-headed sympathy.

But suffering is not limited to the crowd; it is shared by characters of all factions, by Robespierre in his monologue after his confrontation with Danton, by Danton and his friends in the Conciergerie. Thomas Payne's line "The smallest twinge of pain—and may it stir only in a single atom—makes a rent in Creation from top to bottom," symbolizes an attitude and a commitment which underlies Büchner's whole poetic world. This human sympathy which Büchner manifests so all-pervasively is related, I think, to

---

21 "From Georg Büchner's Letters," trans. Maurice Edwards, *Tulane Drama Review*, VI (1962), 134–35.

the dramatic sympathy which he grants his characters and which, in turn, underlies his dramatic technique. Robespierre, Danton, Payne, Marion, Lucile, the starving people of Paris—all are fellow sufferers, whatever their mutual antagonisms and differences in personality. "People call me a scoffer," he once wrote in a letter to his family; "it is true, I often laugh at people; yet I don't laugh at *how* someone is a human being, but simply at the fact *that* he is a human being, for which of course he is not to blame, and I often laugh at myself as one who shares his fate."[22] The piety toward his fellow beings which he expresses here is fundamental to his refusal to pass judgment directly on his characters, but rather to present them in all their immediacy, for what they are; it is an attitude, moreover, which more surely shapes his work than any of the doctrines, political or philosophical, which have been applied to interpret it.

v

In contrast to most of the German Classical dramas, *Danton's Death* is in prose, yet in the impression it leaves it is one of the most poetic of German plays. For one thing, it displays a luxuriance of metaphor which German dramatic blank verse had insisted on doing without. Even the abstract Robespierre muses metaphorically to himself in his monologue: "Night snores over the earth and wallows in wild dreams." Danton's speeches, especially in the prison scenes, not only contain an amazing number of poetic figures, but they also show a complexity of tone and a concentration of language which the rhetorical conventions of German Classical drama normally excluded from dramatic verse. Take the following lines: "It's as if I'm smelling already. My dear body, I'll hold my nose and imagine that you're a woman, sweating and stinking after the dance, and pay you compliments. We've often passed the time with each other already." Fear of death, courtliness of manner, tender regret about the fleetingness of past pleasures—all are fused together in this image with a characteristically

22 Bergemann, pp. 377–78.

Shakespearean boldness. Moreover, the final Conciergerie scene, in which the prisoners voice their fears in a series of lyrical outbursts, has a grandeur of language which Büchner was never to surpass, for the type of dramatic structure toward which he moved in his remaining works left no opportunity for such displays of eloquence.

Yet *Danton's Death* is surely not poetic in the nineteenth-century sense of the term—its bawdiness and its lack of solemnity would hardly have made such a term suitable—but in a peculiarly modern sense, in the way that we think of works such as Joyce's *Ulysses* or the plays of Bertolt Brecht as poetic. Like these works of our own century, it is able to achieve a poetic effect for us only through its conscious refusal to seem poetic in any traditional way. The ironic contrasts, the bantering of the mob, Danton's jibes at Robespierre's pompousness—all these serve as a kind of guarantee that the drama will not get rhetorically out of hand, that the deeply moving dramatic effects toward which the play is building will be backed up by a tough-minded attitude toward all human experience. The pathos of Lucile's and Julie's final speeches, or of Camille's tender expressions about his wife in the last act, is possible only because of the down-to-earth context which Büchner has built up throughout the play. Danton's *de profundis* cry, "Are we children who are roasted in the glowing Moloch arms of this world and are tickled with light rays so that the gods amuse themselves with the children's laughter?" carries such great emotional weight precisely because of the surprise we feel at words like *roasted* and *tickled*, which would seem quite indecorous in more conventionally poetic surroundings. Like innumerable modern writers, Büchner allows himself to release feeling by first assuring his audience, as it were, that he has properly screened the feelings he chooses to display.

In something of the same way he allows Danton to achieve the stature of a hero only by first refusing him the conventional heroic attributes. At first glance, Danton, with his continual complaints of ennui, seems like one of the early examples in drama of the hero as aesthete. The notions he voices—on the meaninglessness of ordinary routine, on the burdens of time, on human loneliness—have much in common with the views of a whole tradition of characters from Werther through J. Alfred Prufrock.[23] Yet Danton maintains a sturdiness and a dignity uncommon among such heroes. We find in him none of Werther's helplessness or self-pity, none of Prufrock's absurdity, nor does he indulge in the self-glorification of Byron's various marked men, or in the over-refined sensibilities of Chekhov's superfluous country gentlemen. What ties him to this tradition of characters, besides some of the generalities on life they express in common, is the fact that he impresses us at first as a consciously conceived anti-hero.

The anti-hero is only possible in a literary tradition which has already represented real heroes—successful men of action such as Goethe's Götz von Berlichingen, or heroes of the mind such as Schiller's Mary Stuart and Joan of Arc, who by dint of will achieve at least an inward victory in the face of inevitable doom. By presenting an anti-hero such as Danton, Büchner implies that such earlier forms of heroism were possible only in a less self-conscious stage of human development; being a hero in Büchner's world means being a bit crude and even ludicrous. The men of action and the men of will in *Danton's Death* are characters such as Robespierre and St. Just. Robespierre's success in getting the crowd under control in the second scene contrasts startlingly with the loquacious passivity which Danton had demonstrated at the opening, yet through Danton's insights into Robespierre's motives (as well as through the crudity of the rhetoric with which the latter exposes himself), Robespierre ultimately seems somewhat naïve and absurd in his busy political doings. Danton impresses us throughout as mentally and morally superior to his opponent and thus makes the value of political activity seem at best a questionable one. "I don't give him six months. I'm dragging him down with me," Danton says of Robespierre just before his execution, and the audience, with its hindsight into subsequent history, sees yet another confirmation of the uselessness of all Robespierre's efforts. (One might note that Danton's prophecy of Robespierre's imminent end was contained in

---

[23] See, for instance, Rudolf Majut's detailed study of the literary traditions—both before and after Büchner—to which characters such as Danton and Leonce belong. *Studien um Büchner: Untersuchungen zur Geschichte der problematischen Natur* (Berlin, 1932).

Büchner's sources and was thus no mere contrivance by which he could gain an easy plus-mark for his hero.)

The superiority we see in Danton is earned not only through his exposure of the absurdity of Robespierre and others, but through the honesty with which he views even his own absurdity and that of the whole human condition. Among the many metaphors he chooses to symbolize the absurdity of human action is the ambition of children to be promoted in school: "From first grade to second, from second to third, and so on? I'm sick of school benches, I've gotten calluses on my backside like a monkey from sitting on them." It is characteristic that Danton's generalizations about life not only take such metaphorical form, but that he places himself in such absurd postures. He resolutely refuses to assume the more comfortable poses to which his unfortunate fate might well have entitled him. He eschews self-pity, but is honest enough about his fears of death. He is never even tempted by the consolations that accompany martyrdom. The closest he comes to a pose—and this only through his refusal to indulge himself emotionally—is Stoicism; yet even this is seen through and rejected: "[The Stoics] worked out for themselves a very comfortable feeling of self-satisfaction. It's not such a bad idea to drape yourself in a toga and look around to see if you throw a long shadow." His only pose, if it is a pose at all, is his joking. His deepest fears are expressed in jokes, his affections toward his friends are conveyed jokingly (though with an underlying seriousness), his last words to the executioner are a joke. To the modern mind joking is perhaps the noblest stance a person can assume in the face of inevitable doom; and Danton, even if he cannot die sword in hand like Hamlet, gains a certain nobility for us through his refusal to assume at least any of the conventional poses.

But Danton's doom is not inevitable at the *start* of the play. By a strange paradox, although the image of the world that we are presented with from the beginning is a hopeless one, it is amply clear that Danton might have avoided death by escaping in time. In contrast to the traditional tragic hero, who comes to see the world as black only when he realizes that his own doom is inevitable, Danton has no illusions about the world from the start and quietly wills his doom. Büchner of course never makes clear to us whether

Danton's failure to save himself was a consequence of his world-view or whether his world-view was a rationalization of a psychological paralysis which precluded even the action of escape: such causal explanations could not (and need not) be made within the confines of the dramatic method to which Büchner subjected himself in writing the play. In something of the same way he never makes clear whether Danton expected that his refusal to escape would result in his arrest, or whether he really believed his much repeated statement that the committee would not dare to arrest an old fellow revolutionary like himself. Both sides of this ambiguity are expressed in his words when he enters the prison: "A stroke is the best death. Would you rather be sick before it? And—I didn't believe they would dare." By leaving both possibilities open (and both possibilities were suggested by Büchner's sources), Büchner is able to maintain our sense of Danton's world-weariness and at the same time to suggest a kind of reckless nonchalance in him.[24]

This nonchalance, combined as it is with an unthinking confidence in his personal security, is the only indication we get in the play of that heroic side of Danton which, two years before, had been able to save the Republic in the face of enemy armies. We are reminded of Danton's past heroism on a number of occasions, but the present Danton generally looks back at his past actions with self-recrimination. As a man of action he had been forced into brutalities —most notably the September Massacres—which, from his present introspective state of mind, haunt him in his sleep with a turbulence reminiscent of the night-thoughts of Lady Macbeth. "You talked of ugly sins and then you moaned, 'September!'" Julie tells him, trying to shake him out of his self-tormenting trance. But later, before the Revolutionary Tribunal, his accusers treat him with such condescension

---

[24] It is worth noting that Büchner chose to omit an important detail which his sources suggested at this point—Lacroix's reproach that Danton's failure to heed the warnings he had received was responsible for the arrest of his friends: "You knew it," cried Lacroix, "and you failed to act! Now see the result of your habitual sloth; it has caused our downfall" (quoted by Thieberger, p. 45). Büchner's inclusion of this reproach would have undercut the audience's sense of the unquestioningly loyal attitude which Danton's friends seem to have toward him.

that his anger is kindled and he displays something of the heroic spirit which he had shown in the past: "On the Field of Mars I declared war on the monarchy; I defeated it on the 10th of August, I killed it on the 21st of January and threw a king's head down as a gauntlet before all monarchs." Several scenes later, when he presents his appeal to the Tribunal (Act III, Scene 9), he accuses his accusers with all the vehemence (though without the clichés) of a Robespierre or a St. Just; his tirade, indeed, is so powerfully persuasive that the audience rallies to his side and the Tribunal is forced to remove him and his fellow prisoners before they can turn the tide to their cause. Even the anti-hero has his moments of traditional heroism.

If Danton displays a heroic quality that sometimes confounds his anti-heroic pretensions, he also possesses an immense vitality which belies the resignation he professes throughout the play. This vitality is inherent in the language he speaks, in the joking, in the poetic evocation of his fears, in the endless succession of metaphors he contrives to express his resignation. One often, in fact, feels as though his general passivity is compensated for by a corresponding degree of verbal activity. But this vitality of language is not confined to Danton alone, it is something one feels in the play as a whole; the very richness of its poetry gives the play a certain exuberance that almost cancels out the cynicism and despair that seem to emanate from it. Indeed, as Egon Schwarz has suggested, wit functions throughout Büchner's dramas as a kind of alternative to the nihilism which they so often attempt to express.[25] Schwarz cites a passage from *Danton's Death* as characteristic: a young man sporting a handkerchief is accosted by the mob, who scream: "He's got a handkerchief! An aristocrat! String him up [on the lamppost]! String him up!" As they are about to string him up, he replies, "All right, but that won't make things any brighter." The mob, surprised by his show of wit, decide to let him go.

Although the wit and the general verbal exuberance suggest at least a possible release from the bleakness of the world which Büchner has created, one must not underesti-

[25] "Tod und Witz im Werke Georg Büchners," *Monatshefte für den deutschen Unterricht*, XLVI (1954), 123–36.

305

mate the dark power which issues from this world. The central image out of which *Danton's Death* is built is that of an upside-down world, one in which all order has been inverted. Büchner sensed the possibilities of this image in a letter he wrote two years before the play:

> I studied the history of the Revolution. I felt as if I were crushed under the terrible fatalism of history. I find in human nature a horrifying sameness, in the human condition an inescapable force, granted to all and to no one. The individual merely foam on the waves, greatness sheer chance, the mastery of genius a puppet play, a ludicrous struggle against an iron law: to recognize it is our utmost achievement, to control it is impossible.

The Reign of Terror, especially in that later stage of it which Büchner chose to depict, provided the perfect scenic embodiment for Danton's notions about the meaninglessness of life. Within this inverted image, all expressions relative to a normal state of things—expressions of affection, petty jealousies, fear of showing bad manners—come to seem hopelessly absurd. "It's really shameful how one's hair and nails grow here," Lacroix complains about his stay in prison, after which Hérault continues the joke: "Watch out —you're sneezing sand into my face."

Lacroix and Hérault of course are conscious of the absurdity of their remarks, but the less shrewd characters of the play—those not capable of the "utmost achievement" of recognizing the "iron law" of which Büchner speaks in the letter quoted above—are trapped by their own absurdity whenever they express themselves in normal terms. Take, for instance, the conversation of three women on the street directly after the execution of Danton and his friends:

First Woman.
A good-looking man, that Hérault.
Second Woman.
When he stood at the Arch of Triumph during the Constitutional Celebration, I thought, "He'll look good next to the guillotine, he will." That was sort of a hunch.

Third Woman.
    Yes, you got to see people in all kinds of situations.
    It's good that dying's being made public now.

Sentiments that would be perfectly acceptable in a normal world—praise for a man's looks, the desire to know what other people are really like—become not only comic and absurd in this abnormal context, but in the light of all that has happened in the play, they achieve a positively chilling effect. Indeed, Büchner's various allusions to a normal world only serve to make the inverted world all the more frightening.

The vision of life that emerges from this collocation of worlds is a profoundly modern one, and but a step or two removed from that of such a modern writer as Kafka. The absurdities out of which Kafka's world is built are obviously far greater in number and intensity than those we find in Büchner. And to achieve his characteristic effects Kafka has had to distort our conceptions of reality to the point where, though we recognize the relation of his world to our everyday world, we are also aware that his world has the essential lineaments of a dream. In Büchner, at least in *Danton's Death*, we are never allowed to feel we are witnessing a dream distortion. The inverted world of the Reign of Terror is presented to us as a mimetic representation of a recognizably real world, with its backgrounds minutely filled in. It is history, after all.

In the final reckoning the only escape from the world of this play is death. Danton made this clear, of course, on the first page of the text, and the play simply goes on to confirm his statement. Of the various ways that the characters in the play go to their death, only Julie's is the kind one is accustomed to find in earlier tragic dramas. Her death has no trace of the absurd about it; she meets it voluntarily, nobly, self-sacrificingly, as though asserting that traditional values still have some meaning. In sharp contrast, Danton and his friends go passively to their death, and in full awareness of its lack of meaning. Unlike such heroes as Goethe's Egmont or Schiller's Joan of Arc they can never tell themselves that they died for any higher cause. The very manner of their execution underscores the meaninglessness of their deaths. "If only it were a fight with hands and teeth! . . . To be killed so mechanically!" Danton cries out in the Conciergerie. In his last words to the executioner, when he speaks of heads accidentally kissing as they fall into the basket, he recognizes the total lack of dignity in such a death.

Had Büchner ended the drama directly after the execution, the effect of the ending would have been similar to the effect of K's death at the end of Kafka's *The Trial:* a passive, meaningless death as a final, none-too-surprising confirmation of the world-view that has been suggested throughout each work. But Büchner chose to work out still another possibility latent within his image of an inverted world; by closing the play with Lucile's death (or, more precisely, her arrest) he was able to give the play a memorably assertive ending that resounded with a series of ironies. I noted earlier that the real-life prototype of Lucile was arrested for far more conventional reasons; but one of Büchner's sources spoke of a number of women who, lacking the courage to take poison, shouted "Long live the king" in full certainty of dying shortly thereafter.[26] Lucile's gesture has the willfulness we associate with many a martyr's death. Yet it is the very opposite of martyrdom: whereas a martyr dies with his most sacred beliefs on his lips, Lucile wills her death by shouting words that mean nothing to her, in fact, words she quite obviously disbelieves in. Moreover, the idea occurs to her quite suddenly, almost as a whim. Her gesture is of course an absurd one, but— quite in contrast to Julie's suicide, which sought to affirm traditional values—it represents the only self-assertive gesture that fully recognizes the absurdity of the inverted world in which she finds herself. In her willful absurdity she has assumed a kind of heroic stance—one which was not granted to Danton and his friends. Yet we must also remember that Büchner depicts her as mad in her final scenes: only in madness, he implies, can one perform an act that has a meaning in a meaningless world.

[26] Thieberger, p. 52.

CORRESPONDENCE ON *DANTON'S DEATH*

[Büchner wrote *Danton's Death* in approximately five weeks during January–February 1835 while living at home. The circumstances were doubly trying. He had already been interrogated by the authorities concerning his revolutionary activities in Giessen, and he was in constant fear of arrest. By writing and finding a publisher for his play he hoped to acquire enough money to flee to Strasbourg, but the plan had to be kept secret from his father. With the help of his brother Wilhelm he managed to write the play while giving his parents the impression that he was immersed in his studies of anatomy. The manuscript was mailed to another young author, Karl Gutzkow (1811–1878).

At this time Gutzkow was a contributor to *Das Literaturblatt* and was acquainted with a number of literary figures and publishers. In 1835 his novel, *Wally the Doubter*, appeared. The heroine of the work is a German girl of good stock who comes into fatal conflict with the mores of her time. The novel was regarded as a glorification of sensuality, and Gutzkow was sent to jail for a month. After his release he became the editor of the literary supplement (*Phönix*) of a Frankfurt newspaper and of *Deutsche Revue*. He was a leading figure among the journalistically oriented "Young Germans," a group of liberal reformers. Later he became a court playwright at the Dresden Theater. His most successful drama was *Uriel Acosta* (1846), a tragedy dealing with religious tolerance.

The letters document the crises and annoyances surrounding the writing and early reception of the play, which in all likelihood would not have been published in Büchner's lifetime without the help of Gutzkow. In his letters to his parents Büchner hoped to "explain" the play in such a way that they would not be overly offended by it. His father's liberal idealism focused on the heroic figure of Napoleon but did not concern itself with the economic situation of the European masses; his mother, a devotee of the characteristically German Christian-Romantic tradition, harbored a somewhat sentimental attitude to the arts. Of great significance are his views on the dramatist as a writer of history—an extension of the opinions expressed by Camille and Danton in the beginning of Act Two, Scene 3 of *Danton's Death*. (See also the essay on *The Hessian Messenger*, pages 241ff.)]

Wilhelm Büchner to Karl Emil Franzos

[*Pfungstadt, December 23, 1878*]

My father . . . a contemporary of the great French Revolution, had taken part as a military doctor in several campaigns with Dutch troops, which at that time were under French command. . . . He liked to recount and elaborate on his experiences by reading to us in the evening from the periodical *Our Times*. We responded with great enthusiasm. Considering the liberal spirit of our family, it is probable that these readings had a particular influence on Georg and inspired *Danton's Death*.

Georg Büchner to Wilhelm Büchner
(QUOTED BY KARL EMIL FRANZOS)

I'm writing in a fever, but that's not hurting my work— to the contrary! Besides, I have no choice, I can't afford to rest until I've put Danton under the guillotine, and most of all I need money, money!

Wilhelm Büchner to Karl Emil Franzos

[*Scheveningen, September 9, 1878*]

What could he do in Strasbourg without any financial means? This desire to earn money motivated him to set down in great haste the drama *Danton's Death*, which he had long been carrying around in his head. And how little money, for so much work! One hundred guilders! The last days of my stay in Darmstadt passed in terrible excitement. I had mailed the manuscript for him, and then came moments of release and expectation. At that time he asked me for two coins which would suffice to allow him to cross the border.

Georg Büchner to the publisher Sauerländer

[*Darmstadt, February 21, 1835*]

Most honored Sir: I am privileged to send you a manuscript along with this letter. It is an attempted dramatization of recent history. If you should be inclined to undertake its publication, then I beg you to inform me as soon as possible. . . . I would be very grateful if you would send the enclosed letter [see below] and the drama to Mr. Karl Gutzkow for his perusal.

Georg Büchner to Karl Gutzkow

[*Darmstadt, February 21, 1835*]

Dear Sir: You may have possibly made the observation, or in more unfortunate circumstances experienced, that there exists a degree of misery which silences all attempts at consideration and feeling. There are people who say that in this case one ought rather starve oneself out of existence, but I could pick a refutation of this idea off the streets: a captain, recently gone blind, explains that he would shoot himself if only he were not forced to remain alive so that his pension could support his family. That is horrifying. You will realize that similar circumstances may exist which restrain one from throwing one's body from the wreck of this world into the water like an anchor, and you will therefore not be surprised that I open your door, step into your room, place a manuscript on your chest, and ask for alms. I beg you to read the manuscript as quickly as possible, to recommend it to Mr. Sauerländer if your conscience as a critic should allow you to do so, and to answer immediately. Concerning the work itself I can only say that unfortunate circumstances forced me to write it in about five weeks. I say this to influence your judgment about the author, not about the drama in and of itself. I do not know myself what I should do with it; I only know that I have every reason to blush before history, but I console myself with the thought that all poets, excepting Shakespeare, stand before history and nature like schoolboys.

I repeat my plea for a speedy response. In the event of a favorable reaction, a few lines from your hand—if they reach me before next Wednesday—would save an unfortunate man from very sorry circumstances.

If the tone of this letter should disturb you, please consider that it is easier for me to beg in rags than to present a plea in a frock coat, and almost easier to say, with a pistol in my hand: your money or your life! than to whisper with trembling lips: may God reward me!

Karl Gutzkow to Georg Büchner

[*Frankfurt, February 25, 1835*]

Honored Sir: A few words in great haste. I like your drama very much, and I will recommend it to Sauerländer; however, theatrical pieces are not enticing commodities for publishers. You must therefore be content with modest payments. It would please me if this preliminary review would help raise your spirits somewhat. More in a few days!

Karl Gutzkow to Georg Büchner

[*Frankfurt, February 28, 1835*]

Honored Sir: You should have written to me what you expect as a payment for *Danton*. Sauerländer cannot give much (least of all what your work is worth). It is a difficult decision for him to publish your manuscript, for however favorable the reviews may be, plays sell very poorly these days. The paper hardly pays for itself. I know that. These are no figures of speech. Calculate the smallest amount you need at present, resign yourself to no great expectations, and try to assure yourself an income through additional writings, such as for the *Phönix*, to which I invite you.

Karl Gutzkow to Georg Büchner

[Frankfurt, March 3, 1835]

Honored Sir: Sauerländer will give you ten Friedrichsdor under the condition that he may use parts of the drama for the *Phönix*, and that you agree to the elimination of your imaginative "buds of mercury" and of all that reminds one of the gutters of Frankfurt and Berlin. I am content with what you have written, but Sauerländer is a family man who has produced seven legitimate children in the holy bed of matrimony. I am already a nightmare to him with my ambiguities; how much more so are you with your blunt and obvious references to one particular subject! So this, then, is very necessary.

It seems as if you are in a great hurry. Where do you wish to go? Is the ground really burning under your feet? I can accept any decision you make—unless you go to America. You must remain in this area (Switzerland, France), where you can weave your marvelous talents into German literature, for your *Danton* reveals a solid foundation that can sustain and produce a great deal . . .

. . . I cannot forgive you for forcing me to take the side of prudishness as a translator and mediator.

Georg Büchner to His Family

[Strasbourg, May 5, 1835]

In case you should come across my drama, I beg you to consider in your judgment of it that I had to remain true to history and present the men of the Revolution as they were: bloody, slovenly, energetic, and cynical. I view my drama as a historical portrait that must resemble its original.

Georg Büchner to His Family

[Strasbourg, July 28, 1835]

I must say a few words about my drama. First I must point out that my permission to make several changes was

313

used to ·excess. Omissions and additions occur on almost every page, and almost always to the great disadvantage of the whole. Sometimes the sense is completely distorted or missing entirely, replaced by pure nonsense. Besides, the book is teeming with the most execrable typographical errors. I received no proofs. The title [*Dramatic Scenes of the French Reign of Terror*] is tasteless, and my name is under it, which I had explicitly forbidden; it was not on the title of my manuscript. The editor has moreover credited me with several obscenities I never would have said in my life.

Karl Gutzkow to Georg Büchner

[*Wiesbaden, July 23, 1835*]

Sauerländer delayed the printing of *Danton* for a long time. I had nothing to do with the "terror" title: that is a publisher's atrocity one no longer permits with one's second book. You will receive copies now, along with my review, decimated by the censors. I asked Sauerländer to send you proofs, for I have a bad conscience.

Georg Büchner to His Family
(CONTINUED FROM ABOVE)

I have read Gutzkow's brilliant reviews and noticed, much to my pleasure, that I have no inclination to vanity. Regarding the so-called immorality of my book, I have the following to say: The dramatic poet is in my eyes nothing but a writer of history. He is superior to the latter, however, in that he re-creates history a second time for us. Instead of telling us a dry story, he places us directly into the life of earlier times, giving us characters instead of characteristics and figures instead of descriptions. His greatest task is to come as close as possible to history as it actually happened. His book must be neither more nor less moral than history itself. God did not create history as suitable entertainment for young ladies, and for that reason I cannot be blamed if my drama is equally unsuitable. I cannot make a Danton and the bandits of the Revolution into virtuous heroes! To show their decadence I had to let them be decadent, to show their godlessness I had to let them speak like atheists. Should you discover any improprieties, then think of the notoriously obscene language of that time. Whatever my characters say is only a weak approximation of it. One might reproach me for choosing such material. But such a reproach has long been refuted. If we were to let it stand, then the greatest masterpieces of literature would have to be rejected. The poet is not a teacher of morality: he creates figures, he brings past times to life, and the public ought to learn from that, as well as from the study and observation of history, what is going on around them. If you wished it otherwise, you shouldn't be permitted to study history at all, for it tells of many immoral acts. You would have to walk blindfolded down the street, for you might see indecencies. You would have to cry out against a God who created a world in which so much dissoluteness occurs. If someone were to tell me that the poet should not depict the world as it is but as it should be, then I answer that I do not want to make it better than God, who certainly made the world as it should be. As far as the so-called idealistic poets are concerned, I find that they have produced hardly anything besides marionettes with sky-blue noses and affected pathos, not men of flesh and blood, with whose sorrow and happiness I sympathize and whose actions repel or attract me. In a word, I think much of Goethe or Shakespeare, but very little of Schiller. Moreover, it is obvious that highly unfavorable reviews will appear, for the governments must have their paid writers prove that their opponents are either idiots or immoral people. I do not in any way judge my work to be perfect, and I will accept any truly aesthetic criticism with thanks.

Karl Gutzkow to Georg Büchner

[*Frankfurt, June 10, 1836*]

Your *Danton* did not attract attention—maybe you do not know the reason? Because you did not cheat history, because a few of the well-known *heroice dicta* crept into your comedy, and from your dialogue it seemed that the wit was all your own. People tended to forget that actually more came from you than from history itself, and they called the whole thing a dramatized chapter from Thiers.

LENZ

O what a noble mind is here o'erthrown! ...
Now see that noble and most sovereign reason
Like sweet bells jangled, out of tune and harsh,
That unmatched form and feature of blown youth
Blasted with ecstasy; O woe is me
To have seen what I have seen, see what I see!
                            (*Hamlet*, Act III, Scene 1)

Critics often speak of *Danton's Death* as the result of a
sudden creative impulse. This may be so, but it is equally
relevant to recall that this play, as well as *Lenz* and *Leonce
and Lena*, were written in considerable haste for financial
reasons—Büchner needed money to escape to and survive
in Strasbourg. He was fortunate to find as his literary
sponsor the liberal writer and editor Karl Gutzkow, a man
scarcely older than he. After Gutzkow had secured the
publication of *Danton's Death*, he invited Büchner to contribute regularly to his literary magazines *Phönix* and
Deutsche Revue. Büchner promptly agreed to translate two
dramas by Victor Hugo, and in early May 1835 he announced to Gutzkow that he was planning to write a prose
piece about the Storm and Stress poet Jakob Michael Reinhold Lenz.

There is no mystery about Büchner's affinity to this
iconoclastic, tragic figure, whose poetry imitated the lyrical
clarity and energy of the young Goethe and whose dramas
brought to life with bitter realism the ambitions, failures,
and conflicts of the middle classes. The Storm and Stress
is one of the shortest epochs in German literary history;
Lenz was its only major exponent who was unable to "out-

grow" it by mellowing his radicalism and conforming to his social environment. Difficulties early in life aggravated an inner imbalance which eventually drove him insane. Born in Livonia in 1751, he endured a rigidly pietistic upbringing. He studied theology at the University of Königsberg but left before his examinations to accompany two noblemen to Strasbourg as a traveling companion. He remained there for five years, writing, working intermittently as a tutor, and participating actively in literary salons. Goethe became his friend, patron, and idol, whom Lenz in turn slavishly imitated and envied. Lenz's erratic behavior more than once strained Goethe's patience, as Goethe recalled in his memoirs (*Poetry and Truth*), written about forty years later. Goethe attempted there to assess his former colleague (who bore the nickname "Goethe's ape") as fairly as possible:

> Small, but of pleasant appearance, a dear little head whose delicate form perfectly matched his dainty, somewhat blunt features; blue eyes, blond hair . . . a gentle, almost cautious gait, a pleasant, hesitant manner of speech, and behavior alternating between reserve and shyness, most appropriate for a young man. . . . For his disposition I know only the English word "whimsical," which, as the dictionary indicates, combines many sorts of peculiarity in *one* term. . . . He showed a definite tendency toward intrigue, intrigue against himself, in fact, without any reasonable, self-serving, achievable purpose; he always set out after something bizarre, which for that reason was his constant amusement. . . . His love and hatred were fictions of his imagination, he was capricious in thought and feeling in order to have something to do at all times.

While admiring his talent and encouraging him to discipline himself for his own good, Goethe could not fully understand the nature of Lenz's turbulent personality; as a result, Goethe's portrait of him became rather patronizing. Lenz could neither control nor sublimate the conflict between his strongly moralistic upbringing and his instincts. He seemed to thrive on pain. He fell in love with several women,

318

among them Goethe's sister, but he inevitably undermined his credibility through his willful behavior. After Goethe had ended his relationship with Friederike Brion, a pastor's daughter who lived in the village of Sesenheim, Lenz visited her with the apparent intent of reading Goethe's letters to her. He fell in love with her so tempestuously (as Goethe later cynically remarked, "to learn her secrets") that she was considerably embarrassed by his presence. In 1776 he followed Goethe to Weimar but soon fell into disgrace for social improprieties. As he wandered through Switzerland, staying with friends, he suffered attacks of insanity, and he attempted suicide. During January and February of 1778 he lived with Pastor Johann Friedrich Oberlin in Waldbach; his brother then brought him home to Livonia. He recovered sufficiently to attempt a new start in St. Petersburg and Moscow. Aided by patrons, he found employment again as a tutor, but insanity overcame him anew. In 1792 he was found dead on a street in Moscow.

Pastor Oberlin (1740–1826) had settled in the remote and inhospitable village of Waldbach in 1767. In subsequent years he established a model of community improvement that eventually earned him an international reputation. He built schools for the workers' children, supervised the construction of roads and bridges, modernized farming methods, coordinated agricultural experiments, and founded a bank. He received commendations from the French government, and a college in Ohio was named after him. Coincidentally, his funeral oration was delivered by Pastor Johann Jaeglé, the father of Georg Büchner's fiancée. Oberlin's diary and several unpublished letters written by Lenz came into the hands of the Stöber family, close acquaintances of Büchner who lived in Strasbourg. With such material within reach, Büchner was in a privileged position to inform as well as entertain his reading public. He chose, however, to concentrate only on Lenz's stay with Oberlin, instead of developing the vaguely conceived "memories of Lenz," as Gutzkow had requested. Büchner's manuscript of *Lenz* has been lost, and the work first appeared two years after his death.

The novella has been lauded for its profound insights into schizophrenic dissociation, for its moving portrayal of the suffering poet's existential loneliness, and for its innovations in narrative technique. (One critic went so far as to say that its seventh sentence, "He felt no fatigue, but at times he was irritated that he could not walk on his head," marks the beginning of modern European prose.) Its subject matter was by no means new; during the latter half of the eighteenth century, European authors of various antirationalist schools analyzed and often glorified the abnormal individual, the social outcast, as they probed for a deeper understanding of the human psyche and its potential. Fictitious diaries and letters became popular as "confessional" prose forms that attempted to create an illusion of spontaneity and psychological realism. The reader was expected to feel that he was partaking in an experience instead of reading an account of a past event. Unlike the moralizing writers of the Enlightenment, the Sentimentalists sought to arouse empathy for the joy and pain of human experience through an intensely emotional style. In Germany the supreme example of such confessional literature is Goethe's *The Sorrows of Young Werther,* which obviously influenced Büchner yet provides an illuminating contrast to his approach.

Werther's letters to his friend are documents of frustration—frustrated love, social adjustment, artistic creativity. At times he loses his bearings, dramatizing his inner affliction, drowning in sentiment; at other times he is rational and ironically self-critical—a tension that permits never more than momentary progress toward clarity or control. As his condition deteriorates, so does his objectivity. The turmoil within him is projected outward to the degree that his environment shrinks to a mere backdrop for his sensibilities:

And then when the moon came out again and rested over the black cloud and the flood rolled and resounded before me in terrible, grandiose reflection: then trembling and longing once more seized me! Ah, with open eyes I stood at the abyss and breathed down! down! and drowned myself in the delight that my pain, my sorrow would be hurled down! to surge away like the waves!

320

Ostensibly, Werther is on the verge of suicide, but in fact he is ecstatically magnifying himself to titanic proportions. He maintains throughout that the intensity of his suffering sets him apart from his fellow men—and above them as well. He sublimates his pain through an exaggerated pose ... and exaggerated prose. That is, while he is still able to write letters, he can hold himself at arm's length and admire himself, but at last he loses even this objectivity, and an unnamed narrator must intercede to provide the final chapter of his self-destruction. Once insanity sets in, an irreparable rift occurs between the irrational mind and the rational observer. Goethe's narrator cannot nor does he wish to penetrate into the "sick" aberrations of his protagonist. (Goethe turned away from Lenz for the same reason—see *Poetry and Truth*.)

Büchner rejects this clear-cut distinction. Lenz's distorted perception of reality dominates our vision, it becomes the narrative truth without a rational counterweight, challenging our complacent, enlightened saneness by obscuring the distinction between normal and abnormal. *Lenz* contains no sentimental posturing for a literary audience, no suffering-for-the-sake-of-art, no self-irony. It is a testament to Büchner's remarkable stylistic control that between *Danton's Death* and *Leonce and Lena*, where wit is the food of life, he was able to write such an unmercifully serious work as *Lenz*. It resembles a psychiatric case history that records (mostly in the third person) the subject's impressions and significant dialogue, except that Büchner, unlike a psychiatrist, does not pass judgment on Lenz, does not assume a superior stance—and thereby implies that we should not do so either. He imposes an additional hardship on his reader: the novella begins, "On the 20th Lenz went through the mountains," and nowhere do we encounter a formal exposition. He severs the present from the past and future, depriving us of the assurance that events are occurring in a logical, comprehensible progression, coercing us to doubt our traditional belief in cause-and-effect relationships. It might even be argued that total ignorance of the background material would heighten the impact of *Lenz* as a parable of insanity. But the fact remains that Büchner chose to retain the real names of his figures, as he did in *Danton's Death* and

Woyzeck, to preserve the dialectical tension between fiction and historical reality.

From the outset, he concentrates on the single yet ever-changing moment of perception. The second sentence, for example, contains no verbs, merely a list of objects, as if a dispassionate eye were taking inventory of a landscape, seemingly without purpose, finding neither cohesion nor significance in what it sees. Then: "Pine branches hung down *heavily* in the moist air. Gray clouds moved across the sky, *but everything so dense,* and then the fog steamed up, *oppressive* and damp, trailing through the bushes, *so sluggish, so shapeless* [italics mine]"—this is more than neutral description; it alerts us to a human presence that senses and interprets the scene. Büchner evokes a vague sense of discomfort, but its source is unclear. He shifts back to the third person, and, in a matter-of-fact way, he reveals Lenz's derangement: "He felt no fatigue, but at times he was irritated that he could not walk on his head." The effect is grotesque (which is never entirely free of humor), much like the first sentence of Kafka's *Metamorphosis:* "As Gregor Samsa awoke one morning from uneasy dreams he found himself transformed in his bed into a gigantic insect."

The syntax of *Lenz* has an alienating quality rarely found in Kafka, however. Like the mind of the protagonist, sentences are disjointed; although overtly factual, the style does not flow smoothly. (As far as possible, Büchner's punctuation and grammatical ambiguities have been preserved in the translation.) A series of events is often compressed into a single sentence, generating haste that vividly mirrors Lenz's impulsive behavior. Just as Lenz loses the ends of his sentences, the reader of *Lenz* can never be sure in which direction Büchner's seemingly unpremeditated style will lead him. Scorning transitions, Büchner slips in and out of his protagonist's mind, as we have seen in the opening passage, pinpointing the essential detail: "He went through the village, lights shone through the windows, he looked in as he passed by, children at the table, old women, girls, all calm, quiet faces, it seemed to him as if the light must radiate from them, he felt at ease, he was soon in the parsonage at Waldbach."

Lenz perceives reality in terms of drastic contrasts. At

times his environment threatens to overwhelm him, at times the entire universe seems to shrink into insignificance. Forest sounds, landscape patterns, weather changes, light and darkness often trigger violent reactions; there are subtle structural parallels in Büchner's use of these objects which belie the seemingly episodic, aimless nature of the narrative (see "Structural Parallels in *Lenz*," pages 328–31). In one instance, he consolidates a multitude of changing natural phenomena into a monster sentence (in the original it is two hundred fifty words long) that focuses on a single point: "pain tore through his chest." To alleviate this inescapable psychosomatic pain, Lenz clings to nature (as he will cling to Oberlin later on), but the spiritual support he so desperately seeks is never more than transitory. Adrift on an endless ocean, he sees distorted, terrifying shapes below the surface, but his vision is too limited to overcome his fear.

Upon Lenz's arrival at Oberlin's parsonage, Büchner began to borrow copiously from Oberlin's diary. In fact, fully a third of the novella is either inspired by or quoted verbatim from it. As in *Danton's Death* and *Woyzeck*, Büchner blends his source seamlessly into his work, often making only minor changes that eliminate naturalistic detail in favor of realistic typification. Interestingly, the fusion of Oberlin's account with freely invented descriptions of Lenz's hallucinations tends to put Oberlin in a negative light without any editorializing by Büchner. The well-meaning Oberlin (like Goethe!) can sympathize with but cannot really comprehend Lenz's madness. In Oberlin's eyes, Lenz was a lovable but slightly ludicrous figure. For instance, after Lenz threw himself into the fountain, Oberlin remarked that he splashed around "like a duck," a comparison that Büchner understandably omitted. Oberlin's person, his family, his environment—rather than his advice—had a calming effect on Lenz, providing him with a physical and spiritual home. The family scenes as Büchner describes them have the repose and warmth of the Dutch paintings that Lenz so admires. For a time, he begins to recover, especially when he is given something to do, such as preparing and delivering a sermon. By affecting and helping others, he can overcome his morbid isolation—a characteristic trait

323

of the historical Lenz as well, who deeply desired to improve society, but his cynicism and emotional temperament inevitably worked at cross-purposes to his reformist impulses. When Büchner writes, "the world he had wished to serve had a gigantic crack," he bares the root of Lenz's frustration, and neither human nor divine solace can dispel it. "But I, if I were almighty, you see," Lenz says to Oberlin, "if I were, I couldn't bear this suffering, I would save, save, I just want nothing but peace, peace, just a little peace and to be able to sleep." "Save" connotes spiritual redemption, salvation that Lenz, "damned for eternity," believes is unattainable. We recognize this as the *cantus firmus* (or *cantus infirmus*, to coin a phrase) of Büchner's philosophy; Danton, Robespierre, Leonce, Lena, Woyzeck, and Büchner himself sing the same melody.

Besides his abysmal despair, Lenz has burdened himself with imagined guilt, also deriving from his frustrated desire to find peace with others. Calling himself Friederike Brion's murderer—although she was still alive at the time—he flagellates himself figuratively and literally for his "sin," and with the obsessive logic of a schizophrenic, he tries to revive his lost love in the form of a dead child. (Although Oberlin notes that the child was also named Friederike, Büchner omitted the name from his manuscript. He may have found the coincidence too blunt and confining for his purposes.) Once this fails, he stands face-to-face with his own mortality, and this disappointment, too deep for rage, generates a kind of demonic euphoria:

Hell's song of triumph was in his breast. The wind sounded like a song of titans, he felt as if he could thrust a gigantic fist up into Heaven and tear God down and drag Him through His clouds; as if he could grind up the world in his teeth and spit it into the Creator's face; he swore, he blasphemed. So he came to the crest of the mountain ridge, and the uncertain light spread down to the white masses of stone, and the sky was a stupid blue eye and the moon hung in it most ludicrously, foolishly. Lenz had to laugh out loud, and in that laughter atheism seized and held him quite securely and calmly and firmly.

At one point, however, all signs of his mental disease disappear, and he is able to hold forth at length on his specialty: aesthetics. This episode, more than any other, represents a release of tension for Lenz, during which he momentarily "forgets himself" and reveals the qualities of a now almost destroyed intelligence. A brief discussion with Oberlin introduces a *leitmotiv* evident in much of modern German literature: the schizophrenia of the intellectual who through his acquired wisdom and sensibility feels divorced from nature, from his childhood, from the simple life of the common folk. At heart a rationalist who "comprehends with more organs but was consequently far more sensitive," Lenz envies those who, as he believes, enjoy a peaceful, mystical communion with nature. Clearly Büchner is expressing his own dualism here, for behind these abstractions lies the recurring man-woman contrast in *Danton's Death* and *Leonce and Lena:* the introspective, self-doubting male versus the instinctual woman, the idealized child of nature, harmonious unto herself. The polarity also resembles Schiller's distinction between the naive and the sentimental poet, except that Schiller equated sentimental, "cultured" man with Kantian ethics, which Büchner could not accept. His antipathy toward Schiller comes to light in Lenz's discussion of aesthetics, in which Büchner combines ideas from Lenz's *Comments on the Theater* with his own anti-idealistic credo, and Lenz in effect becomes his mouthpiece. (See the discussion of art in Act II, Scene 3 of *Danton's Death,* and Büchner's letter to his parents on pages 314–15.) The result is somewhat anachronistic, since the "idealistic period" was not beginning in 1778, as he maintains, but apparently he wanted to seize this opportunity for some polemicizing. The artist's duty to imitate Creation, the emphasis on the individual rather than on abstractions, the puppetlike figures of idealistic drama —this all derives from Lenz's essay. Büchner points to Lenz's best-known plays, *The Tutor* and *The Soldiers,* as models (which manifestly influenced Büchner himself). The partly autobiographical *The Tutor* relates with acerbic realism the misfortunes of an exploited private tutor in a middle-class household; *The Soldiers* demonstrates the fatal consequences attending the seduction of a naive middle-class girl by an aristocratic officer. Both Lenz and Büchner, especially in *Woyzeck*, created figures that were not classical embodiments of ideas but instead were multidimensional, contradictory, fundamentally unpredictable as products of their environment. The *sine qua non* of their dramaturgy was close, unprejudiced observation and sympathy for the downtrodden, insignificant, or unattractive individual.

As such, Büchner's aesthetic has distinctly sociopolitical implications. He disallowed the premise that classical idealism is a universal and therefore apolitical or suprapolitical philosophy. Such idealists, he maintained, were elitists, apologists for the aristocracy, oppressors of the poor. A properly democratic form of art was obliged to reveal the truth of existing social relationships (*cf. The Hessian Messenger*) instead of positing a hypothetical ideal. In his works he endeavored to "let the figures come to life without copying anything into them from the outside" in order to diminish the gap between reality and art, to allow the work to appear as spontaneously real as possible. This explains why he often incorporated his sources for *Danton's Death, Lenz,* and *Woyzeck* directly into the works. Reality meant impenetrable complexity—impenetrable in that no single being (not even an author who feels there is a touch of divinity in his art) can presume to reduce existence to simple formulas. Art therefore does not merely teach lessons, construct a moral code, or send us to the barricades; it enlightens us by challenging our intellect and sharpening our sensibilities, showing forces in conflict without foreseeable resolution. In other words, it reveals a "possibility of existence."

No aesthetic can avoid a definition of beauty, and in Lenz's monologue Büchner provides several: there is beauty in human contact (the girls sitting on a rock, the painting of "Christ and the Disciples at Emmaus"), in simple, peaceful devotion (the painting of the woman with her prayer book), in the uniqueness of each individual, and, most significantly, in the endless metamorphosis of forms and images, which art can never fully capture nor transmit. His yearning for purity and simplicity in art and nature is fundamentally Romantic—the antithesis of the suffering caused by man's innate inability to exist without harming himself and others. The Büchner-Lenz aesthetic does not fully resolve this contradiction, nor does it explain their frequent use of exaggerated characterization for polemical effect. In practice, both writers were not wholly impartial, of course; they clearly took sides and demolished social stereotypes with bitter caricature. Yet despite its inconclusiveness, the discussion on aesthetics is exceedingly valuable simply because there is so little in Büchner's extant writings that illuminates his artistic principles.

When Lenz wanders off into the mountains after Oberlin's departure to Switzerland and comes upon a hut, he encounters several forms of spiritual ecstasy that make his own affliction seem almost normal. The mystical experiences of the people in the hut intensify the feeling of insufficiency that arises when an individual attempts to comprehend and interpret his surroundings through the limited faculty of his reason. As in Goethe's *Werther,* such encounters function as variations on the primary theme of the work. Unlike the episodes in a typical *Bildungsroman,* they are not ascending steps in the hero's intellectual growth; they lead him instead in the opposite direction by concretizing and intensifying his self-destructive impulses. After leaving the hut, Lenz feels "a stirring and crawling toward an abyss to which an inexorable power was drawing him." This decline is somewhat accelerated by Oberlin's absence, but it is not very significant because from the start, the feeling of repose that Lenz had been able to derive from him was never more than momentary. It is not so surprising, then, that Lenz is upset at Oberlin's early return. Oberlin himself becomes more distantly patronizing, his attempts to console Lenz become ineffective clichés ("He told him, 'Honor your father and mother' and more of the same"), for simple piety can no longer reach him. His behavior becomes increasingly extreme and repetitive; he is emptier, more withdrawn than before, capable of feeling only through self-inflicted pain. To others, his actions appear comically grotesque—e.g., his mad chase with his guards, his demand to be tied up, his battle with Oberlin's cat. His isolation is so impenetrable that Büchner can only describe it from the outside, and in consequence he relies more than ever on Oberlin's diary. He merely adds a few incidents, a few poignant conversations with Oberlin here and there as he hastens to his conclusion. Stylistic monotony sets in with a proliferation of hyperbole: "gigantic," "terrible," "horrible," "indescribable," "unspeakable," "utter," "dreadful," "appalling," "immense." Finally he breaks off in mid-sentence (as far as we can judge) and adds a masterful final paragraph in which a beautiful evening landscape contrasts downright spitefully with Lenz's catatonic state. The ever-changing play of light and color on form prevails while the perceiver remains inanimate. Lenz does not die, he merely lives on (an approximation of the final untranslatable sentence: *So lebte er hin* can imply "thus he lived himself out" or "vegetated"). There is no classical resolution; Lenz must continue to endure his fate: death-in-life. (Oberlin, on the other hand, is sufficiently detached to be able to write in his diary: "everything ended admirably.")

Why, ultimately, did Büchner write *Lenz* in this manner? The work is disturbing precisely because it lacks the reassurance of a moralizing stance or of self-conscious artistry. We cannot distance ourselves from it as much as we might like. Büchner compels us to accept Lenz as a "possibility of existence" only a step removed from our own sanity, rather than as a self-indulgent aberration. In a school essay on suicide written in his teens, Büchner concluded: "A suicide from physical and mental suffering is no suicide, he has only died from an illness." Our pity for Lenz is mixed with fear because we could easily share his fate—the familiar Aristotelian definition of tragedy—but the hero is not larger than life and thus not remote from our frame of reference. And finally, we are left with no catharsis, no return to universal order, but with the open wound of despair.

STRUCTURAL PARALLELS IN *LENZ*

[Despite its fragmentary appearance, Büchner's novella is a carefully wrought entity, bonded by parallel and contrasting episodes and motifs. If we assume its fulcrum to be Oberlin's departure for Switzerland

—the episode is simultaneously the halfway mark in the narrative, its chronological midpoint, and a turning point in Lenz's deterioration—then *Lenz* divides cleanly into two parts. Part Two is essentially a darkened mirror image of Part One, structurally underscoring Lenz's inevitable descent into insanity. (This was first suggested by Erna Kritsch Neuse in "Büchners *Lenz:* Zur Struktur der Novelle," *German Quarterly,* 43 [March 1970], 199–209.) The following outline illustrates correspondences in sequential order, based on the paragraph numbers indicated in the translation. A chart of this sort inevitably tends to oversimplify, since it does not take all structural elements into account. Yet Oberlin's diary does not yield these correspondences, and it is quite unlikely that they are merely accidental. They point to the conclusion that *Lenz* is more closely linked to Classical and Romantic models than critics have previously believed.]

Part One

1: Lenz alone in the mountains.
"He went on indifferently, the path did not matter to him, up or down."

"It had grown dark. . . . At last he heard voices, he saw lights . . . ."
". . . children at the table, old women, girls, all calm, quiet faces, it seemed to him as if the light must radiate from them . . . ."
He is warmly received by Oberlin and his family.

(2 & 6: Oberlin tells of his visions, which strengthened his faith.)

Part Two

10: Lenz alone in the mountains.
"Sometimes he sat, then he went on again, but slowly, dreaming. He did not look for a path."

"It was dark when he came to an inhabited hut on a slope toward the Steintal."
"[A lamp's] light fell on the pale face of a girl resting behind it . . . ."

10–12: He remains a detached observer of the family in the hut.
The man in the hut tells of his frightening visions in the mountains.

Lenz enters his room: "the light was out, darkness swallowed everything; an inexpressible fear seized him." Self-inflicted pain restores him to consciousness, and he "come[s] to his senses again."

2: He accompanies Oberlin on his duties; "it all had a beneficial and soothing effect on him." He has bouts of despair, but the shock of throwing himself into the fountain restores him; "the more he accustomed himself to this way of life, the calmer he became . . . ." He has a reassuring vision of his mother.

3–5: He prepares and delivers his sermon. "A sweet feeling of endless well-being crept over him." The cathartic effect of the experience clears his mind, and he sleeps peacefully.

6: He dreams that his mother has died: "the roses had slowly grown over her . . . he was quite calm about it."

6–7: Discussion with Oberlin about the "elemental" character and its closeness to nature, the innate

Lenz returns home, "and within himself he felt a stirring and crawling toward an abyss to which an inexorable power was drawing him." When he regains his strength, he is "cold and indifferent."

13–14: He spends time with Madame Oberlin and the children, "clutch[ing] at every diversion. Always hastily from one thing to another."

14–16: He is tormented by his memories of Friederike (see below).

17–20: "Meanwhile his religious torments continued." His spirit is dead; begging God for a sign, he sets out for Fouday to resurrect a dead child. Frustrated and desperate, he is seized by "atheism . . . securely and calmly and firmly." He is terrified by his "sin against the Holy Ghost"; he is "the wandering Jew."

21–23: He presumes Friederike to be dead and castigates himself: "oh, good mother, she loved me too. I'm a murderer."

24: Cynical discussion with Oberlin about boredom: "I don't even want to kill myself: it's too boring!"

peacefulness of the "lower forms."

8: Kaufmann arrives. Lenz is irritated by the intrusion.

But in Kaufmann's presence he speaks eloquently about literature and art; "often smiling, often serious . . . he had completely forgotten himself."

Kaufmann tells him to return home. Lenz angrily refuses because he "feel[s] comfortable here."

9: Oberlin departs. Lenz is terrified in anticipation of his absence.

The schoolmaster becomes his guardian. Lenz tries to shake him off; he "got on his nerves."

24–27: He continues to deteriorate, becoming less coherent; "he had lost the end of his sentence." His impressions and reactions are meaninglessly fragmented; "it was the abyss of incurable insanity."
He is compelled to leave because Oberlin can no longer control him. (This corresponds to the gap in Büchner's text—see the passage from Oberlin's diary on the following pages.)

28: Lenz departs "in cold resignation . . . a terrible void inside him." (Compare with paragraph 2 and especially paragraph 1: the landscape no longer affects him; the cycle is complete.)

FROM PASTOR OBERLIN'S DIARY

[The events described here fill the gap in Büchner's text immediately prior to Lenz's departure from Waldbach.]

. . . The nursemaid, deathly pale and trembling all over, came to my wife: Mr. Lenz had thrown himself out of the window. My wife called to me in confusion—I ran out, but

Mr. Lenz was already back in his room. I just had a moment to tell a maid: "Go quickly to the bailiff and have him send two men," and I ran up to Mr. Lenz's room.

I led him to my room with friendly words; his whole body shivered. Above the waist he wore only an undershirt, torn and completely soiled like the rest of his clothes. We warmed a shirt and a robe for him, and we dried his clothes. We discovered that during the short time he was outside he must have attempted to drown himself again, but God had provided once more. His clothes were soaked.

Now, I thought, you have deceived me enough, now *you* must be deceived, now it's at an end, now you must be watched. I waited for the men with great impatience. Meanwhile I continued to write my sermon as Mr. Lenz sat at the stove, a step away from me. I didn't dare leave him for a moment, I had to wait. My wife stayed also, worried about me. I really would have liked to send for the men again, but I could not speak of it to my wife or anyone else. If I had spoken openly he would have understood; we didn't want to speak in secret, because the slightest opportunity for suspicion excites such people far too much. At eight-thirty we went to eat. My wife trembled in fear and Mr. Lenz in cold and confusion.

After less than fifteen minutes he asked me whether he could go up to my room.—What do you want to do, my dear friend?—To read something.—Go in God's name.—He went, and pretending I had eaten enough, I followed him.

We sat: I wrote, he leafed through my French Bible with terrifying speed and finally grew quiet. I went for a moment into the study without delaying in the slightest, only to get something from my desk. My wife stood at the door and watched Mr. Lenz. I was stepping out of the study when my wife screamed in a gruesome, hollow, broken voice: "Lord Jesus, he's going to stab himself!" Never in my life have I seen such an expression of deathlike, despairing terror as in that moment, in the wild, horribly distorted features of my wife.

I was outside.—What are you up to, my dear friend?—He put down the scissors. He had been looking about with dreadful, rigid glances, and since he saw no one in his bewilderment, he had quietly picked up the scissors, placed them with a tight fist against his heart——all this so quickly that only God was able to prevent the blow until my wife's scream frightened him and returned him somewhat to his senses. After a few moments I took away the scissors, as if lost in thought and paying him no mind. Since he solemnly assured me that he hadn't intended to kill himself with them, I didn't want to act as if I didn't believe him at all.

Because all previous arguments against his suicidal mania had been fruitless, I tried another tack. I said to him: "You were a total stranger to us, we didn't know you at all, we had only heard your name once before we knew you, we took you in with love, my wife cared for your injured foot with such patience, and you do us so much harm, you cast us from one fright into another." He was moved by this, jumped up, wanted to beg my wife's pardon, but she was still so afraid of him and ran out the door. He wanted to follow, but she held the door shut. Now he wailed that he had murdered my wife, the child she was carrying——everything, he killed everything wherever he went.——No, my friend, my wife is still alive and God can temper the harmful consequences of her fright, nor would her child die nor be harmed by that.——He calmed down again. Soon it was ten o'clock. Meanwhile my wife had sent for urgent help among the neighbors. Everyone was in bed, but the schoolmaster came, pretending as if he had something to ask me, gave me some news, and Mr. Lenz, becoming active again, took part in the conversation as if nothing had happened.

Finally I received a sign that the two men had arrived ——oh, how happy I was! It was time. Mr. Lenz had just asked to go to bed. I said to him: "Dear friend, we love you, you know that, and you love us, we are certain of that, too. Your suicide would worsen, not improve your condition; we must therefore be concerned about your survival. But when depression overcomes you, you lose control of yourself. That's why I've asked two men to sleep in your room (to watch, I thought to myself), so that you have company and help if necessary." He agreed to this.

One should not be surprised that I spoke to him and treated him in this manner. He was always quite reasonable and had an exceptionally sympathetic heart. When the attacks of depression had passed, everything seemed so secure, and he was so amiable that one almost had a bad conscience while suspecting or troubling him. Add to that our fondest pity for his immeasurable torment, that we had so often witnessed. What he endured was terrible and hellish, and it pierced and broke my heart when I was compelled to suffer with him the consequences of his disobedience toward his father, his erratic way of life, his aimless occupations, his frequent association with women. I was horrified and felt tortures never experienced before when he was on his knees, his hand in mine, his head resting on my knee, his pale face covered with cold sweat, hidden in my robe, trembling and shivering all over—not confessing, but not able to contain the outpouring of his tormented conscience and unfulfilled longing. The more difficult it became to calm him, the more pitiable he was to me, since our respective attitudes were in strong opposition—or at least appeared to differ.

Now back to the facts: I said he permitted two men to be in his room. I accompanied him into it. One of his guards stared at him with rigid, frightened eyes. To calm the guard somewhat, I said to Mr. Lenz in French in the presence of the two guards what I had already told him in my room . . . . I concluded with several kisses which I pressed on the unhappy youth's mouth with all my heart, and I went to bed with exhausted, quivering limbs.

While in bed he said among other things to his guards: "Listen, we don't want to make any noise, but if you have a knife, give it to me quietly and without fear." After he had requested this time and again without a response, he began to beat his head against the wall. In our sleep we heard much thumping, appearing to increase and decrease, which finally woke us up. We thought it was in the attic but could not guess the cause. The clock struck three and the thumping continued. We rang for a light; our servants were all deep in horrible dreams and had difficulty waking up. We discovered at last that the thumping was coming from Mr. Lenz and in part from the guards, who were summoning help by stamping on the floor, since they could not leave him alone. I rushed to his room. As soon as he saw me, he stopped trying to struggle out of his guards' arms. They then also stopped restraining him. I gave them a sign to let him go, sat on his bed, talked with him, and prayed with him as he requested. He stirred a bit, and once he smashed his head against the wall with great force. The guards jumped up and held him again.

I went to summon a third guard. When Mr. Lenz saw him, he mocked them all, saying that all three would not be strong enough for him. Secretly I ordered my coach to be made ready, to be covered over, to have two extra horses brought besides mine. I sent for Sebastian Scheidecker, the schoolmaster of Bellefosse, and Johann David Bohy, the schoolmaster of Solb, two sensible, determined men whom Mr. Lenz was fond of. Johann Georg Claude, Waldbach's churchwarden, came as well; the house was astir although it was not yet day. Mr. Lenz noticed this, and whereas earlier he had shown such cunning, such violence to free himself, to smash his head, to obtain a knife, he was now suddenly so quiet.

After I had arranged everything, I went to Mr. Lenz, saying to him that I had asked several men to accompany him to Strasbourg in my coach so that he might receive better care in accordance with his condition.

He lay quietly with only one guard sitting by him. At my words he sobbed, asking for only one more week's patience with him (one had to cry at his demeanor.) But he said he would think about it. Fifteen minutes later he sent word: yes, he would go; he stood up, got dressed, was quite reasonable, packed his things, thanked everyone individually most tenderly, including the guards, looked for my wife and the maids who had concealed themselves from him, because just previously his rage had increased whenever he heard or believed to have heard a woman's voice. Now he asked to see everyone, thanked them, begged their forgiveness; in short, he took leave from everyone so movingly that all eyes were bathed in tears.

And so the pitiable youth departed from us, with three companions and two coachmen. During the journey he never became violent, seeing himself outnumbered, but he attempted various ruses, especially at Ensisheim where they spent the night. But the schoolmasters matched his cunning politeness with their own, and everything ended admirably.

LEONCE AND LENA

During the first five months of 1836, Büchner wrote a dissertation in French on the nervous system of fish and delivered three well-received lectures on this topic before the Strasbourg *Société d'histoire naturelle*. He announced in a letter to a friend that the thesis was completed on May 31, and "when I've paid for my doctorate, I won't have a cent left, and I haven't been able to write anything [i.e., for money] during this time. For a while I have to live from dear old credit and see how in the next 6–8 weeks I'll cut a coat and pants for myself out of the large white sheets of paper that I have to scribble full." The sheets were soon filled with the comedy *Leonce and Lena;* several witticisms from this letter, in fact, appeared in it. Presumably he had been planning the comedy while working on the dissertation. The project was inspired by a competition announced on February 3 by the Cotta publishing house for "the best German comedy." He unfortunately missed the deadline, and the play was sent back unread. Like *Lenz*, the manuscript is lost, and the work was not published in his lifetime.

Leonce and Lena is his only work that originated from literary rather than documentary sources. Romantic comedy would seem to be a genre vastly remote from his usual literary and political concerns, and Büchner scholars of various persuasions have had difficulty coming to terms with the play, calling it structurally deficient, too wordy, too lightweight, too derivative (it does in fact borrow heavily from Shakespeare's *As You Like It* and *Hamlet*, Clemens Brentano's *Ponce de Leon*, and Alfred de Musset's *Fantasio*). On the other hand, it has been laboriously dissected, defended, and categorized—far more so than its companion works—so that it might occupy a suitably profound position among them. These investigations tend to come to the paradoxical but by no means misguided conclusion that this frothy playlet may well be Büchner's most pessimistic creation.

Each of his previous works left its traces in *Leonce and Lena*—even *The Hessian Messenger*. The political satire in the play brings up the question whether he was now attempting to reform society through the theater instead of sending pamphlets to workers' huts, relying on ridicule instead of polemics. The mad antics of King Peter and his court seem to be a distorted reflection of the Grand Duchy of Hesse-Darmstadt. King Peter's tiny kingdom lies in a land where it is possible to walk "through a dozen principalities, half a dozen grand duchies, and several kingdoms with the greatest haste in half a day." The King, an ineffective buffoon, rules over a court of automatons, recalling the "puppets on strings" in the *Messenger*. Peasants are forced to line up along the streets to greet the royal couple, and their reward shall be that once in their lives they will smell a roast; the pamphlet described with bitter irony how the peasants' children might once go to Darmstadt "when a royal heir and a royal heiress want to devise means to produce another royal heir, and your children can look through the open glass doors and see the tablecloth on which the lords dine and smell the lamps that shine from the fat of the peasants." Yet the comedy is clearly not in the first instance a satirical dramatization of social conditions. Less than a quarter of the play deals with courtly life. Besides, the satire is applied with such broad strokes that it cannot injure. King Peter's subjects are even more ludicrous than their ruler; they are burlesque marionettes, devoid of stature, barely able to think or communicate. As clowns in a knockabout farce, they evoke no sympathy, for they do not really suffer, and their "oppressors" therefore cannot be called villains. In none of his works, in fact, did Büchner create a Machiavellian aristocrat who destroys innocent virtue, a familiar figure in the plays of less radical writers such as Lessing, Goethe, and Schiller. He tended to dismiss the aristocracy as a class with a wave of the hand; they appear only once in

Danton's Death, as impotent fools. One wonders why the leaders of the Revolution are making such a fuss about them. He waged war instead against the self-appointed "military policeman of heaven," the egotistical moralist, the intellectual elitist, regardless of class.

Nevertheless: Leonce, the hero of his comedy, its most sympathetic figure, is an aristocrat. Here social rank is oddly divorced from social implications and becomes a form of wish fulfillment. Leonce's high status frees him from the need to work for a living; his whims become reality upon command. He is a Faust served by a court instead of a devil. Yet this freedom is a curse that threatens to undermine his sanity. He has no antagonist except himself. His identity crisis—not the society in which it occurs—is the nucleus of the play. By diminishing the Kingdom of Popo to weightless insignificance so as to avoid any serious confrontation between the self and its environment, Büchner created a comedy which lacks the element for which Leonce is so desperately searching: meaningful action.

The plot is easily told: Leonce and Lena flee their respective kingdoms to avoid a forced marriage; they meet, fall in love, and return to discover that they had been intended for each other from the start. Trying to evade fate, they rush headlong into its arms—an archetypal comic situation. The complex intrigue characteristic of comedy from Shakespeare to de Musset is nowhere in evidence, however; there is no bustling, vibrant world in which men and women progress from confusion and despair to happiness and regeneration. Instead, solitary figures contemplate the void, play verbal games, seek diversion, but never totally overcome their inner emptiness. The play begins with a dissertation on boredom. Leonce comments ironically about the importance of spitting on a stone, asks himself whether he is an idler, is himself bored by his parrotlike tutor, and concludes that "idleness is the root of all vice." He yearns to be able to see the top of his head, to view himself from a different, "impossible" angle, quite like Lenz, who wanted to walk on his head. (*Auf den Kopf sehen* and *auf dem Kopf gehen* rhyme in German, and they appear in nearly identical locations in their respective texts.) Best of all would be a total escape from his identity: "Oh, to be someone else for once!" But he is not merely flaunting nor playing with these insights—he is their prisoner: "Why must *I* be the one to know this? Why can't I take myself seriously . . . ?" and in his subsequent monologues he discourses further on this theme: "If only I knew of one thing under the sun that could still make me run. . . . It's as if I were sitting under a vacuum pump. . . . My life yawns at me like a large white sheet of paper that I have to fill, but I can't write a single letter. . . . Oh, I know myself, I know what I'll be thinking and dreaming in a quarter of an hour, in a week, in a year." He is trapped in the vicious circle of the endlessly introspective mind. He embodies Büchner's own intellectual radicalism, rejecting limitations and conventional solutions in his Faustian quest for experience and knowledge, searching for essences as far as his rational powers will allow. Through Leonce, Büchner reveals the danger behind such endeavors: as we strip away surfaces, we self-destruct, we relativize ourselves out of existence. Leonce's rootless, probing mind therefore falls prey to existential anxiety: "I hardly dare stretch out my hands, as if I were in a narrow room of mirrors, afraid of bumping against everything—then the beautiful figures would lie in fragments on the floor and I'd be standing before the bare, naked wall." He strains to avoid the sort of insanity that befell Lenz; like Danton he refuses to succumb to utter fatalism. He possesses a life-force, an optimistic energy ("I still have a certain dose of enthusiasm to use up") that drives him from experience to experience, although inevitably they all seem to grow stale. But somewhere, he hopes, he will find *substance* in this universe of mirrors, be it ever so insignificant: "Oh God! I'll spend half my life in prayer if I only could have a blade of straw on which to ride as on a splendid steed, until I lie on the straw myself."

As he muses his way through Act I, he considers and rejects various means of escape, finally settling on a mode of existence anticipated by the motto of this act: "O that I were a fool!" His anguish would cease if he could immerse himself in the blissful security of a permanent *idée fixe*. In the words of Danton's friend, Camille Desmoulins: "The happiest of all men was the one who could imagine

he was God the Father, the Son, and the Holy Ghost."
Such a man is Leonce's companion, Valerio, a Shakespearean fool of sheer intellect without substance, a figure
who can play the game of life endlessly without ever feeling its weight. He is a match for Leonce in wordplay, but
he lacks Leonce's insatiable spiritual hunger and thus feels
not a trace of anxiety. He lives from meal to meal, a
creature of instinct, jest, and fantasy. It has been claimed
that the Leonce-Valerio relationship is outlined in Büchner's rather obscure prologue to the play: "Alfieri: 'And
fame?'/Gozzi: 'And hunger?'" Büchner may have wished
to establish a sort of preliminary dialectic; at any rate, no
clarification has been found in the heroic tragedies of Vit-
torio Alfieri (1749–1803) nor in the satiric comedies of
Carlo Gozzi (1720–1806). It seems unlikely that "hunger"
refers to Valerio's devil-may-care materialism. (At best, it
appears to anticipate Brecht's famous line about poverty:
"First we eat, then we moralize.") The mirage of fame
and the hunger for baser pleasures are but two of the human drives that Leonce and Valerio analyze and ridicule.
In their verbal games of thesis-antithesis, they set up poses
and illusions for the other to destroy—a ceaseless duel of
ironic refutation. Valerio needs no synthesis, and Leonce
cannot find one. Their common denominator, the quality
that in effect makes Valerio an extension of Leonce, is wit.
Leonce and Valerio belong to the tradition of romantic
ironists who depend upon wit as an antidote to suicidal
despair, as a means of demystifying reality by destroying
the alienating "otherness" of the non-self. People and objects become part of the game and are thereby "control-
lable"; the threat and anguish of the unknown disappear.
Yet this is merely a transitory stage, for the ironist realizes
that the medium of control, namely language, is itself in-
tangible, unreliable, and can only yield insufficient answers.
Thus his grip upon reality remains tenuous, fundamentally
devoid of meaning. In this context, Leonce's and Valerio's
characterizations of each other are devastatingly accurate:

Leonce.
Man, you are nothing more than a bad pun. You
have neither father nor mother—the five vowels
gave birth to you.

Valerio.
And you, Prince, are a book without words, with
nothing but dashes.

("Dashes" is a pale approximation of *Gedankenstrichen*—
literally, "thought-dashes" or "thought-lines.")

Puns and irony are poor meat for a drama, as Büchner
surely discovered while studying one of his sources for
Leonce and Lena, Brentano's *Ponce de Leon.* He overcame
the danger of stagnation, pretension, and archness through
his characteristic economy and variety; no two episodes or
soliloquies are sufficiently alike to admit of any cutting.
His Leonce is a figure of many facets, superbly sensitive to
himself and his surroundings. His poetic imagination keeps
pace with the labyrinthine path of his intellect; he comes
to life as a dramatic figure through his stylistic vitality and
originality. In contrast to his fellow Popoians, he faces the
anguish of existence head-on, grappling with its endless
contradictions.

Appealing as these traits may be, there is no denying
that Leonce is a capricious and even cruel person. He is
aware of this; he also knows that his behavior emanates
from a fundamental pleasure-pain duality: "How vilely I
played the cavalier to those poor devils! And yet there's a
kind of pleasure in a certain kind of vileness." He hints at
the consequences of being tempted by sadism as an escape
from boredom: "Gentlemen, gentlemen, do you know
what Caligula and Nero were? I know." Finally, only one
possible role remains: he shall not become a scholar, a
hero, a poetic genius, nor a useful member of society, but
a beggar, free to enjoy the intoxicating atmosphere of the
south, free from his role as Prince. In other words, a sublimely liberated fool.

His father, King Peter, is a fool as well, but a pathetic
one. Doggedly unaware that he is an inept ruler of a realm
of idiots, he clings to ritual as an assertion of his self-
importance. Worse yet, he is an amateur philosopher. Having ingested a bit of Kant and Fichte, he has developed a
mania for categorizing: "Now for my attributes, modifications, affections, and accessories: where is my shirt, my
pants?" A misplaced snuffbox threatens universal disorder.
Büchner obviously relished this opportunity to spoof philo-

sophical jargon, as his letters testify. While he was "throwing [himself] with all [his] might into philosophy," he complained that "the artificial language is awful—for human affairs I think one should find human expressions . . . . I'm getting an insight into a new aspect of the poverty of the human mind." Nevertheless, there is a trace of compassion in Büchner's characterization of King Peter. As an unskilled laborer in the art of self-expression, he is dimly aware that he cannot fully sustain himself through the ritualized language of his role; at times the mask slips and he becomes confused, even anxious:

> My dear and faithful subjects, I wish you to know by these presents, to know by these presents—because either my son marries or not (*Puts a finger next to his nose.*)—either, or—you understand, of course? There is no third possibility. Man must think. (*Stands musing for a while.*) When I speak out loud like that, I don't know who it really is—I or someone else: that frightens me. (*After long reflection.*) I am I.—What do you think of that, President?

Despite the farcical overtones, King Peter shares with Danton, Lenz, and Leonce a painful search for identity. Valerio, on the other hand, toys with the question in a supremely detached manner as he confuses King Peter with his masks in Act III.

The contrast between Acts I and II is quite Goethean: the systolic confinement of the court gives way to the diastolic expanse of nature. Valerio establishes the change of atmosphere immediately—"the world is an incredibly spacious building"—albeit on a purely physical level, and the sensitive Lena enters already rejuvenated in spirit:

> Oh, the world is beautiful and so vast, so infinitely vast. I'd like to go on like this day and night. Nothing is stirring. Look how the red glow from the orchids plays over the meadow and the distant mountains lie on the earth like resting clouds.

Leonce, however, is at first still the same Leonce, joking with Valerio, musing about his anxieties, but gradually the landscape begins to draw him out of himself, muting the sterile, solipsistic introspection of Act I:

> What an uncanny evening! Down there everything is quiet, and up there the clouds change and drift and the sunshine comes and goes. Look what strange shapes chase each other up there, look at the long white shadows with horribly skinny legs and bats' wings— and all so swift, so chaotic, and down there not a leaf, not a blade of grass is stirring. The earth has curled up like a frightened child, and ghosts stalk over its cradle.

As usual, Valerio deflates the image:

> I don't know what you're after—I feel very comfortable. The sun looks like the sign of an inn and the fiery clouds over it like the inscription: "Inn of the Golden Sun."

. . . and he concludes with a playful allegory. This banter is familiar to us by now, and we know it can only lead nowhere. What Leonce truly seeks and, within this act, appears to find, is again anticipated by the motto which precedes it:

> Did not once a voice resound
> Deep within me,
> And instantly within me drowned
> All my memory.

Loss of memory, *forgetting oneself*, is the ultimate escape from pain. Danton ruminates about this at length, Lenz is truly at peace only when he can achieve it, and Woyzeck suffers because he can no longer regain it after Marie has deserted him. Despite their dissimilarity in character and social standing, Büchner's heroes constantly thirst for spiritual intoxication, but they are inevitably burdened with oppressive existential hangovers. Leonce tries to intoxicate himself artificially by summoning up a romantic atmosphere at the beginning of the Rosetta scene in Act I, but in vain. In Act II, Valerio literally tries to intoxicate Leonce with a glass of wine, but Leonce has already rejected this alternative: "Which bottle has the wine that will make me drunk today? Can't I even get that far anymore?" True intoxication finally arrives in the person of Princess Lena.

Except for Woyzeck's Marie, Büchner's women tend to have an aura of idealized, incorporeal purity about them. One might be tempted to search for parallels in Büchner's relationship with Minna Jaeglé, but be that as it may, Julie Danton, Lucile Desmoulins, the prostitute Marion, Lena, and Friederike Brion (as Lenz describes her) are all "naive" in their uncomplicated spontaneity; their rapport with reality (and especially with nature) is far more immanent than that of the men, whose self-conscious intellectualizing alienates them from their environment. The women do little else than bloom and wither like flowers, reacting rather than acting, providing a lyrical, memory-erasing refuge for the contemplative male.

Lena's life in the Kingdom of Peepee is sheer agony, since she cannot cope through wit as Leonce can. She is nothing but an ornament, "a poor, helpless stream whose quiet depths must reflect every image that bends over it . . . less than a flower . . . a lamb to the slaughter." Unlike Leonce, who plans his own escape, she is led out of her prison by her masculine Governess, her Valerio. Once freed, she floats through the landscape, an adagio in a minor key. When she and Leonce meet, it is not her physical presence but her voice that strikes a responsive chord in Leonce ("Did not once a voice resound/Deep within me . . ."). He becomes ecstatic not about her but about his reaction to her: "What ferment in the depths, what growth in me, how the voice pours through space!" and the two go their separate ways. When they meet again that night, they are still a pair of disembodied voices, speculating about dreams and death, interacting only through wordplay and rhythmical speech. Leonce indeed seems incapable of doing anything without shrouding it in metaphors and burying it in contradictions: "Let me be your angel of death! . . . Dear corpse, you rest so beautifully on the black pall of night . . . ," etc. In the midst of passion, he rhapsodizes about its cessation. When this ironically morbid love-duet is consummated with a kiss, Lena rushes off.

Leonce grows unselfconsciously exuberant, no longer able to hold himself at arm's length. But it is difficult to empathize with his romantic elation, for his exaggerated pathos makes him appear slightly ridiculous. The experience itself is deeply felt, but it cannot be properly expressed. Emotion turns into melodrama: "Down with you, holy chalice!" but Valerio soon brings him back to his senses, and Leonce jokes about the weather and the man whose suicide he almost imitated, Goethe's Werther. Lena is forgotten, and the two men simply go to sleep.

There is no further development of the ethereal relationship between Leonce and Lena—how could it have been developed further?—and we are soon presented with a *fait accompli:* they are to be married. It is a union of melancholy poets. Lena loves Leonce as a fellow-sufferer; her characterization of him is perhaps the most poignant moment in the play:

> He was so old under his blond hair. Spring on his cheeks and winter in his heart. That's sad. A tired body finds a pillow everywhere, but when the spirit is tired, where shall it rest? I've just had a horrible thought: I think there are people who are unhappy, incurable, just because they *exist*.

Leonce presumably loves Lena for the same reason, as well as for her spirituality. He is rather patronizing about the latter, reducing the poor woman once again to a flower: "Try asking a carnation and a dewdrop what their names are." (In an earlier draft, Leonce says: "She is so much a flower that she can hardly have been baptised, a closed bud, still completely shut by the morning dew.")

The denouement is held in abeyance while King Peter and his court indulge in their customary slapstick. Act III resembles the closing pages of *Lenz* in that Büchner seemed to have tired of his material somewhat and was merely going through the motions before ending with a masterful flourish. One episode stands out, however: Valerio's satiric presentation of the protagonists as marionettes. Leonce and Lena take on the guise of what they feel they already are. Deceiving the court (and each other as well) as to their true identities, they fall unwittingly into an apparently happy ending because King Peter, of all people, uncovers the truth by decreeing an illusion: "We shall celebrate the wedding in effigy." Once unmasked, the pair are playfully ambivalent and mannered, as if they cannot stop playacting:

Leonce.
Why Lena, I think that was an escape into paradise. I've been deceived.
Lena.
I've been deceived.
Leonce.
Oh, Fortune!
Lena.
Oh, Providence!

After he sends off the automatons he now rules, he suggests to Lena various games they might enjoy—no trace of an enlightened social conscience here, for he was and remains totally self-centered. But she rejects them all, including, ironically, the theater, the medium of their existence. He concludes with a paradisiacal fantasy: total sublimation of the self in nature, permanent destruction of time, memory, and identity. Valerio gaily takes up the conceit as the curtain falls. A happy end? It would seem so—yet there are signs throughout the play that Büchner did not want his audience to accept it as such. First of all, Leonce's hyperbolic final speech expresses the "comic enthusiasm" so consistently undermined in previous scenes. Now it simply stands without contradiction, but the illusion-disillusionment pattern has been too firmly established for us to believe in his sincerity. Then, one wonders how long figures with such piercing insight can sustain themselves with a castle in the air. Finally, the ending does not sufficiently lay to rest Leonce's doubts about the permanence of love, eloquently expressed in Act I, Scene 3. Since Büchner's characters often complain about the monotonous repetitiveness of existence, it seems justified to view Lena as a figure in an early stage of Leonce's love experiences, eventually fated to be cast aside—just like Rosetta.

Despite the ambrosian atmosphere of the Rosetta scene, Leonce cannot conquer his boredom. His uninvolved, aesthetic contemplation of her is decadent in a literal sense: he revels only in the beauty of life fading into death:

Oh, a dying love is more beautiful than a growing one. I'm a Roman—for dessert at our lavish banquet golden fish play in their death's colors. How her red cheeks fade, how softly her eyes dim, how gently her swaying limbs rise and fall! *Addio, addio,* my love, I shall love your corpse.

. . . which is precisely how he visualizes Lena in Act II. If indeed "the most insignificant human being is so great that life is far too short to love him," then any hope of salvation through Lena is nothing more than self-deception. His eulogy about his dead love for Rosetta subverts his infatuation for Lena. It seems to be merely a matter of time before the cycle will begin again:

Love is a peculiar thing. You lie half-asleep in bed for a year, then one fine morning you wake up, drink a glass of water, get dressed, and run your hand across your forehead and come to your senses—and come to your senses.—My God, how many women does one need to sing up and down the scale of love? One woman is scarcely enough for a single note. Why is the mist above the earth a prism that breaks the white-hot ray of love into a rainbow?

His despairing relativism allows no hope of a miraculous transformation, for this would be entirely contrary to his nature. Yet Büchner did supply a happy end, possibly because he felt the play would otherwise have been unacceptable to the judges of the Cotta competition. In context, the happy end is the ultimate irony, a cynical parody of the cathartic reaffirmation of existence typical of traditional comedy. Like *Lenz*, therefore, *Leonce and Lena* is to be read as a warning, as a "possibility of existence" that in this particular case leads to a dead end.

WOYZECK

THE *WOYZECK* MANUSCRIPTS

The history of *Woyzeck* is a history of textual contamination. To be sure, some editorial manipulation is inevitable if a stageable drama is to emerge from the various manuscripts of this incomplete work. But in the strictest sense, the publication of *Woyzeck* in any form transgresses against the author's intentions. It renders permanent what he regarded as provisional; it imposes a rigid sequence upon episodes whose position in a final version had not yet been determined. Büchner's drafts are sketches of events, characters, and motifs which he freely transposed from one context to another, constructing scenes from nuclei of sometimes little more than a single line of dialogue. In print, the forty-nine extant scenes, grouped in four (or perhaps five) drafts, fill approximately thirty-five pages. The final draft is obviously a revision of earlier attempts, but it contains gaps and breaks off before Marie's murder. To be properly understood, then, the work should be reproduced in its natural state—as an incomplete creative process. The reader's encounter with the text should approximate the flexibility and uncertainty that existed in Büchner's mind when he prematurely laid down his pen.

Not until recently did *Woyzeck* editions begin to reveal the fragmentary nature of the play accurately. For nearly a century, editors had presented to the public ostensibly finished versions. They promoted themselves in effect to co-authors by not clearly indicating their alterations and additions. They modernized orthography, standardized punctuation, rearranged the scene sequence, and even included entire scenes of their own. Reshaping the work according to classicistic standards, they blocked access to Büchner's dramaturgical workshop. As a result, a number of widely held misconceptions have arisen around the play. It is believed, for instance, that the drafts are a chaotic accumulation of episodes that give no indication whatsoever of scene sequence; that the protagonist is actually named Wozzeck or Wozzek (although scholars disproved this more than fifty years ago, the popularity of Alban Berg's opera *Wozzeck* still causes confusion); that he drowns in a pond at the end of the play; that the work begins with the scene "The Captain. Woyzeck."; and that—to return to the original point—Büchner wrote a play called *Woyzeck* with a beginning, a middle, and an end, consisting of twenty-five to twenty-seven scenes. These misunderstandings have influenced the reception of the drama considerably since its initial publication in the 1870's.

Büchner's extant letters contain no direct reference to the work. Before June 10, 1836, he had evidently written to Karl Gutzkow about his forthcoming "swinish plays"; then in a letter to his brother Wilhelm on September 2, he claimed to be busy "letting several people kill each other or get married on paper, asking the dear Lord for a simple-minded publisher and a large audience with as little good taste as possible." That he was contemplating a happy end to his *Woyzeck* is unlikely; he may have been referring to his lost drama about the Renaissance satirist Pietro Aretino. During the same month he wrote to his parents: "I have not yet released my two dramas, I'm still dissatisfied with several things, and I don't want it to go like the first time [i.e., the publication of *Danton's Death*]. These are works which cannot be completed at a specified time, like a tailor with a dress." Just before the onset of his fatal illness, he mentioned to his fiancée his "joy in creating [his] poetic products" and announced in another letter that *"Leonce and Lena* and two other dramas would be ready for publication in a week at most." Evidently, he considered *Woyzeck* to be on the verge of completion.

The first edition of Büchner's works, produced by his

brother Ludwig in 1850, did not contain the play at all. Ludwig later claimed that he had not been able to decipher adequately his brother's nearly illegible shorthand. Besides, he considered the content "trivial" and "cynical." For a generation the manuscripts lay in an attic, exposed to rain, dust, and rodents, until they came into the hands of Karl Emil Franzos, a prolific Jewish novelist. He had known and admired *Danton's Death* since his student days. With the excitement of discovery, he set to work on *Woyzeck;* his transcription was subsequently published in two installments by the Viennese newspaper *New Free Press* in November 1875. *Woyzeck* reappeared in his complete edition of Büchner's works (1879)—the edition that established Büchner's reputation as a forerunner of modern literature.

Franzos rescued *Woyzeck* from almost certain oblivion, yet he was responsible for inaugurating a long tradition of *Woyzeck* falsifications. The ink on the forty-year-old manuscripts had faded considerably by the time they were rediscovered; to make them more legible, he treated them with chemicals that hastened their further deterioration. Being an author himself, he allowed his enthusiasm and inventiveness to prevail over editorial accuracy, liberally altering and adding to the text, clarifying where he thought the play needed clarification. He did this "for aesthetic reasons," despite his avowal that he was reproducing the text with literal fidelity. Büchner had not indicated a title, so, misreading the protagonist's name, Franzos provided one: *"Wozzeck:* a Fragment of a Tragedy." Although the misspelling was corrected in 1920 by Georg Witkowski, Franzos's arbitrary choice of title has hardly ever been questioned. Perhaps he chose it with *Lenz* in mind, but it is conceivable that—analogous to Büchner's other works— *Woyzeck and Marie* or *Woyzeck's Death* (if the drama had been completed according to its historical sources) might have been appropriate. (This somewhat tongue-in-cheek speculation is meant to underscore the inconclusiveness of the textual evidence. It would therefore be correct—but, I admit, unbearably pedantic—to refer to the play henceforth as "[*Woyzeck*].")

Fritz Bergemann's edition of 1922, containing all of Büchner's writings and correspondence, textual variants, deleted passages, and much documentary material, was heralded as the last word in Büchner scholarship, despite its normalization of orthography and other minor editorial contaminations. His meticulous scholarship produced an edition far superior to Franzos's, but in subsequent printings he, too, let himself be guided by aesthetic considerations and altered the scene sequence. Following Franzos's initiative, he reinstated "The Captain. Woyzeck." as the first scene of the play, for which the drafts give no justification. Editorial intrusions of this sort—and there have been many others since—are invariably based on subjective considerations of literary and theatrical effectiveness. They imprison Büchner's work within the aesthetic standards of a particular era. This is indeed unavoidable in a theatrical production that necessarily reflects the interpretation of a director and his cast, but the lasting value of a textual edition resides in its fidelity to the original manuscripts. It must present with as much exactitude as possible the raw material of literature, from which elucidation, reception, and theatrical realization can then proceed.

Such demarcation between text and interpretation was not adequately preserved in *Woyzeck* editions until the appearance of the first volume of Werner R. Lehmann's *Georg Büchner. Sämtliche Werke und Briefe* in 1967. Lehmann correctly maintained that the drama should be published in three different forms: (a) in the unaltered drafts, to clarify the genesis of the work; (b) in a synopsis, to illustrate the interrelationships among the scene fragments; (c) in an unauthentic reconstruction that deviates as little as possible from Büchner's intentions while providing a readable and actable whole. "The user," Lehmann wrote, "always has the opportunity to turn from the suggestions offered here and . . . return to the sources." Scholars subsequently took him at his word and criticized him for taking unnecessary liberties in his reconstruction. Two newer editions avoided this pitfall by taking a more conservative stance toward the text than he. Egon Krause's *Woyzeck* (1969) might be considered a positivistic antipode to Franzos's freewheeling contaminations. Krause maintained that any attempt at a reconstruction is a falsification of the text, and he simply published the drafts in their chronological order. He bolstered his argument that the Fourth Draft is by itself a nearly complete drama by analyzing the biblical passages in the various drafts and concluding that Woyzeck is not preparing to murder Marie but to reconcile himself with her. I shall take issue with this view in the following essay; suffice it to say that among Büchner critics, Krause stands alone on this point. Lothar, Bornscheuer's reconstruction (*Woyzeck,* 1972) is the sparest of all those published or suggested recently. He omits the scenes from the Third Draft, the "Fair booth. Lights. People." scene from the Fourth Draft (because Büchner never completed it), and, for reasons discussed below, the "Court Clerk . . ." scene (1,21) from the end. Klaus Kanzog, David G. Richards, and Wolfgang Wittkowski have offered other solutions, all differing in minor details. While benefiting from their insights, I found I could not accept any of the suggested reconstructions without reservations. What may seem here like scholarly hairsplitting to the nonspecialist is in fact an earnest attempt on all sides to approach a legitimate compromise between a readable and an authentic *Woyzeck.*

Despite the aforementioned editorial disagreements, there are only a few significant aspects of the *Woyzeck* manuscripts that are still subject to controversy. Editors have overcome the difficulties of Büchner's handwriting to the extent that the text can be considered "secure." Granted, there are and will remain disputed readings of nearly illegible passages; it is, for example, difficult to tell from the squiggles in the manuscript at the end of Scene 4,7 whether Woyzeck says: "With my own eyes!" or "You'll learn how to see!" or "You've got to die, bitch!" as various commentators have suggested—or whether in Scene 4,11 he says: "He—he's got her now, like I used to have her!" or: ". . . like it always is at the beginning!" (*wie ich zu Anfang* vs. *wie immer zu Anfang*). The vast majority of the passages, however, are not nearly so questionable. It is incumbent upon the editor to isolate these passages as being unresolved, so they are not given equal weight with the rest of the text. How these considerations can affect interpretation is especially evident in Scene 1,17. Most editors have assumed that Katey sings the songs injected into Woyzeck's monologue, but Büchner did not indicate this. It is possible that Woyzeck talks *and* sings, compulsively, in fragments, to overcome his memory of Marie's murder, while Katey stares at him, shocked and uncomprehending.

The *Woyzeck* manuscripts consist of five double-pages in folio format (First and Second Drafts), one page in quarto format (Third Draft), and six double-pages in quarto format (Fourth Draft), written in varying degrees of legibility. There is general agreement about the order in which the drafts were written and the arrangement of pages within them. Using as a guide the incomplete revision (Fourth Draft) and the assumption that Büchner indeed planned to include Marie's murder in the drama, we can roughly determine the work's genesis: Büchner first sketched out the middle and end of the plot (First Draft), then he added a beginning (Second Draft), followed by revisions of the beginning and middle (Fourth Draft). It is therefore incorrect to describe the drafts as a welter of scenes which merely provide material for a do-it-yourself *Woyzeck,* irrespective of sequence, material clearly deleted by the author, etc. An accurate reconstruction must clearly indicate that it is an unauthentic version based on certain interpretative decisions. It would seem prudent to follow Lehmann's example and assign the reconstruction to an appendix, or at least place it after the authenticated drafts. But since my edition is designed primarily for nonspecialists, I have decided to spare their patience by placing it first, with the indication that it consists of a combination of various drafts. A theater director can of course "solve" the problems of scene sequence any way he wishes; he may, for instance, want to reinstate the two scenes from the Third Draft that I omitted from the Reconstruction. This edition is based on the premise that the reader must be given a clear picture of the available textual evidence in order to perceive the fragmentary continuum present in the drafts.

THE FIRST DRAFT

Several interpreters have called *Woyzeck* a "dramatic ballad." With its connotation of folksy simplicity, the term does not do justice to the sophistication of Büchner's revision, but it does describe well the intensely concentrated

353

infidelity-jealousy-murder action in the First Draft. The plot unfolds in spurts, without exposition or motivation. Louis and Margret (prefigurations of Woyzeck and Marie) go to a fair where she meets a Sergeant, whom she admires while Louis grows restless. He sees her dancing with the Sergeant at the inn, has visions of blood, and hears voices commanding him to murder her. He describes his hallucinations and suspicions to his unconcerned friend Andres. Undecided at first, he gradually resolves to kill her. After the murder he rushes off to the inn, but his conscience drives him back to the scene of the crime, where he disposes of the knife and tries to wash the blood off his hands. The draft ends with a fragmentary scene that hints at an impending trial. Interspersed in this mini-drama of passion and revenge are scenes of generalized, often ironic commentary: the Announcer at the fair and the Barber (in Scene 1,10) discourse on the beastly nature of man, the Grandmother tells a Dantonesque fairy tale of abject loneliness.

Wilfried Buch and Lothar Bornscheuer have recently suggested that the manuscript of the First Draft can be divided in two, and that the second half (Scenes 1,11–20) was written before Scenes 1,1–10. (The "Court Clerk . . ." scene [1,21] is therefore not a part of the so-called murder-complex.) The arguments for and against their hypothesis are in my opinion ultimately inconclusive. I incline toward retaining the traditional sequence, so the draft is printed here as it appears in the Lehmann and Krause editions.

Scene 1,10: Is the Barber a precursor of Woyzeck? In later drafts, Woyzeck does indeed shave his Captain and becomes an object of scientific experimentation, but the differences between the two personalities are more striking than the similarities. The Barber is eloquent, arrogant, secure in his social milieu. Later drafts indicate that he was a tentative characterization which Büchner eventually dismantled, transplanting aspects of his personality to the Apprentices, the Drum Major, the Captain, the Doctor, and to Woyzeck himself.

Scenes 1,18–20: If the children (1,18) already know that Marie's body has been discovered ("Everybody's gone out there already"), how can Woyzeck be alone with her in 1,19, noticing "people—over there" only at the end of his monologue? Besides, what are a group of children doing on the street at this time of night? These three scenes are crammed onto a single page of the manuscript, perhaps as an afterthought, so their sequence cannot be precisely determined. Lehmann and Kanzog place 1,18 after 1,20, implying that Marie's body is discovered the following morning. Wittkowski argues for a sequence of 19-18-20. A director of a *Woyzeck* production may well incline toward these plausible alternatives; I prefer to adhere to the original order, because these chronological enigmas would seem to lose significance upon consideration of the expressionistic quality of these final scenes. Their frenzied pace, their nightmarish abruptness—in short, their form symbolizes and intensifies Woyzeck's desperation, his inner derangement. In consequence, it seems singularly inappropriate to pause and ask the time of day.

Scene 1,20: Like Lady Macbeth, Woyzeck tries to cleanse himself of guilt, but there is no indication whatsoever in the text that he drowns. This myth, initiated by Franzos and immortalized by Alban Berg, has been consistently supported by those who see in Woyzeck's demise an appropriately classical tragic closure. Woyzeck pays for his sins with his life: accounts are closed, and an aesthetically satisfying catharsis occurs, expressing the preservation of natural/social order through divine retribution. The play thereby implicitly reaffirms the principles of Aristotelian and Shakespearean tragedy. Besides violating Büchner's analytical, open-ended approach to social conflict, this interpretation ignores his explicitly stated technique of dramatizing historical material (see the letter to his family, pages 314–15), to which he faithfully adhered in *Danton's Death* and *Lenz*. It seems quite improbable that he was thinking of deviating so drastically from his sources here. The three murderers from whose case histories he drew material for *Woyzeck* were, after all, arrested and tried for their crimes. However, it is equally true that the manuscripts do not indicate beyond a shadow of a doubt that Woyzeck was to survive after his search for the knife. According to the text, he simply disappears after the line "There's a spot—and there's another."

Scene 1,21 does not resolve the problem. The presence of a Judge and a Doctor indicates that a trial might be forthcoming, but Woyzeck is absent. What role the Barber was meant to play is unclear (unless the scene takes place in an autopsy room), nor can one make sense out of the final word, which is either "science," "scientist," or "scientific." This scene appears at the beginning of a new set of pages, so it is assumed that Büchner proceeded immediately with:

THE SECOND DRAFT

Unlike its predecessor, the Second Draft lacks dramatic action. An appropriate title for it—borrowed from Act I of Berg's *Wozzeck*—would be: "Woyzeck and his environment: character sketches." (The name "Woyzeck" appears here for the first time, linking the drama directly to its primary historical source, the case history of Johann Christian Woyzeck. His execution in 1824 was still a matter of controversy in the 1830's.) Generally longer and more coherent than before, the scenes of the Second Draft place Woyzeck in confrontation with figures that serve to clarify his social context. The "insolence of office" that he must endure, his economic dependence, his anxieties and feelings of inferiority become reality. He cuts branches "for the major" and eats nothing but peas in order to collect a few extra pennies a day from the Doctor with a mania for peculiar scientific experiments. He suffers the taunts of the Captain, his military superior, and the sarcasm of his mistress, Louise. A mere silhouette in the First Draft, she acquires here a personality of tragic proportions: the final scene fragment hints at a conflict of conscience that Büchner later expanded into the poignant Scene 4,16.

While preparing his revision, Büchner crossed out all but Scenes 2,3 and 2,7, transplanting much of the material to the beginning of the Fourth Draft. Environmental factors thus became the expositional basis for the drama of elemental passion already outlined in the First Draft.

We do not know where Büchner might have planned to incorporate Scenes 3,1 and 3,2 in his final version. They appear in most reconstructions because editors can understandably not bear to part with them. I have omitted them, although with considerable regret, because their inclusion would destroy the sanctity of authorized textual material and would represent an interpretation of the drama that transcends the author's declared intentions.

Scene 3,1: The memoirs of an acquaintance of Büchner's indicate that the ear-wiggling incident was based on an episode that took place during an anatomy lecture at the University of Giessen. The professor in question, J. B. Wilbrand, was indisputably the model for Büchner's Doctor. He brought his son to class to demonstrate that "the ear muscles have become obsolete among human beings. Man cannot wiggle his ears, only the apes can do that." Then his son was obliged to stand and wiggle his ears. Büchner transforms this prank into a scene of callous exploitation of a man victimized to the point of collapse. Since the designation of the Wilbrand-figure changes abruptly from "Professor" to "Doctor" during the scene, critics have concluded that it was written before Scene 2,6, in which "Doctor" is used exclusively. It is possible, however, that Büchner may have momentarily forgotten the appellation he used earlier, correcting his mistake as he wrote (after all, Wilbrand was called "Professor"), and the argument becomes invalid. Although Scene 3,1 does not introduce significantly new material, it is dramatically more effective than the other Woyzeck-Doctor scenes (2,6 and 4,8), and I strongly encourage its inclusion in a stage production. In the Berliner Ensemble's *Woyzeck*, this scene was performed first, establishing a note of icy detachment that reappeared in the final "Court Clerk . . ." scene.

Scene 3,2: Editorial controversy begins with the first line, "He fell in the water. . . ." On the one hand, Karl might be referring to Woyzeck's damp appearance after returning from the pond, which would necessarily place the episode after Scene 1,20. On the other hand, it has been pointed out that these lines are children's counting rhymes, similar to "This one has a golden crown . . ." in Scene 4,16. Karl may be foretelling Woyzeck's search for the knife. As I noted above, the First Draft gives no indication about his fate after the scene at the pond. Although it is most unlikely that he drowns, the placement of Scene 3,2 after the end of the First Draft irrevocably brings him back, limiting the alternatives set by Scene 1,20. Scene 3,2 might well appear before the Inn scene (1,17), as Richards suggests, but I prefer to leave this decision to the theater director. Using my earlier reconstruction (Avon Books, 1969), the National Theatre of the Deaf performed Scene 3,2 last; in an emotionally shattering ending, various characters joined Karl in a wild dance, shouting, "Hop-hop! Horsey! Horsey!" around the isolated figure of Woyzeck.

Finally, an economic inconsistency: can Woyzeck afford to buy his son a hobbyhorse—even if it is merely a stick with an imitation horse's head at one end? Perhaps—the text literally reads, "Christian, you'll get a *rider*." I had originally translated this as "cookie," after hearing that a *Reuter* can refer to a cookie baked in the shape of horse and rider, but this alternative obscures the transition to Woyzeck's "hop-hop" game.

THE FOURTH DRAFT AND THE RECONSTRUCTION

The term "draft" has been used to describe the subdivisions of the *Woyzeck* manuscripts, but it is nevertheless somewhat misleading. The First, Second, and Third Drafts reveal, with shifting emphasis, a gradual development of action, character, and theme. Taken together, they comprise the first version of the work. Except for Scene 2,3, Büchner did not pause to revise earlier material until he began the Fourth Draft, the second version. Working from the First and Second Drafts, he crossed out earlier scenes once revision was complete (see the Synopsis on page 229). A few scenes were incorporated into the Fourth Draft with only minor changes (e.g., Scenes 4,1–2), some were considerably altered or expanded (e.g., Scenes 4,14 and 4,16), five were completely new (Scenes 4,4–6, 4,15, and 4,17). Scene 4,5 ("The Captain. Woyzeck.") was probably added to balance the Woyzeck-Doctor encounter in Scene 4,8. On the whole, episodes become less fragmentary, extraneous material disappears, and the plot is tightened. Woyzeck's reflections on his condition become less abstractly philosophical, more concretely related to his social standing. Epigrammatic lines such as "Is no to blame for yes, or yes for no?" and "Everyone's a chasm. You get dizzy when you look down into it" give way to more characteristic ruminations about the injustices perpetrated upon "us poor people."

Scene 4,3: As noted in the text, Büchner wrote the title "Fair booths. Lights. People." and left one and a half pages blank. None of the corresponding scenes in the first two drafts is crossed out, implying that Büchner was undecided about their eventual revision. In my Reconstruction I have followed Richards's suggestion that Scene 2,3 is clearly a reworking of Scene 1,1 and must therefore take precedence. (A director might wish to reinstate the brief dialogue between Woyzeck and Marie that concludes 1,1.) Several unclear or disputed passages have been omitted. The Reconstruction then continues with the Sergeant–Drum Major dialogue from Scene 2,5. Whether Büchner intended to cross out this scene is still a matter of controversy; the line eliminating Scene 2,4 extends halfway through this scene, so the deletion may have been unintentional. The final segment, "Inside the booth," reproduces Scene 1,2 in its entirety.

Scene 4,9: Since Woyzeck does not appear here, the vaudevillian encounter between the Captain and the Doctor seems incomplete compared to its source, Scene 2,7. Three-quarters of a page remains blank after Scene 4,9, meaning that Büchner either had left it incomplete and planned to return to it. or that he had allotted a certain amount of space to it (cf. Scene 4.3) and the scene. written in later, did not fill it. That he did not cross out Scene 2,7 does not settle the problem either way. It is inappropriate to supplement Scene 4.9 with the Woyzeck-Captain-Doctor dialogue of Scene 2.7 because there is a stylistic discrepancy between Woyzeck's philosophical speculations in the earlier version

359

and his blunt manner of speaking in the Fourth Draft. More important, the Captain's taunts have lost their motivation: in the Fourth Draft, Woyzeck becomes aware of Marie's infidelity in the previous scene. In Scene 2,7 he was still unsuspecting because the equivalent confrontation with Marie occurred *afterward*. Büchner was probably aware of this inconsistency but seemed unwilling to eliminate entirely the Captain-Doctor repartee.

Adding the so-called murder-complex (Scenes 1,14–21) to the Fourth Draft in a reconstruction brings about an unavoidable stylistic anomaly: after the introspective Scenes 4,16–17, the tempo suddenly intensifies. In a theatrical production, the break after Scene 4,17 would be practically unnoticeable, but the reader must be aware that the murder-complex derives from an earlier stage of conception and is being grafted onto Büchner's revision. But is this combination of drafts at all legitimate? It appears valid to assume that Büchner intended to depict in some fashion Woyzeck's murder of Marie. The murder-complex is in itself a coherent dramatic unit that corresponds to the historical sources upon which the play was based. Büchner's statement that *"Leonce and Lena* and two other dramas would be ready for publication in a week at most" implies that he was not contemplating major changes in his conception of the drama. That is, the alterations in the murder-complex would probably have been minor. The Reconstruction offers an approximation of his final plan without attempting to simplify the issues he left unresolved.

A bibliography (in chronological order) of *Woyzeck* editions and recent secondary literature referred to in this essay follows:

EDITIONS

Büchner, Ludwig. *Nachgelassene Schriften von Georg Büchner.* Frankfurt a.M., 1850.

Franzos, Karl Emil. *Georg Büchners Sämtliche Werke und handschriftlicher Nachlass.* Frankfurt a.M., 1879.

Witkowski, Georg. *Georg Büchner. "Woyzeck."* Leipzig, 1920.

Bergemann, Fritz. *Georg Büchner. Sämtliche Werke und*

Briefe. Leipzig, 1922. Also: Wiesbaden, 1958; Munich, 1965 (paperback edition).

Lehmann, Werner R. *Georg Büchner. Sämtliche Werke und Briefe.* Vol. I. Hamburg, 1967. Also: *Textkritische Noten. Prolegomena zur Hamburger Büchner-Ausgabe.* Hamburg, 1967.

Krause, Egon. *Georg Büchner. "Woyzeck."* Frankfurt a.M., 1969.

Schmidt, Henry J. *Georg Büchner: "Woyzeck."* New York: Avon Books, 1969.

Bornscheuer, Lothar. *Georg Büchner, "Woyzeck." Kritische Lese- und Arbeitsausgabe.* Stuttgart, 1972.

Bornscheuer, Lothar. *Georg Büchner, "Woyzeck." Erläuterungen und Dokumente.* Stuttgart, 1972. (See also my review of the Bornscheuer volumes in *Monatshefte,* 65 [Winter 1973], 425–28.)

SECONDARY LITERATURE

Richards, David G. "Anmerkungen zur Hamburger Büchner-Ausgabe, den *Woyzeck* betreffend." *Euphorion,* 65 (1971), 49–57.

Lehmann, Werner R. "Repliken: Beiträge zu einem Streitgespräch über den *Woyzeck.*" *Euphorion,* 65 (1971), 57–83.

Kanzog, Klaus. "Wozzeck, Woyzeck und kein Ende. Zur Standortsbestimmung der Editionsphilologie." *Deutsche Vierteljahrsschrift für Literaturwissenschaft und Geistesgeschichte,* 47, No. 3 (1973), 420–42.

Richards, David G. *Georg Büchners "Woyzeck." Interpretation und Textgestaltung.* Bonn, 1975.

Wittkowski, Wolfgang. *Georg Büchner.* (unpublished manuscript)

(I wish to express my gratitude to Professors Richards and Wittkowski for allowing me to consult their manuscripts before publication.)

WOYZECK

In Pastor Oberlin's diary, Büchner found a detailed record of J. M. R. Lenz's aberrant behavior during his stay at the parsonage in Waldbach. Adhering closely to its source, Büchner's novella focused on the denouement of an outcast, omitting the dramatic turning points that had helped precipitate Lenz's mental deterioration—in short, exploring its effects while hinting only vaguely at its causes. *Woyzeck* depicts antisocial behavior on a broader scale than *Lenz;* it seeks out its roots and examines its context. Of all of Büchner's works, *Woyzeck* reveals most clearly the fundamental relationships among his political and literary activities, his study of science and philosophy. Like *Danton's Death* and *Lenz, Woyzeck* is not a piece of freely invented fiction. It is based on the documented histories of three men who killed their mistresses.

Büchner probably first encountered the case histories of the murderers Daniel Schmolling, Johann Diess, and Johann Christian Woyzeck in the *Journal of State Pharmaceutics.* His father was for a time a member of its staff and possessed a complete set. The question of a criminal's sanity, of his legal and moral culpability for his actions, had long been a matter of heated public debate. In the 1820's the German judicial system had become liberalized to the extent that no criminal whose sanity was in doubt was sentenced without extensive medical examinations. A private citizen could challenge the findings of a court and initiate an appeal. Capital punishment, even for such crimes as murder, had become a rare occurrence. The beheading of Johann Christian Woyzeck on August 27, 1824, took place only after repeated investigations into the defendant's situation and character, and the arguments about his mental stability continued after his death. Schmolling and Diess were involved in equally controversial cases that were resolved by imprisonment rather than execution.

The thirty-eight-year-old Daniel Schmolling, formerly a

soldier, was employed in a tobacco factory near Berlin when he stabbed his mistress, Henriette Lehne, to death with a single thrust on September 25, 1817. He had first met her while he was living with her stepmother—Henriette was an illegitimate daughter of her stepmother's late husband. After the stepmother died, Schmolling married and divorced another woman. When he met Henriette again some years later, he was nearly penniless and was not providing support for the three children he had produced in his previous liaisons. According to his testimony, he was deeply in love with Henriette and planned to marry her. He claimed that their affection was mutual, and that he had no cause to suspect infidelity. His acquaintances reported that they had noticed no signs of mental imbalance or melancholia in his behavior, describing him as a calm, cheerful individual. His motive for the crime was a puzzle even to himself. He declared bluntly: "I had absolutely no reason to murder Miss Lehne [and kill himself afterward]; the thought came to me by itself, and I have no idea how." The only abnormality he sensed before the deed was great anxiety, which he attempted to dispel by singing songs together with his fellow workers. On the afternoon of the murder he went into the woods with Henriette to collect pinecones, but he could find no appropriate opportunity to murder her, since he wanted to cause her as little pain as possible. They went for a walk that evening. He asked her to sit by him "because I could kill her more easily sitting than standing." Announcing that "this is the spot where we both shall die," he stabbed her once. About to kill himself, he was frightened off by approaching people, ran into the woods, lost his knife, then looked for a stone with which to smash his head. But wanting to prevent a false arrest, he returned to the scene of the crime. He declared himself the murderer and even asked his dying victim for corroboration.

Johann Diess was drafted into the military when he was twenty years old. His undisciplined behavior soon made him notorious; he was imprisoned for a year for desertion and other infractions of regulations. After his discharge he pursued his trade as a linen weaver, eventually entering into a stormy relationship with Elisabeth Reuter in Darmstadt (Büchner's birthplace). He was violently aggressive

363

toward her, toward strangers, toward himself. He made several attempts on his life. In 1830 their daughter, born out of wedlock, was four years old; Diess, thirty-seven then, was passionately attached to her. Early that year, he almost killed Elisabeth with a cobblestone. Then, on August 15, he murdered her on the street after an argument, stabbing her repeatedly with a pipe-borer. He fled into the woods, reappearing after several days to turn himself in to the authorities.

On January 3, 1780, Johann Christian Woyzeck was born in Leipzig of moderately well-to-do parents, who had both died by the time he was thirteen. He began traveling around in Germany as a wigmaker, barber, and illuminator of copper engravings. Unable to find permanent employment, he enlisted in the army, serving in various German, Dutch, and Swedish regiments. In 1810, while in Stralsund, he met and fell in love with a woman named Wienberg, who subsequently bore him a child. He discovered that she was cuckolding him with other soldiers. For a while he had considered marrying her, but his disappointment drove him to reenlist. In 1818 he returned to Leipzig, where he led an impoverished and aimless existence. He moved from place to place seeking employment, unable to pay his rent. He began an affair with a Mrs. Woost, the widow of a surgeon. She also had the habit of consorting freely with soldiers, and although she was five years older than he and "not at all attractive," according to reports, he often flew into jealous rages and attacked her. It was said she scorned him because of his poverty. On one occasion he beat her with a shattered pot; at another time, finding her dancing with a rival, he threw her down a flight of stairs. On June 21, 1821, he had arranged a rendezvous with her, but he waited in vain because she had decided to go for a walk with a soldier named Böttcher. Toward evening the enraged Woyzeck had a wooden handle affixed to a knife blade he owned. Shortly afterward, he met her and accompanied her home in a calmer frame of mind. But upon reaching the entrance to her house, she said, "What do you want from me? Go home! What if my landlord comes out?" Losing all control, Woyzeck stabbed her seven times, killing her immediately. He was apprehended a few minutes later, before he was able to dispose of his knife. To his captors he said: "God hope she's dead. She deserved it!"

Three impoverished former soldiers stab their mistresses to death: an excellent subject, it would seem, for a fictional treatment of Danton's question, "What is it in us that whores, lies, steals, and murders?" But *Woyzeck*'s scope is not confined to psychological or philosophical speculation about human nature in an ahistorical vacuum. Büchner clearly did not intend to isolate the tragic action from its social context in this manner. He did not simply wish to dramatize *what* had occurred, exploiting its sensationalistic potential, but to analyze *how* and *why* it had occurred. The striking parallels among the Schmolling-Diess-Woyzeck cases were to be interpreted not as mere coincidences but as symptoms typical of a diseased society. In consequence, extrinsic environmental factors were to play as important a role in the drama as the tragic conflict on an individual level. Is society aware of its responsibility for such deviant behavior? Does it examine critically the nature of its justice? *Woyzeck* poses these questions from the start. It is evident, then, that not just the murders themselves but their aftermath, the manner in which society came to terms with them, was instrumental for the concept of the play. *Woyzeck* was in essence Büchner's rebuttal of the verdicts reached against Schmolling, Diess, and Woyzeck in the courts of Berlin, Darmstadt, and Leipzig.

Schmolling was interviewed by a court-appointed medical examiner, who subsequently absolved him of responsibility for his act under the assumption that it had been committed in a moment of "hidden insanity." Schmolling's defense lawyer recommended protective custody. However, a death sentence was decreed by the Municipal Court of Berlin and sustained by the Crime Council of the Berlin Supreme Court. Its presiding adviser was the noted Romantic poet E. T. A. Hoffmann, who maintained that the law cannot declare a man inculpable for his actions merely because "the motivation could not be ascertained, and because the otherwise mentally and physically sound criminal simply states that a blind, irresistible force had driven him to it." The sentence was appealed—against Schmolling's will, incidentally—and a second opinion on behalf of the defense found him to be lacking in "the freedom of spirit

necessary to evaluate the nature of one's acts properly."
The verdict was upheld nonetheless; the Board of Appeal
noted that "the intention and the motivation for the act do
not influence the proper judgment of the crime. Whether
the murder was committed because of love, hatred, weari-
ness of life, or self-interest is a totally indifferent matter."
His sentence was then commuted to life imprisonment. The
rejection of his lawyer's prescient demand for protective
custody soon had violent consequences: Schmolling murdered a fellow prisoner of high social standing. It is assumed
he died in jail.

Diess's lawyer also requested protective custody for his
client. Although a medical examiner did find Diess accountable for his actions, the Grand Ducal Court in Darmstadt pronounced a sentence of only eighteen years'
imprisonment. He died in jail on May 23, 1834, and his
corpse was shipped to the anatomical laboratory at the
University of Giessen, where the medical student Georg
Büchner may have taken part in the postmortem examination.

The temperament of Johann Christian Woyzeck appeared to be a complex amalgam of the inscrutable Schmolling and the hot-tempered Diess, and it was in this figure
that Büchner took the most interest. Two months after the
crime was committed, J. C. A. Clarus, a prominent Saxon
court physician, was asked to prepare a report on Woyzeck's
mental condition. After extensive examination and interrogation, he concluded that the prisoner was of sound
mind and body, and Woyzeck was sentenced to "die by the
sword." Numerous appeals for clemency and further investigation were denied, until a private citizen stepped forward with witnesses who could testify to Woyzeck's mental
derangement. The court again turned to Clarus, who re-
interviewed the prisoner and wrote a far lengthier report
that supported his earlier conclusions.

To ascertain Woyzeck's legal responsibility for his act,
Clarus interrogated a number of witnesses and investigated
Woyzeck's life and medical record. He found the prisoner
to be physically healthy except for evidence of high blood
pressure. Woyzeck's memory was good; he was receptive to
questions and spoke clearly and openly about events and
motives leading to the murder, but he insisted that he felt

no remorse for his deed. Clarus stated that Woyzeck was by nature not a violent man—his jealous rages were isolated exceptions—and although he occasionally drank heavily, he was not a confirmed alcoholic. The only indication of possible insanity was his assertion that he was plagued by hallucinations and voices.

He often dreamed about the Freemasons. In one such dream he saw three fiery faces in the sky, causing him to believe that in some way the secrets of this organization were being revealed to him. Voices, he said, spoke to him from walls. These fantasies were usually accompanied by an accelerated heartbeat, dizziness, hissing in his right ear, and temporary loss of memory. These symptoms seemed to be related at least in part to Mrs. Woost's infidelity. One night he was lying in bed, thinking that at that moment she might be dancing with another man, and he seemed to hear the sounds of violins and basses accompanying the words "On and on! On and on!" (*"Immer drauf,"* similar in meaning to Büchner's *"immer zu."*) On another occasion he heard a voice saying, "Stab Mrs. Woost to death!" and he thought to himself, "You won't do it." The voice responded, "Yes, you will." He was disturbed and depressed by these experiences, but he testified that he was usually able to conceal his unease from his acquaintances. Speaking about the murder, he said that during the act he had had no idea what he was doing.

Clarus maintained that such manifestations were a form of self-delusion; Woyzeck was unconsciously externalizing his doubts and fears, which were intensified by his superstitious nature and by disorders in his circulatory system. Since on his own admission he had heard no voices on the day of the murder, and since he had acquired a knife for the purpose of killing Mrs. Woost, he was demonstrably sane, the crime was to be considered premeditated, and he must suffer the consequences. As a result, the death sentence was upheld, and on August 27, 1824, more than three years after the murder, Woyzeck was beheaded in a Leipzig public square filled with onlookers.

Clarus's investigations raised a storm of controversy. Before and after his reports were published in full in the *Journal of State Pharmaceutics,* there were several rebuttals. Dr. C. M. Marc wrote in 1825 that the documentation provided by Clarus proved that Woyzeck was indeed mentally disturbed and that his emotional outbreaks were caused by his psychological disorders. Marc was in turn attacked by Dr. J. C. A. Heinroth, who insisted that Woyzeck's symptoms were the result of his "moral decrepitude." As a rational being and a Christian, he should not have harbored such hatred against Mrs. Woost. The debate continued into the 1830's.

That Clarus had a sizable reputation to protect is evident from the title of his second report: *The Soundness of Mind of the Murderer Johann Christian Woyzeck, Proven on the Basis of Documents According to the Principles of State Pharmaceutics, by Dr. Johann Christian August Clarus, Councillor to the Royal Saxon Court, Knight of the Fourth Class of the Royal Saxon Order of Civil Merit and of the Royal Russian Order of Vladimir, Professor of the Clinic, the District Government, the University, and the City of Leipzig, Physician and Doctor at Jacob Hospital, Etc.* In his introduction, written with righteous pathos, he assumed a stance of moral indignation that contradicted most of his findings. While declaring that no sensible person could remain unmoved by the prisoner's impending execution, he cast Woyzeck in the role of social deviant, placing the onus of guilt upon him alone:

The educated and sensitive person is seized with profound pity, since he still sees in this criminal a human being, a former citizen, a benefactor of the charity of our common religion, of our blessed and mild government, and of many local advantages and comforts of our immediate environment. This man, who in the course of an uncertain, desolate, thoughtless, and indolent life sank from one level of moral degeneration down to the next, who finally in the dark tumult of primitive emotion destroyed a human life, shall now, rejected by society, lose his own on the scaffold by human hand.

But besides the pity and emotion generated by the horror and repugnance of the death sentence . . . we must remember the *unassailable sanctity of the law.* Subject like humanity itself to continuing moderation and improvement, it must decide in strict justice, for the protection of the throne and the huts, where to be lenient or punitive.

Woyzeck's death was to serve as an example:

> May everyone return from this terrible event [the execution] with the firm decision to become better so that conditions may improve.

The throne-huts imagery, the insistence that social conditions are determined by the innate morality of the individual—in truth, Clarus's introduction reads like an inverted *Hessian Messenger*. He sanctifies the status quo (from which he has derived much personal benefit), equating existing law with an abstract moral code, damning Woyzeck as a transgressor against both. Woyzeck appears as a man who willed his own "degeneration" because he was too obstinate—or perverse—to accept the benefits of a "blessed and mild government," etc. This unreasonable individual is thus declared an outcast from a society which righteously refuses to take any responsibility for his conditioning. That Woyzeck's desperation might have been caused in large part by poverty and hardship—that is, by a grossly unequal distribution of wealth upheld by a repressive social order—is a question that Clarus ignores.

In one of his earlier letters (see pages 244–45), Büchner declared his opposition to laws that protect exploiters from the exploited, to laws that sustain the hugely disparate way of life between aristocrat and peasant—the "long Sunday" versus the "long workday," according to *The Hessian Messenger*. His dramatization of the Schmolling-Diess-Woyzeck cases was a means of analyzing social mechanisms beyond the self-protective boundaries established by the courts. He pursued the issue as a scientist, as an observer of behavior, and as a committed humanitarian. His sources indicated that most of the medical consultants involved in the criminal cases (with the notable exception of Clarus) had come to a deeper, more objective understanding of the criminal mind than had the courts. Unaware of the genetic effects of heredity or of chromosomal abnormality (which may well have been a cause of Diess's violent outbreaks), Büchner was engrossed in the investigation of the organic

369

nature of behavioral response, beginning with the nervous system of fish, his dissertation topic. In *Woyzeck* he re-created the psychosomatic afflictions, the erratic behavior, the visions, the anxiety he found documented in his sources, intending neither to condemn nor to idealize abnormality but to pose with scientific objectivity the question "Why?" In this light, Danton's remark, "A mistake was made when we were created—something is missing," can be read not only as a philosophical statement but as the outcry of a scientist whose discipline cannot yet provide him with the answers he is seeking.

Through such varied characterizations as the prostitute Marion, Lenz, and Woyzeck, Büchner challenged generally accepted distinctions between normal and deviant behavior. If behavior is defined by the individual's reaction to his environment, then the formative social determinants must be included in the analysis. *The Hessian Messenger* proves that Büchner was aware of the class differences that compelled the overwhelming majority of the population to struggle daily for a minimal existence within a society that manipulated and subjugated their human instincts. These insights established the analytical foundation of *Woyzeck*. Yet, of equal formative importance to the drama is Büchner's personal commitment to the poor. His obvious partisanship enables him to avoid false objectivity, which in its presumed neutrality "explains" and thereby excuses acts of repression and injustice. From first to last, his letters give evidence of his humanitarian impulse. One letter in particular, although written to his family more than two and a half years (February 1834) before he began his work on *Woyzeck*, is of such pertinence to the drama that it deserves to be quoted at length.

Having apparently been accused of coldness toward old acquaintances, he replied:

I scorn no one, least of all for his reason or his educa-tion, for it lies in nobody's power not to become an idiot or a criminal, because in similar circumstances we would all be equal and because the circumstances lie outside ourselves. Reason is in fact only a very small part of our mental self, and education is only an incidental form of it.

370

His premise is that of an anti-idealistic determinist. He continued:

> Whoever accuses me of such scorn maintains that I would kick a man because he wears a shabby coat. This kind of brutality, which one would never be considered capable of in the physical sense, is here transposed into the sphere of the intellect, where it is all the more base. I can call someone an idiot without scorning him for that; idiocy belongs to the general characteristics of human nature. I can't change their existence, but no one can prevent me from calling everything that exists by its rightful name or from avoiding whatever I don't like. . . . People call me a scoffer. That's true, I often laugh; but I do not laugh *about* a human being but *because* he is a human being, which he cannot help, and I thereby laugh about myself, for I share his fate. People call that ridicule; they do not tolerate it if one acts like a fool and talks to them familiarly. They are arrogant scorners and scoffers because they search for foolishness only *outside themselves*.

These "scorners and scoffers" were to take form as *Woyzeck*'s Doctor, Captain, and Drum Major. In the following passage Büchner anticipated the polemic intent behind these caricatures:

> I have in truth another kind of ridicule, but its origin is not contempt but hatred. Hatred is as acceptable as love, and I direct my hate in fullest measure against those *who scorn others*. There is a great number of them, endowed with a foolish superficiality called education or with that dead stuff, learning, who sacrifice the great masses of their fellow men to their scornful egotism. Aristocracy is the most despicable contempt of the holy spirit in man. Against this contempt I turn its own weapons: arrogance against arrogance, ridicule against ridicule.

Turning from negation to affirmation, Büchner let slip a trace of condescension:

371

You had better consult my shoeshine-boy about me: my arrogance and contempt of the poor in spirit and of the uneducated would find their best subject there. I beg you, ask him sometime . . . I still hope that I have looked more often with pity at suffering, oppressed beings than have said bitter words to cold, aristocratic hearts.

But two years later (to his family, January 1, 1836), he was more concrete, less righteous than before:

I just came from the Christmas displays: everywhere groups of ragged, freezing children who were standing with bulging eyes and sad faces before those wonders of water and flour, dirt and gold foil. The thought that even the most paltry delights and joys are unattainable for most people made me very bitter.

Peasants and laborers, *The Hessian Messenger* had proclaimed, are "creeping things" over which the princes and aristocrats have dominion. The laborer whose "body is a callus," whose "sweat is the salt on the aristocrat's table," was soon to come to life as Woyzeck in a drama that gave voice to the author's strongly felt empathy for the lower classes.

Woyzeck's social standing is determined by what he owns. The verb "to have" acquires a leitmotivic function in the play, emphasizing the oppressive power of a social order that robs him of those human and civil rights for which the *Messenger* had agitated. The chasm between the "haves" and the "have-nots" gapes most visibly during Woyzeck's confrontation with his Captain (Scene 4,5). Woyzeck has no morality, says the Captain, ostensibly appealing to ethical and religious standards but in actuality employing the sophisticated mechanism by which the lower classes are manipulated into feelings of inferiority. Woyzeck's single "acquisition" independent of his economic status is his relationship with Marie and the child they produced. They presumably could not afford to marry, so their union becomes a transgression, according to the Captain, for it does not have "the blessing of the church."

Thought-control thus invades the most private sphere of Woyzeck's life. Insecure about their morality—a quality they know they must have in order to be considered "good" —both he and Marie turn to the Bible for guidance. It alone provides them with a sense of identity and purpose that transcends their immediate suffering. While it fails them at the critical moment of indecision (Scenes 4,16– 17), it gives them a basis from which to strike back: "Suffer little children [i.e., the poor, in their self-debasing image] to come unto me."

Confronting the Captain directly, Woyzeck pinpoints the critical factor: "Us poor people. You see, Cap'n— money, money. If you don't have money . . ." For the poor, even morality is a luxury, affordable only by those with "a hat and a watch and a topcoat" and refined speech. Economic considerations bind him to the Doctor as well: he sells him his body for a few pennies. His "natural" transgression here—urinating on the street—is a contractual violation, to which the Doctor responds with outrage. He has a contract, the Captain has a moral code, and Woyzeck simply has his own nature, which he cannot comprehend. Yet despite his appearance as a relatively incoherent thinker, Woyzeck *can* communicate his awareness of his poverty—but only to the audience, not to his unaffected oppressors. Therein lies the essence of Woyzeck's tragic situation.

The acquisition of forbidden wealth signals the rift between Woyzeck and Marie. The earrings Marie receives from the Drum Major tempt her, and Woyzeck immediately recognizes the threat they pose: "I've never found anything like that. Two at once." They prompt Marie to class-conscious self-recognition; echoing the "child of man under the princely cloak" image from *The Hessian Messenger*, she protests against social inequality based on the superficial trappings of wealth. Büchner found his model for the scene in Goethe's *Faust:* Gretchen laments over her casket of jewels, albeit more poetically than Marie but without consequence for the succeeding action:

> If these earrings were only mine!
> One looks quite different right away.
> What's the use of looks and youth?

It may be well to wonder at,
But people let it go at that.
They praise you half in pity.
For gold contend,
On gold depend
All things. Ah, we poor!

Marie is the poor man's Manon Lescaut, profligate because she cannot help herself. With his money and status, the Drum Major offers her an irresistible opportunity to be liberated from the constraints of her poverty, to be one of the "chosen"—and to be emotionally liberated from her brooding, preoccupied common-law husband. Once she achieves fulfillment, her self-consciousness dissolves, and with it all thoughts of Woyzeck and her son. "On! and on, on and on!" is all she wants. Her attempt at repentance (Scene 4,16) is futile because she is incapable of such a change: "My God, I can't!" Frustrated like *Hamlet*'s Claudius, her "words fly up, [her] thoughts remain below;/ Words without thoughts never to heaven go." Her son personifies the bond between her and Woyzeck, and her motherly love conflicts painfully with her admission of guilt: "The boy is like a knife in my heart." Her ultimate tragedy is not her death for a sin but her despairing recognition that, given another chance, she would again succumb.

Weakened by his labor and by the Doctor's experiments, degraded by his superiors, Woyzeck falls prey to visions caused by repressed anxieties. He believes himself pursued by demonic forces, declining like Lenz into schizophrenia as his anchor in reality loses its grip. His dementia represents the terminal stage of his alienation; not even Marie can penetrate it. Once his suspicions of her infidelity are confirmed, his visions center on revenge for the loss of the only possession that gave his life meaning. Without her he would simply vegetate, "living on" like Lenz, but whereas Lenz can inflict pain only upon himself, Woyzeck has a target for his retribution. In Scene 4,2, before we are even aware of their relationship, Marie "kills" him by responding to the advances of the Drum Major. The inexplicable "must," the uncontrollable drive to kill her is but a symbolic realization of his own spiritual death; in other words, by killing her he avenges—suicidally—what she has already done to him. The inevitability of his act is intensified by his calmness in the Barracks scene with Andres, as he distributes his remaining property and closes accounts on his existence.

The tragic quality of *Woyzeck* lies, as I said before, not just in the infidelity-jealousy-murder action but in the *vacuum* in which it occurs. No one mourns for Woyzeck; no chorus, no Horatio is at hand to "explain" his fall. He suffers and kills without causing more than momentary interest in the men-marionettes around him. The sublimely complacent Doctor simply subordinates man to a formula that denies the complexity of man's nature and conceals the true causes of his behavior. (The caricature clearly parodies Clarus, as well as Büchner's Professor Wilbrand of Giessen —see page 357.) Andres is a good-natured simpleton, truly little more than a folk song. The Jew is a Hessian Shylock whose *idée fixe* is money. The Drum Major, who directly perpetrates the tragedy, is ironically a petty antagonist. He is a decorated phallus whose outer appearance reflects the single drive that defines his existence. His self-esteem is based on the approbation of his superiors, and as such he is merely a strutting puppet of absolutism. The Captain, a self-satisfied Philistine, is a more complex character than the other stereotypes, for he, like King Peter, is a caricature of the Büchnerian thinker. He is vaguely aware that all is not right with his world, that his control of self and environment is essentially illusory. He suffers like Leonce from the recognition that life is a vast expanse of time that he must somehow fill. Rather than face such anxiety directly, he prefers to adopt a grave expression and strike a moral attitude: "But Woyzeck, virtue, virtue! How else could I make time go by?" Since he does not need to live solely from the fruits of his own labor, time lies heavily on his hands, and he can afford the luxury of boredom. In short, he is a farcical embodiment of the bourgeois intellectual. His character suggests that Büchner might have been indulging here in a bit of self-parody.

These caricatures are basically comic figures, stock types patterned in the tradition of the *commedia dell'arte*. At first glance they seem totally out of place in the tragedy of *Woyzeck*. By allowing these ludicrous puppets to dominate

Woyzeck's environment and showing them to be embodiments of the factors causing his downfall, Büchner suffuses his play with an atmosphere alien to that of classical tragedy: it is the mood of the grotesque, wherein a perversion of rational order, a world-out-of-joint becomes the accepted norm. Woyzeck's apocalyptic visions, his fear that the ground beneath him lacks substance, that he is pursued by an inexpressible "it" are symptoms of deteriorating belief in an ordered universe, typical of much nineteenth-century European literature and philosophy. It was no longer inevitably taken for granted, as in classical tragedy, that antagonistic conflicts would resolve into and reaffirm a stable collective whole—that is, the unquestioned legitimacy of a particular society, religion, or ethical code. The decay of legitimacy produces alienation; in *The Hessian Messenger* Büchner had attempted to demonstrate the sociopolitical nature of this alienation to Hessian peasants and laborers. In *Woyzeck* it is not merely described, but it is expressed through metaphor, through dialogue and scene structure, thereby determining the manner in which character, action, and context are communicated to the audience.

Most of *Woyzeck*'s scenes show the central figure either in open or implied conflict with his surroundings. Three episodes—the Barker/Announcer's oratory at the fair (Scene 4,3), the speech of the First Apprentice (Scene 4,11), and the Grandmother's fairy tale (Scene 1,14)—do not involve Woyzeck directly. They are metaphorical extrapolations of his situation. The scene at the fair is a multilayered parody of social behavior. The satiric technique of debasing a man to an animal becomes yet more ambivalent here through the transformation of an animal to resemble a man, since we cannot be sure whether the animal itself is being elevated or debased in this process. The animal's nature is perverted by the artificial human trappings it must bear. The monkey can be made to adopt any role its master wishes. He "is already a soldier. That's not much—it's the lowest level of the human race!" A mere gesture (i.e., an acquired social grace) transforms him into a baron. The horse is guilty of the same "crime" of which the Doctor accuses Woyzeck later on: they are both "unideal nature," imperfect because they lack the veneer of social propriety—which is, however, "unhealthy."

The drunken First Apprentice parodies the "wisdom of God," Woyzeck's and Marie's spiritual (yet ultimately fallible) sustenance. Here the question "Why does Man exist?" leads only to absurd conclusions. The transience of mortal existence becomes perversely ambiguous: even money, the source of happiness *and* misery, must eventually decay, implying that change is inevitable yet purposeless. Finally, perversity yields to depravity, manifest as lower-class anti-Semitism: "let us piss crosswise so that a Jew will die."

The Grandmother's fairy tale has often been considered to be *Woyzeck in nuce*, a summation of Woyzeck's essential condition: an individual in existentialistic isolation within a meaningless universe. Can the drama be reduced in this manner to a metaphysical parable? First, we must remember that the fairy tale occurs toward the end of the First Draft. Subsequent drafts emphasize the social influences upon Woyzeck's situation, and we cannot be certain that Büchner would have retained the fairy tale unaltered in his revision. In any case, it must be regarded within the drama's continuum of action as a single episode, a single "possibility of existence" that may be modified or even refuted by its context. Reducing the play to a simple Woyzeck-child analogy would signify for Büchner an uncharacteristic leap into the nebulous abstractions of "eternal truths." The Grandmother's tale is indeed fatalistic, employing the uncomplicated imagery and paratactic syntax of the traditional fairy tale to parody and negate the wish fulfillment it normally expresses. The abandoned, weeping child is a nightmarish projection of Woyzeck's anxiety, a symbolic warning rather than an explanation. After its wanderings, the child lapses into an eternally passive state of suffering—a drastic realization of Lucile Desmoulins' "I suppose we must bear it." All of Büchner's literary works bear witness to his preoccupation with sterile resignation, the antithesis of self-confident activism. In no work, however, does he cast his lot irrevocably with either alternative.

Woyzeck's lack of self-confidence is apparent in his fragmentary, hesitant utterances, that contrast sharply with traditional classical style. Implicit in the measured rhetoric of classical drama is the belief that rational communication is possible, and that a nonrealistic, "spiritualized" style can impose meaningful order upon the fragmented chaos of human experience. Classical soliloquies display the dialectical process of self-reflective logic: alternatives are weighed, leading to conclusions that are in turn challenged by new alternatives. The form sustains an aesthetically harmonious balance between progression and closure. *Woyzeck*, on the other hand, exhibits the disjunctive technique of *Aneinandervorbeireden* ("talking-past-one-another"). J. M. R. Lenz was probably the first European dramatist to employ it consistently; it subsequently became a common characteristic of modernist drama through the highly influential works of Chekhov. Instead of creating suspenseful, dramatic confrontations, the dialogue of such anticlassical plays is largely static. Their figures generally ruminate to themselves, unconcerned about and alienated from others. Like Büchner's Lenz, they are more or less consciously aware that they can no longer provide mutual support or even communicate with each other. Andres, for instance, is so blissfully indifferent to his friend's anxieties that he becomes a caricature of the classical confidant. The Doctor is so obsessed by his experiments that he is nothing more than the embodiment of a fixed idea, an inhumanly narrow character who cannot respond to the human needs of others. The Captain is a prisoner of bourgeois clichés and self-doubt; any response by Woyzeck simply confuses him. Woyzeck himself can speak only obliquely with Marie, since their basis for communication is deteriorating rapidly. All that remains between them is a residue of sympathy, of human warmth that is constantly threatened by the fear of betrayal and loss.

Equally anticlassical are Woyzeck's unpremeditated, spontaneous outbursts. He pauses only rarely to reflect upon his situation. In his speech, the patterned structure of language loses its communicative function and becomes a gesture, an immediate expression of the inner self distilled to the purity of an exclamation. When he is confused, he stammers, seizing first on the concept, then gradually arranging his thoughts in syntactic order: "Us poor people. You see, Cap'n—money, money. If you don't have money . . . Just try to raise your own kind on morality in this wo ld." Like the disjointed narrative style of *Lenz*, his

378

halting speech symbolizes his groping through the darkness of an irrational, alien environment, reacting rather than acting as he sees the source of his happiness slipping away. When he does assert himself he either fails miserably (the fight with the Drum Major), or he is not sure why he is doing so (Marie's murder).

Büchner uses language-as-gesture to powerful effect in the murder scene. As he leads Marie into the woods, Woyzeck seems to be possessed by a sense of inevitability. His apparent detachment then explodes into violence. Marie does not die a "clean" death; she and Woyzeck struggle like animals:

Woyzeck.
Take that and that! Can't you die? There! There! Ah—she's still twitching. Not yet? Not yet? Still alive? (*Keeps on stabbing.*) Are you dead? Dead! Dead!

For him, even murder is hard work. The act is all the more terrifying because its visualization is left largely up to the reader's imagination. With characteristic restraint, Büchner adds only a single stage direction to his dialogue—an effect that is downright Aristotelian in its avoidance of excess (or in modern parlance, cheap sensationalism).

While Woyzeck persistently searches for answers in his disintegrating world, Marie becomes lyrical when introspection has ceased. In accordance with her social status, she sings traditional folk songs, which indirectly express her fears and wishes. Within these lyrical interludes Büchner strives for artless, genuine simplicity while allowing the action and Marie's mood to coalesce realistically in a poem. Her utterances, like Woyzeck's, are rooted in the present. That is, neither figure is sufficiently detached from its immediate situation to reflect meaningfully about the past or the future. Their speech is spontaneous yet eloquent, devoid of the trivial, revealing only the essence of action, character, and emotion; "the figures come to life without copying anything into them from the outside" (*Lenz*). Their silences are as profound as the brilliant word-cascades of Danton and Leonce.

Such economy of technique determines the composition of *Woyzeck* as a whole. The brief scenes are often subdivided into even smaller units of only a few lines. For instance (Scene 1,14):

Woyzeck.
  Marie!
Marie.
  (*Startled*.) What is it?
Woyzeck.
  Marie, we have to go. It's time.
Marie.
  Where to?
Woyzeck.
  How do I know?

In contrast to the linear, architectonic structure of classical drama, whose scenes are as rigidly fixed as the blocks of an arch, *Woyzeck*'s episodic form is composed of largely autonomous slices-of-life. Within the restrictions of plot, their sequence is variable, since they are linked less to each other than to the central, unifying theme: the person and situation of Woyzeck. They begin *in medias res* and end abruptly. Instead of being led smoothly from event to event, the audience is compelled to provide its own transitions, to interpret, to think each action through to its possible conclusions. The play becomes an experience of empirical observation, in which certain phenomena are presented *as they are*—that is, in seemingly random, disjointed fashion. Woyzeck's fragmented perception and the irrational social structure in which he exists are thus mirrored and intensified by the formal structure of the work.

Woyzeck's episodic composition is marked, like that of *Danton's Death,* by contrastive juxtaposition, in which satiric, tragic, grotesquely comic, intimate, and "public" moments alternate with unexpected suddenness. As Herbert Lindenberger points out (page 276), these contrasts are not restricted to scene divisions but often occur within them as well. Through such simultaneity, ironic tension arises that is not resolved by scene endings. Irony in *Woyzeck* is therefore largely a structural phenomenon and lies outside the figures—that is, they are not self-consciously ironic like the supersensitive protagonists of *Leonce and Lena*. Yet, as in the earlier plays, irony functions as a *relativizing* factor, as a constant calling-into-question of anything that smacks of conclusiveness. Büchner thereby avoids reducing *Woyzeck* to a polemical tract, while at the same time he diminishes the possibility of unreflected emotional response to familiar dramatic situations. He does not allow his audience to become enthusiastic about glorious heroes, sentimental about fallen virtue, nor refreshed by the liberating effect of comedy. Instead, fluctuating perspectives and moods interact in constant dialectical play, evoking the multifaceted reality of individual and collective conflict. Not only do such figures as Danton, Leonce, and Woyzeck embody provocation and challenge of accepted norms, but the very fabric of the dramas itself serves to unsettle our expectations by inciting within us contradictory mental and emotional impressions.

That Büchner was able to achieve this in *Woyzeck* on a subliminal as well as on an intellectual level is particularly evident in Marie's "repentance" scene (4,16). As she leafs through the Bible seeking expiation for her adulterous act, she realizes that her rejection of Woyzeck's love cannot be healed simply by divine example: " '. . . And Jesus said unto her, "Neither do I condemn thee: go, and sin no more." ' . . . My God, I can't." Spiritual solace has become merely an artificial literary construct from which she is hopelessly alienated. At that moment, their child snuggles up to her, and the pain becomes nearly intolerable. But they are not alone—Karl the idiot is lying in the sun telling himself fairy tales on his fingers. His presence intensifies Marie's isolation; unlike her, he can respond to the child without guilt. Where she so desperately needs sympathy and support, she has only an uncomprehending fool as a companion, much like Woyzeck's Andres. Yet the fool's prattle has a deeper, more ironic function: since it is juxtaposed with the Bible passages, it seems to parody them, implying that the texts Marie reads are as meaningless as Karl's fairy tales. Parody blunts the scene's high potential for sentimentality, generating through ironic contrast a more deeply tragic commentary on Marie's situation.

Woyzeck's disparate, antilinear scenes are linked not only by theme, as I indicated before, but by leitmotivs. Colors, sounds, phrases, and objects appear in various, often metaphorical guises. Some examples: Marie's red lips and black hair are associated through color with passion, blood, and guilt (the red thread around her neck in Scene 1,19 is the German equivalent of a scarlet letter); her "on and on!" pursues Woyzeck into an open field; the knife that kills her is both vision and reality. In consequence, the environment often appears to be demonically alive, an active participant in the action. But despite such evidence of aesthetic unity, the semiautonomous segments of the work do not combine in any way into a classical semblance of closure. In fact, dramas of this type are often called "open-form." *Woyzeck* is a radical example of this genre, although partly by accident—the drama would naturally be less open-ended if Büchner had succeeded in completing it. To shed some light on the controversies over the ending, I must elaborate on several points raised in the previous essay (see pages 351–53, 355, 360).

Büchner's revision ends with the Barracks scene, in which Woyzeck distributes his belongings to Andres and experiences premonitions of death. Although this may well have been the last scene Büchner was able to write, it hardly seems an appropriate conclusion, since it resolves nothing. To argue (as Egon Krause has done) that this and the previous scene suggest a tendency toward reconciliation between Woyzeck and Marie not only runs counter to Büchner's sources but misinterprets the action: Marie cannot shed her guilt, and Woyzeck, in effect resigning from the military, is taking leave of his accustomed way of life. The murder-complex of the First Draft is equally inconclusive. Whether Woyzeck drowns or survives to be brought to trial is mere speculation; the fact remains that his existence as a fictitious character ceases after Scene 1,20. The action ends as unexpectedly as any scene in the play. If it is true, as stated above, that *Woyzeck*'s form and content were designed to provoke and unsettle the expectations of Büchner's audience, then it is illogical to attempt to find a resolution where there is none. The assertion that Woyzeck simply disappears from view disallows various conclusions proposed by critics: that he drowns accidentally in the pond, suffering divine retribution for his crime; that he drowns himself in recognition of his transgression; that he survives, only to remain in a state of alienated loneliness like the child in the Grandmother's tale; that he is caught and punished by a society too narrow-minded to understand the causes of his misfortune. Such interpretations seem to indicate dissatisfaction with the facts of the text—namely, that Büchner's fragment leaves us with an unpunished murderer. We are compelled, in his words, "to pursue the thought." Ironically, this may not have been his ultimate intention, yet the open ending is perfectly characteristic of this voracious student of history, philosophy, sociology, literature, and medicine who scorned pat answers, slogans, clichés—all that reduces human existence to formulas that deny its boundless diversity. Woyzeck's inconclusive fate challenges the reassuring balance achieved by social or metaphysical forces when they bring an evildoer to justice. As in *Lenz* and *Leonce and Lena*, Büchner once again denies us cathartic relief, drawing us as judges into the unresolved action rather than leading us out of it into a world of restored order.

Seen in this light, the ending contradicts the commonly held view that the drama is fatalistic. Implicit in the final scenes and in the fabric of the play as a whole is the conviction that an audience, observing Büchner's dramatization of the Woyzeck-Schmolling-Diess cases, can come to a more enlightened assessment of their motives than the courts that sentenced them. Although he did not say so explicitly, the nature of Büchner's dramaturgy indicates that he shared with Bertolt Brecht the belief that social conditions are potentially alterable and that drama can serve as a factor in their alteration. The ultimate proof of this rests in the figure of Woyzeck himself. Despite his servile posture, despite the demeaning references to his animalistic state and his childlike loneliness, there is heroism in him: he works himself to exhaustion for Marie and the child, he asserts himself before the Captain and the Drum Major, he struggles to remain sane in the face of overwhelming adversity and loss. In contrast to all but Marie, he is admirably human. Büchner was not the sort of radical determinist who denies categorically the possibility of free will; Woyzeck is free will in its unrealized potential, suppressed and distorted by a society that fears its liberation.

SUGGESTED MELODIES FOR THE FOLK SONGS

[With the possible exception of "A hunter from the west" (Scene 4,11), all songs should be sung unaccompanied. The melodies derive from the sources of Büchner's verses; however, some of the original folk songs have more than one tune, so absolute authenticity cannot be guaranteed. A few of the sources could not be located. In performance, an appropriate extant or even improvised folk melody can easily fill the gaps.]

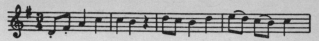

I saw two big rab-bits Chew-ing up the green green grass,

Chew-ing up the green green grass Till it all was go-one.

Scene 4,1, Andres

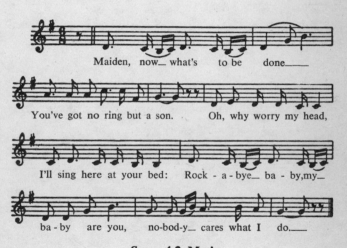

Maiden, now— what's to be done—

You've got no ring but a son. Oh, why worry my head,

I'll sing here at your bed: Rock - a - bye— ba - by, my—

ba - by are you, no-bod-y— cares what I do.—

Scene 4,2, Marie

Our host-ess has a pret-ty maid, she's in her gar-den night and day, She sits in-side her gar-den Un-til the bells have all struck twelve, And stares at all the sol-diers.

Scene 4,10, Andres

A hun-ter from the west Once went ri-ding through the woods. Hip hip hoo-ray! A hun-ter has a merry life, O'er mead-ow and o'er stream, Oh, hunt-ing is my dream!

Scene 4,11, drinkers' chorus

Oh, brand-y, that's my life, Oh, brand-y gives me cour-age!

Scene 4,14, Drum Major

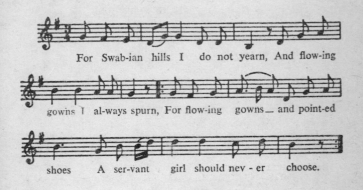

For Swab-ian hills I do not yearn, And flow-ing gowns I al-ways spurn, For flow-ing gowns — and point-ed shoes A ser-vant girl should nev - er choose.

Scene 1,17, Katey

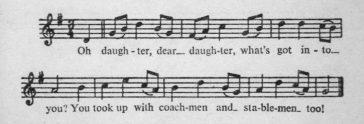

Oh daugh - ter, dear — daugh-ter, what's got in - to — you? You took up with coach-men and — sta-ble-men — too!

Scene 1,10, Barber

ALBAN BERG'S *WOZZECK* (1921)

The extent of an author's influence is measured by the convergence of the literary work with public taste. In Büchner's case, the two did not significantly coincide until the early twentieth century. The history of Büchner's reception (see pages 399–410) reveals that his long neglect was caused in large measure by the dominance of classicistic style on German stages throughout the nineteenth century. The theater was unable and unwilling to come to terms with his innovative dramas; consequently, his works did not begin to reach a wide audience until nearly four generations after his death. For similar reasons, Büchner's modernism did not find its musical equivalent until the Classical and Romantic traditions had been superseded by new modes of composition that corresponded more closely to his realistic, open-form dramaturgy.

Both classical music and classical literature display a progression from dissonance to consonance, from unrest to stability. The "home key" in music corresponds roughly to the resolution of a dramatic conflict into harmonious order which is either purely aesthetic (music) or aesthetic and moral (literature). It appears obvious that a nineteenth-century composer schooled in the classical tradition could not have found an adequate musical correlative for the profoundly anticlassical qualities of *Danton's Death, Leonce and Lena*, and especially *Woyzeck* without revolutionizing his art at the same time. In *Woyzeck* there is no equivalent of consonance, there are only lighter and more acute stages of dissonance. The play's language is neither elevated nor "beautiful"; it is harsh, common, realistic, at times grotesque. In its sensory effect, it corresponds remarkably to atonality in music. That this is not merely a theoretical speculation was demonstrated masterfully by Alban Berg, a student of Arnold Schoenberg, the founder of twelve-tone music.

Deeply affected by a performance of the play in 1914,

Berg (1885–1936) determined to transform it into an opera, despite Schoenberg's objection that it was too realistic to set to music. Berg arranged the libretto himself from Franzos's reconstruction (retaining the misspelling "Wozzeck"). He was aware that beneath the drama's apparently loose structure lay a unity of theme and mood, of characterization and leitmotivic repetition that a musical adaptation would necessarily have to preserve, because a through-composed atonal opera would inevitably fall into incoherent fragments. He divided the play into three acts of five scenes apiece, calling the acts, respectively, "Five Character Studies," "Symphony in Five Movements," and "Six Inventions" (one invention is an orchestral interlude; see pages 394–98). Each scene was composed according to a specific classical (!) model: suite, rhapsody, march, passacaglia, sonata, etc., that would govern the musical delineation of dramatic action.

Besides omitting several scenes to compress the action, Berg made few alterations in Franzos's text. (To conform to public taste, he bowdlerized "pissing on the wall" to "coughing.") Although the Franzos reconstruction lacked the rough-hewn, staccato force of the later Bergemann and Lehmann readings, Berg nevertheless transformed Büchner's understated drama into a work of strident, Expressionist intensity. The musical interludes between scenes propel the action relentlessly forward; the listener can barely pause to reflect or to observe with cool detachment. This stylistic contrast was noted by the eminent baritone Dietrich Fischer-Dieskau: "Where Büchner inwardly withholds his accusation in a sober and restrained manner, remaining calm and objective, Berg paints all the colors of the . . . palette of experience within this new century onto his picture, with numbing complexity, incapable of stopping, directing, or containing the flow." Pain, rage, and psychological disorder dominate in Berg's opera. He intensifies to brilliant effect the grotesque qualities of Büchner's caricatures. The harshly arrhythmical laugh of the Captain is simultaneously cruel and absurd, his whining pathos becomes all the more repulsive as banal singsong. The Doctor's prattle dashes grotesquely across the chromatic spectrum, and the drunken revels of the Inn scenes are an immense conglomeration of dissonances. In the second Inn scene, the featured instrument is an out-of-tune pianino played onstage. Berg's emphasis on hysteria, perversion, and sustained insanity achieves an effect similar to that of the contemporary Expressionist film *The Cabinet of Dr. Caligari*, with its distorted sets. Yet Berg never allowed bombast to overpower his acutely evocative realization of textual nuance.

At the opera's climax, he employs relatively simple yet graphic musical devices: insistent beating of the tympani during Marie's murder; a long, terrifying crescendo in unison on one note after her death. Like an Expressionist artist isolating and intensifying a pure color, he concentrates the scene's horror into a single stab of pain. In the epilogue, Wozzeck's and Marie's child plays on a hobbyhorse as other children rush in and tell him that his mother is dead. They go out to see the corpse, leaving the child to hop about alone onstage until he runs off after the others. Flutes quaver irresolutely, and the opera is over. As Berg describes it: ". . . although the cadence proceeds clearly to the final chord, it almost appears as if it were to continue. And it does continue! The beginning measures of the opera would in fact easily connect to these final measures, and the circle would be complete." Yet the listener cannot possibly be aware of this cyclical link without studying the score, nor is the harmonic resolution obvious. The quavering rhythm does indeed make it "appear as if it were to continue," and Berg thereby achieves an effect of inconclusiveness remarkably similar to that generated by the final scenes of Büchner's play . . . even though Berg's last scene was not written by Büchner at all, but by Franzos.

Vocal expression in *Wozzeck* includes singing, speech, and *Sprechgesang* ("sung speech," a Schoenberg innovation), wherein the pitch is indicated but the singer is to follow the natural intonation of speech. This hinders the possibility of tonal blending, for the voice and its accompaniment are harmonically disconnected, moving in two "antagonistic" horizontal lines instead of establishing vertical chordal unity. Such technical demands placed an extraordinary burden on Berg's singers; only after one hundred thirty-seven rehearsals did the premiere take place under Erich Kleiber in Berlin on December 14, 1925.

Five months later another *Wozzeck* was presented in

Bremen—an opera composed by the relatively obscure Manfred Gurlitt (born in 1890). Except for a recent revival by the Metropolitan Opera Studio, his opera has been forgotten. Musically, he stands closer to Strauss and Hindemith than to Schoenberg. His instrumentation is less sophisticated and complex than Berg's; his orchestra is subordinated to an accompanying role in the drama, and the scenes stand as autonomous units. He chose eighteen scenes from the Franzos text, making considerable cuts and, like Berg, adding an epilogue preceded by a lengthy musical interlude (called "Sorrow for Wozzeck"). He makes extensive use of an offstage soprano choir as a sort of universal commentary on the action; the opera begins and ends with the choir singing "We poor people" in measured tones. The Grandmother's tale is accompanied by ethereal offstage sighs, and after Marie's murder, the entire chorus screams "Murderer! Murderer!" at Wozzeck. To underscore the ecstasy of Marie's seduction by the Drum Major, the sopranos occasionally contribute a joyful "Hei a ja hei!" which bears an unfortunate resemblance to Brünnhilde's cry in *Die Walküre*.

Although Gurlitt's dramatic additions may on occasion be in questionable taste, he is not an incompetent composer; his inadequacy lies in his inability to reproduce the power and complexity of Büchner's play. Alban Berg's genius, however, produced a work of subtle expressivity and theatrical impact that deserves to stand beside its source as an artistic achievement. As one of the few masterpieces of twentieth-century opera, it has persistently overshadowed *Woyzeck* in popularity, especially in non-German-speaking countries, where it has served for many as an introduction to Büchner. Unfortunately, it has become an all-too-common practice to compare the two works qualitatively while ignoring the basic dissimilarity of form, technique, and effect between drama and opera. Such comparisons, focusing on purely aesthetic criteria, fall victim to excess subjectivity and overlook the differing cultural and historical contexts of both works. As a librettist-composer, Berg was conscious of his function as an "ideal director" who interprets and prepares a work for an effective performance before an audience of contemporaries, whose expectations naturally differ from those of the author's audience. *Woy-*

zeck is a product of 1830s' radicalism, ideologically still part of the legacy of the French Revolution; *Wozzeck* is a late Expressionist work of the post–World War I era. A truly comprehensive analysis of both must be founded on these realities.

"PROBLEM OF THE OPERA"

Alban Berg

PRO MUNDO

". . . What do you think about the present-day evolution of the opera?"—the same as I think about all evolution of the arts: that one of these days, a masterpiece will be written which points so directly into the future that on the basis of its existence one can speak of an "evolution of the opera." The use of "present-day" media, such as films, revues, loudspeakers, jazz, just proves a work is modern. Yet we cannot call that real progress, for we have already arrived there and cannot progress further through these media alone.

In order to be able to say once again that the art of opera has evolved—as it evolved, for example, through Monteverdi, Lully, Gluck, Wagner, and recently through Schoenberg's works—other means are necessary than merely the use of the latest advances and whatever is currently popular.

But must there always be "evolution"? Is it not enough to write beautiful music for good theater, or, to put it better: to write such beautiful music that—despite all—good theater ensues?

I have arrived at my own views on the "problem of the opera," about which I must comment in order to correct the widespread false conception of my ideas which arose concurrently with the performance of my opera *Wozzeck*. Therefore please excuse this

PRO DOMO

I did not dream of wanting to reform the art of opera with the composition of *Wozzeck*. This was not my intention when I began it, nor do I regard the finished work as being exemplary for future operatic writing—neither my own nor that of other composers. Nor did I assume nor expect that *Wozzeck* would set a precedent.

Aside from the desire to write good music, to realize musically the intellectual content of Büchner's immortal drama, to transform his poetic language into a musical one, I imagined at the moment when I decided to write an opera nothing more (even relating to the techniques of composition) than to give the theater what belongs to it. That means forming the music in such a way that it is always conscious of its duty to serve the drama. Moreover, that it derives from itself everything which this drama demands for its transformation to the reality of the stage, thus demanding from the composer all the essential tasks of an ideal director. In fact, all of this at once—without detracting from the otherwise absolute (purely musical) justification of the existence of such music, without detracting from its own life, unhampered by nonmusical attributes.

It was a foregone conclusion that this would be accomplished by applying more or less old musical forms (this was considered one of the most significant of my so-called operatic reforms).

The necessity of choosing a selection of Büchner's twenty-six loose, partially fragmented scenes for my libretto, avoiding repetitions which did not allow musical variation, connecting the scenes to each other and grouping them into acts, required of me a musical rather than a literary solution, whether I liked it or not. This problem was to be solved by the laws of musical structure, not dramaturgy.

In order to provide variety for my grouping of fifteen scenes, whereby their musical clarity and memorableness would be guaranteed, I was prevented from simply "through-composing" them according to their literary content, as is so often done. Be it ever so rich in structure or appropriate in illustrating dramatic events, absolute music would not have prevented a feeling of musical monotony —even after a short number of scenes composed in this manner—a feeling of aversion which would have unavoidably grown to boredom, resulting from a series of a dozen entr'acte pieces, formally offering nothing more than the consequences of an illustrative musical style. And boredom is the last thing which one must experience in the theater!

By following the demanding task of giving each scene and each entr'acte piece (either as preludes, postludes, transitions, or interludes) its own unmistakable musical countenance and unity, the use of whatever means could show such characteristics and unity was a foregone result: namely the often-debated use of old and new musical forms, and in fact those used only in absolute music.

Relating these forms to the field of opera to such a great extent may have seemed unusual or new, but this was no new accomplishment! I can and must thereby refute the opinion that I had reformed the art of opera through these innovations.

Since I do not want to belittle my own work with this explanation (which others, who do not know it as well, can do much better), I would like to reveal what I believe to be my exclusive accomplishment:

No matter how much one might know about the musical forms within the framework of this opera, how everything is strictly and logically "worked out," what skill lurks in all details . . . from the moment when the curtain goes up to the moment when it goes down for the last time, no one in the audience should be aware of these diverse fugues and inventions, suite and sonata movements, variations and passacaglias—no one who is suffused with anything besides the central idea of this opera, which transcends far beyond the single fate of Wozzeck. And that—I believe—I have accomplished!

Neue Musik-Zeitung, Vol. 49, No. 9
(Stuttgart 1928).

BERG'S RECONSTRUCTION OF THE PLAY
FOR HIS OPERA *WOZZECK*

1. Scenes
2. Time and Place of Action

3. Characters
4. Plot
5. Musical Forms

ACT ONE: "Wozzeck and his Environment (Exposition)"
        —Five Character Sketches

1. Scene One.
2. The Captain's room. Early morning.
3. Wozzeck and the Captain.
4. We learn a few things about Wozzeck. He is a soldier. He is poor. He lives with Marie. They have a child. He must earn money. Every morning, like this one, he shaves his Captain.
5. "The Captain." Suite: Prelude, Pavane, Cadenza, Gigue, Cadenza, Gavotte-Double I/II, Air, Prelude in retrogression.
CHANGE OF SCENE
1. Scene Two.
2. Open field, the town in the distance. Late afternoon.
3. Wozzeck and Andres.
4. Wozzeck cuts branches for his Captain. Andres helps him. We learn more about Wozzeck: he has visions. He has fixed ideas. He must be sick.
5. "Andres." Rhapsody on three chord progressions and Andres' hunting song in three stanzas.
CHANGE OF SCENE
1. Scene Three.
2. Marie's room. Evening.
3. Marie, Margret, the Child; later Wozzeck.
4. Marie stands at the window of her room, her neighbor Margret is outside. The "music" arrives. Marie sees the Drum Major for the first time.
5. "Marie." Military March, Cradle Song.
CHANGE OF SCENE
1. Scene Four.
2. The Doctor's study. Sunny afternoon.
3. Wozzeck and the Doctor.
4. We see why Wozzeck is sick: in his free time he does not go to Marie or to his child but to the Doctor. He allows himself to be experimented upon, for three cents a day.

5. "The Doctor." Passacaglia (Chaconne): twelve-tone theme with 21 Variations.
   CHANGE OF SCENE
1. Scene Five.
2. Street in front of Marie's house. Twilight.
3. Marie and the Drum Major.
4. Marie is often alone. The Drum Major stands before the door. The drama begins.
5. "The Drum Major." Andante affettuoso (Rondo).

ACT TWO: "Dramatic Development (Peripeteia)"—Symphony in Five Movements

1. Scene One.
2. Marie's room. Morning, sunshine.
3. Marie and the Child; later Wozzeck.
4. Wozzeck comes to Marie, to the Child. He brings them money. He sees the earrings.—She can still make excuses.
5. Sonata movement: Exposition (main, secondary, final movement), First Reprise, Development, Second Reprise.
   CHANGE OF SCENE
1. Scene Two.
2. Street in the town. Daytime.
3. The Captain and the Doctor; later Wozzeck.
4. The world of the townspeople: The Captain and the Doctor. Wozzeck goes past. The Captain makes fun of him. He speaks of a beard's hair in the soup. He speaks of the Drum Major. The little world that Wozzeck thinks he owns collapses around him.
5. Fantasy and Fugue on three themes.
   CHANGE OF SCENE
1. Scene Three.
2. Street in front of Marie's house. A dismal day.
3. Marie and Wozzeck.
4. Wozzeck acts. He goes to Marie. She lies to him. But she does not let him touch her anymore.
5. Largo (a chamber orchestra in the instrumentation of Arnold Schoenberg's Chamber Symphony).
   CHANGE OF SCENE
1. Scene Four.

2. Garden at the Inn. Late evening.
3. Apprentices, Soldiers, and Girls, the First and Second Apprentices, Andres, the Drum Major, and Marie; a little later Wozzeck, finally the Fool.
4. Wozzeck continues to act as well as he can. He cannot do very much. He can only run after her. He watches her at the dance ("On and on, on and on . . ."). A Fool sees him and smells blood.
5. Scherzo: Scherzo I (Ländler), Trio I (Second Apprentice's Song), Scherzo II (Waltz), Trio II (Apprentices' Hunting Chorus and Andres' Song), Scherzo I (variation of the Ländler), Trio I (Song variation on the Sermon of the Second Apprentice), Scherzo II (Waltz with development).
CHANGE OF SCENE
1. Scene Five.
2. Guardroom in the barracks. Night.
3. Soldiers, Wozzeck, and Andres; later the Drum Major.
4. Wozzeck fights with the Drum Major in the guardroom of the barracks. Wozzeck loses. His opponent beats him up. "One thing after another," says Wozzeck.
5. Rondo martiale con Introduzione.

ACT THREE: "Denouement"—Six Inventions

1. Scene One.
2. Marie's room. Night, candlelight.
3. Marie and her Child.
4. Marie reads in the Bible about Mary Magdalen, the sinner.
5. Invention on a Theme: Theme, seven Variations and Fugue.
CHANGE OF SCENE
1. Scene Two.
2. Forest path by a pond. It is getting dark.
3. Wozzeck and Marie.
4. There is no way out. Wozzeck must act. He kills Marie with the knife.
5. Invention on a Tone (B).
CHANGE OF SCENE
1. Scene Three.

2. Inn. Night, weak light.
3. Apprentices and bar girls, Wozzeck and Margret.
4. Wozzeck in the Inn. Blood on his arm betrays him. He thinks of the knife. He runs off to look for it.
5. Invention on a Rhythm.

CHANGE OF SCENE

1. Scene Four.
2. Forest path by a pond. Moonlit night.
3. Wozzeck; later the Captain and the Doctor.
4. Wozzeck throws the knife in the pond. He goes after the knife into the water. He drowns. The Captain and the Doctor come walking by.
5. Invention on a Sixth Chord.
   Invention on a Key.

CHANGE OF SCENE

1. Scene Five.
2. Street in front of Marie's house. Bright morning, sunlight.
3. Marie's boy, Children.
4. The Children play in front of Marie's house. Marie's son plays with them. They call to each other: "Hey, your mother is dead." This is a sensation. They have to run off for a look. Marie's son keeps on playing: "Hop, hop— hop, hop."
5. Invention on a Quaver Rhythm.

GEORG BÜCHNER'S RECEPTION
AND INFLUENCE

I shall begin with a thesis: Georg Büchner's writings already contain in condensed form all of the fundamental compositional elements of our century's modern literature.

—Wilhelm Emrich, *Georg Büchner und die moderne Literatur*

Emrich's claim would seem to be all out of proportion to its subject: Büchner's writings, after all, consist of a mere one hundred fifty pages of text, produced in less than two years by a man who died before his twenty-fourth birthday. And is it conceivable that an author who died a half century before the emergence of modernism in Central Europe could have anticipated the exceptional *diversity* of expression characterizing twentieth-century literature? A close examination of his works and their influence proves that Emrich's bluntness is not misplaced. Rejected and ignored by his contemporaries, Büchner is in many respects a writer more of our century than his own. Without question, he fits Nietzsche's definition of the "untimely" author who "writes against his time and thereby influences it, in the hope of benefiting a future time." He challenges prevalent ideologies, accepted norms, and long-held patterns of association by causing his readers to alter their perception of reality, to experience a learning process through which they may emerge from their "self-incurred immaturity" (Kant). Among Büchner's contemporaries, only Heinrich Heine and, to a lesser extent, Christian Dietrich Grabbe achieved an equivalent reputation of "untimeliness." Writing against the time during the 1830's meant writing against a bourgeois value system strongly influenced by the German Enlightenment and its apotheosis, Weimar Classicism.

At an age when the political unification of Germany was still a utopian dream, Weimar Classicism appeared to have achieved a cultural unification of the German spirit, a Golden Age of literature of the highest moral standards. The writings of Goethe and Schiller were regarded as a culmination of enlightened rationalism and middle-class individualism, as a synthesis of Greek and French classical tradition with German poetic genius. In pure and harmonious classical form, their works asserted the primacy of free will, the autonomy of the creative artist, the moral, spiritual, and aesthetic perfectibility of mankind, and they gradually came to be viewed as universal models for individual betterment. The transcendent nature of their humanistic idealism soon elevated Goethe and Schiller—who had created a modern mythology out of the myths of the past —into mythical figures themselves, whose cultic, norm-giving influence has not changed appreciably in Germany since the early nineteenth century.

To be sure, there were coexistent alternatives to Classicism among Romantic writers and the Jacobin Left, both of which left their mark on Büchner. But the formative anticlassical influence upon the young playwright derived from the Storm and Stress dramatist, poet, and essayist J. M. R. Lenz. He was a zealous reformer who used drama to shed light on social injustices. In such plays as *The Tutor* and *The Soldiers*, he demonstrated how poverty, narrow-minded education, and class prejudice affect social behavior, transforming human beings into caricatures of themselves. His realistic, slice-of-life dramaturgy challenged the ideological foundations of the enlightened bourgeoisie by uncovering patterns of repression that Enlightenment literature had overlooked in its pursuit of a perfect society. His dramas consist of seemingly unpolished scene fragments whose unsettling ambivalence is not dissipated by the didactic solutions Lenz incorporated into the works at their conclusions. In the 1770's, conditions for a favorable reception of Lenz did not exist. He remained an outsider, gradually driven insane by his inability to cope with a hostile environment. Bourgeois idealism and the largely unchallenged authority of the feudal power structure proved to be fertile soil for the preservation, not overthrow, of Enlightenment attitudes, and Weimar Classicism consequently began to bloom in the 1780's.

Büchner was one of the few nineteenth-century writers who recognized and expanded upon the political and aesthetic ramifications of the Lenzian alternative. Refusing to "bow down to the parade horses and cornerstones of history," he created art forms whose epic, open structures mirrored the crumbling belief in transcendent systems of order, the alienation of the individual in an industrial society, the manipulative nature of language and its imprisoning effect on human perception. In short, his art replaced the synthetic "answer" and the security of myth with the rigorous dialectic of scientific observation. The unique epic-contrastive style of *Danton's Death* and *Woyzeck*, for example, propels the reader not toward inner resolution but outward into the contradictions of his own reality. For sociopolitical art of this sort, the dialectical interaction between author and audience becomes crucially important: through critical response to his work, the author gains experience and his technique matures. But Büchner was fated to write in almost total isolation. Besides, whatever he managed to get into print during his lifetime was scarred by precensorship. His essay on Hessian conditions was severely edited by Pastor Weidig before it was incorporated into *The Hessian Messenger*, and most of the copies fell into the hands of the police. *Danton's Death* appeared in expurgated form under the unauthorized title *Dramatic Scenes of the French Reign of Terror;* it was received with enthusiasm by an audience of one: Karl Gutzkow.

For four decades after his death, Büchner was virtually unknown. The only edition of his works to be published before 1879 was prepared in rather arbitrary fashion by his younger brother Ludwig. *Danton's Death* was not performed, although several imitations of it appeared, only to be quickly forgotten. During this era, the German theater was undergoing a reactionary phase, conforming to audience demand for classicistic drama that did not offend refined sensibilities nor tax the public's intelligence. Stage design was painstakingly realistic, requiring ponderous sets; the production of a play like *Danton's Death* with many

401

scene changes was therefore impracticable. But these were merely symptoms of the deeper cause of Büchner's neglect. Conservative public taste and the sterile theater reflected German political conditions after the revolutions of 1848; despite rapid industrialization, the intellectual climate had not changed appreciably since the 1830's. The forces of reaction had succeeded in reestablishing priorities set forth by the Congress of Vienna in 1815, maintaining détente through autocratic, antiliberal rule. For post-'48 society, the French Revolution was an antiquated theme. Büchner's works were obliged to wait for the emergence of a new audience.

After the mid-1880's, cultural foundations began to crumble. The German proletariat was beginning to make itself heard as a potent force of opposition, challenging Establishment politics and art. The influence of Ibsen and Zola helped instigate in Germany the literary revolution called Naturalism. The stage reforms of Gordon Craig and Max Reinhardt created a more flexible and progressive theater that was receptive to experimentation with new forms of drama. These converging factors rapidly created a "timely" environment for Büchner. A favorable reception of his works was practically assured when Karl Emil Franzos rescued *Woyzeck* from oblivion and published the first truly complete edition of his works in 1879. For forty years they had lain in neglect—after another forty years, they were established classics.

One would expect Büchner's reception history to reflect his extraordinary versatility as a writer. Considering that he produced a historical drama, a psychological novella, a Romantic comedy, and a proletarian tragedy, it is hardly surprising that later generations would create differing images of him, corresponding to their philosophical and aesthetic preferences. But the diversity among Büchner images from the 1880's through the 1920's is such that one begins to lose sight of the common denominator. I offer a few of the most prominent examples: Gerhart Hauptmann became an immediate convert and promptly raised Büchner to the level of a deity (see below, pages 404–05). Büchner was also to be found on Georg Heym's altar (*sic*), who visualized him as a proto-Expressionist *poète maudit*: "I love all those whose heart is torn, I love Kleist,

Grabbe, Hölderlin, Büchner, I love Rimbaud and Marlowe. I love all those who are not worshiped by the masses. I love all those who despair, as I do daily." Hauptmann's archrival, the dramatist Frank Wedekind, claimed that *Woyzeck* and *Leonce and Lena* belonged to his "literary shrine." Without *Woyzeck*, he is reputed to have said, his first drama, *Spring's Awakening*, would not have been written. Alban Berg was moved by *Woyzeck*'s expressionistic qualities to transform it into a "timely" opera. (His second opera remained in the Büchner tradition: he set to music the two plays comprising Wedekind's *Lulu* tragedy.) Meanwhile, Rainer Maria Rilke was placing Woyzeck next to his blind man on the *Pont du Carrousel:* ". . . around Wozzek (*sic*) stands all the grandeur of existence; he cannot help that here and there, before, behind, beside his gloomy soul, the horizons tear apart into violence, into monstrousness, into endlessness. It is a drama without compare how this misused being stands in the cosmos wearing his worker's jacket, *malgré lui,* in the endless order of the stars." Like Rilke and Berg, the young Bertolt Brecht attended one of the earliest productions of the play and came away with the impression that Büchner was one of the few true realists of the nineteenth century. He counted Büchner and Wedekind as the most important influences upon his early antiexpressionist (!) dramas. Contemporary Socialists and Communists hailed Büchner as a pre-Marxist voice of revolution, a champion of the oppressed lower classes.

To pursue the history of Büchner's influence beyond fragmentary impressions and questionable generalizations would require a second book of this size. An exhaustive study—which does not yet exist—would have to investigate his reception by audiences and theater critics within and outside Germany, his direct and indirect influence upon literary production since his death, his changing image within the historical development of twentieth-century literary criticism (which seems to produce books about Büchner on a monthly basis), and—perhaps the highest form of tribute to the artist—the approximately twenty-five novels, plays, and poems that have been written about him. Finally, there is the current phenomenon of Büchner as a cultural institution in the Federal Republic of Germany and the German Democratic Republic. In the space remaining here, I will resort to brief overviews: first, a chronology of his emergence from obscurity to immortality; second, a résumé of characteristics that comprise what is now considered to be Büchnerian literary tradition. One should not assume from the résumé that every literary innovation it enumerates necessarily originated with Büchner, nor that every work listed below each category was verifiably influenced by him. The works have been selected to suggest close parallels and affinities to Büchner as an aid to further study, and to demonstrate that Büchner's works did indeed anticipate a remarkable variety of modern forms, techniques, and themes.

BÜCHNER'S RECEPTION

1879	First publication of Büchner's complete works (Karl Emil Franzos, editor).
1885	Premiere of *Leonce and Lena* in an outdoor performance by Munich's "Intimate Theater."
c. 1886–1910	Bismarck's *Sozialistengesetz* (an edict prohibiting Socialists the right of assembly) compels workers and leftists to form "culture groups" that will not attract the suspicions of the police. Searching for literature that reflects their own social realities, they call for performances of dramas by Ibsen, the Naturalists, and earlier writers of a "revolutionary spirit" such as Büchner.
1886	First American publication of *Danton's Death* (in German) as No. 10 in a series called "Socialistic Library."
1887	Gerhart Hauptmann (whose *Before Sunrise* was to inaugurate the Naturalist movement with a theater scandal) delivers an enthusiastic lecture on Büchner to a group of young Berlin writers and visits his grave in Zurich. Hauptmann claims to have begun a "heroic cult" dedicated to "this poetic spirit cast up like glowing lava from chthonic depths (*sic*)." Büchner's grave "became a constant Mecca

for our circle." Thus Büchner—who would not bow down to the parade horses and cornerstones of history, who demythologized the heroes of the French Revolution—becomes a cultic figure at the very dawn of his reception.

1902   Premiere of *Danton's Death* by the "Free Folk-Theater" in Berlin.

1905   A Yiddish translation of *Danton's Death* is published in London by the "Workers' Friend Press."

1909–25   Six complete editions and twenty-two editions of single works by Büchner are published in Germany.

1910–33   Büchner's dramas conquer the German stage. The earliest productions of *Danton's Death* emphasize the play's atmospheric, expressionistic qualities; directors experiment with highly stylized stage settings and contrastive lighting. The work is nevertheless bowdlerized: passages considered too blatantly political, philosophical, obscene, or anti-Christian are cut. Max Reinhardt achieves spectacular success with the play in 1916 and again in 1921. Premiere of *Woyzeck* by the Munich Residenztheater on the centenary of Büchner's birth in 1913; the production is initiated and the text prepared by the Austrian poet Hugo von Hofmannsthal. After Germany's defeat in 1918, *Danton's Death* and *Woyzeck* are staged repeatedly as a call to revolution. To stimulate the workers' sense of class consciousness, productions emphasize the starving masses in *Danton's Death* and the effects of economic deprivation in *Woyzeck*. Danton appears as a moderate Socialist, Robespierre as a Communist dedicated to the vision of a proletarian state. Communist songs are inserted into the play. Less political stagings continue to attract audiences as well. Max Reinhardt takes *Danton's Death* to America in 1926–27. In all, from 1910 to 1933 there occurred in German-speaking countries ninety-seven different productions of *Danton's Death,* seventy-five of *Woyzeck,* and fifty-five of *Leonce and Lena.*

1923   The State of Hesse establishes a George Büchner Prize, to be awarded yearly to a native Hessian in the creative arts. Suspended in 1933.

1925   Premiere of Alban Berg's *Wozzeck* in Berlin.

1933–45   A few attempts are made to claim Büchner as a "folk poet," but his dramas are performed only sporadically under the Nazis. *Danton's Death* appears in painstakingly historical guise, remote from immediate realities.

1945–   Federal Republic of Germany: once again, the Socialists are the first to resurrect Büchner, performing *Danton's Death* in Hamburg (1946). A short time later, German prisoners of war produce both *Danton's Death* and *Leonce and Lena* in an English internment camp. The numerous subsequent stagings in the FRG reflect the ideological pluralism of the postwar era. *Danton's Death* is staged as an anticommunist and/or existentialist play; fatalistic-deterministic productions of *Woyzeck* abound; *Leonce and Lena* appears in playful or serious guise. Performances range from the routine to the experimental. Examples of both: an uninspired production of *Woyzeck* in Darmstadt, Büchner's birthplace, becomes interminable when the curtain is lowered after every scene; a theater in Recklinghausen performs *Leonce and Lena* and *Woyzeck* simultaneously by intermixing scenes from both plays, employing identical casts. The German Academy of Language and Literature reestablishes the Georg Büchner Prize in 1951. No longer restricted to artists of Hessian birth, it becomes the FRG's most prestigious literary award. Among the recipients: Gottfried Benn, Max Frisch, Paul Celan, Hans Magnus Enzensberger, Günter Grass, Heinrich Böll. The prizewinners' acceptance speeches testify to Büchner's wide-ranging appeal across the political spectrum.

German Democratic Republic: although Bertolt Brecht valued Büchner's plays as models for epic dramaturgy and *Woyzeck* in particular as a technical masterpiece, none of the works was performed at the Berliner Ensemble during his lifetime. The GDR Büchner reception continues the tradition established by the German Left before 1933: he is esteemed as a precursor of Marxism, as the first major writer to create a realistic proletarian hero. Only *Woyzeck* is performed with any frequency.

Other countries: Jean Vilar stages an impressive production of *Danton's Death* in Paris (1952), using the translation by the Absurdist dramatist Arthur Adamov (who once wrote: "Between Shakespeare and Molière's *Don Juan* to Brecht there is nothing but Büchner"). An Italian theater performs all *Woyzeck* drafts in sequence. In America, Büchner thrives particularly on college campuses (numerous performances in both English and German), but he is not unknown to Off-Broadway, Off-Off-Broadway, radical theater groups, and independent companies. In 1965 he achieves nationwide attention as the centerpiece for a major cultural event: *Danton's Death* is performed at the opening of the Vivian Beaumont Theater in New York's Lincoln Center. The National Theatre of the Deaf tours the country with *Woyzeck* in 1970–71.

1947   Premiere of Gottfried von Einem's opera, *Danton's Death*, in Salzburg.

1961   Premiere of Kurt Schwaen's opera, *Leonce and Lena*, in Berlin.

1. Non-Aristotelian techniques of open-form drama (*Danton's Death, Woyzeck*). Antilinear, autonomous scenes; fragmented, paratactic dialogue. Unity achieved through leitmotiv, variation, and contrast.

—From Büchner and his contemporary, Christian Dietrich Grabbe, the tradition extends over Frank Wedekind to the epic and dialectic theater of Bertolt Brecht, who more than any other playwright influenced the development of postwar European drama.

2. Antiheroic historical drama (*Danton's Death*). The material origins and dialectical conflicts of revolution. Individual moral responsibility versus the welfare of the collective. Hedonism (Danton) versus asceticism (Robespierre).

—Gerhart Hauptmann, *The Weavers* (1892); Ernst Toller, *Mass-Man* (1921); Bertolt Brecht, *The Measures Taken* (1930) and *The Days of the Commune* (1949); Carl Zuckmayer, *The Devil's General* (1946); Peter Weiss, *The Persecution and Assassination of Jean Paul Marat as Performed by the Inmates of the Asylum of Charenton under the Direction of the Marquis de Sade* (1964); Tankred Dorst, *Toller* (1968); Peter Weiss, *Trotzky in Exile* (1970); Heiner Müller, *Mauser* (1970); Gaston Salvatore, *Büchner's Death* (1972).

3. Direct incorporation of documentary sources into literature to emphasize historical realities behind the fictional construct (*Danton's Death, Lenz, Woyzeck*). "The dramatic poet is in my eyes nothing but a writer of history . . ." (Büchner's letter of July 28, 1835).

—Erwin Piscator's dramatic productions during the 1920's; Rolf Hochhuth, *The Deputy* (1963); Heinar Kipphardt, *In the Matter of J. Robert Oppenheimer* (1964); Peter Weiss, *The Investigation* (1965); Hans Magnus Enzensberger, *The Havana Trial* (1970).

4. Clinically dispassionate analysis of schizophrenic

alienation (*Lenz*). Interior narrative perspective that "sweeps away the smokescreen . . . of fabricated emotions" (Christa Wolf on *Lenz*).

—Gerhart Hauptmann, *Flagman Thiel* (1887) and *The Apostle* (1890); Alfred Döblin, *The Murder of a Buttercup* (1910); Georg Heym, *The Madman* (1911); Hugo von Hofmannsthal, *Andreas* (1913); Georg Trakl, *Dream and Derangement* (1914); Peter Schneider, *Lenz* (1973); Volker Braun, *An Unfinished Story* (1975).

5. Self-conscious role-playing (*Leonce and Lena*). Wit as defense against ennui. The genesis of absurdism from Romantic irony: the deceptive nature of linguistic communication.

—Theater of the Absurd in France and Germany; Friedrich Dürrenmatt, *Romulus the Great* (1949); Max Frisch, *Don Juan or The Love of Geometry* (1953); Tom Stoppard, *Rosencrantz and Guildenstern Are Dead* (1967); Peter Handke, *Kaspar* (1968).

6. Use of grotesque distortion as intensified form of social criticism, as perversion of natural order (*Danton's Death, Leonce and Lena, Woyzeck*). Man as animal.

—Frank Wedekind, *Spring's Awakening* (1891) and *Earth Spirit* (1895); Bertolt Brecht, *In the Jungle of Cities* (1924) and *Man Is Man* (1926); Friedrich Dürrenmatt, *The Visit of the Old Lady* (1956); Peter Weiss, *Song of the Lusitanian Bogey* (1967); Heiner Müller, *Germania* (1971); contemporary radical theater.

7. The tragedy of the oppressed proletarian (*Woyzeck*). Environment as antagonist: social and economic determinism. Use of dialect to enhance realism of "folk play."

—Bertolt Brecht, *Baal* (1918) and *Drums in the Night* (1920); Ernst Toller, *Hobbleman* (1923); Ödön von Horváth, *Sladek or The Black Army* (1927); Georg Kaiser, *Lieutenant Welzeck* (1939) and *The Soldier Tanaka* (1940); Wolfgang Borchert, *The Man Outside* (1947); Max Frisch, *Andorra* (1961); Martin Walser,

Oak and Angora (1962); Franz Xaver Kroetz, *The Nest* (1975).

8. The author as political educator (*The Hessian Messenger*). Techniques of investigative journalism. Direct involvement in political activities (*cf.* Büchner's "Society for the Rights of Man").
—Political writings of Günter Grass, Hans Magnus Enzensberger, Günter Wallraff.

BIBLIOGRAPHY

Listed below are books, essays, and articles on Georg Büchner in English, arranged chronologically within each category. Dissertations, reviews of theatrical performances, and introductions to editions and anthologies (except where otherwise noted) are not included. Asterisks denote books and longer essays of a general nature.

I. GENERAL

Vickers, L. "Georg Büchner." *Nation*, 32 (1880), 224.

*Dunlop, Geoffrey, trans. "Introduction." *The Plays of Georg Büchner*. London, 1927, pp. 7–65.

Hauch, Edward E. "The Reviviscence of Georg Büchner." *Publications of the Modern Language Association of America*, 44 (1929), 892–900.

Kresh, Joseph G. "Georg Büchner's Reputation as an Economic Radical." *Germanic Review*, 8 (1933), 44–51.

*Kresh, Joseph G. "Georg Büchner." *Dialectics*, 1, No. 6 (1938), 1–11; No. 7 (1938), 19–31.

Kaufmann, Friedrich W. "Georg Büchner." *German Dramatists of the 19th Century*. Los Angeles, 1940, pp. 103–11.

Meyer, Erwin L. *The Changing Attitude Toward Georg Büchner*. Bloomington, Ind., 1945.

Rosenberg, Ralph P. "Georg Büchner's Early Reception in America." *Journal of English and Germanic Philology*, 44 (1945), 270–73.

Zeydel, Edwin H. "A Note on Georg Büchner and Gerhart Hauptmann." *Journal of English and Germanic Philology,* 44 (1945), 87–88.

*Knight, Arthur H. J. *Georg Büchner.* Oxford, 1951.

*White, John S. "Georg Büchner or the Suffering Through the Father." *The American Imago,* 9 (1952), 365–427.

Majut, Rudolf. "Georg Büchner and Some English Thinkers." *Modern Language Review,* 48 (1953), 310–22.

*Jacobs, Margaret, ed. "Introduction." *Georg Büchner: "Dantons Tod" and "Woyzeck."* Manchester, 1954, pp. ix–xxxiv.

Majut, Rudolf. "Some Literary Affiliations of Georg Büchner with England." *Modern Language Review,* 50 (1955), 30–43.

Furness, N. A. "Georg Büchner's Translations of Victor Hugo." *Modern Language Review,* 51 (1956), 49–54.

Closs, August. "Nihilism and Modern German Drama: Grabbe and Büchner." *Medusa's Mirror: Studies in German Literature.* London, 1957, pp. 147–63.

*Hamburger, Michael. "Georg Büchner." *Evergreen Review,* 1 (1957), 68–98.

*Hamburger, Michael. "Georg Büchner." *Reason and Energy: Studies in German Literature.* London/New York, 1957, pp. 179–208.

Peacock, Ronald. "A Note on Georg Büchner's Plays." *German Life and Letters,* 10 (1956–57), 189–97. Also in *The Poet in the Theatre.* New York, 1960, pp. 181–93.

Steiner, George. *The Death of Tragedy.* London, 1961/New York, 1963, pp. 270–81.

Benn, Maurice B., ed. "Introduction." *Georg Büchner: "Leonce und Lena" and "Lenz."* London, 1963, pp. ix–xxxi.

Hartwig, Gilbert F. "Georg Büchner: Nineteenth Century Avant-garde." *The Southern Quarterly,* 1, No. 2 (1963), 98–128.

*Lindenberger, Herbert S. *Georg Büchner.* Carbondale, Ill., 1964.

*Stern, J. P. "A World of Suffering: Georg Büchner." *Seven Studies in Nineteenth-Century German Literature.* London, 1964, pp. 78–155.

*Spalter, Max. "Georg Büchner." *Brecht's Tradition*. Baltimore, 1967, pp. 75–111.

Böll, Heinrich. "On Georg Büchner." *Delos*, 2 (1968), 105–10.

Cowen, Roy C. "Identity and Conscience in Büchner's Works." *Germanic Review*, 43 (1968), 258–66.

MacEwen, Leslie. *The Narren-motifs in the Works of Georg Büchner*. Bern, 1968.

Benn, Maurice B. "Anti-Pygmalion: An Apologia for Georg Büchner's Aesthetics." *Modern Language Review*, 64 (1969), 597–604.

*Schmidt, Henry J. *Satire, Caricature, and Perspectivism in the Works of Georg Büchner*. The Hague, 1970.

Bell, Gerda E. "Georg Büchner's Translations of Victor Hugo's *Lucrèce Borgia* and *Maria Tudor*." *Arcadia*, 6 (1971), 151–74.

Bell, Gerda E. "Traduttore-Traditore? Some Remarks on Georg Büchner's Victor Hugo Translations." *Monatshefte*, 63 (1971), 19-27.

Burwick, Frederick. "The Anatomy of Revolution: Beddoes and Büchner." *Pacific Coast Philology*, 6 (1971), 5–12.

Murdoch, Brian. "Communication as a Dramatic Problem: Büchner, Chekhov, Hofmannsthal, and Wesker." *Revue de Littérature Comparée*, 45 (1971), 40–56.

Bell, Gerda E. "Windows: A Study of a Symbol in Georg Büchner's Work." *Germanic Review*, 47 (1972), 95–108.

Brustein, Robert. "Büchner: Artist and Visionary." *Yale/Theatre*, 3, No. 3 (1972), 4–7.

Fischer, Heinz. "Some Marginal Notes on Georg Büchner." *Revue de Littérature Comparée*, 46 (1972), 255–58.

Gilman, Richard. "Georg Büchner: History Redeemed." *Yale/Theatre*, 3, No. 3 (1972), 8–34.

Schechter, Joel. "Pietro Aretino: Georg Büchner's Lost Play." *Yale/Theatre*, 3, No. 3 (1972), 94–98.

Benn, Maurice B. "Büchner and Gautier." *Seminar*, 9 (1973), 202–07.

Bell, Gerda E. "Georg Büchner's Last Words." *German* (1973), 202–207.
Life and Letters, 27 (1973–74), 17–22.

*Hauser, Ronald. *Georg Büchner*. New York, 1974.

Wells, George A. "Büchner as Tragedian." *Erfahrung und Überlieferung: Festschrift for C. P. Magill*. Cardiff, 1974, pp. 100–12.

*Benn, Maurice B. *The Drama of Revolt: A Critical Study of Georg Büchner*. Cambridge, 1976.

*Richards, David G. *Georg Büchner and the Birth of the Modern Drama*. Albany, 1977.

II. *Danton's Death*

Rosenberg, Ralph P. "Problems in Translation with Reference to *Dantons Tod*." *German Quarterly*, 15 (1942), 19–27.

Knight, Arthur H. J. "Some Considerations Relating to Georg Büchner's Opinions on History and the Drama and to His Play *Dantons Tod*." *Modern Language Review*, 42 (1947), 70–81.

MacLean, H. "The Moral Conflict in Georg Büchner's *Dantons Tod*." *Journal of the Australasian Universities Modern Language Association*, 6 (1957), 25–33.

Baxandall, Lee. "Georg Büchner's *Danton's Death*." *Tulane Drama Review*, 6, No. 3 (1961–62), 136–49.

Fleissner, E. M. "Revolution as Theatre: *Danton's Death and Marat/Sade*." *Massachusetts Review*, 7 (1966), 543–56.

Cowen, Roy C. "Grabbe's *Don Juan and Faust* and Büchner's *Dantons Tod*: Epicureanism and *Weltschmerz*." *Publications of the Modern Language Association of America*, 82 (1967), 342–51.

Cowen, Roy C. "Grabbe's *Napoleon*, Büchner's *Danton* and the Masses." *Symposium*, 21 (1967), 316–23.

Milburn, Douglas, Jr. "Social Conscience and Social Reform: The Political Paradox of *Dantons Tod*." *Rice University Studies*, 53, No. 4 (1967), 23–31.

Lindenberger, Herbert S. "*Danton's Death* and the Conventions of Historical Drama." *Comparative Drama*, 3 (1969), 99–109.

Beacham, Richard. "Büchner's Use of Sources in *Danton's Death*." *Yale/Theatre*, 3, No. 3 (1972), 45–55.

Houseman, John. "Orson Welles and *Danton's Death*." *Yale/Theatre*, 3, No. 3 (1972), 56–67.

Simon, John. "On *Danton's Death.*" *Yale/Theatre*, 3, No. 3 (1972), 35–44.

Bodi, Leslie. " 'Sensualism' and 'Spiritualism' in Büchner's *Danton's Death.*" *Komos*, 3 (1973), 17–19.

Malkin, Michael R. *"Danton's Death:* Büchner's Unidealistic Danton." *Studies in the Humanities*, 3, No. 2 (1973), 46–48.

Roberts, David. "Büchner and the French Revolution: Two Arguments." *Komos*, 3 (1973), 24–27.

Rose, Margaret. "Messianism and the Terror: Desmoulins' and Büchner's Use of a New Messiah *Figura.*" *Komos*, 3 (1973), 27–30.

Teichmann, Max. *"Danton's Death:* An Early Psychodrama." *Komos*, 3 (1973), 21–23.

Worrall, G. S. "The Historical Background to *Danton's Death.*" *Komos*, 3 (1973), 19–21.

Holmes, T. M. "The Ideology of the Moderates in Büchner's *Dantons Tod.*" *German Life and Letters*, 27 (1973–74), 93–100.

Waldeck, Peter B. "Georg Büchner's *Dantons Tod:* Dramatic Structure and Individual Necessity." *Susquehanna University Studies*, 9, No. 4 (1974), 211–25.

Grimm, Reinhold. "The Play within a Play in Revolutionary Theatre." *Mosaic*, 9, No. 1 (1975), 41–52.

Swales, Martin. "Ontology, Politics, Sexuality: A Note on Georg Büchner's Drama *Dantons Tod.*" *New German Studies*, 3 (1975), 109–25.

III. *Lenz*

Parker, John J. "Some Reflections on Georg Büchner's *Lenz* and Its Principal Source, the Oberlin Record." *German Life and Letters*, 21 (1968), 103–11.

Harris, Edward P. "J. M. R. Lenz in German Literature: From Büchner to Bobrowski." *Colloquia Germanica*, 3 (1973), 214–33.

King, Janet K. "Lenz Viewed Sane." *Germanic Review*, 49 (1974), 146–53.

Jansen, Peter K. "The Structural Function of the *Kunstgespräch* in Büchner's *Lenz.*" *Monatshefte*, 67 (1975), 145–56.

IV. *Leonce and Lena*

Shaw, Leroy R. "Symbolism of Time in Georg Büchner's *Leonce und Lena.*" *Monatshefte,* 48 (1956), 221–30.

Hauser, Ronald. "Georg Büchner's *Leonce und Lena.*" *Monatshefte,* 53 (1961), 338–46.

Macay, Barbara. *"Leonce and Lena." Yale/Theatre,* 3, No. 3 (1972), 68–82.

Lamb, Margaret. "That Strain Again: 'Shakespearean' Comedies by Musset and Büchner." *Educational Theatre Journal,* 27 (1975), 70–76.

V. *Woyzeck*

Blackall, Eric A. "Büchner and Alban Berg: Some Thoughts on *Wozzeck." German Quarterly,* 34 (1961), 431–38.

Kayser, Wolfgang J. *"Woyzeck." The Grotesque in Art and Literature.* London/Bloomington, Ind., 1963; New York, 1966, pp. 89–99.

Perle, George. "Woyzeck and Wozzeck." *Musical Quarterly,* 53 (1967), 206–19.

Stein, Jack M. "From *Woyzeck* to *Wozzeck:* Alban Berg's Adaptation of Büchner." *Germanic Review,* 46 (1972), 168–80.

Wiles, Timothy. *"Woyzeck,* immer zu." *Yale/Theatre,* 3, No. 3 (1972), 83–89.

Stodder, Joseph H. "Influences of *Othello* on Büchner's *Woyzeck." Modern Language Review,* 69 (1974), 115–20.

Baumgartner, Ingeborg. "Ambiguity in Büchner's *Woyzeck." Michigan Germanic Studies,* 1 (1975), 199–214.

For books and articles in German consult:

Schlick, Werner. *Das Georg Büchner-Schrifttum bis 1965.* Hildesheim, 1968.

Mayer, Hans. *Georg Büchner und seine Zeit*. Frankfurt a.M., 1972.

Knapp, Gerhard P. *Georg Büchner. Eine kritische Einführung in die Forschung*. Frankfurt a.M., 1975.

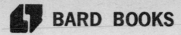 **BARD BOOKS**

the classics, poetry, drama and
distinguished modern fiction

FICTION

SUN CITY Tove Jansson	32318	1.95
THE LANGUAGE OF CATS AND OTHER STORIES Spencer Hoist	14381	1.65
THE LAST DAYS OF LOUISIANA RED Ishmael Reed	35451	2.25
LEAF STORM AND OTHER STORIES Gabriel García Márquez	35816	1.95
LESBIAN BODY Monique Wittig	31062	1.75
LES GUERILLERES Monique Wittig	14373	1.65
A LONG AND HAPPY LIFE Reynolds Price	17053	1.65
LUCIFER WITH A BOOK John Horne Burns	33340	2.25
THE MAGNIFICENT AMBERSONS Booth Tarkington	17236	1.50
THE MAN WHO WAS NOT WITH IT Herbert Gold	19356	1.65
THE MAZE MAKER Michael Ayrton	23648	1.65
MEMENTO MORI Muriel Spark	12237	1.65
MYSTERIES Knut Hamsun	25221	1.95
NABOKOV'S DOZEN Vladimir Nabokov	15354	1.65
NO ONE WRITES TO THE COLONEL AND OTHER STORIES Gabriel García Márquez	32748	1.75
ONE HUNDRED YEARS OF SOLITUDE Gabriel García Márquez	34033	2.25
OUR TOWN Thornton Wilder	26674	1.25
PARTIES Carl Van Vechten	32631	1.95
PATHS OF GLORY Humphrey Cobb	16758	1.65
PNIN Vladimir Nabokov	15800	1.65
REAL PEOPLE Alison Lurie	23747	1.65
THE RECOGNITIONS William Gaddis	18572	2.65
SLAVE Isaac Singer	26377	1.95
A SMUGGLER'S BIBLE Joseph McElroy	33589	2.50
STUDS LONIGAN TRILOGY James T. Farrell	31955	2.75
SUMMERING Joanne Greenberg	17798	1.65
62: A MODEL KIT Julio Cortázar	17558	1.65
THREE BY HANDKE Peter Handke	32458	2.25
THE VICTIM Saul Bellow	24273	1.75
WHAT HAPPENS NEXT? Gilbert Rogin	17806	1.65

Where better paperbacks are sold, or directly from the publisher. Include 25¢ per copy for postage and handling, allow 4-6 weeks for delivery.

Avon Books, Mail Order Dept.
250 West 55th Street, New York, N.Y. 10019

BD(2) 11-77

BARD BOOKS

DISTINGUISHED DRAMA

 **BARD BOOKS**

distinguished poetry

EVANGELINE
Henry Wadsworth Longfellow · 01669 · .60

LEAVES OF GRASS Walt Whitman · 02154 · .60

THE RIME OF THE ANCIENT MARINER
Samuel Taylor Coleridge · 36830 · 1.25

THE RUBAIYAT OF OMAR KHAYYAM
Edward Fitzgerald · 18770 · .70

SHAKESPEARE'S SONNETS
Ed. by Barbara Herrnstein Smith · 08904 · 1.25

A SHROPSHIRE LAD A. E. Housman · 02139 · .60

**SONGS OF INNOCENCE AND OF
EXPERIENCE** William Blake · 18762 · .70

SONNETS FROM THE PORTUGUESE
Elizabeth B. Browning · 19836 · .75

YEVTUSHENKO'S READER
Yevgeny Yevtushenko · 14811 · 1.45

THE LONG WAR DEAD
Bryan Alec Floyd · 27615 · 1.50

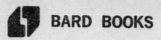 **BARD BOOKS**

DISTINGUISHED
LATIN-AMERICAN FICTION

BETRAYED BY RITA HAYWORTH
Manuel Puig | 36020 | 2.25

THE FAMILY OF PASCUAL DUARTE
Camilo José Cela | 11247 | 1.45

**THE EYE OF THE HEART: SHORT
STORIES FROM LATIN AMERICA**
Barbara Howes, Ed. | 20883 | 2.25

GABRIELA, CLOVE AND CINNAMON
Jorge Amado | 18275 | 1.95

HOPSCOTCH   Julio Cortázar | 36731 | 2.95

THE GREEN HOUSE   Mario Vargas Llosa | 15099 | 1.65

LEAF STORM AND OTHER STORIES
Gabriel García Márquez | 35816 | 1.95

NO ONE WRITES TO THE COLONEL
Gabriel García Márquez | 36748 | 2.25

ONE HUNDRED YEARS OF SOLITUDE
Gabriel García Márquez | 34033 | 2.50

62: A MODEL KIT   Julio Cortázar | 17558 | 1.65

Where better paperbacks are sold, or direct from the publisher. Avon Books, Mail Order Dept., 250 West 55th St., New York, N. Y. 10019. Include 25¢ per copy for postage and handling; allow 4-6 weeks for delivery.

BLA 11-77